# WAR OWL FALLING

*Maya and Mesoamerican Studies*

UNIVERSITY PRESS OF FLORIDA

Florida A&M University, Tallahassee
Florida Atlantic University, Boca Raton
Florida Gulf Coast University, Ft. Myers
Florida International University, Miami
Florida State University, Tallahassee
New College of Florida, Sarasota
University of Central Florida, Orlando
University of Florida, Gainesville
University of North Florida, Jacksonville
University of South Florida, Tampa
University of West Florida, Pensacola

# WAR OWL
# FALLING

Innovation, Creativity, and Culture Change
in Ancient Maya Society

## MARKUS EBERL

Foreword by Arlen F. Chase and Diane Z. Chase, Series Editors

University Press of Florida
Gainesville · Tallahassee · Tampa · Boca Raton
Pensacola · Orlando · Miami · Jacksonville · Ft. Myers · Sarasota

All drawings, diagrams, photos, and tables are by the author unless otherwise noted.

First cloth printing, 2017
First paperback printing, 2025

30  29  28  27  26  25   6  5  4  3  2  1

Library of Congress Cataloging-in-Publication Data
Names: Eberl, Markus, author. | Chase, Arlen F. (Arlen Frank), 1953– author
  of foreword. | Chase, Diane Z., author of foreword.
Title: War owl falling : innovation, creativity, and culture change in
  ancient Maya society / Markus Eberl ; foreword by Arlen F. Chase and Diane
  Chase, series editors.
Other titles: Maya studies.
Description: Gainesville : University Press of Florida, 2017. | Series: Maya
  studies | Includes bibliographical references and index.
Identifiers: LCCN 2017016670 | ISBN 9780813056555 (cloth) | ISBN 9780813080802 (pbk.)
Subjects: LCSH: Mayas—History. | Mayas—Antiquities. | Maya art. |
  Inscriptions, Mayan.
Classification: LCC F1435 .E24 2018 | DDC 972.81—dc23
LC record available at https://lccn.loc.gov/2017016670

The University Press of Florida is the scholarly publishing agency for the State University System of Florida, comprising Florida A&M University, Florida Atlantic University, Florida Gulf Coast University, Florida International University, Florida State University, New College of Florida, University of Central Florida, University of Florida, University of North Florida, University of South Florida, and University of West Florida.

University Press of Florida
2046 NE Waldo Road
Suite 2100
Gainesville, FL 32609
http://upress.ufl.edu

# Contents

# Figures

# Tables

# Foreword

Rarely does a book on the ancient Maya cross-cut a wide array of disciplinary boundaries. Yet, that is precisely what Markus Eberl's *War Owl Falling* does. It includes material from archaeology, anthropology, ethnohistory, history, art history, epigraphy, and philosophy. Using the concept of innovation as a focus, the book examines how Maya society changed over the course of the Late Classic Period. Brought to bear on this concept are philosophical discussions over perception as well as modern examples of political change in which societal rules were followed, but within a different interpretational framework from the original cultural intent. Eberl weaves all of these various threads into a well-written and engaging narrative.

Eberl uses his previous archaeological work at the sites of Nacimiento and Dos Ceibas in the southeastern Peten of Guatemala to structure his arguments about innovation and societal change. He also brings archaeological data from Copan, Honduras, and Tikal, Guatemala (along with some comparative data from several other sites) into his discussion. The title decribes how the icon of the owl over time became more broadly distributed in ancient Maya society. An elite symbol of war at the onset of the Late Classic Period (ca. A.D. 550), the war owl was transformed into an artistic motif that was stamped on Maya pottery vessels used in normal residential contexts towards the end of the Late Classic Period (ca. A.D. 760). By using this example, he argues that the Maya war owl rises to become a symbol over time that represents both change and innovation in ancient Maya society just as it falls from elite to common use.

When we began the series on Maya Studies with the University Press of Florida almost a decade and a half ago, we envisioned a set of monographs that included books that dealt with archaeology, ethnography, and broader, more integrative topics. Markus Eberl has provided the series with a work that overcomes polemical confines. His tome should be of interest to scholars both within and outside the field of Maya Studies. This book is not parochial, and, because it transcends disciplinary boundaries, it raises many questions that future generations of researchers will strive to answer.

*Diane Z. Chase and Arlen F. Chase*
*Series Editors*

# Acknowledgments

The war owls swooped in on a gloomy afternoon. I was sitting in the laboratory sorting through ceramic sherds I had excavated in ancient Maya villages. I eliminated the eroded ones, separated the remaining ones into different types, and counted as well as weighed each pile. That afternoon, I had slogged through many bags full of sherds when a stamped sherd caught my attention. It dated to the eighth century A.D., when the villagers were only decades from abandoning their homes for good as the Maya collapse set in. On its stamped surface two circles peered from ski goggles over and over again. The Classic Maya would have recognized this motif as the head of an owl. They saw in this nocturnal bird of prey a messenger from the otherworld and associated it with darkness and war. Until this stamped sherd, owls had only been associated with Maya rulers and nobles. My discovery posed intriguing questions: Why did Maya villagers employ elite imagery? Why did owl motifs appear suddenly during the eighth century A.D.?

It soon became clear the stamped ceramic sherd was not unique. I found more war owls and other equally interesting motifs. My search for answers forced me to face a central challenge of archaeology. Labels like "Classic Maya" or "ancient Egyptians" suggest homogeneous societies that were stable for hundreds or thousands of years. Nonetheless, their material cultures changed continuously. Archaeologists look for these changes especially in ceramic vessels and sherds because ancient potters played with their forms, material compositions, and decorations. In my case, hand-modeled decorations prevailed until stamping emerged as a new technique during the eighth century. From these developments archaeologists distill changes over time and reconstruct culture history.

Unlike earlier geometric decorations, the war owls and other eighth-century motifs relate to Classic Maya art and writing. I can probe their meaning by comparing where they occur and by situating them in social structures that circumscribe individual action. I can aim to understand how material changes link to social changes. At last, ancient cultures show themselves to be more complex than their labels. I doubt that "the Classic Maya" existed in the sense that every member of Classic Maya society had similar cultural experiences. The war owls exemplify my goal to reveal what differentiated villagers from one another and what united them. In this book I deploy innovation as a way to understand social change in the past. The war owls are at the intersection of active individuals, dynamic processes, and constraining structures in Classic Maya society.

In "Digging," Seamus Heaney recalls how his father and grandfather deftly handled spades to dig potatoes and peat. As a writer, he no longer has a "spade to follow men like them" (Heaney 1966:14). Instead, a squat pen rests between his finger and thumb. Whereas his forbears dug into the earth for a living, he digs into the past. I similarly look out my window and recall how this book came to fruition. Here is the place to cast my eye over the people who shaped this book, often imperceptibly.

Jack Sasson urged me over a Noshville brunch to critique the idea of genius that often drives models of innovation. Bryan Lowe inadvertently exposed me to Saba Mahmood's work and stimulated me to consider how individuals creatively manipulate complex structures. With her unsurpassed knowledge of colonial and modern Yucatec Maya, Vicki Bricker provided feedback on linguistic issues and their cultural relevance, most memorably on *nen*, "mirror." Norbert Ross discussed with me Frank Cancian's and Dan Sperber's work on innovation and culture change. John Weymark pointed me to different measures of social inequality. Arlen Chase reminded me of the complex social structure of Classic Maya society. During a pleasant walk, Ted Fisher and I canvassed structuralist theories. Vera Tiesler, Janice Jun, and Andrew Scherer contributed their insights on tooth implants and other medical issues. David Freidel and Arthur Demarest worked behind the scenes to support my work. I crafted several maps with the help of Sarah Levithol and Scotti Norman. Beth Conklin made money available to pay the latter. Takeshi Inomata contributed a photo and allowed me to use Aguateca's petrified wood. He and Antonia Foias probed my take on Maya ceramics. Jan Gasco sent me unpublished materials on Soconusco biodiversity. Takeshi Inomata and Maria Mayo read the manuscript before submission and gave much-appreciated editorial advice. Meredith Babb enthusiastically propelled this project from prospectus to book. I am thankful for her patience when I responded slowly with revisions. Two reviewers—Andrew Scherer and Scott Hutson as I eventually learned—tackled this book twice and heaped extensive remarks on it. "Curt cuts of an edge / through living roots awaken in my head" (Heaney 1966:14). These scholars challenged me and corrected me. They improved this book and I thank them all. What follows emanates from my privilege to wield a pen as well as a spade. Thank you, fathomless and unnameable, for making it possible. 你令我开心。

# 1

## Flower Mountain Revealed

### Innovation and Social Change in Ancient Societies

Wild animals dwell on the Flower Mountain (Figure 1.1). Slithering from a tree trunk, a snake strikes a bird; a jaguar preys on more birds that flap around their nest. A lizard and another snake peek out of a cave opening. The Flower Mountain mural, found at San Bartolo in the northwestern Peten, shows the cave as an animate being: Its back wall and roof form a menacing mouth with a stalactite fang. Vapor clouds—depicted as red swirls—are the cave's breath. The Flower Mountain is a wild and threatening paradise that protects the cave's riches.

A couple emerges from the cave. The young man carries a gourd of water on his head while the woman holds up a vessel full of maize tamales. These two are the ancestors of humankind who had ventured to the Flower Mountain to find sustenance (Saturno et al. 2005). What they bring back are common stock, which I mean here in the archaic sense as the food and things shared and created in joint human labor: the gourd that holds the water is the oldest domesticated plant of the Americas; maize was domesticated almost as early and became so important that the Maya still call themselves the Maize People; the ceramic vessel that holds the corn tamales had to be molded from clay by a potter. The murals of San Bartolo show how the ancient Maya became human. Their ancestors turned raw into cooked, matter into shape, nature into culture. This process of becoming requires innovations. Agriculture and crafts enabled a settled life and a complex society. Yet too often these inventions are treated as strictly technological advances. The San Bartolo mural reunites the inventions with the humans who thought of and propagated them. This book follows their lead. I ask how human creativity comes up with inventions and how these inventions change society.

Figure 1.1. The founder couple emerges from the cave in the Flower Mountain carrying corn tamales and water. (Detail from the north wall of the San Bartolo murals; based on the Heather Hearst rendering appended to Saturno et al. 2005.)

Dating to about 100 B.C., the San Bartolo murals signal a profound transformation of ancient Maya society. The west wall depicts how a supernatural being is crowned. Within a few centuries, human rulers take its place and claim divine status as they ascend to the throne. The Classic Maya kings and queens were never able to unify the Maya Lowlands politically. Instead, they ruled over what eventually became dozens of kingdoms (Figure 1.2). In their capitals, they assembled nobles, scribes, artists, and officials in royal courts while lively farming communities dotted the hinterland. Over the course of the first millennium A.D., this setting gave rise to art and architecture that remain widely admired.

A painted ceramic vessel draws back the curtain from a Maya palace where a ruler straddles his throne-bench (Figure 1.3). A pillow supports his back and several ceramic vessels offer food (the plate at his feet contains

Figure 1.2. The Maya area. (The image of Chaak, the rain god, is from Codex-style vessel K1152.)

Figure 1.3. K'awiil Chan K'inich, the last king of Dos Pilas (A.D. 741 to c. 761), surrounded by court officials in A.D. 735. The upper right inset is an enlargement of the artist's signature. (Drawing of polychrome vessel K1599 after rollout photo in Kerr 1989:100; the provenance of the vessel is unknown.)

tamales just like the vessel shown in the San Bartolo mural; the now-ubiquitous tortillas seem not to have become popular until later). The ruler's breast pendant shows a stylized face with two circles as eyes, a triangular nose, and a round mouth. The same face appears in Maya hieroglyphic texts as the word for *ajaw,* "lord." Here it confirms the ruler's noble status. To his right are two men holding flower bouquets. The hieroglyphic caption between both identifies them as *k'inich chok,* "sun-eyed princes." The larger L-shaped text dates this scene to 3 Ben 6 K'ank'iin, or A.D. October 27, 735. It goes on to identify the ruler as K'awiil Chan K'inich, the fourth ruler of the Dos Pilas dynasty. He calls himself captor of the Ahkul Lord and divine ruler of Dos Pilas.

Unlike many premodern cultures in which individuals remain nameless, among the Maya hieroglyphic writing preserves individuals' names and deeds. Their role in creating and maintaining culture is graspable. Unseen yet present is the artist who made the ceramic vessel and painted it. His or her signature appears behind ruler K'awiil Chan K'inich (enlarged inset in Figure 1.3). Similar to *fecit,* "(s)he made it," in medieval European art, the Maya artist declares the ceramic vessel as *u tz'iib,* "the writing or painting of" Ahkan . . . , his or her name (the ellipsis alludes to the second glyph whose reading remains debated). Ahkan's painting captures a divine Maya ruler and his court nobles in their eighth-century glory.

The artist Ahkan also left a mystery. The palace scene is dated six years *before* K'awiil Chan K'inich became divine lord on A.D. June 21, 741 (Martin and Grube 2008:62–63). Ahkan compressed history and depicted a ruler-to-be as ruler. The conflation of present and future, fact and potential, is typical for Maya art (Baudez and Mathews 1980:32; M. E. Miller 1986:98; Miller and Houston 1987:50–51). It illustrates the human ability to imagine possible worlds that may or may not come to pass. Creativity challenges models of society that emphasize the force of habits. Social structures imperceptibly guide human behaviors. Through habits, individuals reproduce these structures in their daily lives. Yet, as self-reflexive agents, they are also able to reflect on their habits. In this book, I argue that this ability for metadiscourse enables creativity and the creation of inventions that change social structures.

Material cultures are dynamic and "always in the process of becoming" (Pauketat 2001:80). Material culture changes are particularly evident to archaeologists, whose temporal frameworks tend to encompass hundreds if not thousands of years. The transformation of traditions calls attention to innovation (Lemonnier 1993; van der Leeuw and Torrence 1989). By innovation, I mean the processes of invention and adoption; that is, the creation of novel goods or services and their wide social acceptance (Torrence and van der Leeuw 1989). I contend that innovation shaped Classic Maya society just as it has any other ancient or modern society. However, I disagree with evolutionary models of continual technological progress and point to the necessity to study the cultural logic and power structures that promote or stifle innovation.

## Sand Grains in the Desert

Innovation is a Western concept and applying it to an ancient and non-western society raises the question: Did the Classic Maya innovate? Some anthropologists would shake their heads and point to, for example, the modern Mopan Maya, among which "the ability to imagine and bring into existence what has not before been seen is indeed negatively evaluated" (Danziger 2013:256). In the 1950s, Ruben Reina (1963) visited the small Maya town of Chinautla, just a few miles north of bustling Guatemala City. The locals clung to *costumbre,* or "custom," as Reina found out when he met

Dolores and Jesús. Both came up with novel ideas: Instead of the traditional large water jars, Dolores made fancy ceramic figurines and miniature vessels for tourists. Jesús abandoned the traditional milpa and grew vegetables in irrigated raised beds. Their success bred suspicion among locals, who began to scrutinize and spread rumors about Jesús. Some neighbors practiced *envidia*, "magic," to ruin him. Slowly the community turned against him. Jesús failed to secure Dolores's hand, he became sick, and he gave up his vegetable business. He returned to milpa agriculture and planted maize and beans to sustain his family.

Reina concludes that *costumbre* smothered innovation at Chinautla. His understanding of *costumbre* has been very influential. For example, Danziger emphasizes that Mopan Maya must unconditionally accept what their ancestors tell them. "To 'obey' a cultural rule in Mopan is prototypically also to 'believe' something about it: that it is part of the body of Law handed down as *kostumbre* by the elders, whom *kostumbre* also instructs us to respect, believe, and obey" (Danziger 2013:257). Reina's cautionary tale has a surprising ending, though. A generation later, Maya have succeeded where Jesús and Dolores had failed. Chinautla potters now sell urban wares in markets (Reina and Hill 1978:262; Rice 1987:452–453) and Maya farmers plant flowers, broccoli, and more for export (Annis 1987; Collier 1994:101–106; Fischer and Benson 2006; Ross 1994). Change and innovation are possible even in a traditional society.

Reina's skepticism reflects the then widely held belief that innovation disturbs society. Many of his contemporaries saw society as a thermostat-like system that balances out intrusions and remains stable. Held together by what Émile Durkheim (1982 [1894]) calls *l'âme collective*, "the collective conscience," every individual works to maintain social solidarity. Any behavior that departs from established norms and values arouses suspicion (Linton 1936:308). Instead of gaining prestige, innovators risk ridicule and, correspondingly, only people who have nothing to lose are assumed to innovate (Barnett 1953; Linton 1936:310; Park 1928). From the perspective of these scholars, innovation can come only from the margins of society.

In recent decades, a factious model of society has replaced Durkheim's consensus-based model. It originated with Karl Marx and Friedrich Engels (1998 [1846]) who emphasize how division of labor creates different forms of ownership. Since in their view material conditions determine social structure, have and have-nots are locked in constant class conflict. The idea that dissonance is inherent to social life resonates with modern scholars. Drawing an analogy from nation-states in which capitalism and other forces compete, some see society as under constant strain. Innovation facilitates creative destruction and maintains progress (Acemoglu and Robinson 2012). From this perspective, societies fail if they impede the clashing of economic, political, and social forces. Their corpses litter history's battlefield as a stark warning for the generals of our future: Innovate or die!

This autopsy of ancient societies has a catch, though. Are societies coherent wholes? Scholars grapple with this question as they ponder the modern world. People, ideas, money, and goods move across the globe ever more freely and ever more frequently, without regard to boundaries, institutions, and customs. Globalization exposes nation-states as political constructs and social *imaginaires*, detached from yet imposing themselves on everyday life (Appadurai 1990). Neither stability nor change are natural; both phenomena require explanation (Sperber 1996). A society can be compared to a desert whose sand dunes stretch to the horizon. From a bird's-eye view, the desert radiates permanence and coherence; yet, from a closer view myriad details appear, down to individual sand grains. Wind gusts chip away at the dunes, constantly changing their shape. From close up, the desert is impermanent, dust to dust.

Like honing in from the desert to sand grains, social theorists now focus on the role of individuals in creating society. Anthony Giddens (1984) developed one of the most influential such models. He emphasizes that instead of taking society for granted, humans reproduce social systems through their behavior across time and space. Individuals are rational and reflexive actors; that is, they consider what they do while they do it. They know how to behave properly in different social situations. Daily activities are repetitive and ingrain habitual responses. Individuals act by heart. Their awareness of the structural properties of society is practical and often not made explicit. These properties consist of rules and resources (Sewell [1992:5–13] discusses Giddens's variable definitions). Here, I define rules as generalizable procedures that apply to different contexts and that methodically continue an established sequence. Resources, on the other hand, materialize structures in human and nonhuman forms. Virtual rules interlink with actual resources. For example, if workers are expected to clock in at 9:00 a.m., this rule requires a punch clock or similar resource. The rule and the resource reinforce each other to make going to work a habit that structures every workday.

The *costumbre* that Ruben Reina (1963:20) encountered in Chinautla can be seen as the native equivalent of Giddens's structure because the local Maya (like many other Latin Americans) understand structure both as rules ("our ancestors did it this way") and as resources in the forms of unique clothing, foods, or products. The Chinautlecos insisted on following the ways of their ancestors to continue their way of life, as Reina observed. More formally stated, "The rules and resources drawn upon in the production and reproduction of social action are at the same time the means of system reproduction" (Giddens 1984:19). Structure performs a dual function in Giddens's model. It is a representation of and for reality; it represents the past and guides future decisions.

Through their behavior and ideas, humans not only reproduce society, they also change it. This means that society is neither inherently stable nor constantly changing (Sperber 1996). Instead, we have to ask why society may appear stable or dynamic. More precisely: Which human actions create continuity and which create change? This question is at the heart of my book. The duality of structure explains how individuals maintain social systems. My challenge is to explain change within Giddens's framework.

## Why the Yir Yoront Have No Canoes

Archaeologists study the material record of ancient societies to see how new technologies emerged: the first corn, first wheel, first writing. In *Man Makes Himself*, V. Gordon Childe (1936) deduced from these firsts a series of technological, economic, and social revolutions. Agriculture emerged during the Neolithic revolution, cities during the urban revolution, and capitalism during the industrial revolution.[1]

Around the same time, Leslie White (1943) correlated human development with the amount of energy that a culture is capable of harnessing. Technological advances mark the individual stages that lead to the industrial revolution. The evolutionary approaches of Childe and White are rooted in historical materialism. What people are coincides "with their production, both with *what* they produce and with *how* they produce" (Marx and Engels 1998:37; emphasis in the original). By arguing that the material conditions of life determine social classes and political structures, Marx and Engels cast the traditional understanding of history aside. Changing modes of production—not events—make history. The models of Childe and White adopt Marxist materialism and tie social progress to technological advances.

More recently, archaeologists have moved away from these and similar evolutionary approaches because they obscure the diversity in the archaeological record and create abstract categories at the expense of historical detail (for example, Pauketat 2007; Yoffee 2005). Technological advances like agriculture, the wheel, or writing appear worldwide, but a closer look reveals distinct local developments. After Middle Eastern foragers domesticated wheat, barley, sheep, and goats, they quickly settled down and became full-time farmers. Foragers in Central America, on the other hand, domesticated and used corn, beans, and squash for thousands of years before founding villages. Plant and animal domestication differed in kind, timing, and social impact in the Middle East versus Central America. This and other examples contradict the idea that technological progress was globally uniform and linear (Pfaffenberger 1992). The material conditions of life are also less determining than often thought. For example, Anga groups in Highland Guinea exploit the same environment with different technologies. They use three types of traps to catch wild pigs (Lemonnier 1986): a stake-lined trench with a covered opening, sharp stakes hidden behind a low barrier, and a dead-fall trap. In most Anga groups, the trapper decides which type of trap to use. Langimar trappers do not use the dead-fall trap, however, despite knowing how it works and having seen it among the neighboring Kapau and Menye. When Lemonnier (1986:165) asked why not, they responded "our ancestors did not use it." Their answer links the use of technology to culture-specific ideals.

In western societies, technology is understood as the study of material goods with little regard for the makers of those goods. This reflects the separation in modern western thought between society and technology (Dobres and Hoffman 1994:228, 230). Martin Heidegger (1977) develops a holistic view in which technology is not simply a means to an end but rather a mode of human existence (Godzinski 2005). He calls the essence of technology *Gestell*, or "enframing," because it orders all material things into a framework or configuration (Heidegger 1977:17–20). Through their work, traditional artisans bring objects out of concealment and reveal their potentiality.[2] Limiting technology to objects and relations among objects neglects the people who develop or use these objects (Ingold 1993; Spector 1993). English and other languages derived the word *technology* from ancient Greek *tekhnología* (τεχνολογία) but narrowed its meaning. The suffix *-logy*, or Greek *logía*, refers to the "study of." *Tékhnē* translates as an inborn skill, a learned craft, and a set of rules; it also means handiwork, work of art, or grammar (Liddell and Scott 1996:1785). For the ancient Greeks, technology encompassed ideas and their material realization, or what Gilbert Simondon (1958) calls the *concrétisation* of ideas. I adopt this holistic perspective. This means that I no longer see the environment and the resulting necessities for survival as the mother of invention (see also Pfaffenberger 1992:495–502). The environment provides crucial resources, but humans have been able to minimize environmental limitations through trade and exchange with other regions and by transforming raw materials technologically. Culture, not nature, defines how humans satisfy their needs. Studies of technology therefore have to deal with the ways in which humans think about and employ technology. More formally stated, the emphasis shifts to cultural reason and social agency.

The Yir Yoront band of Australian Aborigines cling to wood logs while swimming. Neighboring bands have, as the Yir Yoront know, bark canoes and can therefore do what they cannot: fish midstream or out at sea, and cross over crocodile- and shark-infested waters. The Yir Yoront's environment contained all the necessary materials for making canoes. Since they had the knowledge and the resources to build canoes, anthropologist Lauriston Sharp (1952:22) asked them why they didn't. Their answer: We have no canoes because our mythical ancestors did not have them. It is not sufficient to make the canoe, it is also necessary to explain it through a myth and by associating it with an ancestor. Yir Yoront society had yet to accept the idea of a canoe. Their case exemplifies how technology relates to mythological beliefs and other socially constructed forms of knowledge. From a western perspective, it is often more convenient to keep myths separate from technology. Seen by themselves myths appear quaint or primitive. Yet, studying the intersection between technology and belief opens an understanding of native science and its cultural logic (Fischer 1999; Hutson and Stanton 2007; Sahlins 1976, 1999).

The material and immaterial aspects of a culture influence each other. Instead of privileging ideas or things, as in Hegel's idealism and Marx's materialism, respectively, I follow Martin Heidegger (1977:13) in emphasizing the dialectic of creator and created. The intentions of makers cannot be separated from the things they make. Technology and society are mutually linked (Annis [1985] and Papousek [1989] provide examples). "People construct their social world using the social resources and structures at hand, but their activities modify the structures even as they are reproduced" (Pfaffenberger 1992:500). A study of technology has to move away from the end product and uncover the process of becoming. This is undeniably a difficult undertaking. Reina (1963), Lemonnier (1986), and Sharp (1952) were told that "our ancestors did not use it," but this is not so much an explanation as "the polite response to any stupid question from the ethnographer on the origin of things, when such questions deserve no comment" (Lemonnier 1986:165). Creating an object welds a craftsperson's inspiration to material potential; innovation articulates otherwise tacit knowledge.

## From Rule to Strategy

For the better part of the twentieth century, social theorists observed Kant's divorce of subject from object and, divided into the camps of phenomenology and structuralism, stressed each side differently. Here, humans have free will and choose what they want to do; there, society runs like a clock according to overarching rules. By the end of the twentieth century, social theorists had begun to bridge the subject-object gap. In *The Constitution of Society*, Anthony Giddens (1984) developed one of the most influential recent models. Agency is for Giddens (1984:3) not simply bodily abilities or individual acts that align linearly in time. Instead, humans carve actions out of lived experience. They identify what they do and in which context they are acting. Agency is an ability, as much physical as cognitive, that embeds humans in society. Agency and structure complement and presuppose each other (Joyce and Lopiparo 2005).

Humans are knowledgeable agents. This means that they are not only capable of acting, but that they also reflect on their own behavior and the behavior of others. Humans have free will, yet they are at the same time tethered to a society and its conventions. Agency rests on a cognitive model of the human mind. I differentiate among perception, memory, and imagination as the mind's three faculties (Gell 1992:231; Neisser 1976). Perception is the use of bodily senses in a given moment and at a specific location; it contextualizes human beings and allows them to monitor their current experiences. Memory is the ability to recall past events and behaviors; it emphasizes past contexts and the human ability to discursively identify acts in the continuous experience of reality. For individuals it also serves to rationalize action through comparison with their own behaviors in the past. Finally, imagination allows humans to plan future behaviors and situate them in desired contexts; it motivates action. Unlike Husserl (1966), who assigns perception a central role, I see perception, memory, and imagination as three phases of a single cognitive process.

The three human faculties of the mind are not passive; that is, they go beyond registering sensual inputs, reproducing past experiences, and extrapolating the future from past behaviors. Instead they influence each other to form a constructive process (Neisser 1976:20). For example, when walking around a shopping mall, with every step we see the building from a different angle. Instead of mistaking it for a different mall, we correlate our changing visual impressions with the sense of our moving body and know that we are in the same building. We navigate successfully from one store to the next by orienting ourselves through recalling past impressions and forecasting how the mall will look around the next corner. As we move through the mall, we are not aware of the perceived (mall, in this case) "in an abstractly empty way; any awareness has a constitutive structure" (McCumber 2011:140). The mind's faculties interlink to form a constructive process. Since we continually engage with the outside world, our behavior does not follow predetermined rules. Instead, we develop strategies and react to changing circumstances.

## Mental Frameworks

When navigating the world we create an internal map—be it of a mall or someplace else—on which we rely to orient ourselves. Our internalized map is imperfect and we sometimes need to consult prominently displayed maps with store locations (compare Hutson 2010:17–18; Martin 2006:57). Humans are unable to comprehend an external reality—in my example, the mall—in its entirety and objectively. Instead, they create a mental image that approximates reality. By constantly refining their mental image, humans are capable of at least bridging, though not closing, the subject-object gap.

Humans generate a mental approximation of the world, an insight that cognitive scientists have appropriated in different ways. Associationist theories posit that mental representations directly reflect the external world (Anderson and Bower 1973; Ebbinghaus 1885, 1964; see also Hastie 1981:41–43). Subject and object are different, but they stand in a one-to-one relationship to each other. Many scholars find these associationist models too simplistic because human behavior is more complex than a reaction to external changes (Casson 1983). They insert schemas or conceptual abstractions that mediate between sensory stimuli and behavioral responses (Minsky 1975; Ross 2004:163–172; Rumelhart 1980). Rumelhart (1980:34) defines schemas as "data structure(s) for representing generic concepts stored in memory" and suggests that these concepts are so general that they apply to all possible contexts (later, I elaborate on the implied procedural role of schemas). Like Minsky (1975:212), Rumelhart identifies particular variables or slots for each schema. For example, a commercial transaction has the five slots BUYER, SELLER, MONEY, GOODS, and EXCHANGE (Rumelhart 1980; the upper case identifies conceptual units). In the schema BUYING, a BUYER EXCHANGEs MONEY for GOODS from a SELLER. Particular elements—actual people, money, actions, and goods—have to bind to all slots to enable, or "instantiate," this schema. Schema theories also specify the conditions that elements have to meet in order to fit into slots; namely, their values (for example, BUYER and SELLER are humans) and their relationships (for example, X amount of MONEY buys Y amount of GOODS).

Schemas exemplify two crucial aspects of humans' mental images of the world: framing and classification. Gregory Bateson (1955) introduces the frame concept through the Epimenides Paradox. This ancient Greek philosopher is claimed to have said, "All Cretans are liars." Since he was from Crete, Epimenides must have lied and his statement is not true—however, this means that he is not lying and told the truth. Before succumbing to an oxymoron, one needs to step out of the funhouse of mirrors and realize that the Epimenides Paradox requires a particular frame to work. Epimenides's statement becomes understandable only if readers connect it to what is unsaid; namely, the birthplace of Epimenides. In turn, they have to know that Epimenides was born on Crete. The paradox exposes how individuals interpret a situation based on their interests and knowledge. Erving Goffman (1974:10–11) describes how this framing, or defining of situations, builds up "in accordance with principles of organization which govern events—at least social ones—and our subjective involvement in them." An intuitive comparison is the movie director who defines a shot with hands forming a rectangular view. Humans frame their outlooks on life similarly, with the additional complexity that, unlike the movie director, they are part of the shot. Everyday life confronts humans with an infinite number of people, objects, and events. Through framing, humans select specific facts and create causal relationships among them.

Schemas are less about sets of slots (for example, D'Andrade 1995:122) than about how these slots relate to each other (Medin and Ross 1996:298; Ross 2004:167). The statement "All Cretans are liars" resonates only with readers who know that Epimenides was Cretan and elicits shrugs from everybody else. At the same time, all readers can debate what this statement means and can adjust their frames to understand the Epimenides Paradox. Schemas are flexible and humans modify them. While individuals identify unique relationships, they can still participate in a social discourse about the Epimenides Paradox or any other fact. Humans recognize shared sets of facts and the different interpretations of these facts.

If framing provides the proper perspective just as a movie shot does, then classification is the camera's focus, spotlighting some aspects in a frame while blurring others. The human ability to identify unique characteristics of people, objects, and events requires the ability to discern sameness; that is, to put these peoples, objects, and events into categories. Buying apples exemplifies these processes (Gell 1992:71). Seen up close, every apple is unique; for example, a particular green apple may have two white flecks, a cut stem, and an off-round shape. For us, the apple is simply a grade A Granny Smith, and its specifics are uninteresting unless it is bruised. Cognitively, we evaluate the apple that we hold in our hand against the token apple, which represents a class of objects. The real-world object and the token require each other if they are to make sense for us.

Schemas provide general organizing principles for classification. Modern Q'eqchi' Maya grow cacao (*kakaw*), vanilla (*che'sibik*), and annatto (*xayaw*), a red food coloring and condiment, in specialized house-gardens then mix all three into flavored chocolate drinks (Caso Barrera and Aliphat Fernández 2012). The Q'eqchi' trace the mixed cultivation of the three plants to the *ch'olkuinq*, "Ch'ol people," who developed Classic Maya civilization and were annihilated after the Spanish conquest. They identify different varieties of cacao and annatto: *kaq*, *saq*, and *rax kakaw*, "red, white, and green-blue cacao"; *kaq*, *saq*, *rax*, and *q'an xayaw*, "red, white, green-blue, and yellow annatto" (Caso Barrera and Aliphat Fernández 2012:296). The Q'eqchi' classify varieties of both cacao and annatto by color—an example of an overarching schema—even though the actual plants diverge substantially from their designated colors. Classification rests on identifying shared and unique structural features of an object (Sperber 1975:65). Positive criteria are resemblance and contiguity; that is, what makes an object similar to other objects in the same class. Negative criteria are opposition and inversion; that is, characteristics that set an object apart from others.

## Structure and Agency

In *The Constitution of Society*, Anthony Giddens (1984) distills the structure of social systems into rules (what I previously called *schemas*) and resources. Schemas are virtual and context-independent, whereas resources are actual and realized in human and nonhuman forms (Sewell 1992, 2005).

In Sewell's concept of complex structures, schemas are transposable since "they can be applied to a wide and not fully predictable range of cases outside the context in which they are initially learned" (Sewell 1992:17). An example of a schema is the colonial Kaqchiquel Maya concept of *patan,* "burden" (for its Classic Maya equivalent see Stuart [1995:352–374]). *Patan* describes the obligations of life in the literal sense as tribute and in a metaphorical sense as humans' subordination to gods and lords (Hill 1992:138). It implies a superior and an inferior in an asymmetrical relationship and reflects the social, political, economic, and religious responsibilities of community members. Kaqchiquel society changed from an elite-dominated hierarchy into an egalitarian cargo system over the course of the colonial period (Hill 1992:153). *Patan* continued as a key schema, however; native lords and gods disappeared, but Spaniards and the Christian God took their place. Schemas are generalizable frames that apply to different contexts and methodically continue an established sequence. They are general enough to articulate logically with historical change and allow room for reinterpretation over time.

Resources are actual (Sewell 2005:133). They materialize, embody, and evoke schemas on particular occasions and in particular environments. Resources accumulate unpredictably because the enactment of schemas can have unforeseen consequences (Sewell 1992:18). Resources are also polysemic in that their meaning is open to interpretation (Sewell 1992:18–19). Kaqchiquel Maya society became poorer and predominantly peasants during the colonial period (Hill 1992). Noble families like the Xpantzay and Pirir struggled to maintain control over their lands, as testaments, court records, and other historical documents attest (Hill 1992:53–55, 60–64). By the end of the colonial period they had lost their lands and had become subsistence-oriented peasant farmers. This socioeconomic leveling affected resources involved in landholding, political office-holding, sponsorship of endowed shrines, and service in religious brotherhoods (for details see Hill 1992:153–154). Virtual schemas and actual resources affect each other to form the structuring properties that allow societies to exist across time and space and thus continue as systems.

Social systems are maintained by individual agents. Individuals use their cognitive facilities to recall and apply schemas, within the guidelines of resources. Structural properties therefore have two functions: They serve as models *of* reality—individuals use them to comprehend the world—and they are models *for* reality because they provide a blueprint for social action (see also Geertz 1966:7). The continuation of a social system is not simply the persistence of a structure, and social change is not simply the application of agency. Structure requires agency, and vice versa, in order to explain both tradition and innovation (Joyce and Lopiparo 2005; Sperber 1996).

## The Fading Wealth of the House of Ziani

Our understanding of society has shifted over the last decades from the level of the desert to the grain of sand; that is, from society as a whole to the individuals who create it. Earlier models, like Durkheim's (1982 [1894]) consensus, assumed that social norms determined individual choices. These models reflect the strict social orders and coherent nation-states of nineteenth-century Europe and are projects of totalization that reflect elitist desires but not reality. No social system can control its members completely but must leave room for individual freedoms (Leach 1962). Giddens (1984) developed the duality of structure around the idea that individuals reflect on their own behavior and that of others and then act knowledgeably. The shift to the individual does not imply an atomistic view of society; rather, individual action can only be understood within society at large. Public institutions, regulations, and customs shape innate skills and allow individuals to flourish. Society provides a framework that constrains but also liberates.

The social fabric into which every individual is woven contains opportunity structures where agency and aspiration play out. During the Middle Ages, sea trade with the Levant made Venice an extremely rich city-state. Sebastiano Ziani, who served as the doge, or chief magistrate, of Venice in the twelfth century was politically and economically cunning. Not only did he reconcile Pope Alexander III and Holy Roman Emperor Frederick I Barbarossa in 1177, but his business deals were so successful that Venetians came to compare fabulously wealthy compatriots to *l'haver de chà Ziani*, or "the wealth of the house of Ziani" (Lane 1973:52). These Venetian Rockefellers amassed their fortune in part from financial and economic innovations (Acemoglu and Robinson 2012:152–156).

Merchants financed their trading expeditions by forming a *commenda*, a rudimentary joint stock company. Instead of a fixed return on investments, they were promised between half and three-fourths of the profit; if the merchant made no profit, the investors came away empty-handed (Lane 1973:52). In this way merchants spread commercial risk while drawing in ever more investors. As new entrants gained wealth and rose socially, the establishment became increasingly nervous because new rich people meant new competitors. At the end of the thirteenth century, the elites closed their ranks and curtailed social mobility during La Serrata, "the Closure." A newly created police force clamped down on unrest. The publication in 1315 of the *Libro d'Oro,* or "Golden Book," the formal directory of nobles, transformed the republic into an oligarchy. The Closure extended into Venice's economy, too. The ruling elite banned *commenda* and similar contracts and nationalized trade by building state galleys and taxing merchant traders. Eventually, Venice's social, political, and economic institutions calcified and its fortunes declined. Venice's rise and fall shows that sociopolitical structures and innovation are linked.

Innovation is a triangulation of novelty, an individual, and society. In modern western societies, patent laws differentiate these three aspects: the invention as a unique object or service, the individual as the inventor, and society as the adopter. The three aspects are much more dynamic in pre-industrial and even some modern societies. Production tends to be less centralized and at least partially in the hands of individual craftspeople. Among the Classic Maya, households produced and consumed many of the goods they needed (King 2015; Scarborough and Valdez 2009; Sheets 2000; Sheets et al. 2015). The lack of legal frameworks comparable to modern patents allowed individuals to modify inventions to suit their particular tastes and circumstances (see also Schiffer 2005). They could be adopters and adapters. Innovation bridges, not separates, individuals and society. Technology connects individual behavior and the social framework; it thus contributes to the production and reproduction of society.

## Innovation in Ancient Maya Society

Modern societies stand on the shoulders of their predecessors. This book does not treat innovation as an exclusively modern concept but projects it back into the past. In this way, it emphasizes how the ideas that materialize in inventions have changed societies for centuries and millennia. The archaeological record attests to inventions in ancient societies, yet objects by themselves testify only vaguely to the ideas that created them. This creates a quandary for any attempt to write a history of innovation. Should one cherry-pick the successful inventions and trace how they spread across time and space? An approach like this tends to emphasize the material side of innovation at the expense of the people who died long ago and took their ideas into the otherworld. Here, I choose to study the material and conceptual aspects of past innovation. To do so, I focus on a specific cultural and historical context. The Classic Maya (A.D. 250 to 900) not only offer a rich archaeological record but also allow me to delve into the conceptual side of innovation through their elaborate art and writing.

The Classic Maya wrote in hieroglyphs. Rather than an alphabet in which each letter represents a sound, the Mayas used word signs and syllables (Coe and Van Stone 2005). A hieroglyphic word sign, or logograph, stands for an entire word. The head of a jaguar is *bahlam,* "jaguar"; analogous examples in western writing are *1* for "one" and *$* for "dollar." Syllables in Maya hieroglyphs combine a consonant with a vowel. For example, a stylized fish fin that looks like a comb is the syllable "ka." To be fully literate, a Classic Maya scribe had to learn about four hundred hieroglyphs, or ten times more signs than an American student must. Correspondingly, few Maya were proficient readers and writers; widely known were perhaps the numbers—a dot for one and a bar for five—and a few prominent hieroglyphs. Calligraphy was highly esteemed. In fact, writing was art and art, writing. *Aj tz'iib*, the Maya scribe's title, translates as "writer" and "painter."[3] The decipherment of Maya hieroglyphs has shown them to be a fully functional script (Coe 1992). The underlying language is closely related to the Ch'olan languages—in particular Ch'orti'—spoken today in the southern Maya Lowlands (Houston et al. 2000). Classic Maya scribes could express every thought in written form (Bricker 1995; Houston 2000). Their hieroglyphic inscriptions preserve crucial insights into ancient Maya concepts that relate to creativity and innovation.

Classic Maya culture is a context in which I can detail how innovation took place. For example, the medical literature credits the ancient Maya with humankind's first tooth implants (Figure 7.1). Skeletons found at Copan and Playa de los Muertos contain artificial teeth made of stone and shell. In Chapter 7, I discuss their function and native explanations for this innovation. It makes little sense to separate this or any other innovation from its social and historical context. Instead, I understand innovation as a social process.

## Maya Lowlands

The ancient Maya flourished in the tropical lowlands where modern Mexico meets its Central American neighbors (Figure 1.2; Sharer 2006). The Yucatan Peninsula jutting into the Gulf of Mexico, the Isthmus of Tehuantepec, and the western borders of modern Honduras and El Salvador delineate the area settled by speakers of Mayan languages. In precolumbian times, goods, people, and ideas flowed across the Yucatan Peninsula from the settled cultures of Mesoamerica to the west, and from Caribbean and lower Central American peoples to the east. Mayan-speaking ancestors emerged about four thousand years ago and splintered into more than thirty language groups as they settled an area slightly larger than modern New Mexico. They adapted to three different environmental zones.

The Pacific coast is a thin strip of fertile but often hot and humid land. Cacao, which the Maya highly esteemed, thrives here alongside more recently introduced sugarcane and cattle. Fish and other maritime resources are abundant. Extensive exchange networks connected the ancient Maya in this area with other Maya groups and with outsiders. The Pacific coast provides the easiest and quickest route for commerce and migration between North and South America. Early sites like Takalik Abaj and Izapa attest that these advantages created a seedbed for the rise of Maya civilization.

Tectonic plates grinding against each other off the Pacific coast force up highlands that contain a string of volcanoes. The piedmont rises steeply from sea level to several thousand feet. Modern Guatemala City, which overlies the ancient city of Kaminaljuyú, is at an altitude of 1,500 meters and its surrounding volcanoes reach almost 4,500 meters. As the elevation increases, the climate becomes more temperate—Guatemala advertises itself as the land of eternal spring—and then cold. The dangers of volcanic eruptions and earthquakes counterbalance advantages of fertile soils and other crucial resources. In the absence of significant ore deposits, the precolumbian Maya substituted obsidian or volcanic glass found in the highlands for metal. They fashioned manos and metates, the tools for grinding, from basalt. Jade and other greenstones served them for tools and ornaments. The rich and diverse highland valleys sustained dense populations early on. Kaminaljuyú and Chiapa de Corzo emerged as centers in the first millennium B.C. The highlands remained important even as the development of Maya civilization shifted to the north in the first centuries A.D. Rivers like the Río Motagua facilitated exchanges of raw materials, goods, and people between the highlands and the lowlands.

The northern two-thirds of the Yucatan Peninsula, known as the Maya Lowlands, is a limestone plateau that rises only a few dozen meters above sea level. Extending over 225,000 square kilometers, this area is approximately the size of Minnesota. Altitude and rainfall range from high in the south, where the lowlands transition into the highlands, to low at the northern tip of the peninsula. The climate is generally hot and humid; the central lowlands have an annual average temperature of 26°C and an average relative humidity of 83 percent. Rainforests cover the southern part of the Yucatan Peninsula, where the annual rainfall exceeds 2,000 mm. These forests are semi-deciduous; that is, some trees shed their leaves because rainfall varies markedly across the two seasons. The dry season, from January to April, leaves parched soils whose cracks reminded the ancient Maya of a turtle shell, while the rainy season brings smothering rainstorms. With his axe—thunder and lightning—Chaak, the precolumbian rain god, cracked the turtle shell open so that maize and other plants could sprout again (inset in Figure 1.2). Differing soils and uneven drainage create a diverse environment with many ecological niches. As part of the Mesoamerican biodiversity hotspot, the lowland rainforests contain more than 5,000 (1.7 percent) of the world's plants and more than 1,100 (4.2 percent) of the world's vertebrates as endemics (Myers et al. 2000). This area is one of the most biodiverse yet also most threatened areas in the world. Less than one-fifth (18 percent) of the original rainforest remains, and the annual deforestation rate is very high, at up to 3 percent.

The lowlands have rich plant and animal resources. For example, according to Naranjo Stela 32, the king of Naranjo received tribute in the form of *k'uk' bahlam,* "quetzal [and] jaguar," or more freely, "feathers and pelts." In A.D. 1635 Antonio de León Pinelo claimed of the lowlands "the climate (though hot) is healthy and fair; the fertile soils bear fruits, maize, cacao, achiote [a red pigment and spice], honey, wax, salt, and other esteemed and useful things; with numerous natives that have been mentioned; divided and irrigated by abundant rivers; beautified with mountains, plains, valleys, and gentle hills; in summary, a land very suited for human habitation" (Scholes and Adams 1960:270; my translation). León Pinelo tried to entice Spaniards to conquer the Maya Lowlands, describing a land of opportunity but omitting that the rich resources aboveground contrast with a relative lack thereof below. Metal ores are too scarce to warrant mining; limestone and chert abound throughout the lowlands, but other non-metallic minerals are rare (for example, slate and granite are found only in the Maya Mountains of modern Belize).

The ancient Maya obtained many resources through exchanges within the lowlands and with the highlands. The Pasión and Usumacinta rivers were transport arteries between the Guatemalan highlands and the Gulf Coast. In precolumbian and into colonial times, obsidian, greenstone, and other raw materials were brought down to the lowlands. A Lowland Maya told Martín Tovilla in A.D. 1635 that they "communicate with the natives of Tabasco and they receive from them some axes and tools to work their milpas; it takes them thirty-five days to reach the people in Tabasco" (Scholes and Adams 1960:210; my translation). Colonial Lacandon Maya traveled sixteen days—the first two days on land, then four days by boat and ten more on land—from their homes in the western Petén to obtain salt (Scholes and Adams 1960:210–211). The ancient Maya mastered the lowlands by maximizing available resources and complementing them through trade and exchange.

## Maya Civilization

Maya culture crystallized over thousands of years. Maize was domesticated in east-central Mexico and arrived in the Maya Lowlands together with manioc, a plant domesticated in South America, around 3000 B.C. (Pohl et al. 1996). Unlike the Old World, where domestication and agriculture went hand in hand, the foragers in the Maya Lowlands used domesticates long before they settled down. They cleared rainforest patches to plant fruits and vegetables. By the second millennium B.C., foragers had reached all parts of the Maya Lowlands. They favored swamp margins and other locales with rich plant, animal, soil, and water resources. Wetland cultivation complemented slash-and-burn agriculture and initiated the intensification of agriculture.

Farming became widespread during the Early Preclassic, or after 1000 B.C. (Lohse 2010). Some foragers settled down in villages and adopted a sedentary lifestyle. Others continued to hunt and gather and coexisted with farmers for centuries. Proto-Mayan, the ancestor of all Mayan languages, split into separate languages around 2200 B.C. and Mayan speakers spread across the highlands. They moved into the lowlands by 1400 B.C. and reached Yucatan's northern tip within a few hundred years (Kaufman 1976). They established the three language families that are spoken today in the Maya Lowlands: Yukatekan in the north, Ch'olan in the south, and Tzeltalan in the southwest. The earliest pottery appeared in distinct traditions. The Xe sphere in the Pasión River valley shows similarities to pottery in the Isthmus of Tehuantepec (Andrews 1990). Non-Mayan Mixe-Zoquean speakers arguably brought it and other ceramic spheres to the Maya Lowlands. Alternatively, the early ceramic spheres could reflect the interaction of lowland inhabitants with the outside world. Local development, immigration, and diffusion contributed in different and so far little-understood ways to Maya culture.

The distinctive traits of Classic Maya civilization appeared during the first millennium B.C. Intensive forms of agriculture, including household gardens, terraces, and raised fields, became common and provided the necessary surplus for an increasing population. The lowlanders expanded from coastal and riverine settings into the forested interior. Exchange networks linked previously isolated groups. Their outward sign is the Mamom Ceramic Complex (c. 700–400 B.C.) that unified and replaced earlier distinct ceramic traditions. Settlements grew from villages into towns. Ceibal began around 1000 B.C. with low platforms made of clay and marl; over the next centuries, the site grew into a massive center with multiple ceremonial constructions (Inomata et al. 2013). Astronomically aligned buildings in so-called E Groups and temple-pyramids in triadic arrangements characterize Preclassic centers. Public art adorned monumental architecture. Life-sized stucco masks depicted deities and elemental forces. Carved stone monuments—stelae and altars—on plazas became popular by the end of the Preclassic. The standing figures on these monuments combine human with divine aspects. Lowland Maya developed hieroglyphic writing influenced by the Epiolmecs farther west. Early texts are incompletely deciphered; readable glyphs refer to timekeeping, rituals, titles, and deities. Preclassic architecture, art, and writing differentiated settlement centers and documented a stratified society.

During the Classic period (A.D. 250–900), rulers differentiated themselves from their shadowy Preclassic forerunners as k'uhul ajaw, or "divine lords" (Figure 1.4; Martin and Grube 2008). Classic Maya kingdoms extended over a few thousand square kilometers, and their inhabitants numbered in the tens to hundreds of thousands. Farming villages dotted the hinterlands of royal capitals. Agricultural surpluses supported a complex stratified society. Divine lords employed artisans, priests, warriors, and bureaucrats at their courts. Craftspeople in palace workshops produced the polychrome ceramic vessels, carved monuments, and other artifacts that Classic Maya culture is famous for. In public ceremonies, rulers celebrated victories, life events of rulers, and period endings. The royal court, with its palaces, temple-pyramids, and plazas, formed the core of each city with a large population. For example, between forty and sixty thousand people lived at Tikal. Since many households had gardens and even fields, Classic Maya cities spread out and have been called garden cities (for example, Chase and Chase 1998). Several dozen kingdoms existed in the lowlands. Marriages, exchanges, diplomacy, and alliances wove Maya nobles into an elite subculture. A Ch'olan language served as the lingua franca across the various languages spoken in the Maya Lowlands (Houston et al. 2000). At

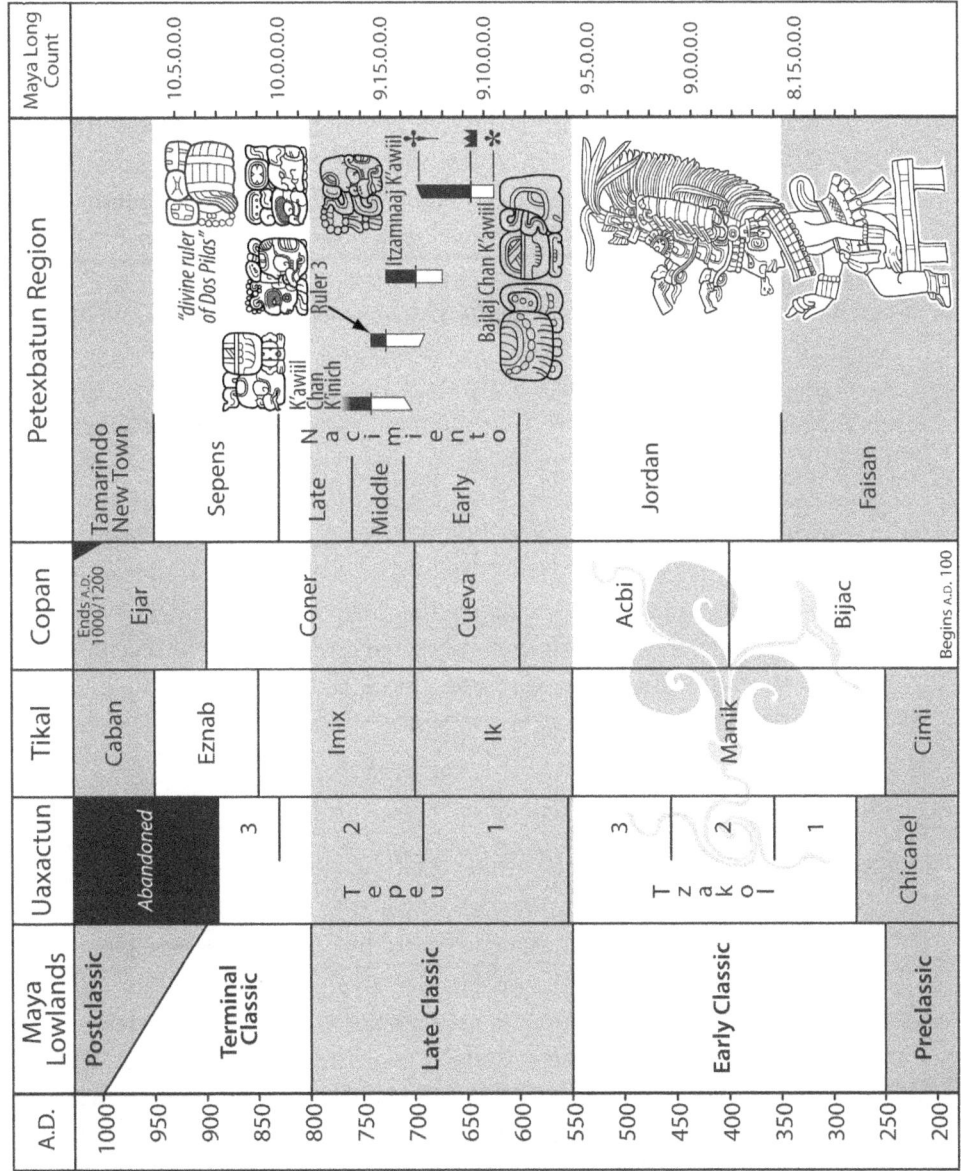

Figure 1.4. Classic Maya history with time periods, ceramic sequences from selected sites, and the dynastic sequence of Dos Pilas. (Uaxactun ceramic sequence after R. Smith [1955:106] with a 9.6.0.0.0 beginning date for Tepeu 1 after Willey et al. [1967:Figure 10]; Tikal sequence after Culbert [1993:4]; Copán sequence after Fash [1991:16] and Willey et al. [1994:12]; Petexbatún sequence after Foias [1996:1011] and Inomata [2010]; Dos Pilas Emblem Glyph and names of Dos Pilas rulers after Martin and Grube [2008:56–63]; fleur-de-lis from vessel K4991; seated ruler from slate scepter K3409.)

| A.D. | Maya Lowlands | Uaxactun | Tikal | Copan | Petexbatun Region | | Maya Long Count |
|------|---------------|----------|-------|-------|-------------------|---|-----------------|
| 1000 | Postclassic | *Abandoned* | Caban | Ends A.D. 1000/1200 Ejar | Tamarindo New Town | | 10.5.0.0.0 |
| 950 | Terminal Classic | | | | | | |
| 900 | | 3 | Eznab | | Sepens | | 10.0.0.0.0 |
| 850 | | | | Coner | | | |
| 800 | Late Classic | Tepeu 2 | Imix | | Late | "divine ruler of Dos Pilas" | |
| 750 | | | | | | | |
| 700 | | 1 | Ik | Cueva | Middle | Ruler 3 | 9.15.0.0.0 |
| 650 | | | | | | Itzamnaaj K'awiil | |
| 600 | | | | | Early | Bajlaj Chan K'awiil | 9.10.0.0.0 |
| 550 | Early Classic | Tzakol 3 | Manik | Acbi | | | |
| 500 | | | | | Jordan | | 9.5.0.0.0 |
| 450 | | 2 | | | | | |
| 400 | | | | Bijac | | | 9.0.0.0.0 |
| 350 | | 1 | Cimi | | | | |
| 300 | Preclassic | Chicanel | | | | | |
| 250 | | | | Begins A.D. 100 | Faisan | | 8.15.0.0.0 |
| 200 | | | | | | | |

the same time, Maya rulers competed against each other. Tikal and Calakmul shepherded Maya elites into two competing blocs (Martin and Grube 2008:17–21). Wars erupted frequently between these blocs. Into these battles, warriors wore the war owl among other insignia that signal death, prowess, and the otherworld (Figure 6.9). The Classic Maya created a civilization of urbanized state-level societies whose unique art and architecture continue to evoke wonder.

Many major centers were abandoned at the end of the first millennium (Culbert 1973; Demarest et al. 2004; Webster 2002). Most divine rulers and their royal courts faded away—not at once but over several generations; not everywhere but specifically in the southern and central lowlands. The Maya Collapse was a drawn-out process that varied locally. Explanations correspondingly invoke multiple factors (Turner and Sabloff 2012): internal warfare, overpopulation and excessive numbers of nobles, epidemic diseases, failing trade and exchange networks, overused soils in degrading environments, lessening rainfall, and drought. The ancient Maya survived by adapting and transforming. *Aj k'iinob*, "daykeepers" or priests, continued hieroglyphic writing after the Classic scribes vanished together with the royal courts; now however they recorded mundane rituals instead of kingly deeds. Warriors, merchants, and priests gained prominence in Postclassic Maya society. Competing lineages established Mayapan as the capital of the northern lowlands and governed until the 1440s. When the Spaniards arrived during the sixteenth century, they encountered a mosaic of hostile societies and needed decades to conquer them. The last independent Maya kingdom in the heart of the lowlands yielded in 1696. Over the next centuries, the Maya became subjugated first to the Spanish Crown and then to modern nation-states.

## Rulers and Peasants

To study innovation among Late Classic Maya, I employ case studies from the entire social spectrum. This includes villages in the Petexbatún region of the southwestern Maya Lowlands (Figure 1.5). There, the Petexbatún River snakes north along a sixty-meter-high escarpment to meet the Pasión River, one of the major arteries between the highlands and lowlands. Two royal dynasties controlled the region at different times. Tamarindito and Arroyo de Piedra served as capitals of an Early Classic kingdom, which kings who established a new dynasty at Dos Pilas and Aguateca brought under their control during the Late Classic. Hieroglyphic inscriptions

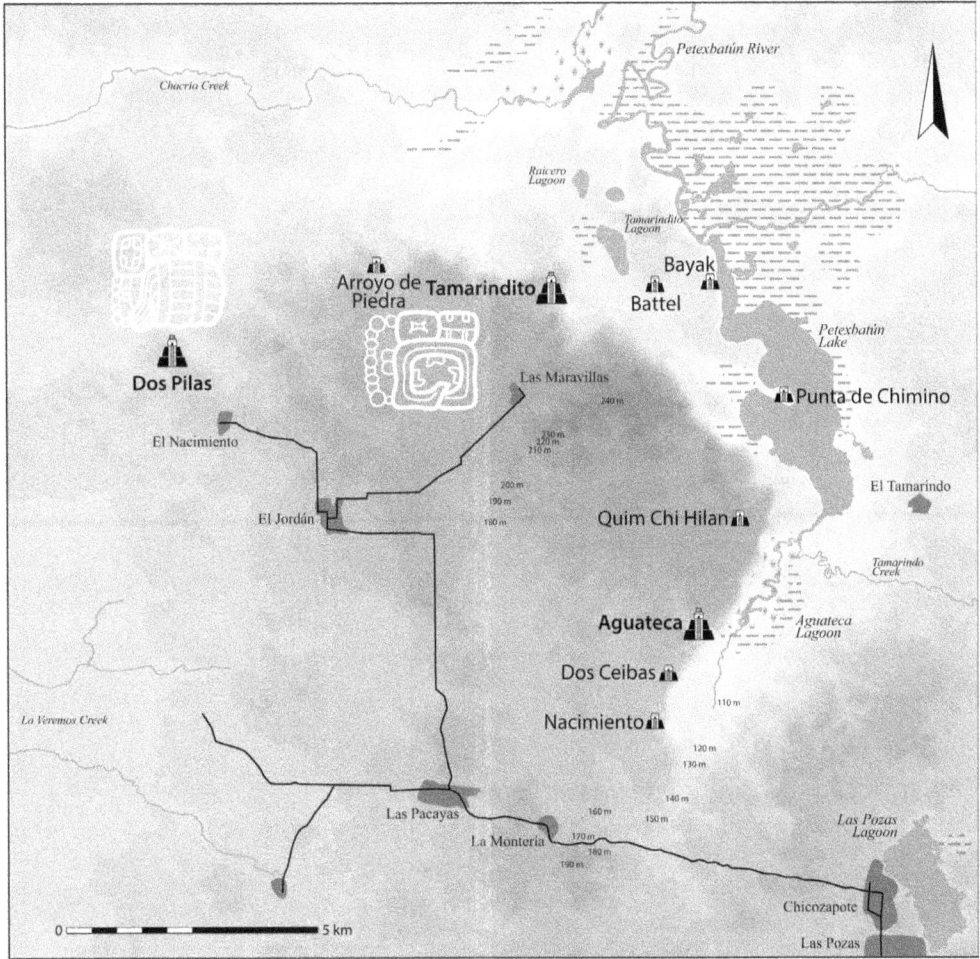

Figure 1.5. The Petexbatún region in the southern Maya Lowlands; insets show the emblem glyphs of Dos Pilas (*left*) and Tamarindito (*right*).

detailed the history of the two kingdoms (Houston 1993; Martin and Grube 2008:54–67). Archaeological investigations took place at the major centers of the Petexbatún region during the 1980s and 1990s (Demarest 1997, 2006). More recently, I studied two villages—Nacimiento and Dos Ceibas—south of the royal capital of Aguateca (Figures 1.6 and 3.6; Eberl 2014a). While small, both had a surprisingly complex social structure.

The archaeological site of Copan is on the border between Guatemala and Honduras where the Copan, a tributary to the Motagua River creates a narrow valley with a fertile alluvial plain (Figure 1.7; Fash 1991). About twenty thousand people formed settled residential groups in several

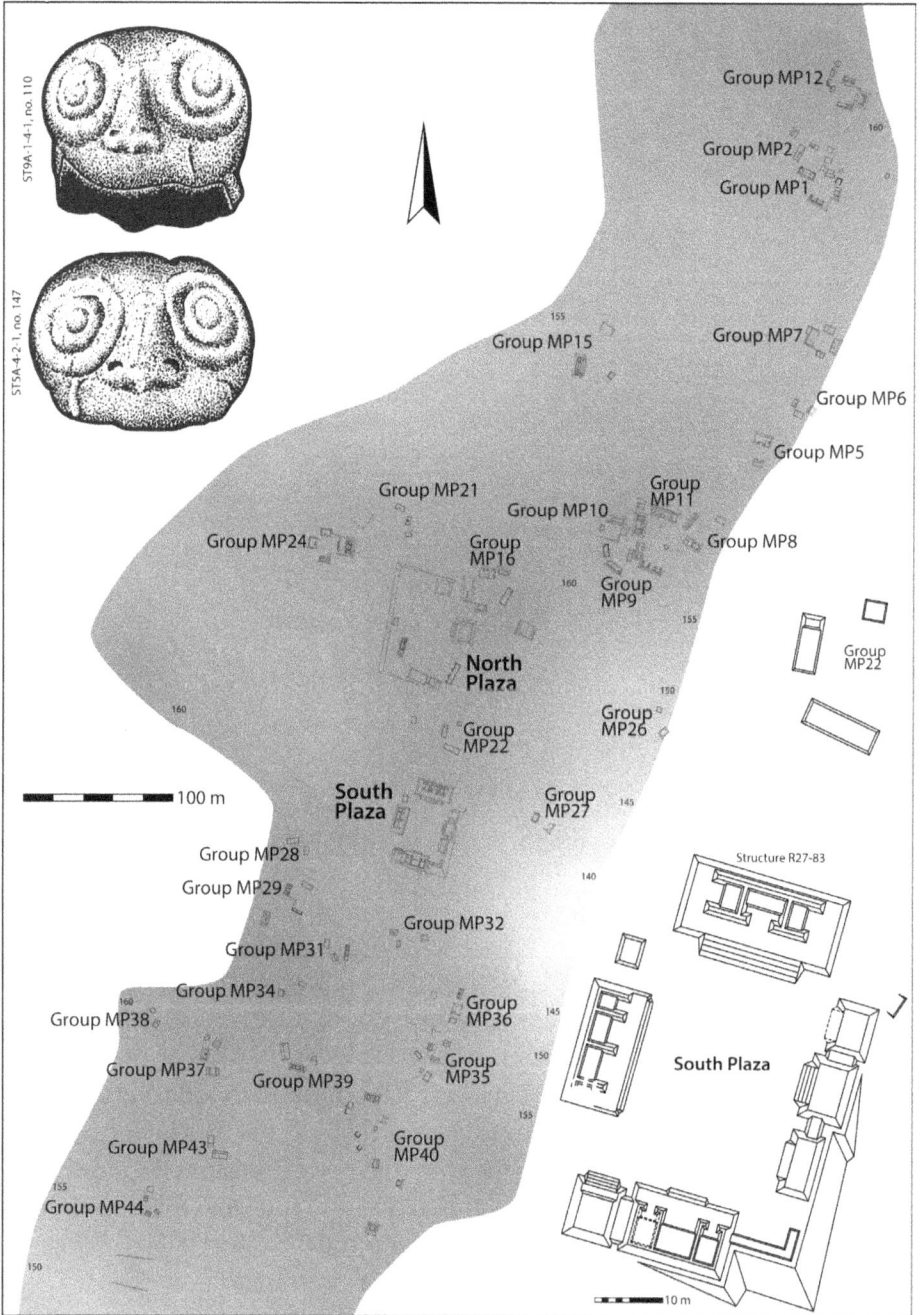

Figure 1.6. Map of the Late Classic village of Dos Ceibas in the Petexbatún region; lower right inset shows the South Plaza and Group MP22; upper left insets show owl figurines that were made from the same mold and found in Group MP22 (*top*) and the South Plaza (*bottom*).

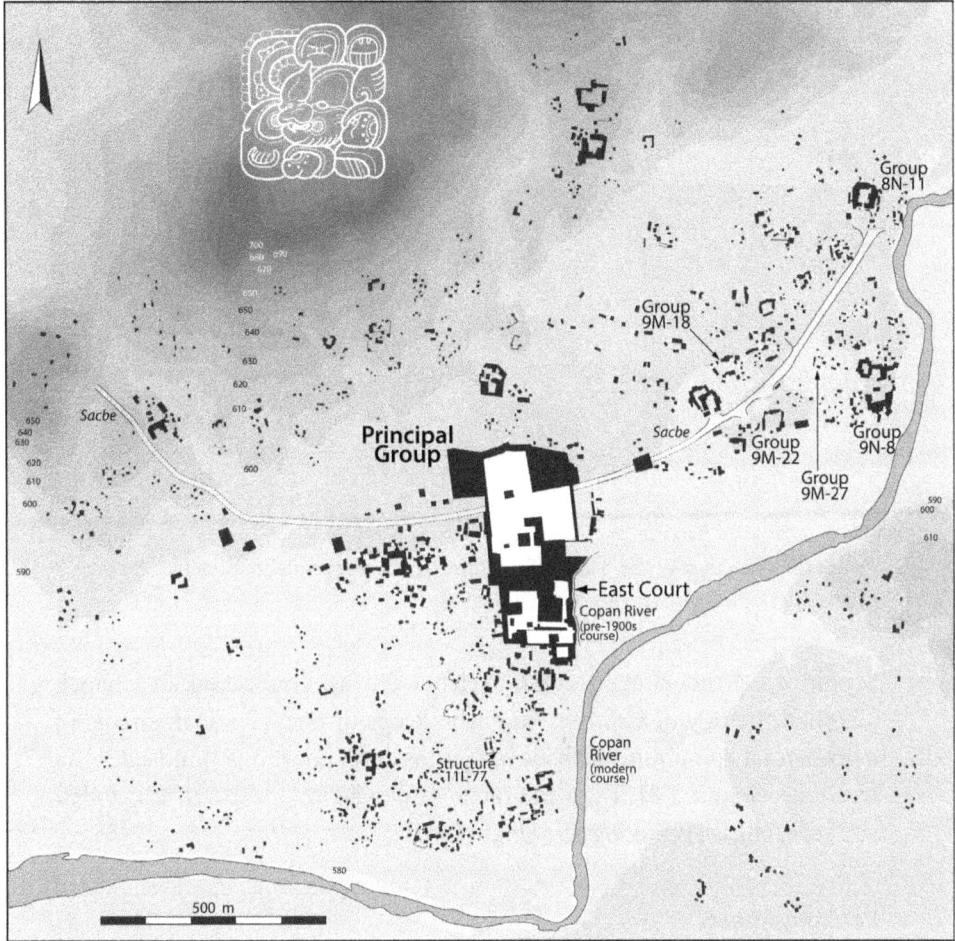

Figure 1.7. The Copan Valley in the southeastern Maya Lowlands; inset shows the Copan emblem glyph. (Map modified after Fash [1991:155 Figure 96]; Copan emblem glyph from Copan Stela I, glyph D6.)

neighborhoods like Las Sepulturas and El Bosque (Figure 1.8). The Principal Group in the valley center was the seat of the royal dynasty. In their heyday, the sixteen kings of the dynasty dominated the southeastern part of the Maya Lowlands (Figure 1.9; Fash 1991; Martin and Grube 2008:190–213). Archaeological investigations have covered the entire Copan Valley and thus have provided insights into all segments of Copan's society (Baudez 1983; Fash 1991; Sanders 1986–2000; Webster, Fash, Widmer, and Zeleznik 1998; Webster, Freter, and Gonlin 1999; Willey et al. 1994). A *sacbe*, or plastered causeway, connects the Principal Group with Group 9N-8 in Las

Figure 1.8. The House of the Bacabs (Structure 9N-82), the residence of noble Mak'an Chanal, in Copan's Group 9N-8 (see Figure 5.1).

Sepulturas (Sanders 1986–2000; Webster 1989a). Noble Mak'an Chanal, who had the title *aj k'uhuun*, "one who keeps or obeys," was in charge of a residential compound with eleven patios and almost one hundred stone buildings (Figure 1.8). The wide range of people in Group 9N-8 included craft specialists and foreigners (Figure 4.5).

## Looking Ahead

Earlier I introduced the question: How can innovation explain change in an ancient society? In Chapter 2, I discuss the theoretical foundation of modern models of society. By emphasizing habits or routines, these models explain the reproduction of social systems across time and space. As knowledgeable and self-reflexive agents, individuals can act against external constraints but social rules guide their behavior as tacit knowledge. The famous rabbit-duck illusion, in which people see either a rabbit or a duck, visualizes the assertion that people not only live in different worlds of meaning but are also unaware of doing so. I counter this interpretation with a dialectical approach. While individuals perceive only a rabbit or a duck at a given moment, most if not all can also see the other animal. What looks first like a rabbit turns into a duck, and vice versa. Switching back and forth between rabbit and duck creates consciousness about knowledge. I locate

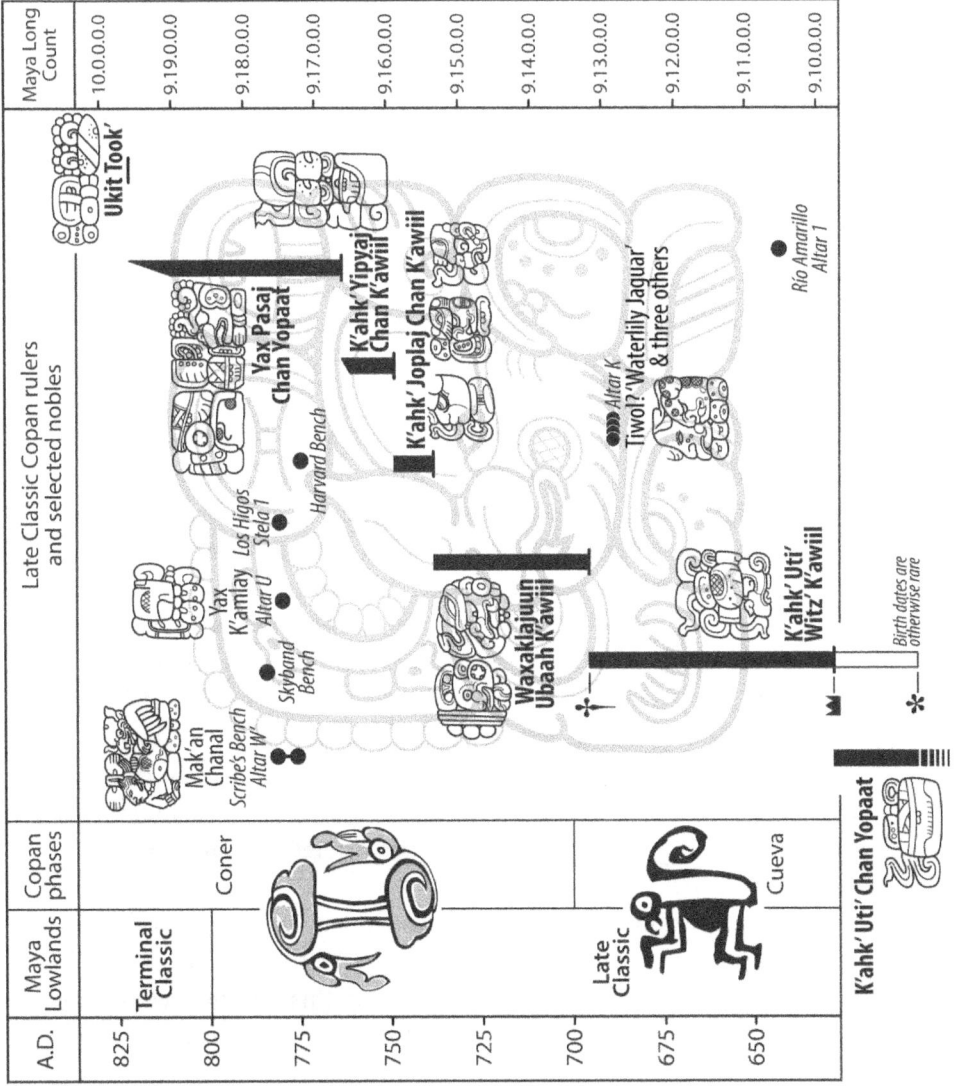

Figure 1.9. Late Classic kings and nobles of Copan; only selected nobles with datable monuments are shown. (Royal biographic data from Martin and Grube [2008:200–213]; Cueva-phase ceramic motif from a Gualpopa Polychrome sherd [Willey et al. 1994:133 Figure 64j]; Coner-phase motif from a Copador Polychrome vessel [Viel 1983:584 Figure S–17d].)

the possibility of change in the meta-awareness that individuals form about themselves and their actions.

I apply the dialectical approach to a symbolic model of creativity. By creativity, I refer to the human capacity to question interpretations of the world and to find new relationships among constituent elements. Metonyms and metaphors are fundamental to human discourse and express subtlety, ambiguity, irony, and sarcasm. For example, the metaphor "fishing for information" evokes fisherfolk working at sea to express an abstract and possibly futile search for data. Symbols link knowledge domains in new ways. I argue that metonyms and metaphors create incomplete linkages. By hovering between domains, they build meta-awareness. The ancient Maya creator god Itzamnaaj helps to illustrate key aspects of my symbolic approach. He wears a mirror on his forehead. Unlike the perfect reflections of modern mirrors, this mirror is made of opaque obsidian and its reflections are never perfect or clear. Knowledge is gained by gazing into it and probing its depth. Itzamnaaj's mirror symbolizes the creative process.

The western myth of the genius—inventors like Thomas Edison or Steve Jobs come to mind—individualizes innovation and thus diverts attention from social processes that enable it. To create and to appreciate an invention, members of society employ creativity. In Chapter 3, I look into the social underpinning of Maya creativity: How did the ancient Maya learn? What opportunities for change did Classic Maya society provide? Maya society grew and diversified over the course of the Classic period. Even hinterland villages changed economically as well as socio-politically and provided individuals with opportunities to advance their interests. I contrast book learning from situated learning. In the former, learning takes place in a hierarchical environment (for example, teachers and students interacting in a classroom) whereas in the latter apprentices observe and imitate masters in a work-related setting. Maya learning still tends to be embedded in communities of practice. For example, girls help modern midwives like ancient carvers worked under the supervision of older artists. Imitation is often derided as mere copying, but in fact following in the footsteps of masters is a dialectic and ongoing process. It facilitates the meta-awareness that forms the foundation of creativity.

Unlike earlier conceptions of society as homogeneous, modern models emphasize its factious nature. Correspondingly, a society cannot be reduced to a single structure but instead contains multiple, coexisting, and even overlapping structures. In Chapter 4, I visualize complex structures as a Garden of Forking Paths in which worlds—some real, others imaginary—coexist. To plan their actions, individuals trace a coherent path between worlds. Their actions adhere to cultural but not necessarily practical logic. They deal with worlds differently and apply what logic calls different modalities. These modalities distinguish innovators from others. The material nature of inventions exhibits interaction and adoption publicly. Therefore, individual decision-making interweaves with decisions of others. Gardens of Forking Paths overlap and the resulting interferences map the structural changes in society.

Individuals make their decisions in the context of entangled social and political relationships. In Chapter 5, I address power and status. Earlier approaches consider status as an objective measure of innovative spirit: the poor are lacking and the wealthy dominate the necessary resources. Innovation then becomes socially dichotomized. These models fail to capture the more complex reality in which all members of society control resources, albeit to differing degrees. Power involves not only the imposition of one's will on others but also (and possibly even more so) the subtle shaping of the framework in which individuals make their decisions. The powerful are choice architects. I apply Thaler and Sunstein's (2008) six principles of decision-making to the changing relationships between kings and their people at Late Classic Copan. As members of society negotiate power, they shape the Garden of Forking Paths that delineates the space for individual decision-making.

In Chapter 6, I discuss how innovation changes social structures. Fault lines traverse societies like the Classic Maya. Their structures are complex, their statuses differentiated, and their power structures unequal. Just as language and speech depend on each other, social structures, statuses, and power exist not in the abstract but are materialized in concrete actions, things, and people. Diacritical consumption sets members of society apart based on culture-specific values. The ancient Maya would have ignored an expensive bottle of wine while westerners would pass by Maya mat iconography. For objects to work as status-differentiating items, members of society must at least partially understand their value. Members of a society develop meta-awareness through their interaction with social frames. For social change, these individual experiences have to convert into a public discourse about structures. Inventions materialize personal visions of society and become novel arguments in the public discourse. As people adopt innovations, they shift the course of their society.

In Chapter 7, I discuss innovation as an intersection between individuals and society. It follows a culture-specific logic that evolutionary approaches easily overlook. Premodern and nonwestern societies encourage tradition (for example, by urging artists to imitate masters) and thus seem to discourage innovation. But this logic should be seen as a culture-specific discourse on social change and order. Structuralist models explain the maintenance of societies by emphasizing habits. Nonetheless, agency includes creativity, that is, the ability to become aware of social structures and to develop new approaches that materialize in inventions. "We live like God wants us to," said Jesús, who built raised beds to grow vegetables in Chinautla. "One knows what one is and this is all" (Reina 1963:30). Jesús placed himself under the authority of God and community, aware of the context in which he was trying to innovate. The material aspect of innovations requires reconsidering the relationship between structures and space-time, the material context of human existence. Instead of being a passive backdrop to innovation, space-time is changed by inventions and adoption. Where Jesús failed in the 1950s, contemporary Maya have succeeded.

# 2

# Wings for Hummingbirds to Fly With

## Creativity as a Play of Symbols

Innovation requires, as the cliché has it, thinking "outside the box." Curiosity comes from the Latin word *cūra,* "concern, attention," and evokes, as Michel Foucault (1997:325) says, "the care one takes of what exists and what might exist." One has to define what makes the box a box (the context of one's knowledge), find the ill-fitting pieces, and look at known things in a different way.

Social continuity flows naturally from the structuralist model since existing norms are tacitly available. On the other hand, social change requires new norms. To introduce the possibility of change, I explore paradoxes and plays. In this chapter, I develop a symbolic model of creativity. "Appropriation, mimicry, quotation, allusion, and sublimated collaboration consist of a kind of sine qua non of the creative act" (Lethem 2007:61). I develop a dialectical approach to individual representations of the other. I illustrate this model with the ancient Maya creator god, Itzamnaaj. He enabled life by, for example, giving hummingbirds their wings and making maize sprout. Scribes, potters, mask makers, and other artisans worked for him at his court. Itzamnaaj served as a role model for creation in ancient Maya society.

## Fishing for Pearls and Information

Figures of speech are fundamental to both communication and creativity. Two operations—relationships of contiguity (or metonymy) and relationships of similarity (or metaphors)—are needed to speak intelligibly (Grigg 2008:151–169; Jakobson and Halle 1956:58; Ricœur 1977; Schmidt 2010; Tilley 1999). Jakobson and Halle (1956:63) distinguished between contiguity and similarity disorders. Stroke patients with the contiguity language disorder known as Broca's aphasia are unable to form coherent words and sentences. The most extreme case was Victor Leborgne, who could hear and understand everything that was said to him but responded to every question with a gesture and *tan, tan*—earning him the nickname Tan (Broca 1861:343). Speakers with a similarity disorder are unable to find alternative words. For example, a patient notes that bachelors live in his apartment building (Jakobson and Halle 1956:60). When asked what a bachelor was, the man became distressed because he could not come up with a synonym or a definition.

Contiguity is associated with metonymy, the figure of speech that relates elements of the same domain; the Greek word μετωνυμία means "a change of name." Similarity is associated with metaphor, the figure of speech that relates elements from separate semantic fields (the original Greek μεταφορά means "transfer"). Someone who "fishes fish" can extend the expression to "fish pearls"; the latter is a metonym that draws on catching things in the sea as a shared domain (Dirven 1999:281). In contrast, "fishing for information" is a metaphor that links the hope of catching something to a new domain unrelated to the sea.

Metonymy and metaphor represent relationships of contiguity and similarity, respectively. Both contain two aspects each. Contiguity involves combination and contexture, whereas similarity involves selection and substitution. To illustrate contiguity, I use novelist Paul Auster's (2008:34) definition of speaking: "Words come out, fly into the air, live for a moment, and die." Each sound combines different features simultaneously (for example, a *t* is a voiceless stop pronounced at the alveolar ridge) while *come out* means "emerge" only if both words are present. In contexture, sounds are joined into words and words are linked into sentences. Words "fly into the air" and are understandable only if spoken in a specific order. Switching places changes the meaning ("words air into the fly") or scrambles it ("words into fly air the"). Any sign consists of constituent signs and occurs in combination with other signs (Jakobson and Halle 1956:60). Metonymy, which is a relationship of contiguity, is transformative (Schmidt 2006:109–111; 2010:133–135). It creates an integrative identity in which dissimilar entities take on mutual attributes (Ricœur 1977).

Metaphors express a relationship of similarity. They imply a choice from alternatives and the possibility of substituting one sign for another. While Auster hears words "coming out," a different writer may prefer them "to emerge." Substitution compares possible similarities and differences in form and meaning. Every utterance reflects two processes. The combinative, or syntagmatic, process places units (for example, sounds and words) from the language's inventory into a higher order (sounds become words, words become sentences); its hallmark is contiguity. The selective, or paradigmatic, process chooses a specific unit from alternatives; its hallmark is similarity.

Metonymy and metaphor allow one to express ambiguity, sarcasm, irony, and semantic subtleties. Contiguity allows for inversion. People may berate a cheating friend as "awesome," expressing their disappointment by exploiting the meanings of *awe* that range from "fear" to "wonder." Similarity allows for opposition. Feminist Irina Dunn employed opposition when she declared that "a woman needs a man like a fish needs a bicycle."

Metonyms and metaphors call attention to five aspects that I develop further in the following sections. First, they bring two or more elements together. Parallelisms are well known in western culture (Ezra Pound's poem "In a Station of the Metro" is an elegant example) and, as I show later, also in Maya culture as diphrastic kennings. Second, figures of speech require linguistic and cultural context to be intelligible. Classic Maya would find the comparison of a man with a bicycle as opaque as westerners find aspects of Maya culture. Third, metonyms and metaphors are open-ended. Inversions and oppositions demonstrate that meanings are not settled. Relationships of contiguity and similarity create a continuous tension (Ricœur 1977). Fourth, metonyms and metaphors require readers/listeners to look beyond the literal. Their interpretation rests on self-reflection and imagination. Fifth, figures of speech raise the question of whether and how metonyms and metaphors can become embodied.

## Rabbit? Duck?

The duality of structure explains tradition (Schwarz 2013). Social systems remain the same because tacit schemas and resources guide human behavior. The mutual dependency of structure and agency makes explaining change difficult (Sewell 1992:14–15). This interdependency rests on the assertion of tacit schemas and resources, that is, structural properties that human beings are mostly unaware of. Instead of following consciously specifiable rules of behavior, humans act on a "gut feeling." The opposition of rules and gut feelings is artificial, however. It reflects Wittgenstein's (2001) concept of *Sprachspiel,* or "language-game," which I discuss to develop a dialectical approach to tradition and change.

Speaking generates the meanings of words by interweaving language with the context in which it is used (Wittgenstein 2001:nos. 7 and 23). Speakers of a language classify and name their worlds not through rules but by recognizing family resemblances (Wittgenstein 2001:nos. 66–67). As an example, Wittgenstein mentions that board games, card games, ball games, and team sports are all games. The large variety of games are connected by a series of overlapping similarities instead of a single essential feature. By emphasizing Saussure's *parole* over *langue*, Wittgenstein moves from rules to tacit knowledge. Later social theorists apply this insight to their models of society (for example, habitus in Bourdieu [1977]; the concept of agency in Giddens [1984]). Humans create meaning through language-games. "It is what human beings *say* that is true and false, they agree in the *language* they use" (Wittgenstein 2001:no. 241; emphasis in the original). Truth then becomes a meaning shared by and restricted to a community of speakers. Wittgenstein's notion of language-games also implies that meaning is no longer universally shared. Speech communities create their own worlds of meaning. Wittgenstein illustrates this with the rabbit-duck illusion (Figure 2.1):[1] "Would it be conceivable that someone who knows rabbits but not ducks should say: 'I can see the drawing as a rabbit and also in another way, although I have no word for the second aspect'? Later he gets to know ducks and says: 'That's what I saw the drawing as that time!' Why is that not possible?" (Wittgenstein 1980:1:16e)

One sees either a rabbit or a duck but not both at the same time. To interpret anything, humans must already understand what they interpret (Heidegger 1962:194; 2006:152). A hermeneutic circle encloses viewers of the rabbit-duck illusion. Although Heidegger (2006:312–314) coined the term "hermeneutic circle," he also saw it as an inapt term. The circle expresses the basic structure of being but does not confine understanding (Heidegger 2006:153). Humans should not try to get out of the circle but rather to come into it in the right way (Heidegger 1962:195; 2006:153). In their quest for understanding, humans realize and consider the existence of the circle. The existential structure of being is therefore a "fore-structure"—it exists before the process of understanding—and the first, last, and constant human task is to work out our fore-having, fore-sight, and fore-conception in terms of the things themselves (Heidegger 1962:195; 2006:153). In other words, Heidegger does not see hermeneutic circles as closed.

How can humans transcend the fore-structures of being? Hans-Georg Gadamer (1990:270–312) develops his answer out of humans' engagement with what Heidegger calls "things themselves," or the context of their

Figure 2.1. The rabbit-duck illusion (adapted from *Fliegende Blätter* 97(2465):147, published on October 23, 1892).

existence. Learning to translate a Latin sentence involves "constructing" the sentence in its entirety before being able to understand its meaning (Gadamer 1990:296). The ability to discern its parts—verbs, nouns, adjectives, and so on—and their relationships requires previous knowledge about grammar and vocabulary. Understanding of the whole rests on its parts while every part can be understood only through its reference to the whole. This hermeneutic circle is not closed, however. Translation involves the application of general rules—the context—to a specific text. Meaning arises from the consideration of context and text. The circle appears, after all, as if printed with a dot-matrix printer; up close every dot is visible yet the shape remains unidentifiable. Only by holding the paper at a distance can one recognize the circle.

The circle and the dot, the whole and its part, form the hermeneutic circle. The hermeneutic process lies in the movement from dot to circle and back. Gadamer (1990:300) identifies the ephemeral space of moving between dot and circle—the in-between—as the true home of hermeneutics. The two poles are the horizon for the oscillating viewer (Gadamer 1990:307). Like watching the sun rise or set on the horizon, contemplating dot and circle makes the interpreter aware of time and space. He or she is then capable of realizing that the process of interpretation is circular only for a godlike entity who looks at the hermeneutic circle from above. For the interpreter on the ground, the process of interpretation unfolds like a spiral that leads to ever-higher levels of understanding.

The concept of horizon emphasizes the context of interpretation. It can be compared to Bourdieu's (1977:4–8) analysis of Lévi-Strauss's (1969) concept of gift exchange. The latter stylizes gift exchange as an eternal giving and taking. Bourdieu criticizes Lévi-Strauss's model for not considering the temporal structure of gift exchange. Participants may delay giving and taking, and they exchange similar but not identical goods. The awareness of the context of each trade makes gift exchange irreversible. What from the outside looks like a circle is for the participants a spiral. Gift exchange requires strategy and not the application of a rule (Bourdieu 1977:9).

## Knowledge about Knowledge

In *One Hundred Years of Solitude*, Colonel Aureliano Buendía has trouble remembering the names and locations of things in his laboratory (García Márquez 1970:46). When he is searching for a small anvil but cannot recall its name, his father suggests "stake." Aureliano writes down "stake" and pastes the piece of paper to the anvil to associate name and object. The stake-anvil paradox recalls the rabbit-duck illusion and allows me to develop another aspect of the hermeneutic circle. One person sees a rabbit, the other, a duck, and both fail to realize that they are seeing the same object. The rabbit-duck illusion fascinates, though, not because one sees a rabbit *or* a duck but because one can see both, switching back and forth from one interpretation to the other. Hermeneutic interpretation rests on this movement between rabbit and duck, between dot and circle, to and from the horizon. Vacillating between rabbit and duck uncovers a paradox: How can the same object permit two distinct interpretations? Which is the true interpretation? As a visual pun the rabbit-duck illusion is similar to the Epimenides Paradox I mentioned in Chapter 1. Both accentuate the playfulness that is implicit in Wittgenstein's *Sprachspiel*, or language-game. Fascinated by plays on language and daily life, Erving Goffman defines them as sets of conventions "by which a given activity, one already meaningful in terms of some primary framework, is transformed into something patterned on this activity but seen by the participants to be something quite else" (Goffman 1974:43).

The rabbit-duck illusion and paradoxes in general magnify the open-endedness of the hermeneutic circle. Every interpretation can be questioned and approached differently. The creation of meaning is inconclusive. Based on Silesius's epigram, Heidegger discusses *a rose is a rose is a rose* as the unending quest for hermeneutic circles nestled inside other hermeneutic circles (Heidegger 1957:68–75; Silesius 1675:58 no. 289; see also Shanks and Tilley 1987:107–108). Paradoxes resist cognitive closure by leaving what if and what is unresolved.

The continual tension inherent in paradoxes makes interpreters aware of the hermeneutic process. "We make the world in which we live and we usually take for granted—the world of the 'natural attitude' . . .—into the object of our thoughts (we make it 'thematic')" (Duranti 2010:27). In this process, perception of the current problem, memory of past interpretations, and imagination of how the problem could be solved are linked cognitive abilities. In this way, an object cannot become fuzzy and fade away but instead the superfluous is excluded. The interpreter recognizes what it takes to solve the problem, defining what is known—the context—in order to be able to step into the unknown. Visual and literal paradoxes go beyond the horizontal relationship between dot and circle and reveal Gadamer's in-between, the liminal state of seeking knowledge, as a meta-level. Cognitive attention creates knowledge about knowledge.

The hierarchical levels can be compared to map and terrain. Hiking requires attention to the immediate surroundings, to trees and other obstacles, to the path; it requires context-dependent or indexical decisions. But this knowledge leads nowhere without a map, that is, non-indexical or context-independent information about the larger area. The map exemplifies the knowledge about knowledge. It enables locating one's current whereabouts (perception), identifying the route that led there (memory), and planning ahead (imagination). Since the map provides more than the immediate context, one can follow an established route or strike out on new routes. Structure—the map in this analogy—allows tradition and innovation.

## Cognitive Coherence

A map depicts a territory but it is not completely removed from it. Whatever route—new or known—I develop, any viable solution is cognitively coherent. Knowledge about knowledge implies not only being aware of the context in which I generate knowledge but also asking how I can confirm knowledge. Human beings share the same world but interpret it in unique ways (Husserl 1950:65; 1960:26).[2] A meaningful sense of reality and objectivity requires transcending unsharable experiences and recognizing that we relate to the same world. In essence, how do I constitute the other within my self (Guenther 2011:268)? Husserl (1950, 1960) bases his explanation on

the lived experience of embodiment. I relate to my body with an imme-
diacy that is distinct from my engagement with all other objects. I can see
a fresh croissant, touch it, hear its crunchy layers, smell its buttery aroma,
bite it, and taste it. My body is integral to eating the croissant; I perceive
my movements and I feel how my senses interact physically with it. Husserl (1950:149–156; 1960:120–128) correspondingly distinguishes the living
body linked to the self (German *Leib*) from the body as externalized object
(German *Körper*). Eating the croissant merges body and self seamlessly.

Self- and object-body are the basis for distinguishing self from other. In
everyday life, I encounter others and I recognize them as object-bodies. For
example, I go to buy a croissant in a café. On entering, I see other customers
and I wait in line to be served. As the line moves slowly toward the counter,
people take eachother's places. I move forward where the person in front
of me was standing and occupy the other's "there" while the person behind
me steps into what was just a moment ago my "here" (Guenther 2011:268).
The deictic switch calls my attention to me as an object-body that is similar
to the object-bodies in front of and behind me. Stepping into the space that
another object-body occupied earlier allows me to experience the world
from that perspective and I infer the other's self-body. Out of this embodied relationality emerges self and other. However, I also understand that my
body can never inhabit the same space as another's body at the same time.
The other is like me but is not me (analogizing transfer in Husserl 1950:140;
1960:111). My bodily experience alternates between the phenomenal and
the objective perspective. I am both rabbit and duck.

The shared movement of people waiting in line harmonizes our bodies and pairs our selves (Husserl 1950:141–143; 1960:112–113). This does not
mean "that we *simultaneously* come to the *same* understanding of any given
situation (although this can happen), but that we have, to start, the *possibility* of exchanging places, of seeing the world from the point of view of
the Other" (Duranti 2010:20; emphasis in the original; the idea of trading
places predates Husserl [Duranti 2010:30 n. 4]). The people waiting in line
move forward by trading places, not by walking through each other; they
rest their hands on the counter and the counter supports them; they order
croissants and coffees and walk away holding both in their hands. I observe
all of these events, and as I step to the counter and replicate their actions, I
know that my mind is not playing tricks on me. Observing others confirms
to me that objects like the counter are real and that I relate to these objects
in the same way as others do. I can never be the other, but my experience interweaves with the other's to form "an invisible net that supports the

coherence of my own experience" (Guenther 2012). Our shared experiences create a harmonious synthesis and a consistent confirmation of my self and my sense of objectivity (Husserl 1950:144; 1960:114). Others may not share my interpretation of the world. Since we recognize each other as inhabitants of the same world, we can at least agree to disagree. "Intersubjectivity is thus an existential condition that can *lead* to a shared understanding—an important achievement in its own terms—rather than being itself such an understanding" (Duranti 2010:21–22; emphasis in the original). The collective perceptual access to the human experience forms the basis for public discourse (Urban 1996:246).

## Social Knowing in Maya Cultures

The ways in which humans understand themselves and others are culturally configured. Empathic processes differ cross-culturally in various respects (Groark 2008:430). First, the relative value of social knowing varies; it may be desirable in some cultural contexts and impossible in others. Second, the mechanisms through which insights into others can be gained vary and involve complex projective-introspective dynamics. Third, empathic knowing is socially relevant; for example, with regard to cooperation and trust. Fourth, members of society know the culturally relevant empathic processes and correspondingly incorporate them in their decision-making; they may frustrate or facilitate what others come to know about them.

Modern and ancient Maya grapple with the epistemological problem of what they can know about others. K'iche' Maya express the limitations of people's knowledge of one another as a fall from grace in the Popol Vuh, their "Book of Council" (Tedlock 1985:165–167). God created their ancestors, or "first mother-fathers," who talked, looked, listened, walked, and worked. "Thoughts came into existence and they gazed; their vision came all at once" (Tedlock 1985:165). These humans had perfect vision and their sight passed through trees, rocks, lakes, seas, mountains, and plains. "As they looked, their knowledge became intense" (Tedlock 1985:165). Their maker worried that they would become as great as gods and decided to take back their knowledge. "They were blinded as the face of a mirror is breathed upon" (Tedlock 1985:167). Their weakened eyes let them discern only nearby things. With that, the humans lost the means of understanding and the means of knowing everything.

The inner states of others are thought to be largely inaccessible in many Maya cultures (Danziger 2013; Groark 2008, 2013; Hanks 1990; Warren

1995). Among the Yucatec Maya, "people interact on the basis of common assumptions and shared codes of proper conduct, summarized in the idea of *legalidad*, 'legality, propriety,' yet they are keenly aware that actors harbor hidden agendas, and that each person 'follows a different road'" (Hanks 1990:93). Correspondingly, social interactions are highly formalized. In conversations, Tzotzil Maya are conspicuously polite while also purposefully opaque so as to reveal as little as possible about themselves (Groark 2013:282; Haviland and Haviland 1983). Danziger (2013:259) argues that speakers cling to conventions to minimize conscious reflection and to facilitate social exchanges. The minds of others may be knowable, but "knowledge of the momentary inner states of individual actors is not considered to be a highly relevant parameter when it comes to interpretation of or, especially, to moral evaluation of others' acts" (Danziger 2013:253–254).

Social opacity characterizes face-to-face interactions among modern Maya. Nonetheless, culture-specific forms of intersubjectivity exist. Prayers express honest emotion and empathic connection. "Only in relationship to the deities—and, indirectly, with family members who might be present to hear these prayers and witness the open expression of intense emotion—is full empathic knowing of one's inner states expected and experienced" (Groark 2008:441). Similarly, Tzotzil Maya curers take a patient's pulse to diagnose sicknesses (Groark 2008:442; J. Nash 1967:133). The blood as well as ritualized confessions tell healers everything about their patient's physical and social state. In public, Tzotzil Maya (especially women) experience anxiety (Groark 2013:283–284). They fear the "hidden words" of people who muster words silently. "When they say something, it seems I feel it in my body" (Groark 2013:284). One's bodily experience embodies and indexes the content of others' hearts and minds. Maya life forces fail to follow the western distinction of body versus soul (Monaghan 1998). In rituals and dreams, some life forces can detach themselves from the body and interact with the life forces of other humans and supernatural beings. Sorcerers and witches try to injure and even kill life forces. "Latent social discord and rancorous feelings can manifest directly in the body as physical or psychosocial symptoms linked to soul-based causes" (Groark 2013:285).

Classic Maya seem to have valued social opacity as well. Nobles displayed themselves in formal poses on public monuments (for example, Figures 1.3, 3.3, 3.4, 6.10, 7.3). They tended to appear in more fluid poses on polychrome vessels and other portable artifacts that presumably were accessible to only few people (compare, for example, the dancer on a Uaxactun vessel [inset in Figure 6.10]). "The corpus of ancient Maya art suggests that, as in

Figure 2.2. The burial of Dos Pilas King Itzamnaaj K'awiil in A.D. 726, glyphs H13–I16 from Dos Pilas Stela 8. The glyph based on the stem *il* or *ila,* "to see, witness" is screened in gray. (Drawing after photos.)

modern ethnographic contexts, the open display of lust, fear, and grief are marked as dangerous and inappropriate for public presentation, though they may be appropriate components of circumstances in which actions are observed by limited audiences or housed in private spaces" (Golden and Scherer 2013:401–402). Empathic processes likely differed for public and private contexts.

Embodied experiences often form the basis of knowing others in Maya cultures. The emphasis in the Popol Vuh on seeing as a way of gaining knowledge applies to Classic Maya culture as well. For example, as I discuss later, rulers gazed into mirrors to divine the future. "When the Classic Maya regarded individual perception, at least in their glyphic texts, it was not simply as a vista or a bracing view of architecture, but as a reciprocal, heavily social context involving other people or beings" (Houston et al. 2006:174). As an example, Itzamnaaj K'awiil, the second ruler of Dos Pilas, passed away in A.D. 726. Twenty-eight lords attended his burial four days later. The corresponding passage on Dos Pilas Stela 8 employs the verb *il,* which means not only "to see" but also "to witness" (Figure 2.2; Houston

1989:39; Houston and Taube 2000:281–289; Stone 1995:165–169; Stuart 1987:25–26). Classic Maya called a shrine *waybil*, or a "sleeping place" of gods (Freidel et al. 1993:188–193; Houston and Stuart 1989:11). Similar to their modern successors, they could communicate with supernatural beings and ancestors when sleeping and dreaming.

Empathic processes foster trust and cooperation in Classic Maya culture (Golden and Scherer 2013). Classic nobles had *way,* or "co-essences," that were extra-somatic life forces (Houston and Stuart 1989). *Way* take fantastic forms and mix supernatural, human, and animal characteristics (Grube and Nahm 1994). In modern Maya cultures, human owners have animal companions, and the two share the same fate (Vogt 1969:371–374). On the other hand, Classic Maya *way* are linked to the divine ruler of a royal dynasty but not to a specific named ruler. This suggests that *way* were shared by multiple individuals and served as emblems of their royal identity.

## Living Body of Christ

The body is not simply a container for consciousness but fuses with consciousness into the self-body. When people perceive the world via the senses, self- and object-body are continuous. People experience their body as object when they interact with others. Standing in line forces people to move forward in unison with others. They step into a place that was occupied by somebody else and pretend to perceive the world from the same perspective. They switch from self- to object-body and back and transfer the experience their predecessor previously had, inferring that they are similar to others. This process of mirroring harmonizes them with others (Husserl 1950:125; 1960:94). Husserl then argues that the pairing of self and other creates an association through passive synthesis rather than active deliberation (Husserl 1950:142; 1960:112). However, experiencing the self- and object-body is an ongoing dialectical process that actively reveals self and other (see also Biceaga 2010). At the same time, self-body and object-body maintain their uniqueness. They are aware that they can never be at the same place at the same time as somebody else. Others are like them but they are not them.

The experience of self- and object-body constitutes the other within the self. But how is this possible if I can only be my self? The Catholic Church resolved this tension through the doctrine of transubstantiation. Jesus Christ took the bread at the Last Supper, blessed it, and gave it to the disciples, saying: "Take, eat; this is my body" (Matthew 26:26, King James

Bible). In the Eucharist, bread and wine transform into the body and blood of Jesus Christ. Transubstantiation states that bread and wine maintain their physical appearance but change in substance to the body and blood of Jesus Christ. The German wording of the liturgy of the Eucharist registers the dogma of transubstantiation precisely. When repeating Christ's words "Take, eat; this is my body," the priest uses *Leib*, or "self-body," instead of *Körper*, or "object-body." Self- and object-body are illusionary experiences, and self is the other. This position ignores the physical experience of the world, as Thomas Aquinas (1964:55, 57) acknowledges: "We could never know by our senses that the real body of Christ and his blood are in this sacrament, but only by our faith which is based on the authority of God."

On the other hand, I emphasize the other within my self as an essential dialectic. The differentiation of self and other is the act of representation (Eberl 2013:455). I create a symbol, or *aliquid stat pro aliquo* "something that stands for something else." Christian baptism makes a child a member of the church and incorporates that child into the "living body of Christ" (1 Corinthians 12:12–14). To become part of the "we" of the Christian community, the child has to emerge as an "I." Instead of relying on belief, I explain the process symbolically. The phrase "living body of Christ" combines metaphor and metonym. Recall that a metaphor relates elements from separate semantic fields and a metonym elements of the same domain. Corinthians 12 links the child to Christ (a metaphor) and expresses the relationship in bodily terms (a metonym). The self projects a symbol upon itself to constitute the other.

Metonyms and metaphors become embodied (for example, Eberl 2013; Schmidt 2006; Tilley 1999; Turner 1991). They are figures of speech but similar processes occur outside of language. Among the Yaka in southwestern Zaire, a diviner-to-be embodies a water shrew (Devisch 1993:44). Its keen sense of smell allows the water shrew, which maintains a burrow with one entrance underwater and another above water, to hunt fish and insects at night. In a trance state, the diviner digs a tunnel with his bare hands and crawls through it; his reappearance concludes his initiation into the *ngoombu* cult. The underground journey serves as a metaphor for death and rebirth while also metonymically imparting on the diviner the shrew's keen sense of smell. Through olfactory, visual, tactile, and verbal stimuli, rituals create multilayered experiences and draw together fields of meaning. In this way rituals represent the meaning of symbols and endow symbols with new meaning (Devisch 1993:43).

A similar symbolic analysis applies to ancient and modern Maya cave rituals. At Chan Kom, ritual foodstuffs are prepared with *zuhuy ha,* or "virgin water." Locals fetch this water from a cenote accessed through a dark and slippery tunnel. "The difficulty of entrance, and the snake-wise movement of the torch-lit procession enhance the awesomeness of the ritual act" (Redfield and Villa Rojas 1934:139). Based on ethnographic comparisons, Brady and Rissolo (2006) argue that the ancient Maya mined caves predominantly for ritual purposes.

Similar to the patient's body in Yaka healing rituals, the child's body is both tool and raw material in birth rituals (Eberl 2013:455). Two processes intersect in children: biologically, they mature as they grow up; socially, they differentiate self from other to become persons. The social and the physical body imply each other (Csordas 1994; Strathern 1992; Turner 1995). Social categories constrain how the physical body is perceived while physical experiences sustain a particular view of society (Douglas 1996:69). The physical experience of symbols bridges the concrete and the abstract (Johnson 1987:xv). On the one hand, symbols project our bodily movements and physical interactions with the world onto abstract domains. Digging the tunnel represents the rebirth of the Yaka novice as a diviner. On the other hand, bodily experience constrains what physical manifestations can be projected on to what symbols. During baptism, the priest anoints a child with chrism to make that child a reincarnation of Jesus Christ, who was anointed priest, prophet, and king.

## Maya Creator God Itzamnaaj

Metonymy and metaphor allow one culture group to spin webs of relationships that remain unintelligible for speakers of a different language and bearers of a different culture. The starting point is the creation myths that serve as the charter for a society (Malinowski 1948). They answer eternal human questions: What is the world? Who made it? How did it happen? Why and when? The Classic Maya myth about the world's origin links creation and destruction (Stuart 2005:60–87, 176–180; Velásquez García 2006). Itzamnaaj oversees the accession of the deity GI in 3309 B.C. or about two centuries before the beginning of ancient Maya time on 13.0.0.0.0 4 Ajaw 8 Kumk'u, or 3114 B.C. Eleven years later and possibly at the hands of deity GI, the cosmic crocodile is decapitated and causes a deluge of blood. (The ancient Maya name for deity GI, or 'God I,' remains debated and scholars continue to use Berlin's [1963] abbreviation.) Its dismembered body parts become the surface of the current world. Hundreds of years into the current

Figure 2.3. Creator god Itzamnaaj brings the decapitated maize god, whose head stands for the maize kernel, back to life. (Detail from vessel K1183; drawing after rollout photo by Justin Kerr.)

era, GI is reborn alongside two new gods, and all three become patron deities of Palenque. They are the creation of a higher deity; the corresponding Maya term, *chab*, means not only "to engender" but also "to sacrifice." Inscribed Stingray Spine 6 from Comalcalco exemplifies the latter meaning in an earthly context. Its text describes how the bones and skull of a sacrificed captive were piled up in A.D. 766 and calls Aj Pakal Tahn, who performed this act, *u baah u chab y-ak'abil* "he is genesis [and] darkness." Births of gods and humans require the shedding of blood. *Chab* epitomizes destruction and renewal as the complementary opposites of creating.

Itzamnaaj contains both aspects. Some traditions identify him as the crocodile whose beheading enables the current world, and they portray him with stingray spines as tools of bloodletting (Taube 1992:37). He also brings back life. An ancient Maya myth recounts how the maize god was decapitated (Taube 1992:44). His head, which symbolizes the maize kernel, ends up with Itzamnaaj, who opens the bundle and reawakens the maize god (Figure 2.3). Harvesting and planting maize manifest the complementary duality of the Maya concept of creation. Both aspects came together when colonial Yucatec Maya honored Itzamnaaj during the Tup K'ahk,' or "putting out the fire" ceremony (Tozzer 1941:162–164). Priests hunted

animals and collected them in the temple courtyard. After setting up a bon-
fire, they cut the animals open and threw their hearts into the fire. When
all the hearts were consumed, the fire was doused with water. The animals'
sacrifice promised a good year of rains and a rich harvest.

Among the Classic Maya gods, Itzamnaaj occupies a central role as creator and facilitator (Taube 1992:31–41).[3] Seated on a throne-bench and surrounded by the luxuries of royal life, he is a senior king (Figure 2.4). To his
forehead are attached a mirror and a tasseled and beaded flower. Both elements relate to Itzamnaaj in metonymic and metaphorical ways. The flower
refers, in the form of dew or nectar, to *itz,* "sap, pitch, and other oozing
fluids," as well as to the first segment of Itzamnaaj's name (see, for example,
Kaufman and Norman 1984:121 no. 174). Maya art expresses beautiful music and dance through flowers (Houston and Taube 2000:265–273). For the
ancient Maya, flowers are more than delicate aesthetic ideals; they emit the
sweet smell not only of having high status but also of being alive. They are
associated with Itzamnaaj because he, as a creator god, gives the breath of
life.

The mirror is Itzamnaaj's tool. The sign for *ak'bal,* "darkness," that is inscribed into Itzamnaaj's mirror recalls the black obsidian or golden brown
pyrite of which the mirror is made. Gazing into the mirror reveals hidden
structures and deep knowledge. For example, mirror gazing allowed colonial curers to discern the causes of a sickness. Their mirror had to be un-
blemished, and the Ritual of the Bacabs advises: *tu pach u wich u pikch'inil
bin chan k'as nen,* "one will have to throw a damaged mirror behind oneself without looking" (my translation after Arzápalo Marín 1987:321). In
colonial Yucatec Maya, *nen,* "mirror," is the root for *nen-ba,* "to look at
oneself (in a mirror or water)," and *nen-ba in cah ti nen,* "I look at myself
in a mirror" (my translation after Arzápalo Marín 1995:557). The mirror
image represents more than a simple reflection. *Nen-olal* means "imagination, amusement, contemplation, consideration" (my translation after Arzápalo Marín 1995:557). *Payal-chi lic u nentic y ol* means "in praying she/he
occupies and amuses her-/himself" (my translation after Arzápalo Marín
1995:557). The ancient Maya are reflected in a mirror and use it to reflect
on themselves and the world. Itzamnaaj carries the mirror as a sign of his
wisdom, insight, and knowledge.

Creation requires deep knowledge and the ability to discern hidden connections. Hieroglyphic texts facilitate both. For one, they record when the
Moon, Venus, and celestial bodies appeared in the sky; and when Maya
individuals went to war, married, and sired heirs. Divination explains

Figure 2.4. Itzamnaaj shows the mask he made to the Monkey Scribe and the Maize God. (Detail from polychrome vessel K8457; drawing after rollout photo by Justin Kerr.)

why these historical events took place and what will happen in the future. Similar events occur on similar dates; events are connected by distance numbers, whose lengths reverberate with calendrical cycles and sacred numbers. At Palenque, rulers and deities often acceded to the throne on Tzolk'iin day 9 Ik', or Nine Wind (Stuart 2005:183–185). Local lore recalls the "first grasping of the K'awiil scepter" on 9 Ik' in 931,449 B.C.; deity GI is seated as ruler on 9 Ik' in 3309 B.C.; another deity becomes ruler on 9 Ik' in 2325 B.C. Based on these precedents, K'inich Ahkal Mo' Nahb legitimized his rule by acceding to the throne on 9 Ik' in A.D. 721 (Figure 3.4).

A well-known example for Maya numerology comes from the Venus pages in the Dresden Codex, where the distance number 9.9.16.0.0 leads to the beginning date of the five-year Venus cycle (Lounsbury 1976:212–213). The distance number is 1,366,560 days long and corresponds to 5,265 Tzolk'iin cycles, 3,744 Haab' cycles, 2,340 Venus cycles, 1,752 Mars cycles, and so forth. Knowledge of writing reveals the mysterious links between calendar, astronomy, and history that explain the past and determine the future. Not surprisingly, Itzamnaaj invented, according to colonial Yucatec Maya, "the characters that served the natives for writing" (translated after López Cogolludo and Ayeta 1685:196). Through writing, he divines why things happened, are happening, and will happen.

According to the ancient Maya everything has life energy or a soul—including the flowery breath of life (Houston et al. 2006:34–35). As creator god, Itzamnaaj overcomes the western separation of inanimate versus animate. For example, he paints a temple in the Madrid Codex (Figure 2.5). This seemingly mundane activity relates to Maya concepts of animation

Figure 2.5. Creator god Itzamnaaj paints a temple. (From Madrid Codex page 23c; drawing based on Lee 1985:96.)

Figure 2.6. The rain god Chaak (glyph A2) plants (*u pak'-a*; glyph A1) sustenance (*tzeen*; glyph B1); the diving god impersonates the plant seedling and holds the glyph for *waaj*, "(maize) tamale," thus clarifying that sustenance refers here to maize. Lacadena (1997:190–191) discusses alternative interpretations for the *pak'* verb. (From Dresden Codex page 15b; omitted are calendrical elements; drawing based on Förstemann 1880.)

(Stross 1998:31–33). Clothing a human being, roofing a house, and painting a temple all enclose, define, and give life. Several polychrome vessels show Itzamnaaj with a mask in his hand and the accompanying hieroglyphic text explains *u pak'-aw,* "he shapes it" (Figure 2.4, glyph A2). In colonial Ch'olti' and modern Ch'orti,' *pak'* means not only "to shape" and "to mold" but also "to plant" (Pérez Martínez et al. 1996:163; Robertson et al. 2010:348; Wisdom 1950:554; Figure 2.6). For ancient and modern Maya, shaping the mask is the same as planting corn. Itzamnaaj makes the mask and imbues it with life.

Masks epitomize the act of creation. Worn during dances, they transform humans into gods (Coe 1978; Looper 2009). Masks both represent and are the deity. In 1562, Francisco Cen testified before the Inquisition that a girl was heart-sacrificed and killed in the presence of "thirty or forty clay idols, small and large, and more than twenty wooden masks" (translated after Scholes and Adams 1938:141). Spanish administrators consequently prohibited all native dances, rituals, and festivals except for the feast day of each town's patron saint, Christmas, and Corpus Christi. The natives were to celebrate these Catholic holidays without renting or bringing masks, feathers, or extraordinary dresses (Scholes and Adams 1960:138).

Western cultures separate the making of objects from the creating of new plant or animal life. Technology therefore differs from the reproduction of society. This distinction fails to apply to the animated universe of the ancient Maya. The creative process is not limited to the material side of an object but extends into metaphysics and imbues the artifact with soul. Itzamnaaj is engineer and priest, creator of novelties and creator of life (Figure 7.4).

## Why Hummingbirds Have Wings

Creation myths work as cognitive structures or schemata through which people understand their world. Some westerners see themselves as the random outcome of a big bang billions of years ago. Christians believe in a God who created the universe in seven days. According to the ancient Maya, Itzamnaaj and other creator gods destroyed what had existed before and created the current world and current era in 3114 B.C. Thus, chaos led to order; destruction turned into creation.

Creation myths are conceptual schemes that blend ontological, theoretical, and methodological principles. Westerners with a scientific bent trace hummingbirds' wings to the hands of Triassic dinosaurs (Weishampel et al.

Figure 2.7. Itzamnaaj grants the hummingbird its wings. Itzamnaaj, wearing the Ajaw plaque, sits in front of the winged hummingbird. The separate image on the left shows the wingless hummingbird. (Details of Tikal's Hummingbird Vessel [K8008]; drawing after rollout photo by Justin Kerr.)

2004:218–220). By invoking evolution, they show how the dinosaurs lost digits 4 and 5 of their hands over millions of years. The ancient Maya describe Itzamnaaj as creator god; the *ajaw* plaque that he sometimes wears identifies him as a supreme king (Figure 2.7). The wingless hummingbird approaches Itzamnaaj with a jar full of *atole* and flowers (Stone and Zender 2011:90). The bird pleads with the god until he grants its wish and gives it wings. Ordinary people would be hard-pressed to empirically test either of these two creation myths and accept them as truth. The myths work as cognitive structures, or schemata, through which people understand their world. I identify four components through which schemata explain the world (based on Kuhn's [1996:181–187] discussion of paradigms).

First, schemata provide symbolic generalizations. For believers in evolution, when dinosaur hands became bird wings, fitness ($w$) increased according to the formula $w = N_{after}/N_{before}$. Since winged animals survived better and had more offspring, their number ($N$) rose within their population over many generations (before/after). This formula integrates fitness, populations, generational change, and phenotypes as key concepts of evolution, and it establishes the relationships among them. The Maya creation myth presents a different generalization. Here, the hummingbird and other animals interact with Itzamnaaj to obtain wings or other essential attributes. This myth centers on individuals, power hierarchies, and social negotiation, and connects them into a story. Both formula and myth identify key elements and the causal relationships among them.

Second, schemata articulate with worldviews. Worldviews are much more comprehensive—one could use the word *culture* instead—but become manifest only through schemata. The hummingbird's pleading with Itzamnaaj exemplifies the animated Maya universe in which animals have agency and the boundary between gods and earthly beings is fluid. For evolutionists, on the other hand, the individual bird disappears in a quantifiable population and across time measured in many generations; genetic makeup determines its behavior and appearance. Paradigms become culturally relevant because worldviews provide appropriate analogies and metaphors. For example, Itzamnaaj is the role model for Maya rulers (see McAnany 2010:213–216). Followers of a particular schema see their approach as superior or, as Kuhn (1996:111–135) argued, as the only true one. From Kuhn's perspective, schemata are incommensurable and science advances in revolutions because new worldviews supplant earlier ones. I disagree on this point. Evolutionists do not share the Maya explanation of a hummingbird's wings but they may at least understand it. Worldviews are relative, not absolute.

Third, schemata define shared values. Scientific models like the theory of evolution emphasize hypothesis testing. If bird wings originated with dinosaur hands, then one should be able to find transitory fossils. In fact, paleontologists have been able to document the loss of two digits and the elongation of the remaining digits across time (Weishampel et al. 2004:219). The ancient Maya creation myth leaves scientists stymied because it lacks a testable hypothesis. Instead, the myth articulates the mutual obligations among all beings in the Maya universe (Monaghan 2000:37–38). The hummingbird gives the god gifts and obtains wings in return. The underlying value is a give-and-take between unequal partners. The differing values that undergird paradigms evoke strong emotional responses, as the current debate between evolutionists and creationists shows. Each community of followers sanctions its shared values.

Fourth, schemata are exemplars that apply to the real world. They not only describe rules, but also encourage learning by doing. Concrete analysis is, for example, common in science. Scholars study the hand-to-wing transition in fossils and skeletons. Through hands-on experience they acquire tacit knowledge that allows them to extend the paradigm and recognize similar situations without having to evoke the underlying rules. Biologists count the five digits of a bat wing and exclude bats from the category of birds. The ancient Maya, on the other hand, view the bat as one of many animals that approached Itzamnaaj to gain their unique characteristics. Their schema serves as a general model that applies to human society. A Maya would approach an earthly ruler (instead of Itzamnaaj) and, with gifts or tribute in hand, ask for favors.

The Maya creation myth and the evolution from dinosaur hand to bird wing are two explanations for a hummingbird's wings. These schemata serve as charters for communities of followers. Their power to convince emotionally and rationally derives from the four ways in which they are cognitively embedded as symbolic generalization, worldviews, shared values, and exemplars. Schemata are key aspects for understanding technology. I mentioned in the introduction that the Australian Yir Yoront lack canoes, not because of missing knowledge or missing resources, but because their mythical ancestors did not have them (Sharp 1952:22). Only a schema that associates canoes with an ancestor would allow the Yir Yoront to accept and integrate this technology. Technological change requires, in other words, not only shifting skills and resources, but also shifting schemata.

## Mambrino's Enchanted Helmet

Creativity is the opposite of a language disorder. The symbolic structure of human discourse collapses in the latter, while creativity establishes and expands it. No one could exemplify this concept better than the ingenious gentleman Don Quixote. Shortly after leaving his village with Sancho Panza, he encounters a glamorous knight with a shiny helmet on a magnificent steed (Cervantes Saavedra 2004 [1605]:187–199). The helmet attracts his attention because he perceives it as the enchanted helmet of the Moorish king Mambrino. Medieval knights of chivalric romances longed for this helmet made of pure gold because it rendered the wearer invulnerable. When Don Quixote readies himself to engage the knight, Sancho holds him back, unsure of what his master sees. Isn't that a barber who has been caught in the rain and who, for an umbrella, has capped himself with the brass basin he uses to bleed sick people and shave men? Don Quixote patiently answers that the golden helmet must have been melted down to make what Sancho thinks is a barber's basin. "But be it as it may; to me who recognizes it, its transformation is irrelevant," and it will at least protect me against a chance blow with a stone (my translation after Cervantes Saavedra 2004 [1605]:190).

Creativity establishes new relationships among elements and thereby creates symbols. Don Quixote is ingenuous—and daft—for envisioning an enchanted helmet where Sancho Panza sees a barber's basin. Schemata provide organizing principles for classification. Sancho Panza explains the brass bowl, the simple man, and the gray donkey as a barber with a tool of his trade. He identifies the round, wide, and concave metal object by connecting it to a typology and considering its context. On the other hand, Don Quixote questions Sancho's coherent interplay among perception, memory, and imagination. Is the world as simple as that? If the basin can serve as an umbrella, couldn't it also be a helmet? Don Quixote exposes the barber's basin as only one of many possible interpretations. In doing so, he also doubts its classification. Like other structures, typologies are neither final nor external but are constituted by humans through their speech and behavior. In the hands of the barber, the basin becomes an umbrella; in the eyes of Don Quixote, it becomes a helmet. Allowing multiple functions for the basin as type creates a quandary. One could close one's eyes and insist that a basin remains a basin no matter what: the classification must remain stable regardless of any contradictory experiences. Alternatively, one could redefine the type basin and include umbrellas and helmets; doing so runs the risk of creating overlapping and overly general classifications. Finally, one could restrict the type basin to objects barbers use for shaving men; all other uses are symbolic. A basin is not, but could be, an umbrella or a helmet. A representation without being defines it as a symbol.

Lévi-Strauss compares mythical thought to bricolage. Elements of a myth are meaningless by themselves, just like jetsam found on a beach. The collector "interrogates all the heterogeneous objects of which his treasury is composed to discover what each of them could 'signify' and so contribute to the definition of a set which has yet to materialize" (Lévi-Strauss 1966:18). Symbols organize the classification system of which they are parts through a comparison of types. Unlike identical types, which share all their characteristics, a nonidentical type represents another type by sharing at least one feature while maintaining differences. A basin is like an umbrella because it is impermeable to rain, yet it is also much heavier and less convenient. Don Quixote's imagination resonates because a basin is solid and potentially protective like a helmet. The comparisons identify shared and different features. Through this differentiation, symbols reveal dormant potentialities (Fernandez 1986:8–11; Ricœur 1977:43). A good example is the invention of the bar code. After World War II, N. Joseph Woodland was asked to create scannable price labels. He spent the winter of 1948 in Miami. Seated in a beach chair, he remembered the Morse code he had learned as Boy Scout. He thought about dots and dashes as he poked his hand into the sand, pulled it toward himself, and drew four lines with his fingers. "Golly!" Woodland thought. "Now I have four lines and they could be wide lines and narrow lines, instead of dots and dashes" (Leibowitz 1999:134).

A comparison of types introduces vulnerability, however. Searching for shared and different features requires me to ask what I know and don't know about the objects in question. I have to evaluate my knowledge and face failure. If I come up with new relationships and convert objects into symbols, the symbols reflect not only my classification system but also the fragile creative process that led to them. This dramatization of risk heightens the sense of a meta-level, or hyper-reality, that enables my dialectic inquiry. The pre-existing classification becomes comparable to a photograph. I can accept what the camera records as a perfect representation of the world. "But this is the opposite of understanding, an approach which starts from *not* accepting the world as it looks" (Sontag 1977:23; emphasis in the original). Modern Ch'ol Maya embed this dialectic into their origin myths. Before the current era and world, there was a "time without time" when words lacked meaning and things had no names (García de León 1988:35). Order—in the form of meaning and classification—arose only when the sun was conceived and rose over the liquid darkness.

Creativity disrupts and then reframes. First, it opens to question one's mental interpretation of the world. Second, it finds new relationships among elements and creates symbols. In the case of Mambrino's helmet, Don Quixote links a barber's basin to a chivalric tale and envisions the basin as a helmet. The basin refers to a helmet but—as even Don Quixote acknowledges—it never becomes one. Though symbols elucidate the classification system, they never provide cognitive closure and so leave the typology in flux. They create meta-awareness about the classification system.

## Reenacting Myths, Becoming Gods

The ancient Maya create symbols by reenacting creation myths and impersonating gods. Their myths are not simply stories but ways to express knowledge through behavior. "The myth does not exist that is not the ever-renewed revelation of a reality, which so imbues the being, that he makes his behavior conform to it," Leenhardt (1979:192) observes. "Short of this, it slowly hardens into a story which will become cold one day." I mentioned earlier that decapitating a crocodile initiated the creation of the current world and era according to Palenque lore. A variant of this myth appears at the nearby site of Yaxchilan. Step VII of Hieroglyphic Stairway 2 recalls three decapitations long before the current era and couches these sacrifices as victories in a ballgame. A distance number links the three mythological victories to a ballgame in A.D. 744 in which King Bird Jaguar IV reenacts the myth. He ties a captive into a ball, pushes him down a stairway, and lets him fall to his death.

Self-sacrifice by bloodletting complements the sacrifice of others. In the sixteenth century, Maya anointed "the face of the idol with blood they drew right there, either from their ears, by piercing them, or from their nostrils or tongue, and even from their private parts" (Tozzer 1941:222). The glyph for *ch'ab*, "to fast" and "to do penance," is fittingly a lacerated male genital (Knowlton 2010:21–25). The ancient Maya saw penance as crucial to the creation of new life. *Ch'ab* describes in hieroglyphic texts how parents engender their children (for example, Copan Altar U, Yaxchilan Lintel 14) and how gods bring forth junior gods (for example, Palenque Temple of the Cross Tablet). Fasting and penance are also components of manufacture. Yucatec Maya artisans carved new wooden god statues while "cutting their ears. And anointing those idols with the blood and burning their incense" (Tozzer 1941:160). Destruction through sacrifice enables creation, not only in the mythological past but also in the historical present.

As part of the reenactment of myths, humans impersonate gods. On carved monuments, *baah*, "self" or "image," often introduces the names of rulers (Houston and Stuart 1996, 1998). *Baah,* and the related term *baah ahn,* thereby identify the ruler as the image of the deity. Humans become the "face" (*ba*) of gods, as modern Tzotzil Maya say (Vogt 1976:205). By wearing masks, humans signal their transformation into gods. Impersonation blurs the boundary between human and divine, between history and myth. Impersonating Itzamnaaj forms part of the reenactment of creation myths. According to the platform in Palenque's Temple XIX, Itzamnaaj oversaw the accession of deity GI to the throne in 3309 B.C. Eleven years later, the latter was then implicated in the beheading of the crocodile, leading to the creation of the current world in 3114 B.C. The hieroglyphic text jumped more than three millennia to connect the creation myth to the accession of King K'inich Ahkal Mo' Nahb in A.D. 721 (Figure 2.8). The king and his court reenacted GI's accession at the hands of Itzamnaaj thousands

Figure 2.8. Disguised as the god Itzamnaaj, nobleman Janaab Ajaw hands Palenque's royal headband to King K'inich Ahkal Mo' Nahb, who impersonates the god GI during his accession in A.D. 721. The hieroglyphic texts begin with *u baahil ahn* (glyphs U1 and W1), which relates to impersonation (Houston and Stuart 1996:297–300; Stuart 2005:118). (Detail of the south face of the Temple XIX platform; Figure 3.4 shows the entire scene; drawing based on photos in Stuart 2005.)

of years earlier. Disguised as Itzamnaaj, the noble Janaab Ajaw hands the royal headband to the royal heir, who impersonates deity GI, thereby installing him as the new king of Palenque. In this moment Prince Chuluk becomes the divine king K'inich Ahkal Mo' Nahb.

Reenactment and impersonation pose difficult questions: Is Janaab Ajaw Itzamnaaj? Is Chuluk deity GI? Can humans be gods? The ancient Maya rituals described previously are mimetic (Durkheim 1995:355–373). Following Frazer's law of similarity, like begets like (Frazer 1905:37–38; see also Hubert and Mauss 1902–1903:61–73). Maya rulers dress as gods to become gods. Yet this mimetic quality underestimates the symbolic process. In Maya hieroglyphic texts humans take on throne names like Sihyaj Chan K'awiil "K'awiil Is Born from the Sky" but also retain their princely names (Eberl and Graña-Behrens 2004); they call themselves divine (*k'uhul*) but never *k'uh*, or gods (Houston and Stuart 1996). The ancient Maya understood the universe to be animated by a divine principle (monistic orientation in Monaghan 2000:25–26). Along with everything else, humans are suffused with this amorphous divine essence, and they employ rituals to give shape to the divine. During impersonation, Maya rulers act like gods but they do not become gods. The transformation of human beings into divine beings is a symbolic process. By replicating gods in speech, appearance, and acts, human-gods claim a priori knowledge of, or even possession of, a divine that seems independent of the ritual that enables their knowledge or possession. The symbolic process creates a circular logic "in which it creatively *brings about* a context and set of identities that it portrays as *already* existing" (Keane 1997:18; emphasis in the original). Impersonators present innovation as a long-standing tradition.

The symbolic analysis of impersonation helps to understand the Maya concept of *costumbre* (see also Chapter 1). *Costumbre* literally means "custom" and refers to practices first instituted by local ancestors or gods (Warren 1978:48–49; Watanabe 2000:230). In modern-day Santiago Atitlán, locals incorporated Catholic saints into their belief system called R'kan Sak R'kan Q'ij, "Footpath of the Dawn, Footpath of the Sun" (Carlsen and Prechtel 1991:36–37). Santiago (Saint James), the patron of the town, is said to have created two enemies and cut each in half with his sword (compare Rowe 2011:23–24). Saint James was one of Jesus's first disciples and supposedly preached the Gospel in Spain before being beheaded in A.D. 44. His body was miraculously brought to Santiago de Compostela, where it became the center of a world-famous pilgrimage. In a fictional battle in A.D. 844, a Christian army invoked the saint to vanquish the Moors. Thereafter, Saint James became known as Santiago Matamoros, or "moor-slayer," and was invoked during medieval battles as Spain's patron saint.

Atitecos ignore Santiago's military prowess and emphasize his regenerative ability. They categorize him as a fertility deity and ask him for rich harvests. The cultivation of maize provides the schema for Maya to integrate this apostle and other saints into pre-existing beliefs. Maya follow the *costumbre,* or schemata, that ancestors and gods established but they do not obey it slavishly. By embedding their practices in rituals, they shape the context in which they act. The circular logic of the symbolic process integrates change while maintaining continuity. The frustrating cul-de-sac "our ancestors did it this way" is not a last-ditch tactic to explain the unexplainable (Lemonnier 1986:165) or cover up unconscious cultural norms (Pfaffenberger 1992:504). Instead, ancestors and gods are crucial participants in native models of change and continuity. They are ritually invoked as role models to achieve consensus in the present.

## Reflections in Itzamnaaj's Mirror

The ancient Maya create resonating symbols through reenactment and im-personation. On his forehead, creator god Itzamnaaj wears a mirror, the tool for divination. Looking into the mirror, and the sense of seeing in general, empowers knowledge. In the sixteenth-century Popol Vuh, cre-ator gods struggled to create the first humans. They succeeded only when *xk'is kilö, xk'is keta'moj*, "completed was their sight, completed was their knowledge" (Hamann 2008b:60; see also Houston et al. 2006:138, 173). This K'iche phrase is a diphrastic kenning, a rhetorical device typical of Maya speech and writing (Edmonson 1985; Edmonson and Bricker 1985; Knowl-ton 2002). Diphrastic kennings were first noticed in Nahuatl literature in examples like *chalchihuitl, quetzalli,* literally "jade, quetzal feathers," for "beauty" (Garibay Kintana 1953–1954; León-Portilla 1963, 1985). The two constituent words or phrases tend to be tangible objects; together they sig-nify a larger abstract meaning. In the K'iche example, sight and knowledge have to be complete to form true human beings. Diphrastic kennings can be based on metonymy by joining two aspects with shared characteristics. Jade and quetzal feathers are blue-green, the color of beauty. Diphrastic kennings can also involve metaphors by bringing two distinct aspects to-gether. In Maya writing, the glyphs for night and day complement each other to read *tz'ak,* "to make whole" (Eberl 2015; Knowlton 2002; Riese 1984; Stuart 2005:99–100).

Maya diphrastic kennings express the symbolic process in a culturally specific way. For Maya, the process of becoming is a process of creating order in time and space. The Books of Chilam Balam describe this pro-cess as the growth of the Yaax Imixché, the green-blue ceiba tree, in the center of the world. The tree "supports the plate and the cup, the mat and the throne of the K'atunes," or twenty-year periods (Barrera Vásquez and Rendón 1948:155). The plate and cup are a diphrastic kenning for heaven and underworld, which the ceiba tree separates. The mat and the throne represent government because the K'atunes order time. Diphrastic ken-nings bring the abstract and the concrete together; or, as the Maya say, their face becomes present and their voice reveals their meaning (Barrera Vásquez and Rendón 1948:69, 95–96).

Itzamnaaj's mirror encapsulates Maya concepts of creativity and learn-ing. For the Maya to see also means to be seen. The colonial Motul diction-ary (folio 326r) calls Itzamnaaj *u nen kah,* "the mirror in which all people see themselves." The creator god wearing his mirror is a role model. Symbolism unfolds fully in Itzamnaaj. Metonymically, rulers impersonate him; metaphorically, Maya look to him as a role model. The Proto-Mayan word *kän, "to learn," survived in modern Ch'orti' as kanin, "to learn, to imitate, to copy" (Kaufman and Norman 1984:122; Pérez Martínez et al. 1996:92). Ch'orti' Maya say, for example, nik'wa'r ukani e ojroner xe' arob'na umen unoy, or "my nephew learned the story that his uncle told him." The Popol Vuh tells the legend of One Hunahpu, a great thinker and midmost seer. With his brother he taught skills to his sons, One Monkey and One Artisan, and the two "became flautists, singers, and writers, carvers, jadeworkers, metalworkers as well" (Tedlock 1985:91). Through these multiple crafts they came to understand the divine force that pervades the Maya universe. Their role models instructed them gently and forcefully. To become great knowers, the Popol Vuh's One Monkey and One Artisan had to master multiple arts and crafts. Learning requires great suffering and pain (Tedlock 1985:104). Similarly, during the feast of the month of Yaxk'iin, Yucatec Maya children received nine slight blows on their wrists "so that they might become skillful workmen in the professions of their fathers and mothers" (Tozzer 1941:159).

Learning from role models seems contradictory to the concept of innovation. How can imitating lead to novel solutions? Creativity explores resonating relationships among elements. To adapt Ervin Goffman's (1974:43) definition, symbols are patterned on one thing, but people see them as something else. Since this process is analogous to music, Goffman (1974:44) calls it keying. In the spirit of the ancient Maya, I compare this process to the reflections in Itzamnaaj's mirror. Its dark obsidian surface mirrors reality in unexpected hues and gives novel clues to the unseen. These representations relate the known in new ways through metonymy and metaphor. Don Quixote's chivalric worldview that sees a barber's basin as an enchanted helmet contrasts with Sancho Panza's premodern realism. For Don Quixote, the brass basin is not what it seems but rather represents Mambrino's melted-down gold helmet. Metonym extends his interpretation into similar domains—the basin could protect his head against a stone's blow—and metaphor associates his interpretation with a new domain—the basin as the sorry vestige of a glorious chivalric past. Metonym and metaphor explore the potentiality of symbolism.

## Analogic Reasoning

The textbook exemplifies a scientific discipline for students and scholars alike (Kuhn 1996:1). It contains the entire knowledge of a discipline by encoding it linguistically, by linearizing it in writing, and by formulating it logically. A textbook should make all its readers fluent in a discipline's schemas, or what Kuhn (1996) calls paradigms. But will an architectural digest necessarily make an architect, or a world history, an archaeologist? Books feed minds but not practice. Successful professionals have practical experience: an archaeologist learns to read the outline of an ancient building from a pile of stones or sees a midden where others step unknowingly on ceramic sherds and other artifacts. Anthropologists encounter this type of knowledge very often in non-western societies. For example, a Malagasy farmer walks through the forest with a friend, who points to a particular spot: "Look over there at that bit of forest, that would make a good swidden" (a piece of land made cultivable by slashing and burning the forest; Bloch 1991:187). To identify a good swidden, Malagasy farmers rely on a schema "partly visual, partly analytical (though not necessarily in a sententious logical way), partly welded to a series of procedures about what you should do to make and maintain a swidden" (Bloch 1991:187). Their knowledge is learned, stored, and transmitted nonverbally.

In non-western societies, students often learn through practice. For example, Ghanaian weavers and Yucatec Maya midwives rarely use questions and answers to teach their apprentices (Goody 1978; Jordan 1989). Apprenticeship learning "involves *the ability to do* rather than *the ability to talk about* something, and indeed it may be impossible to elicit from people operating in this mode what they know (how to do)" (Jordan 1989:933; emphasis in the original). The linguistic model of textbooks is ill-suited for this kind of experiential and multisensory knowledge.

The reasoning that makes sense of this complex knowledge is analogic and employs symbolic connections. In his analysis of Baktaman rituals, Fredrik Barth (1975) contrasted analogic with digital reasoning (see also Tilley 1999:29–31). Linguist Ferdinand de Saussure (1966) noted that the sound of words—linguistic signs—is unrelated to their meaning; instead, their meaning is determined in the context of words in a linear order and as part of a closed code (a dictionary). The Saussurian concept of signs correspondingly separates signifier from signified and sees the relationship between the two as arbitrary and ordered. For example, Lévi-Strauss identifies the elements of Winnebago myths and analyzes their meaning by relating the contexts in which they appear (for example, Lévi-Strauss 1960). By forcing the elements into binary oppositions like life and death, he employs a digital logic in which a string like "0101" has to be understood entirely to know that it encodes the number five. The two principles of these linguistic models—arbitrariness and linear order—are difficult to apply to nonverbal symbols (Barth 1975:207–208).

Nonverbal symbols seldom come in neat packages of arbitrarily linked form and meaning. For example, Barth (1975:235–236) analyzes the symbolic significance of the brushturkey. With its large claws, this chicken-like bird scratches forest debris together to build a large mound; it does this so meticulously that the area around the mound is as tidy and artificial as a weeded garden. It then buries its white eggs in the mound and incubates them for at least two months—allowing them to mature slowly like taro tubers—until fully formed birds hatch. Publicly, Baktaman see brushturkeys as impure because they scratch the ground and eat subterranean grubs and snails; therefore, only women and children eat them or their eggs. During their initiation, novices first learn that brushturkeys are game for the secret hunt and suitable sacrifices for the ancestor. Later it is revealed to them that the secret cache at the sacred fire post shrine includes not only long bones from the ancestor but also the foot of a brushturkey. Through this association with or blessing of the ancestor, brushturkeys transform from impure into pure. For the Baktaman these mound-building and egg-laying birds represent the mystery of agricultural fertility. Observation of their unique behavior leads the Baktaman to see the brushturkeys as symbols. Unlike the case of words, their form and meaning remain linked.

The brushturkey fails to form part of a coherent and totalizing code similar to a dictionary containing all words of a language. Its symbolic meaning arises instead from its differential incorporation into cultural practices and rituals. Women and children eat the bird publicly, novices secretly; various stages of initiation reveal the importance of this "dirty" bird. The emphasis is not on a system of symbols but on transforming an object into a symbol. This process is recognizable in Classic Maya culture. On Yaxchilan Lintel 25, Queen K'abal Xook calls herself y-ohl tahnil, "heart-chest," and uy-ok te'el, "foot-tree," of Yaxchilan. Heart and chest refer to the living body, while foot and tree indicate its root or origin (compare Stuart 2006). Through these phrases Queen K'abal Xook links herself to the city and its inhabitants and embodies them as their representative (compare the moniker altepeyóllotl, "hearts of the people," for Aztec protector gods; López Austin 1980:254, 423).

Nonverbal symbols seldom align linearly the way spoken or written words do. They can involve all the senses, and their color, smell, sound, and texture overlap, as the good swidden or the brushturkey illustrate. It would be difficult if not impossible to fit multisensory symbols into a complete and coherent system. Yet, their multidimensionality allows us to understand such symbols at one glance. For example, we can walk into a room, absorb its furniture, and instantly deduce the owner's social status and aesthetic preferences from style, wear, arrangement, and materials (Miller 1987:101–102).

Analogic reasoning works with incomplete and incoherent systems by transforming objects into symbols; by linking symbols to loose, partial, and shifting meanings; and by employing symbols in different contexts. Rituals and practices create the symbols and allow them to resonate emotionally and cognitively. Analogic reasoning is a process that accommodates old and new.

## Disrupt, Then Reframe

The symbolic axes of human discourse—metonym and metaphor—open up a structure of relationships that collapses in language disorders and is enhanced in innovation. I argue for a symbolic understanding of creativity. First, creativity questions the current mental interpretation of the world. Second, it finds new relationships among elements and converts them into symbols. Out of a dialectical process there arises meta-awareness of the frames in which social action takes place. Creativity disrupts, then reframes. The theme of rebuilding from destruction resonates with the Maya myth of creation. For the ancient Maya, the current era and world began in 3114 B.C., but the destruction of the previous world occurred almost two hundred years earlier when the cosmic crocodile was decapitated. Its dismembered body parts became the surface of the current world. The god Itzamnaaj participated in these events, serving as a role model of creation.

# 3

## Itzamnaaj's Court

### Creativity Embedded in Social Opportunity Structures

Lady 'A'isha Qandisha is a jealous lover, as her husband, the Moroccan tile maker Tuhami, discovers, because she demands absolute secrecy in her marital affairs (Crapanzano 1980:5). He first met her in a dream after becoming sick from a stone thrown at him in a factory: "The woman told me to dress like her. She told me to do what she does and to do everything she says" (Crapanzano 1980:68). Lady 'A'isha is not an ordinary woman, though; she is a camel-footed *jinniyya,* or she-demon, and Tuhami believes himself married to her. But he is not quite sure and would find it much easier to believe in the she-demon wife if he could persuade someone else of her existence (Crapanzano 1980:80–87). Therefore, he tells other villagers about her, trying to make history out of his story.

Tuhami's story demonstrates that as creative as one's personal beliefs are, they reflect, depend, and change with social norms and the opinions of other members of society. Agehananda Bharati (1970:273) calls this the "pizza effect." In Italy, pizza originated as a simple, hot-baked bread without any trimmings. Emigrants brought it to the United States, where it was elaborated with toppings and diversified in shape and flavors. Visiting Italian Americans then reintroduced their new version to Italy and changed pizza for good (for additional examples see Bestor 2006; Hanson 1989). The pizza effect reflects how social interaction transforms personal beliefs and individual inventions.

Innovation rests on the flow of information within society. Inventors have to communicate their ideas to others to find acceptance and encourage adoption. Societies differ, though, in the opportunity structures that they provide. In this chapter, I begin by addressing the size and organization of social groups. In Classic Maya society, Itzamnaaj's court provided the template for royal equivalents that served as nexuses of creation and production. Hinterland settlements were not simply contributors, though; they formed tightly knit communities on their own. Second, I trace the social networks that link individuals and social groups and that enable but also impede the nonlocal flow of information. Third, I discuss different modes of learning and present a practice-based approach in ancient and modern Maya communities.

## Artisans at Itzamnaaj's Court

Creativity is embedded in a specific cultural setting. In ancient Maya thought, the creator god Itzamnaaj is seated on a throne and presides over a court where scribes, artisans, and others assemble at his feet. The God D Court Vessel, which shows Itzamnaaj and his court, records a long and so far largely undeciphered speech that ends with *cheheen Itzamnaaj ti 4 te' chuwen[?]*, "Itzamnaaj says [this] to the four artisans" who are seated in front of him (Figure 3.1; Boot 2008). This and similar scenes situate creation and learning in a community. Three aspects stand out: distinct people join the court, Itzamnaaj engages actively with his retinue, and his followers collaborate.

At his court, Itzamnaaj brings together beings with different backgrounds, like the Maize God and the Monkey Scribe (Figure 2.4). Other depictions add deities like GI and Bolon Okte' K'uh, along with anthropomorphic animals including monkeys, dogs, opossums, and vultures. The colonial-era Popol Vuh explains why the ancient Maya attributed artistic prowess to animals. It tells the story of the originally human One Monkey

Figure 3.1. Itzamnaaj speaks to four artisans; final glyphs of his lengthy discourse from the God D Court Vessel. (After photo in Boot 2008:10, Figure 4; Coe and Houston 2015:190–191.)

Figure 3.2. Creator god Itzamnaaj, identified by the square eye, teaches future scribes. (Detail from vessel K1196, drawn after rollout photo; for comparable vessels see "The Scribes" series in Robicsek and Hales 1981:53–59.)

and One Artisan, who became flautists, singers, writers, carvers of jade, and metalworkers (Tedlock 1985:91). When their younger brothers, the Hero Twins, grew into loudmouths, One Monkey and One Artisan turned jealous and angry. During a bird hunt, the Hero Twins lured their older brothers into a tree and transformed them into monkeys. As gods, One Monkey and One Artisan appear together or in groups as the patron deities of the arts (Coe 1977). Instead of specializing in a single art form, each monkey god excels in various crafts.

The members of Itzamnaaj's court form a visual mélange, but their skills overlap at least partially. The court is a model space for a community-based framework of learning in which participants share enough similarities to communicate and exchange ideas despite their unique backgrounds. Itzamnaaj's courtiers share skills and interests. The court offers them a space for dialogue, while their similarities facilitate effective communication. Nonetheless, each individual has a different background, role, and perspective. The cross-fertilization of their ideas nourishes innovation.

Learning combines abstract understanding with hands-on experience. Itzamnaaj creates and bestows the ability to create on others. As the inventor of writing, he teaches future scribes to read and to write. He complements verbal instruction—note the speech scrolls in Figure 3.2—with practical demonstration. For example, he shows the mask he made to the Maize

God and the Monkey Scribe (Figure 2.4). The two deities dutifully polish their masks in imitation of Itzamnaaj's work. The semantic range of the accompanying verbal expressions combines abstract meanings with tangible objects and observable behavior. Itzamnaaj "shapes" (pak') the mask (Figure 2.4). The alternative translation of "planting" resonates with the concept of animating the inanimate. Similarly, the expression pat translates as "to build, to shape" in the literal sense, as well as to dedicate new buildings and monuments. In other scenes, creating is described as ch'ab or kob. These verbs refer to the genitals and mean "to engender" through sexual intercourse (see Houston et al. 2006:42, 106; Knowlton 2010:21–30; Schele 1993; Stuart 2005:81).

Ritual drinking also appears as part of the collaborative, creative process. Large jars stand between the four artisans on the God D Court Vessel, and the first artisan vomits red liquid. Erik Boot (2008:8) states that they are participating a drinking ceremony. Ritual drinking survived into colonial times, as the Spaniards observed with disgust (Tozzer 1941:91–92). Yucatec Maya made a strong, stinking mead from water, honey, and balche root, and consumed it during sacrifices and ritual dances. "This wine made them healthy, they say, because with it they cleansed their bodies and threw up many worms through the mouth," Spanish conquistadors noted (translated after Garza 1983: 2:39). Drinking was likely part of public and community-affirming rituals among Itzamnaaj's artists. Itzamnaaj's court also models collaborative efforts similar to ones attested in ethnohistoric sources. In the sixteenth century, Diego de Landa narrated that a priest ordered new wooden statues of deities during the month of Mol. After cutting the wood, Yucatec Maya artisans, the priest, and religious officials called Chacs secreted themselves to make the statues (Tozzer 1941:160).

Colorful characters like vultures, monkeys, and dogs populate Itzamnaaj's court and, judging from the accompanying hieroglyphic texts, contributed outrageous adventures. However, myths like these not only make good fireside stories but also serve as templates. Itzamnaaj and his court were for the ancient Maya what chivalric romances were in western literature. The latter memorialized heroic knights and their quests, such as King Arthur and the Knights of the Round Table searching for the Holy Grail. Beneath the veneer of these romances are ideals of gentlemanly behavior and human yearning that appeal to both medieval and modern readers. Don Quixote famously failed to re-create these ideals, but knightly behavior still motivates Renaissance festivals and television series. In a similar vein,

Itzamnaaj's court was the model for Classic Maya society. It laid out the structured and community-based environment for learning and creation.

## Royal Courts as Nexuses of Creation

As a structured environment in which learning and creation take place, Itzamnaaj's court serves as the template for Classic Maya courts (Miller and Martin 2004:51–91). Excavations at Aguateca have revealed King Tahn Te' K'inich's palace and the residences of his court officials (Inomata 1995; Inomata and Triadan 2010, 2014; Inomata et al. 2002). Aguateca was a major Classic center, first serving as the twin capital of the kingdom of Dos Pilas and later as capital of an independent kingdom (Figure 1.5; Houston 1993; Inomata 1995; Inomata and Triadan 2010). Protected by chasms and defensive walls, Aguateca's elite packed themselves into an area of less than four hectares (ten acres). A presumed military attack around the year A.D. 810 forced the nobles and their families to flee, leaving most of their belongings behind (Inomata et al. 2004). Pompeii-like conditions helped archaeologists to identify a scribe in Structure M4-10, a stone carver in Structure M8-8, and a jeweler in Structure M8-4 (Inomata et al. 2002). The artisans and nobles lived within walking distance of each other and the royal palace and formed a tight-knit neighborhood.

Ancient Maya artists not only lived together at the royal court but they collaborated and formed a community of practice. Some left their names and titles on carved monuments. These artists' signatures elucidate the palace schools of the Classic period (see, for example, McAnany 2010:226; Montgomery 1995). Multiple signatures on the same work of art document collaboratives (these signatures are short tags providing the name and titles of the artist). For example, no less than eight artists signed off on Piedras Negras Stela 12. Varying titles point to their division of labor. These artists also worked together in different configurations on other monuments.

A panel from Pomoy illustrates how ancient Maya craftspeople collaborated and were organized (Figure 3.3). The panel shows Queen Yook Ahiin in her fourth K'atun (between ages sixty and eighty). The hieroglyphs in the upper left corner provide her name and titles. Two glyph panels to her left and right identify the artists who created the sculpture. The first is 4 Ajaw from Uxte' K'uh, a polity in the southwestern lowlands (glyphs C1–4 in Figure 3.3). He worked as *anaab*, "stone carver," of the Pomoy queen and formed part of Queen Yook Ahiin's court.[1] The second artist is Ahkal

Figure 3.3. Carved panel from the ancient Maya kingdom of Pomoy, with two artists' signatures enlarged (insets a and b). (Based on photo in Mayer 1995: frontispiece.)

Ich . . . (the second part of the signature is lost; see glyphs F1–5 in Figure 3.3). Ahkal identifies himself as a dwarf and an *anaab*. (Classic Maya respected dwarves as people with unique capabilities and, especially, as mediators with the otherworld [Houston 1992].) His superior was not Queen Yook Ahiin but another artist who worked as *aj yul*, or "polisher," and who, like the queen, was in his fourth K'atun. The polisher further served as *aj k'uhuun*, or "worshipper," and occupied the high-ranking banded bird office (glyphs F6–9 in Figure 3.3).

The Pomoy panel reveals a royal court of nobles and artisans headed by a venerable queen. The titles point to specialization of labor in the form of various priestly offices and craft skills. The court had an internal hierarchy not only between the nobles and the queen but also among the nobles themselves. At least in the case of the four-K'atun polisher, age conferred privilege. The hierarchical environment of Queen Yook Ahiin's court was replicated elsewhere in the Maya Lowlands. Court officials were differentiated by age and status. Living in palaces, they were socially and spatially separated from Maya commoners. Finally, court officials had multiple roles. Nobles were not only craftspeople but also filled priestly functions, social roles, and court offices. Artisans served as ritual specialists. At Aguateca's court, artists seem also to have been farmers and warriors (for example, Aoyama 2007; Inomata and Triadan 2010; Inomata et al. 2002).

The Pomoy artists learned from each other and collaborated for years if not decades. Their experience exposes the challenges of community. Sustained social interaction allows people to address the quandary of personal experience: "Every time I hear a sound and see another person look toward the origin of that sound, I receive an implicit confirmation that what I heard was something real, that it was not just my imagination playing tricks on me" (Guenther 2012). Such observations create a tacit safety net: personal experiences appear coherent and, since we assume that others observe our behavior similarly, we deduce a shared reality. Of course, everyone interprets reality in unique ways, but direct and indirect exchanges allow people to compare their worldviews. Social groups provide an arena in which to confirm personal experiences.

A social group is not simply a sum of individuals. Group norms govern the ways in which group members interact. Whether tacit or openly acknowledged, their impact is profound. Regardless of their unique qualifications, individuals may obstruct or complement each other and fail or succeed as a group. Psychologists identify two crucial aspects of collective intelligence (Woolley et al. 2010). First, individuals differ in their social sensitivity; that is, their ability to intuit how others feel from verbal and nonverbal cues. A group succeeds if its members are attuned to one another. Second, groups differ in the degree to which individuals take turns. Members have different roles and contribute unique talents and skills. Correspondingly, they vary in when and how they participate. To succeed as a team, however, their overall distribution of turn-taking should be equal.

The Pomoy Panel manifests the group norms at Queen Yook Ahiin's court. The artists gave voice to identify themselves. Their signatures reveal their accomplishments and also their intricate social network. The layout of the hieroglyphic texts on the panel replicates the hierarchical structure of the royal court. The artists located their signatures to the left and right of Queen Yook Ahiin but celebrated the queen by placing her name on the top left of the panel, above their names.

For the ancient Maya, the myth of Itzamnaaj's court articulated how the world should be structured. By stressing exclusion and stratification, it biased reality and transformed Classic Maya society in its image. Rulers like Queen Yook Ahiin re-created the myth, putting themselves at the top of a hierarchical environment and surrounded themselves with a menagerie of court officials. Individuals who aspired to be part of the royal court conformed their behavior to the myth. Through works of art, Yook Ahiin's artists reiterated and thereby maintained the myth. Maya royal courts remained nexuses of creation and innovation as long as the myth was believed to reveal reality. As soon as the myth was no longer enacted, it grew stale alongside withering social relations (Leenhardt 1979:192).

## Situated Learning

Collaboration in a community fosters mutual learning (Jackson 1998). This way of learning differs in many ways from traditional western learning, where teachers and students interact in a classroom. Among modern Yucatec Maya, "teaching simply did not occur as an identifiable activity, and whatever instruction I received originated not from a teacher doing teaching but from a midwife doing her work" (Jordan 1989:932). In this decentralized paradigm, "mastery resides not in the master but in the organization of the community of practice of which the master is part" (Lave and Wenger 1991:94; also Costin 1991; Ingold 2000:332–372; Wendrich 2012). Ancient and modern Maya societies illustrate how the transmission of knowledge varies according to the people involved and the setting (see also Hutson 2011:417–420; Miller 2012).

In a learning relationship the participants differ in their social roles. Teacher-student relationships tend to be characterized by power imbalances and vertical flows of information. In the traditional western classroom, this asymmetry manifests in straight rows of desks facing a blackboard. In contrast, the Classic Maya, like their Yucatec descendants, seem to have de-emphasized teachers. On Dos Pilas Panel 19, Ruler 3 and other nobles watch the teenage prince who later became King K'awiil Chan K'inich suffering through his first blood sacrifice (Houston 1993:115). Tijal Hiix, a court noble, kneels in front of the prince holding the bloodletter with which he had pierced the prince's genitals moments earlier. The prince's blood drips into a bowl, later to be burned together with copal as public affirmation of the sacrifice. The two men standing behind the prince seem to provide moral as well as physical support. Inscriptions identify them as the young man's "guardians" or "stewards."

This title can refer to various social others like princes, war captives, and even deities (Houston 1993:116–118). On polychrome vessel K1092, *cha'n,* or *chanul,* seems to describe the efforts of two men to keep a staggering drunkard from falling. The step inscription of Copan Temple 22 identifies patron gods of King Waxaklajuun Ubaah K'awiil as stewards. In Lowland Mayan languages, *cha'n* translates as "to watch (over), to supervise" (Lacadena and Wichmann 2004:140–141). Classic Maya stewardship denoted mutual responsibilities that included protection and tutelage. It required intense social and ritual interaction as well as cooperation. Similarly, modern Tzeltal Maya shamans assign deities and ancestor spirits to objects to animate them and become their guardians (Stross 1998).

Based on ethnographic comparisons, Hayden and Cannon identify various learning modes utilized for many Highland Maya crafts and skills. These modes range from nuclear family to corporate group, extended kin, general community, formal schooling, and specialist training. The modes differ in the social distance between the people involved and in the number of sources from which one learns (Hayden and Cannon 1984:341–355). Individuals learn common crafts from various sources (Table 3.1 displays the top ten crafts). Some teach themselves how to make pottery; others learn from their nuclear family, their extended family, friends, or even non-kin specialists. On average across the ten most common crafts, six out of ten individuals learn from their nuclear family; their situation is similar to that of Yucatec Maya midwives who tend to learn from their mothers. The other three learning sources are less important, accounting for slightly more than one out of ten individuals each. According to my chi-square analysis, six

Table 3.1. Learning sources for the ten most common crafts and skills in three modern Highland Maya villages

| Craft/Skill | No. of individuals | Learning Source | | | |
|---|---|---|---|---|---|
| | | Self-taught | Nuclear Family | Extended Family | Other |
| Sewing | 161 | 8 (5.0%)[†] | 130 (80.7%)[†] | 7 (4.3%)[†] | 16 (9.9%) |
| Pottery making | 97 | 5 (5.2%) | 47 (48.5%) | 37 (38.1%)[†] | 8 (8.2%) |
| Fiber working | 87 | 7 (8.0%) | 57 (65.5%) | 6 (6.9%) | 17 (19.5%) |
| Hunting | 63 | 24 (38.1%)[†] | 27 (42.9%) | 3 (4.8%) | 9 (14.3%) |
| Construction work | 62 | 14 (22.6%) | 31 (50.0%) | 6 (9.7%) | 11 (17.7%) |
| Glass working | 60 | 6 (10.0%) | 42 (70.0%) | 3 (5.0%) | 9 (15.0%) |
| Weaving | 43 | — | 31 (72.1%) | 6 (14.0%) | 6 (14.0%) |
| Bone working | 32 | 6 (18.8%) | 19 (59.4%) | 2 (6.3%) | 5 (15.6%) |
| Basket making | 24 | 2 (8.3%) | 11 (45.8%) | 4 (16.7%) | 7 (29.2%) |
| Furniture making | 22 | 10 (45.5%)[†] | 7 (31.8%) | — | 5 (22.7%) |
| Total and averages | 651[a] | 82 (12.6%) | 402 (61.8%) | 74 (11.4%) | 93 (14.3%) |

*Notes:* Data from Hayden and Cannon (1984:348–349 Table 5). Italics indicate the most common learning source for each craft.

† Learning sources that are significantly more frequent among particular crafts than the ten-craft average (their chi-square value for two degrees of freedom and a 5 percent significance level is higher than 5.991).

a. Because households practice on average four crafts, it is likely that some of the 651 individuals (who come from 154 households) are versed in more than one craft and are counted several times.

out of the ten crafts conform to this distribution of learning sources. Individuals learn fiber, glass, and bone working, as well as weaving, basket-making, and construction within their nuclear family. Four crafts deviate from this pattern. Sewing is highly localized in the family, with eight out of ten individuals learning to sew in the nuclear family. Unusually, many individuals teach themselves to hunt and to make furniture. The extended family plays a bigger role in teaching pottery making. While learning sources differ for the crafts, learning preferably takes place in kin-based social networks. Individuals leave their nuclear or extended family only to learn rare skills like repairing watches and radios. In most cases, Highland Maya acquire knowledge not through formal teaching but through informal and cooperative relationships.

Growing up in a crafting family is the preferred way to learn a craft. Eighteen Highland Maya potters learned their skill between ages two and twenty-five; fifteen of them were less than twelve years old when they made their first pot (Hayden and Cannon 1984:353). As girls and boys they had other potters in their family and observed how these masters made and sold pots. Eventually, they helped out and later even made pots themselves. They learned through participation, first indirectly because the craft formed part of their family life, and then directly. During this lengthy process they absorbed and were absorbed into a culture of practice (Lave and Wenger 1991:95). They learned not only the practical side of a craft but also its social, economic, and political implications: How do masters talk among themselves and to customers? How do they structure their daily work? How do they find and pay for resources? How do other community members judge them? Answers to many of these questions come from social interactions with a wide array of people. Apprentices learn from their masters and, possibly to an even higher degree, from other apprentices and bystanders. Highland Maya households practice on average not one but four crafts. This culture of practice exposes family members to several crafts at once. Individuals can acquire skills through observation and comparison (for archaeological case studies see Hasaki 2012; Kamp 2001; Kelly-Buccellati 2012; Sassaman and Rudolphi 2001).

Social networks replace formal classrooms in Highland Maya communities. Few learners follow a set path or obtain formal schooling (for impeding factors see Offit 2008). Instead, economic status influences individuals' sources of learning. In poor families, nearly nine out of ten individuals (87 percent) learn from family members; in rich families, five of ten (50 percent) learn from non-kin (Hayden and Cannon 1984:351). These differences are statistically significant ($\chi^2 = 7.38$; $p < 0.007$). Wealth influences the size of Maya social networks and the number of learning sources.

Itzamnaaj's court combines different ways of learning. Itzamnaaj gifts his knowledge to artisans; he exemplifies the vertical flow of information with a corresponding imbalance in power. Meanwhile, court artisans practice multiple crafts simultaneously and create a community. They seem to embody the situated learning found in modern Maya societies. In Chapter 4, I discuss how actual Classic Maya workshops reflected this tension between vertical and horizontal transmissions of knowledge. Their artisans were versed in several crafts and lived under the auspices of nobles (Figure 4.5; McAnany 2010).

## Classic Maya Elites Diversify

When K'inich Ahkal Mo' Nahb III became king of Palenque in A.D. 721, Janaab Ajaw handed him the royal headband while five nobles looked on (Figure 3.4). The inclusion of noblemen in this panel deviates from the exclusive emphasis on the divine king that defined earlier Maya art. During the Lat Classic, nonroyal Maya nobles begin to appear on monumental sculptures and are mentioned in hieroglyphic texts (Figure 1.9; Fash et al. 1992; Houston 1993:132; Schele and Freidel 1990:262–345; Webster 2002:138–139). Some nobles even commissioned their own art and inscriptions. Classic Maya society also diversified beyond its highest levels. I introduce the Gini coefficient to measure inequality in Maya villages and show how they became more stratified over the course of the Late Classic. Ancient Maya society was dynamic and provided opportunity structures for innovation.

I start with Classic Maya elites. The number of divine rulers rose steadily during the Late Classic. Around A.D. 400, only a handful of polities existed (as measured by the number of emblem glyphs); they ballooned to several dozen four hundred years later (Mathews 1991). To distinguish themselves, rulers began to add k'uhul, "holy," to their title (Houston and Stuart 2001:59–60). Many kings had several wives and procreated not only heirs but also competing princes and princelings (Grube 2006a:161–164). Hieroglyphic texts and archaeological remains (for example, fortifications) attest to increasing warfare between and more factions within kingdoms (Demarest et al. 1997; Houston 1993; Webster 2000).

At the same time, nonroyal nobles grew in number (Sharer 1977; Webster 1992; Willey and Shimkin 1973). Hieroglyphic texts illustrate their rise

Figure 3.4. Under the eyes of his court nobles, K'inich Ahkal Mo' Nahb III becomes king of Palenque in A.D. 721. Omitted here are the hieroglyphic texts detailed in Figure 2.8. (Detail of the south face of the platform in Temple XIX at Palenque; based on photos in Stuart 2005.)

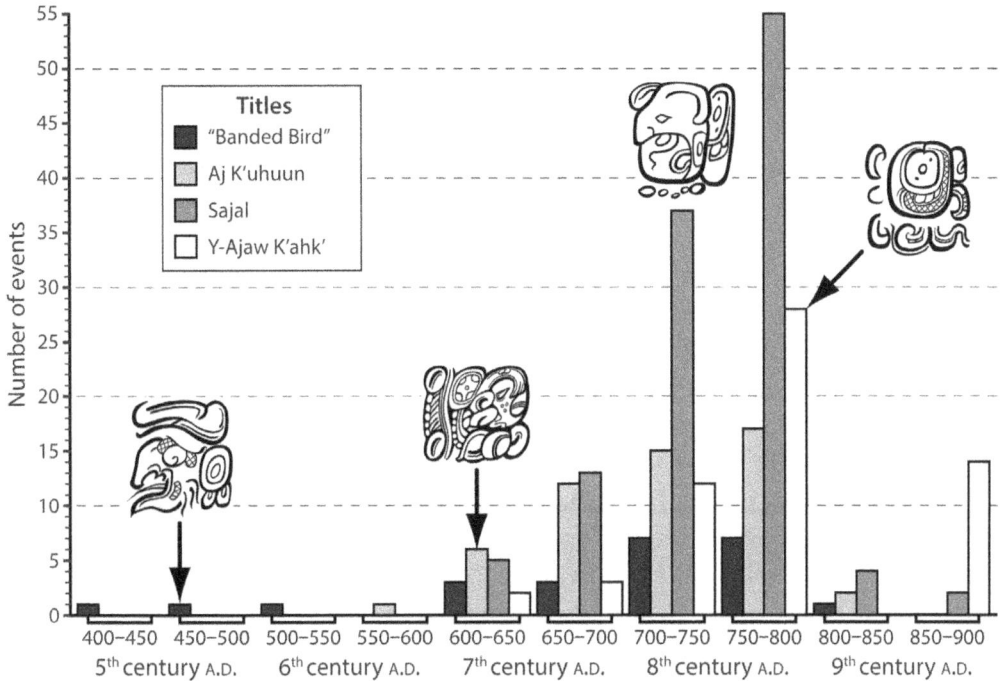

Figure 3.5. The growth of nonroyal elites in Classic Maya society, as illustrated by the number of events that mention individuals with four nonroyal titles from the fifth through the ninth centuries A.D.

(Figure 3.5).[2] Very few nobles are attested until A.D. 600; during the next two centuries, they appear in increasing numbers before they vanish during the Maya Collapse at the end of the first millennium A.D. (Houston 1993:132; Houston and Stuart 2001; Jackson 2013:82–85). Their growth in number coincides with greater diversification. The "banded bird" title, which possibly reads *na'at*, "sage," is one of the most important nonroyal titles (Bernal Romero 2009; Stuart 2005:133–136). For example, Janaab Ajaw, who makes Palenque's K'inich Ahkal Mo' Nahb III king, is a banded bird (Figures 2.8 and 3.4). Banded birds are first mentioned in A.D. 445, and this remains the only nonroyal title until A.D. 587 (Figure 3.5). The remaining titles appear around A.D. 600. *Sajals* emerge as governors of subordinate centers (Schele 1991; Stuart 1984); the *aj k'uhuun*, "guardian or worshipper," title denotes noble overseers of craft production, especially of sacred and luxury goods like paper (Houston 1993:130–134; Jackson and Stuart 2003); *y-ajaw k'ahk',* "fire lord," designates military commanders who waged war in the ruler's name (these include the two men shown to K'inich Ahkal Mo'

Nahb's right, behind Janaab Ajaw, in Figure 3.4). Many more but rarer elite titles are known (Houston and Stuart 2001; Miller and Martin 2004:23–27). They attest to an increasing division of labor. Classic Maya elites grew in number, they diversified, and they became more stratified. Increasing numbers of high-status residential groups and secondary centers mirror these developments archaeologically (Chase 1992; Chase and Chase 1992; Fash and Stuart 1991; Iannone 2005; Taschek and Ball 2003; Webster 1992, 2002). Classic Maya society became top-heavy, factionalized, and decentralized over the course of the Late Classic (Chase 1992; Fash and Stuart 1991:177–178; Schele and Freidel 1990).

The growth in number and kind of nonroyal nobles has traditionally been linked to the procreative powers of Maya rulers, though scholars are beginning to discuss alternatives to this top-down view (Chase and Chase 1996a, 1996b). In the traditional view, since not all of rulers' offspring could become king or queen, new statuses and positions cropped up to keep them occupied (McAnany 1993; Viel 1999). Individuals occupying the *lakam,* "banner," office delivered tribute to rulers and participated in wars. Lacadena (2008) argues that *lakam* were not nobles but middle-class people with economic and military responsibilities to rulers (see, however, Tsukamoto et al. 2015). If so, Classic Maya commoners could move up socially. The following section looks at rural villages to suggest a certain degree of social mobility for all members of Classic Maya society.

### Hamlets Become Villages

Classic Maya society diversified, not only among the highest elites but also more broadly. Here, I describe how two small settlements in Aguateca's hinterland, Nacimiento and Dos Ceibas, developed (Figure 1.5; Eberl 2014a). Nacimiento occupies the top of an escarpment overlooking its namesake spring, one of the major water sources in the Petexbatún region (Figure 3.6). Thirty-nine residential complexes and thirteen isolated structures are dispersed over 1.4 square kilometers, for a low settlement density of 134 structures per square kilometer. Three public groups—a ballcourt, a cave surrounded by a small pyramid and other structures, and a main plaza—form the core of three neighborhoods in the western, central, and eastern sections of the site (two of which are shown in Figure 3.6). Large depressions separate the three neighborhoods. Dos Ceibas is situated between Nacimiento and Aguateca. Its thirty-two residential groups surround a ceremonial complex with a small pyramid, the North Plaza (Figure 1.6). The settlement density

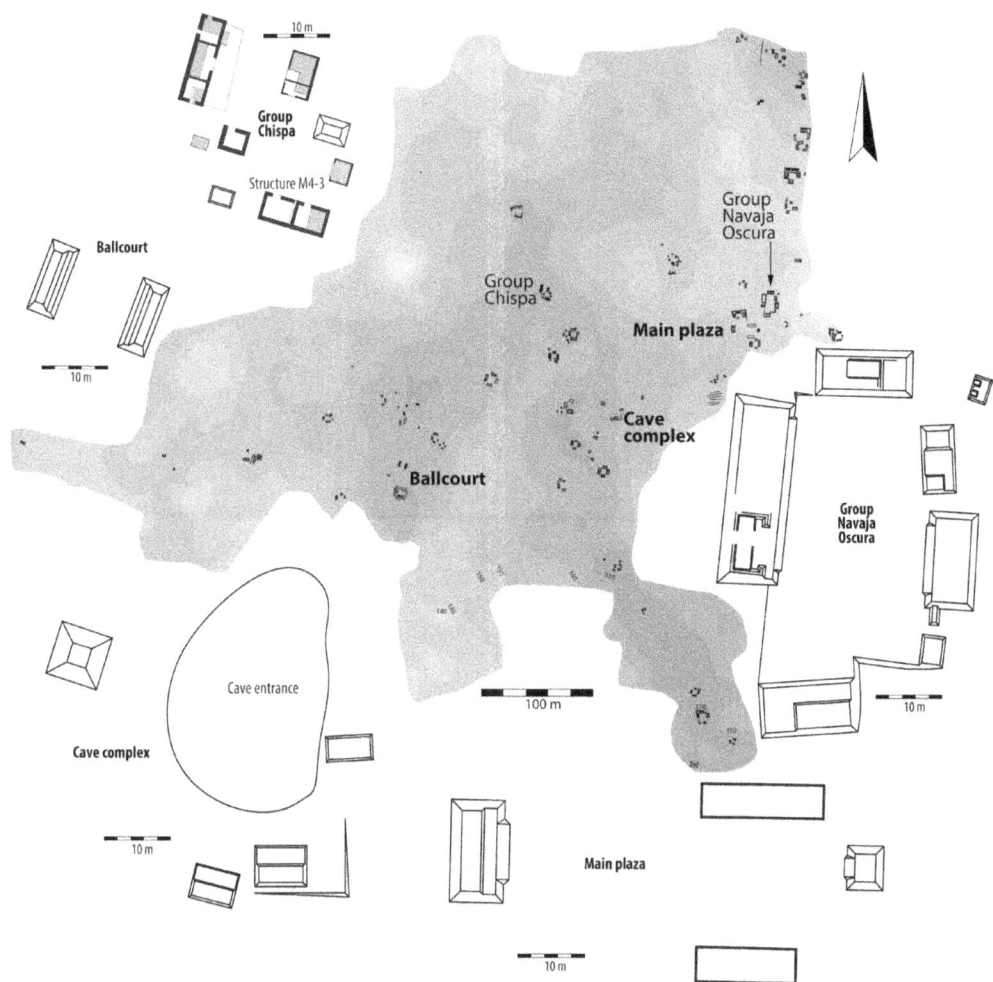

Figure 3.6. The Late Classic site of Nacimiento (5 m contour lines); insets show the three public groups; the largest residential group of Group Navaja Oscura; and Group Chispa, an extensively excavated group (all to the same scale).

of 555 structures per square kilometer is four times higher than that of Nacimiento and puts Dos Ceibas into the category of an urban center.

Nacimiento was founded around A.D. 600, when it consisted of eleven residential groups, three of which surrounded the main plaza. Within a century six additional groups spread out, like seedlings of a plant, in the direction of the eighth-century ballcourt and cave complex. The two remaining residential groups are isolated. During the seventh century A.D., Nacimiento was a hamlet with widely dispersed homesteads and the main

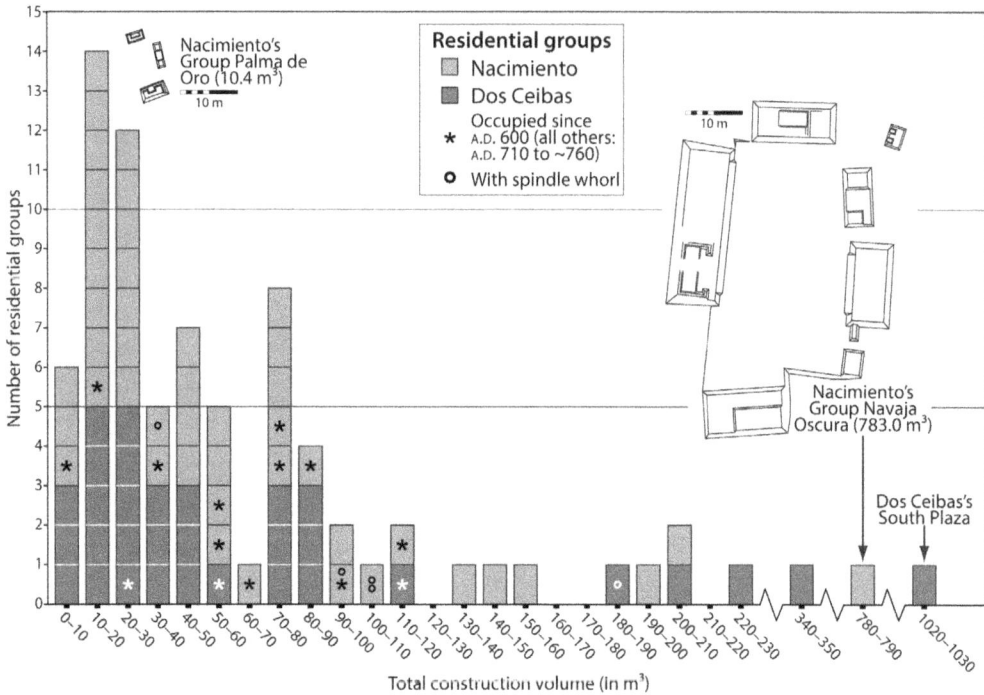

Figure 3.7. The sites of Nacimiento and Dos Ceibas grow from hamlets into villages during the Late Classic. To illustrate the differences, the largest residential group of Nacimiento—Group Navaja Oscura—is shown next to Group Palma de Oro, one of the small residential groups; stars identify groups occupied since A.D. 600. (The diagram excludes public groups; three breaks along the horizontal scale accommodate residential groups with total construction volumes greater than 230 m³. The inset spindle whorls are discussed in Chapter 6.)

plaza as its public space. Over subsequent generations, the settlement grew to thirty-nine residential groups and three public groups (Figure 3.7). In the eighth-century A.D. new neighborhoods largely filled in unsettled areas of the hamlet, and only a few were built outside of existing settlement limits. The early construction technique, which employed largely unworked rocks and boulders, continued into the eighth century A.D. and was applied to a new architectural style that favored residential buildings with three rooms instead of one. Nacimiento became a village and reached its maximum population of four hundred to five hundred people between A.D. 710 and 760.

Located on the same escarpment as Nacimiento and only a few kilometers away, Dos Ceibas has roots that go back to the Preclassic (Eberl et al.

2009). The site was abandoned during the Early Classic then resettled at the beginning of the Late Classic. During the seventh century A.D., building activity occurred in the North Plaza and in three nearby residential groups (Figure 1.6). Within a century, Dos Ceibas grew fifteenfold into a densely populated settlement with thirty-two residential groups. The exponential growth was possibly violent. One of the buildings in the North Plaza was burned down and building activity there—Dos Ceibas's former center—stopped. The focus shifted to the South Plaza, where the terrain was leveled for a three-meter-high platform to support the construction of the largest residential group of the site. Structure R27-83, the South Plaza's largest building, imitated the layout and placement of elite palaces (Figure 3.8). Dos Ceibas also expanded to the north and south along the escarpment. Three-room structures became the signature residence of many residential groups. Cut facade stones gave these and other prominent buildings at Dos Ceibas a refined appearance that set them apart visually from the raw monumentality of comparable buildings at Nacimiento.

During the Late Classic, Nacimiento and Dos Ceibas both grew from hamlets into villages, yet they developed differently (Figure 3.7). Nacimiento quadrupled in size, maintained its settlement layout, and continued earlier construction techniques. In contrast, Dos Ceibas grew fifteenfold, saw shifts in its settlement pattern, and adopted a new architectural style along with new construction techniques. Continuity and gradual growth at

Figure 3.8. Palatial Structure R27-83 in Dos Ceibas's South Plaza. Q'eqchi' Maya sit on the stairway and the center room bench; see lower right inset in Figure 1.6 for a map of the building. (Photo courtesy of Takeshi Inomata.)

Nacimiento contrast with abrupt, perhaps violent, and exponential change at Dos Ceibas.

The differences and similarities between these villages point to a complex social fabric. Both eventually numbered several hundred inhabitants who were living in close proximity with one another. Neighbors could easily peer into each other's courtyards and call out to each other. This setting facilitated the sustained and frequent social interactions that enable community (Redfield 1955:4; Robin 2002:254). Nonetheless, varying settlement densities suggest correspondingly diverse social interactions (Hutson et al. 2008). Residential groups thin out at the edges of both villages (Eberl 2014a:223–224). The narrow separation, perhaps three hundred meters, between Nacimiento and Dos Ceibas is especially remarkable. The environment is similar on both sides but residential groups are absent. An isolated structure at Dos Ceibas's southern end may have marked the boundary. Different construction techniques further set off the villages. At Nacimiento, settlement density is not uniform. Public groups form the core of three neighborhoods. Large depressions separate neighborhoods, and smaller depressions divide residential groups. These spaces granted Nacimiento's inhabitants more privacy than their counterparts at Dos Ceibas. Their residential groups similarly separate outward- from inward-facing. Raw boulders line the outer facades of buildings whereas shaped rocks and slabs project an image of order toward the interior plazas (Eberl 2014a:175–176). The depressions were likely milpas for maize agriculture (Wright et al. 2009). Even if planted and harvested individually, the neat rows of green and gold likely reminded Nacimiento's inhabitants of their shared source of labor and sustenance.

Dos Ceibas, by contrast, was too densely settled to allow for agricultural fields between residential groups. People were living next to one another and consequently intimately witnessed each other's lives. Their construction techniques may reflect the intense social interaction. Dos Ceibas's residential groups employ cut-stone architecture consistently, a different aesthetic than practiced at Nacimiento. Buildings appear finished from all sides and invite close-up appreciation.

The two villages contained public spaces consisting of pyramids, platforms, and a ball court. In construction quality and size these are inferior to the monumental architecture found in royal capitals. Yet, in the Petexbatún region only Dos Pilas, Punta de Chimino, and Nacimiento have ball courts. Regional elites had no monopoly over the ballgame as a sport and as a vehicle to express and create identity. Consequently, the commoners of Nacimiento could use the ball court to foster interaction and integration within their village. Public architecture at Nacimiento and Dos Ceibas included plazas on which the entire community could gather for rituals, feasts, and entertainment. At Nacimiento, three public institutions (ball court, plaza, and cave), each with enough space for the entire village coexisted and possibly competed. At Dos Ceibas, the North Plaza provided the only shared place. These differences point to differing levels of interaction within the two villages.

The populations of Nacimiento and Dos Ceibas multiplied during the seventh and eighth centuries A.D. With several hundred inhabitants each, the villages provided sufficiently large pools of people to facilitate social learning (Marquet et al. 2012:14754). Social interaction and subsequent learning cannot be assumed, however (see, for example, Putnam 2000). Nacimiento and Dos Ceibas grew not randomly but cohesively. Instead of sprawling, their settlements remained dense. Instead of growing apart, their public institutions integrated. Continued proximity enabled frequent face-to-face contacts.

## Diversifying Hinterland

Social inequality is characteristic of complex societies. Wealth roughly measures individuals' differential access to goods and services. Since inequality varies among societies and across time, individual wealth has to be compared within the same population. John D. Rockefeller amassed more than $1.4 billion during the nineteenth and early twentieth centuries (Klepper and Gunther 1996:xi). His wealth appears small compared to modern fortunes; for example, Bill Gates was worth $12 billion in 1995 (Klepper and Gunther 1996:xii). Yet Rockefeller's wealth amounted to 1.5 percent of America's gross domestic product in 1937, whereas Gates commanded 0.2 percent of America's GDP in 1995 (Klepper and Gunther 1996:xi). To understand social inequality, one needs to compare the wealth of all members of society.

The Lorenz curve plots wealth cumulatively from lowest to highest. Wealth and population are standardized on a scale from 0 to 100 percent. Each point along the Lorenz curve indicates the share of total wealth held by a specific percentage of the population. In a perfectly equal population, everybody would earn exactly the same amount; in a perfectly unequal population, one individual would control everything and the rest of the population would be empty-handed. The Lorenz curve varies between

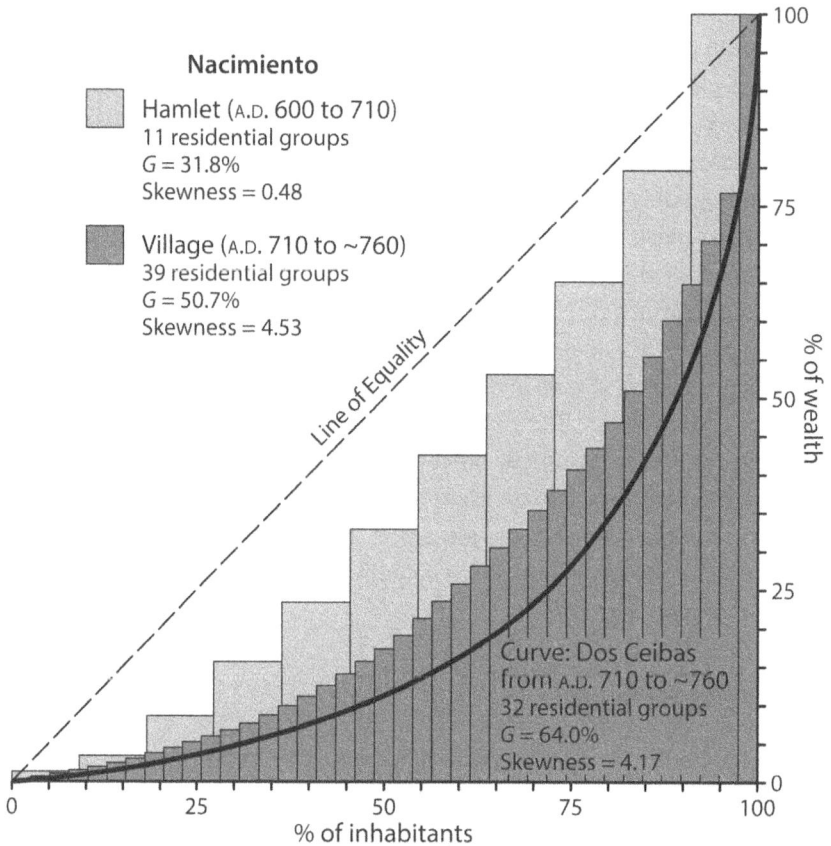

**Nacimiento**

Hamlet (A.D. 600 to 710)
11 residential groups
G = 31.8%
Skewness = 0.48

Village (A.D. 710 to ~760)
39 residential groups
G = 50.7%
Skewness = 4.53

Line of Equality

Curve: Dos Ceibas
from A.D. 710 to ~760
32 residential groups
G = 64.0%
Skewness = 4.17

% of wealth

% of inhabitants

Figure 3.9. A Lorenz curve showing cumulative distribution of wealth, as estimated from the construction volume of residential groups, at Nacimiento and Dos Ceibas. Wealth distributions are shown for Nacimiento as a hamlet and as a village and for Dos Ceibas between A.D. 710 and circa 760 (too few groups date to A.D. 600–710 to compute the Lorenz curve).

these two extremes. The axes describe a perfectly unequal population: Everybody except one has nothing (the population axis), or one person owns everything (the wealth axis). The diagonal Line of Equality corresponds to a perfectly equal distribution: 25 percent of the population has 25 percent of the total wealth, 50 percent has 50 percent, 75 percent has 75 percent, and so on. Real-world wealth distributions oscillate between the two extremes, as Nacimiento and Dos Ceibas show (Figure 3.9).

Unlike modern capitalist societies, Classic Maya society had no legal tender, and it is unclear to what degree cacao beans, shells, and other artifacts may have served as money (Reents-Budet 2006:220). As an alternative

Table 3.2. Characteristics of residential groups at Nacimiento and Dos Ceibas, small settlements in the southwestern Maya Lowlands

| Category (total construction volume) | Site | No. of patio groups[a] | Patio groups with 3-room structures (%) | No. of buildings[b] | Plaza area[b] |
|---|---|---|---|---|---|
| Small (0–60 m³) | Nacimiento | 29 | 3.4 | 4.1±1.7 | 110.3±77.1 m² |
| | Dos Ceibas | 20 | 15.0 | 3.0±1.1 | 98.4±57.8 m² |
| Medium (60–120 m³) | Nacimiento | 11 | 54.6 | 4.9±1.0[c] | 218.1±183.2 m² |
| | Dos Ceibas | 7 | 42.9 | 4.1±1.8 | 183.2±95.3 m² |
| Large (120–340 m³) | Nacimiento | 5 | 20.0[d] | 4.4±1.3 | 276.8±64.7 m² |
| | Dos Ceibas | 4 | 75.0 | 5.0±2.2 | 293.3±163.1 m² |
| Extra-Large (783 m³ and 1,023.6 m³) | Nacimiento | 1 | 100.0 | 7 | 882.5 m² |
| | Dos Ceibas | 1 | 100.0 | 8 | 874.8 m² |

*Source:* Data from Eberl 2014a.
*Notes:* a. Seven of Nacimiento's thirty-nine residential groups have two patios; here, I list each plaza and its associated buildings separately, for a total of forty-six patio groups.
b. Average and standard deviation.
c. Nacimiento's medium-sized residential groups have on average more structures than large residential groups because the count includes isolated structures outside its plaza that in large residential complexes commonly form separate patio groups.
d. Looting affected large residential groups in particular and likely destroyed some three-room structures beyond recognizability.

measure for wealth, I use residential architecture. The great variation in size and quality of housing makes architecture one of the best measures of wealth in agrarian societies (Abrams 1994; Abul-Magd 2002; Blanton 1994; Inomata and Aoyama 1996:293; McGuire 1983; M. E. Smith 1987:301).[3] For example, buildings and land accounted for 55 percent of wealth in late colonial America (Jones 1980). Residential groups at Nacimiento and Dos Ceibas differ in total construction volume, average number of structures, presence of three-room structures, and average plaza sizes (Table 3.2). Total construction volumes range from 5 to 1,024 cubic meters. Breaks at 60 cubic meters, 120 cubic meters, and more than 340 cubic meters distinguish four categories of residential groups (Figure 3.7; Table 3.2; see Eberl 2014a:237–238 for further discussion). Most residential groups have an irregular layout and are small in total construction volume, plaza area, and number of structures. Few groups have three-room structures. Medium and large residential groups increase linearly on all measures. At each site, one residential group is markedly larger than all the others. Nacimiento's Group Navaja Oscura and Dos Ceibas's South Plaza are in volume and plaza area three times larger than the next-biggest group.

Returning to Figure 3.9, the area between the Lorenz curve and the Line of Equality represents the degree of wealth inequality. Named after the Italian statistician Corrado Gini (1912), the Gini coefficient ($G$) is the ratio between the area of inequality and the entire triangle. It ranges from 0 percent (perfect equality) to 100 percent (perfect inequality). Gini indexes can be calculated for various measures of inequality and, correspondingly, vary for the same society. Most research focuses on disposable income (for example, Milanović 2005). Economists James Davies and colleagues calculated the wealth Gini for modern countries (Davies et al. 2008:9–10). In 2000, values ranged from 54.7 percent for Japan to 80.1 percent for the United States and 80.3 percent for Switzerland (income Gini coefficients tend to be at least 10 percent lower; Davies et al. 2008:7).

The wealth Gini for Nacimiento and Dos Ceibas ranges from 31.8 percent to 64.0 percent (Figure 3.9). Maya cities have comparable Gini coefficients (Hutson 2016:156). They range from Mayapan (32 percent) and Dzibilchaltun (39 percent) at the lower end to Palenque (63 percent) and Chunchucmil (57–63 percent, depending on the proxy) at the upper end. Prehispanic Highland Mexican settlements show a wider range of inequality, with Gini indexes for construction volumes varying between 9 percent and 48 percent (Smith et al. 2014). Royal elites did not live in the Petexbatún villages. Therefore, these villages are not representative of Classic Maya society as a whole, and their Gini coefficients are not directly comparable to the wealth Gini coefficients of modern countries.

The Petexbatún villages were not egalitarian but showed a noticeable degree of stratification. Gini coefficients indicate the degree of social inequality but they say little about the ways in which wealth is distributed. A hypothetical population in which ninety-nine people have $1 each and one person owns $108 has the same Gini coefficient (50.7 percent) as the eighth-century village of Nacimiento. The shape of the Lorenz curve, its skewness in particular, differentiates the two. The wealth distribution for the hypothetical population would skew heavily toward the right (skewness of 9.85), whereas Nacimiento's Lorenz curve is more symmetrical (skewness of 4.53). Since both skewness values are positive, the Lorenz curves lean to the right. This means that a smallish segment of the population controlled a disproportionate amount of wealth. The one rich person in the hypothetical population would cause a very steep skew, whereas at Nacimiento wealthy individuals were rarer, producing a shallower skew. Nonetheless, they existed.

Among the eleven Nacimiento residential groups occupied during the seventh century A.D., five are medium-sized and six are small (Figure 3.7). The three contemporary residential groups at Dos Ceibas are small and medium-sized. The Gini coefficient of 31.8 percent and almost no skew (0.48) for the Nacimiento hamlet points to few wealth differences (Figure 3.9; due to the small sample size, no Lorenz curve was calculated for Dos Ceibas).

The populations at both sites grew not only in number but also in diversity during the course of the Late Classic. All large and extra-large residential groups date to the eighth century A.D. The lack of predecessors means that small and medium-sized residential groups did not grow larger over time. This differs from other Maya sites like Copan, where the largest residential groups are the endpoints of gradual growth and transformation over centuries (for example, Fash 1983:354–369; Freter 1992; Sheehy 1991; Webster and Freter 1990). Therefore, buried earlier constructions do not bias the calculation of the Gini index at Nacimiento and Dos Ceibas. The Gini coefficients rise to 50.7 percent for Nacimiento and 64.0 percent for Dos Ceibas. The Lorenz curve for both villages skews to the right. For Nacimiento skewness jumps from 0.48 to 4.53 between the seventh and eighth centuries, indicating the inhabitants of a few residential groups controlled more of the total wealth. The residents of Nacimiento and Dos Ceibas were commoners in comparison to the nearby elites at Aguateca; for example, Aguateca's Palace Group, the residence of divine king Tahn Te' K'inich, is almost fifteen times larger than the largest residential group at either village. Nonetheless, these commoners were internally differentiated. Small, medium, and large residential groups are relatively close together at Nacimiento and Dos Ceibas. They differ on a linear scale in construction volumes, structure numbers, and plaza sizes (Table 3.2). Extra-large residential groups stand apart by all architectural measures. Since only one extra-large group exists in each village, I assume that these two groups served as seats of local gentry. In sum the Late Classic settlements at Nacimiento and Dos Ceibas not only grew into villages but they diversified as well.

William Rathje (1971) suggests that status evolved from acquired to ascribed in Classic Maya society. Early Classic graves tend to contain few grave goods, whereas Late Classic graves are often impressively furnished (Chapman 1987; Tainter 1978). (Other scholars, however, critique the direct correlation of grave goods with status [Binford 1971; Saxe 1971]). According to Rathje, individuals had to achieve status through their own efforts during the Early Classic while their descendants were born into wealth during the Late Classic. This implies that Early Classic Maya society was fluid but social rankings solidified during the Late Classic (Fash 1991:93; Rathje 1971). The Late Classic changes at Nacimiento and Dos Ceibas point to more complex and dynamic developments.

## Impacts of Social Diversification

Social diversification is not unique to the Petexbatún hinterland. Ancient Maya society reached its maximum population density around A.D. 800 (Culbert and Rice 1990). Around fifty people lived on each square kilometer during the Early Classic. Within two hundred years the population density doubled if not tripled, before declining rapidly during the Maya Collapse (the estimates for A.D. 800 range between 116.7 and 149.3 people per square kilometer; Turner 1990:320 Table 15.3). Populations grew commensurably in rural areas. According to large surveys around Tikal and Calakmul and in the Río Bec region, rural populations at least tripled from Early Classic levels (Turner 1990:321–323 Tables 15.4–15.6). The Late Classic population increase at Nacimiento and Dos Ceibas is very similar to the population growth in the Maya Lowlands. At least some Late Classic Maya commoners were socially and economically complex. In the Belize River valley, small settlements in the hinterland of Xunantunich are heterogeneous both internally and in comparison to each other (Yaeger and Robin 2004). In the Copan Valley, Groups 9N-8 and 9M-22 have elite households at their cores; people with different occupations, ethnicities, and statuses occupied the adjacent courtyards (Figure 1.7; Sheehy 1991; Webster 1989b:14–15). The construction of Group 9M-22 over the course of the Late Classic points to a certain degree of diversification that mirrors the pattern observed among the Petexbatún commoners.

The Canadian economist Miles Corak (2006, 2013) has studied the relationship between inequality as measured by the income Gini and social mobility in the form of intergenerational earnings elasticity. The latter compares the earnings of parents and their children and measures how much more the children earn as a percentage of their parents' income. In the United States, an elasticity of close to 50 percent means that relatively wealthy parents, who earn 100 percent more than poorer parents, will see their children earn 50 percent more than the children of the poorer parents. In Denmark, on the other hand, parents account for only 15 percent of their children's income difference (Corak 2013:111). This indicates the United States has much less social mobility than Denmark. Intergenerational earnings elasticity relates inversely to income Gini coefficients (Corak 2013:115). In what is known as the Great Gatsby Curve, low social mobility correlates with high inequality, and high mobility with low inequality. I argue that this inverse relationship also applies to preindustrial Classic Maya society. During the Late Classic, inequality rose and social mobility decreased. However, if Nacimiento and Dos Ceibas are representative of Maya society in general, inequality rose very modestly by modern standards. The Late Classic villages were about as unequal as modern Japan is, and taking Japan's intergenerational earnings elasticity of 34 percent as an estimate, still provided a fair amount of social mobility.

Social diversification affects social learning and innovation. In the modern Highland Maya villages I discussed earlier, poor individuals learn overwhelmingly from kin while wealthy individuals learn to the same degree from kin and non-kin. For example, nobody in these villages knows how to repair radios and individuals have to travel elsewhere to acquire this skill. They can do this only if they have money. Thus, wealth influences what people can learn and from whom. Wealth provides the necessary capital for innovation, and wealthier people tend to be better educated and thus better informed about the potential of specific innovations (Cancian 1979:16). Innovations also affect power relationships. When iron plows were introduced to the Mexican village of Tepoztlán around 1900, only rich landowners could afford them (Lewis 1951). These landowners then proceeded to contract poorer neighbors to work in their fields and forced them to become wage laborers.

At Nacimiento and Dos Ceibas, the degree and kind of social interaction changed over the course of the Late Classic. In both villages, one residential group outsized all others by the eighth century A.D. (Table 3.2). The plaza of this extra-large group rivaled the public places in size. At Dos Ceibas, construction activity in the public North Plaza stopped, possibly violently, during the seventh century. If Dos Ceibas's inhabitants stopped using the North Plaza, they had only the South Plaza as an alternative space for village-wide gatherings. They would have come together under the eyes of, and likely on the terms of, the South Plaza's inhabitants (compare Yaeger 2000, 2003).

## Widening Social Networks

Social interaction enables innovation. Size and connectedness of populations are assumed to correlate with the creation of new and more complex
inventions while reducing cultural loss rates (Boyd et al. 2011; Henrich 2004;
Powell et al. 2009; Shennan 2011). Computer simulations and field studies
have suggested a generally positive effect of population size on cultural
complexity (Derex et al. 2013; Kempe and Mesoudi 2014; Kline and Boyd
2010; Muthukrishna et al. 2013; Powell et al. 2009; see however Collard, Buchanan, and O'Brien 2013; Collard, Buchanan, O'Brien et al. 2013; Vaesen
et al. 2016 for an alternative perspective). In the Classic Maya Lowlands,
populations grew overall, but centers and regions differed in their specific
population developments. "Throughout Classic and Postclassic times, there
are innumerable instances of sudden and geometric population expansion
(even on an archaeological time scale) that cannot be explained by autoch-
thonous growth rates" (McAnany 1995:146). Clearly, people moved across
the lowlands (Inomata 2004; Jones 1982). In doing so, they interacted more
widely socially and likely exchanged goods as well as ideas.

Social networks can be double-edged swords. In fully connected groups,
individuals learn so successfully from each other that the overall cultural
diversity is lower than in partially connected groups (Derex and Boyd
2016). In the modern French village of Pellaport, agricultural innovations
disperse more through interpersonal discussion than through structured
channels like the Chamber of Agriculture (Layton 1989:40–41). The villagers' social contacts widened considerably from the 1940s to the 1960s in
response to the allure of urban employment and an increasing dependency
on imported tractors, mowers, and other farm machinery. This led to networks where, for example, Claude Bavarel's cousin worked in a garage and
told him to buy a diesel instead of a gasoline-powered tractor for lower fuel
costs and better fuel consumption (Layton 1989:39). Wider social contacts
translated to a quicker pace of innovation, but not every villager created
a larger social network. Many villagers remained insular and a handful
of well-connected farmers introduced most of the innovations (Layton
1989:41).

In situated learning, social networks replace classrooms: modern Highland Maya can be asked whom they know and from whom they learn. Of
course, the ancient inhabitants of Nacimiento and Dos Ceibas are long
dead and I therefore rely on indirect evidence to reconstruct their social
networks. Imported materials serve as measures of trade and exchange

among the lowlanders. These include items like obsidian and greenstone ornaments and tools, which were mostly brought from the highlands; and sandstone grinding stones, which presumably came from the area around Altar de Sacrificios. Nacimiento and Dos Ceibas were at the end of a long supply chain, and imported materials were generally scarce (Eberl 2014a:309–313). Nonetheless, access to nonlocal resources did change over the course of the Late Classic. For example, grinding equipment made from sandstone appears only during the eighth century A.D. Ceramic vessels tempered with volcanic ash from the highlands are absent in the seventh century A.D. but present in small quantities during the eighth century A.D. (Eberl 2014a:285 Table 10.16). To a small extent, the villagers of Nacimiento and Dos Ceibas enjoyed broader access to nonlocal resources. In Chapter 6, I discuss how they adopted new iconographic motifs during the eighth century A.D. These motifs relate to key concepts found in Classic Maya writing and art and include the signs for *ajaw* (lord) and the war owl. During the eighth century A.D., they actively engaged with the ideology that sustained Classic Maya society. Their social networks went beyond the limits of hinterland villages and reached into royal capitals.

At Nacimiento and Dos Ceibas, architecture provides another indirect measure of social networks. Three-room structures became the norm during the eighth century A.D. In these rectangular buildings, the center room opens to the plaza while the side rooms open to the front or the sides. The center rooms tend to have higher benches with armrests and niches that resemble thrones. Their doorjambs are usually thin and, for example, occupy 37.1 percent of the center room's width among Petexbatún examples (Eberl 2014a:213 Table 8.3). Wide doorways make the center room's interior easily visible to outsiders.

Nacimiento's Group Navaja Oscura and Dos Ceibas's South Plaza are much larger than the next-biggest groups in these villages. In both these extra-large residential groups, buildings are situated close to each other and in some cases are linked by walls. Platforms and walls in the corners leave only narrow entry passages to the plaza. Since they are low and do not contain defensive features like baffled gates, these structures seem to have controlled access to the plaza. Dos Ceibas's South Plaza replicates the spatial setting and layout of elite palaces (Inomata 2001a; see also Ashmore et al. 2004:312; Andres et al. [2014:55–56] provide a comparable traffic-flow analysis among palaces). Careful staging is palpable in the South Plaza of Dos Ceibas, whose only spacious entrance was in the southwest corner (inset in Figure 1.6). Visitors entering the plaza here encounter parallel buildings on both sides that guide their eyes to the palatial structure at the northern end. There, ample terraces form stages on both sides of a three-room structure. A monumental stairway leads to the central room, which features a wide doorway and a throne-like bench (Figure 3.8). People and their activities in and next to Structure R27-83 were highly visible from the plaza.

Three-room structures and extra-large residential groups appear at Nacimiento and Dos Ceibas only during the eighth century A.D. (for comparable architectural innovation see Schwarz 2013:312). They show how some people in the hinterland transcended their local traditions and adopted elite customs. During the Late Classic, roles became differentiated both within the hinterland villages—at least when the inhabitants of the extra-large groups are contrasted with everybody else—and between the villages and royal capitals. Divine rulers and their households became measuring sticks if not role models. As populations increased, diversified, and built wider social networks in Late Classic Maya society, I suggest that these changes applied not only to elites but also to commoners. In other words, Maya society changed dynamically during the seventh and eighth centuries A.D.

## Beyond Divine Rulers and Royal Courts

Human interactions follow four models (Fiske 1992). In Communal Sharing, individuals see themselves as part of a bounded group and treat each other as equals. Their shared identity as a nation or race overshadows individual identities and feeds communal action. In Authority Ranking, people are in hierarchical relationships, and their rank determines their privileges and duties. Examples are seniority due to age or military rank. The third model is Equality Matching. In these relationships, people track imbalances between themselves and others and make corrections to maintain one-to-one correspondences. Examples include turn-taking in games and term limits for officeholders. Market Pricing is the last model. People reduce social interaction to a single variable like money or pleasure and judge it through ratio values, for example by maximizing profits while minimizing losses. Economically valuable activities lend themselves to this approach.

These four models allow judgments of the forms of sociality that are permissible and fostered in a given society. Of particular interest are the specific rules and domains where these models are present. The myth of Itzamnaaj's court exemplifies the Authority Ranking model in Classic

Maya society. The myth exemplifies the centripetal force of divine rulers and royal courts. Similar to Marcel Mauss's (1990) total social facts, the myth cannot be reduced to its religious meaning but encompasses social, political, and economic domains (see also Wagner 1977:627). It provides a collective image of how individuals interact in Maya society (compare Hunt 1977; Weiner 1988). At the same time, the myth must be understood critically. Although it was presented as a generalizable template, it served the interests of the divine rulers. The question becomes whether alternative forms of sociality existed in Maya society.

The Classic Maya villages of Nacimiento and Dos Ceibas likely each formed a community with a shared identity, fostered by public institutions like ballgames and cave rituals (see also Canuto and Yaeger 2000). The architecture of Nacimiento varied in style and construction technique from that in Dos Ceibas, and I argue that architecture differentiated these two neighboring villages not only visually but also socially, establishing in-group versus out-group distinctions. Community members treated each other as equals, following Fiske's Communal Sharing mode. For example, they enjoyed comparable access to obsidian despite considerable wealth differences (Eberl 2014a:321–322). Each community seems to have had mechanisms to redistribute goods and services.

Tit-for-tat characterizes Equality Matching relationships. It informs the interaction with the divine in past and modern Maya societies (Monaghan 2000:36–39). Prayers and offerings bind deities to respond in kind and grant favors. Maya rulers call themselves caretakers of their patron gods (the latter are *u juntan,* "their cared-for ones"; Stuart 1997:8–9). The myth of Itzamnaaj contains this element of mutuality. As supreme king, Itzamnaaj naturally commands respect and submission; yet, even he gives something in return. The hummingbird obtains its wings, the deer its antlers. In Classic Maya society, tribute seems to have been conceptualized similarly. To fulfill *patan,* "burden," non-elites delivered labor or goods to divine rulers and gained their patronage and benevolence (see also Hill 1992:138–149). Similar patron-client relationships likely existed in the outwardly egalitarian village of Dos Ceibas. The South Plaza was its largest residential group and likely the seat of local gentry (Figure 3.8). Construction bins and multiple stone carvers' marks suggest that the community at large built Structure R27-83, the South Plaza's largest residence (Eberl 2014a:212–213). The gentry who eventually lived in it reciprocated. Figurines from the same mold were found in Structure R27-83 and in a small group immediately to the north (inset in Figure 1.6).

Figure 3.10. Exchanging goods, services, and ideas in Classic Maya society: *a.* Map of the North Acropolis at Calakmul—known anciently as *chiik nahb kot* according to the glyphs at its entrance; *b.* three-dimensional reconstruction of Structure Sub 1-4, showing its southeast corner with the tamale vendor mural (other murals are omitted); *c.* mural of a female tamale vendor and her customer. (Glyph block based on photo in Carrasco Vargas and Colón González 2005:45; map based on Carrasco Vargas and Cordeiro Baqueiro 2012:10; reconstruction based partially on Carrasco Vargas and Cordeiro Baqueiro 2012:14; mural based on photos and drawing in Carrasco Vargas and Cordeiro Baqueiro 2012:28–33; Martin 2012:65.)

Some exchanges in Classic Maya society were nonhierarchical and possibly followed Fiske's Market Pricing model. Calakmul's North Acropolis exemplifies this type of interaction (Figure 3.10). Situated at the core of the site, this 2.5-hectare square contains approximately seventy buildings that align in parallel rows (Carrasco Vargas and Cordeiro Baqueiro 2012). A mural at the entrance repeats the glyphic phrase *chiik nahb kot,* "coati pool wall," amidst images of birds, serpents, and water lilies (Carrasco Vargas and Colón González 2005). Chiik Nahb refers to Calakmul in general, and *chiik nahb kot* specifically to the North Acropolis as the city's public space (Carter 2014:39–44). Murals cover a predecessor of Structure 1 in the center of the North Acropolis (Carrasco Vargas et al. 2009). They show economic transactions. For example, a woman sits in front of a basket full of tamales. She offers a plate filled with tamales to a customer, who probingly bites into one. The caption identifies the woman as *aj waaj,* or "tamale person," without providing her name. People also drink *atole* and offer goods like maize, salt, and tobacco. Porters wait nearby or load, carry, and unload tall bundles. These economic interactions match aspects of Fiske's Market Pricing model. The murals of Structure Sub 1-4 may depict market scenes, an aspect of Classic Maya culture that remains little understood (for example, Dahlin et al. 2007; King 2015). Glyphic captions identify the activities but leave the producers and consumers—many of them likely nonelites—anonymous. The one exception is the name-phrase *ix ? bolon tuun,* "Lady . . . Nine Stones," which appears below the tamale vendor and in several other murals (Martin 2012:79–80). The prominent size and placement of her name suggest a human officeholder or a supernatural patron with some supervisory function. While many questions remain, the Chiik Nahb murals offer an alternative image of sociality.

Social interactions in Classic Maya society are not limited to hierarchical relationships. I argue that Fiske's four models of sociality were present, even if their actualization remains little understood in many cases. The myth of Itzamnaaj's court overshadows these coexisting and overlapping forms of interaction. It provides a convenient image of Classic Maya society not by being more truthful about ancient realities but by being promoted at the expense of alternative discourses. The myth served the interests of divine rulers, and it should be understood as a totalizing ideology (Keane 1997, 2003). Power relationships shape social discourses and authorize forms of sociality.

## Transmission of Knowledge

Societies differ in the ways people learn and develop the self- and meta-awareness that forms the basis for creative thinking. In the West, learning tends to be institutionalized and separated from daily life. Teachers and students occupy clear social roles and are in a hierarchical relationship. Traditional classrooms, exams, and textbooks emphasize a vertical transmission of knowledge. In Chapter 2 I contrasted this with situated learning. Instead of taking classes, Yucatec Maya girls become midwives by accompanying, observing, and copying their mothers. "They know what the life of a midwife is like (for example, that she needs to go out at all hours of the day or night), what kinds of stories the women and men who come to consult her tell, what kinds of herbs and other remedies need to be collected, and the like" (Jordan 1989:932). In situated learning like this, regular daily activities blend with the application of professional skills (Lave and Wenger 1991). Learning results from growing up in a particular environment. "If your mother is a midwife, you are likely to know a lot about midwifery; if your grandmother is a potter, you are likely to know something about making pots; and if you spend most of your childhood in a tailor shop, you are likely to know a lot about what tailors do" (Jordan 1989:932). Apprenticeship learning emphasizes the acquisition of physical skills and the creation of a context in which novices can develop their own skills (Ingold 2001:142). Novices learn how, when, and where to do things.

The ways in which societies transmit knowledge are not fixed. Schooling affects the ways people learn (Correa-Chávez and Rogoff 2005; Göncü et al. 2000; Lancy 2015:354; Mejía-Arauz et al. 2005). Chavajay (2006) studied how highland Guatemalan mothers organized the participation of children in a problem-solving discussion. "Mothers with no or little schooling typically structured children's participation with flexible collaboration that provided children opportunities to decide how and when to participate" (Chavajay 2006:378). On the other hand, mothers with more years of formal schooling managed the children's contributions through individual turn-taking and test questions. Similar developments have been noted among Maya children in Zinacantan (Maynard 2004). The local model of learning stresses observational learning, contextualized talk, bodily closeness between teacher and learner, and multiple teachers (519). While playing, children teach their siblings how to make tortillas or to care for baby dolls. Unschooled children rely on the traditional model. Those who had attended school use a western model of learning by teaching from a distance and using more, and more decontextualized, verbal discourse (Maynard 2004:530). Some realized that their siblings failed to comply and switched back to the traditional model. Situated and didactic learning are not exclusionary but respond to social structures.

Situated learning embodies knowledge. In a Brazilian market, psychologists approached a twelve-year-old boy selling coconuts (Carraher et al. 1985). "How much is one coconut?" they asked him. "Thirty-five." To test his mathematical skills, the scholars then asked for ten coconuts. "How much is that?" The boy paused before replying: "Three will be 105; with three more, that will be 210. [Pause] I need four more. That is . . . [Pause] 315 . . . I think it is 350" (Carraher et al. 1985:23). Instead of applying the arithmetic skills that he had learned in five years at school, the boy solved the problem using his street smarts by calculating based on the units of one to three coconuts he commonly sold. The same researchers came back a week later and presented him and four other market children with the same question, formulated first as a marketplace sales problem, then as a written equation, and finally as a theoretical problem. The results were stunning. Almost all children answered correctly when the problem was phrased in terms selling coconuts (only 2 percent were wrong), but 26 percent got the answer wrong when they encountered the same problem in writing, and 63 percent did so when they were confronted with an abstract arithmetic problem ("How much is ten times thirty-five?"; Carraher et al. 1985:24). The Brazilian coconut vendors are not unique. Street and school mathematical skills diverge similarly in other contexts (Bender Jørgensen 2012; Hutchins 1990; Lave 1977; Rampal 2003; Rocha 1985; Saxe 1991; Scribner 1984, 1985).

Context and rules of knowledge can be viewed as two poles of learning at the extremes of a range (for case studies see Hasaki 2012; Kelly-Buccellati 2012; Maynard 2004). Bottom-up and learner-initiated processes (situated learning) are better for conveying procedural skills, while highly structured and top-down processes (didactic learning) are better for conveying declarative information (Lancy 2015:372). Both approaches have strengths and weaknesses. The Brazilian coconut vendor learned how to multiply by ten in school but failed to apply the rule to his everyday context, nor could he transfer his street smarts to a context-independent rule. His case illustrates the risk that practice-based learning remains tethered to repetition without deep understanding. On the other hand, didactic learning may fail to contextualize abstract rules.

## Haggling over Ideas in Life's Bazaar

Society provides opportunity structures for innovation. As an Illinois state legislator in 1842, Abraham Lincoln pondered how social influence affected people's daily actions. Would a man go to church with his wife's bonnet on his head? He would not; not because it was immoral or uncomfortable but because it was egregiously unfashionable. "And what is the influence of fashion, but the influence that other people's actions have on our actions— the strong inclination each of us feels to do as we see all our neighbors do?" (Lincoln 1920:62). Individuals' novel ideas enter a social contest that is comparable to a Byzantine bazaar. People enter without knowing what ideas they might encounter or what these ideas might be worth. If they are not careful, merchants will cheat them by overpricing yesteryear's novelty. People have to build trust to get honest opinions and fair evaluations. Inventors, on the other hand, have to understand these social processes in order to find acceptance; otherwise, they close their business with a pile of unmarketable ideas. Society may promote or stifle individuals and their novel ideas. At stake are cross-fertilization, comparison, and competition.

Individual creativity resonates within a social context. Mesoamerican ritual specialists face this dilemma daily. In east-central Mexico, they cut figures from paper and use them in sacred ceremonies (for the ritual importance of paper among the past and present Mesoamerican people and the Maya see Sandstrom and Sandstrom 1986:3–34; Stuart 2012). Each paper image represents a spirit in the Nahua pantheon and, after being sacralized, it acquires the power to attract the life force of that spirit (Sandstrom and Sandstrom 1986:74). Apprentices of a Nahua ritual specialist learn from their master and repeat his or her forms. As soon as they begin working on their own they have to attract clients, and they start cutting their paper images in innovative ways in an attempt to do so. These ritual entrepreneurs are not free to create at will, though. "They are constrained by the expectations of the people they serve and by the logical requirements of the philosophical and theological system in which they operate" (Sandstrom and Sandstrom 1986:260). Social learning leads people to adopt the cultural logic of their society.

Even seemingly simple Classic Maya villages were economically and sociopolitically diverse, illustrating that societies are heterogeneous, even fractured. Multiple structures operate on different levels and in different modalities, as scientific disciplines with their fields of knowledge exemplify (Sewell 1992:16, 19). Becoming an expert requires specialization at the risk of constricting oneself to dwelling in a field-specific silo. By contrast, innovators often bridge different fields with their ideas. Their cross-fertilizing approach requires considering which structures exist, how they overlap, and in which contexts they apply. At the same time, it requires them to link with experts who have specialized knowledge. Can these individuals trust each other, work together, and share ideas? Or would they compete out of fear that their ideas will be stolen? Collaboration and competition show how individuals are situated in social, cultural, and historical contexts (Munn 1983:280; 1986:11; 1990:1; 1992:106; Pazos Garciandía 1995:220; Smith 2003:15; Urry 1991:160). For innovation to be successful, information has to flow freely. "We mustn't adopt a protectionist attitude, to stop 'bad' information from invading and stifling the 'good'" (Foucault 1997:326). The size of social groups, the extent of social networks, and the modes of communication impact the flow of information. Through innovation, individuals imagine novel ways to align structures and practices. Whether they can realize them depends on social constraints and opportunities.

# 4

## Bleibt Alles Anders

### Modeling Invention

In 1602, Sebastián Vizcaíno explored the Pacific coast of Mexico with three Spanish ships under his command. After several months at sea, the sailors were dying of hunger. Diego de Santiago, the chief scribe of the expedition, complained in the official diary of "rotten jerked beef, gruel, biscuits, and beans and chick-peas spoiled by weevils" (Bolton 1916:97). When men went ashore for water and food, they were so weak that "the strongest of them could not lift a bottle of water from the ground" (Bolton 1916:98). A mysterious sickness made the situation worse. Many had sore mouths with gums swollen over their teeth. They could hardly sip water and could no longer eat, suffering Tantalus-like pains in view of the little food left on board. Those who were affected the worst died suddenly, sometimes mid-sentence. Sailors had feared the sore mouth sickness for ages without knowing what caused it or how to heal it. By accident, Vizcaíno and his men stumbled across the cure. At one stop along the Mexican coast, while desperately searching for food, they picked cactus fruits. When men with sore mouths sucked the fruits dry, their profusely bleeding ulcers sloughed off. "Within six days," marveled Sebastián Vizcaíno in his diary, "there was nobody left whose mouth was not healed" (translated after Baranowski 2011:68).

The sore mouth sickness is now known as scurvy and its cause is understood to be lack of vitamin C. Alongside others, Vizcaíno is now hailed as a discoverer of a cure for scurvy (Frankenburg 2009:73–75). I would hesitate, though, to feed his finding into an evolutionary model of innovation and assume an unbroken stream of scientific advances. Instead, Vizcaíno exemplifies failed innovation. His sailors saw the effect of eating the cactus fruit and copied each other through situated learning. But their insight never spread beyond this expedition, and the Spanish navy never adopted cactus fruits as a remedy for scurvy. The reason survives in Vizcaíno's diary: "As the father of mercy, God chose to furnish these islands with a small fruit called *jucoystles* that are similar to wild pineapples [*Bromelia pinguin*]" (translated after Baranowski 2011:68). Vizcaíno recognized the role of the cactus fruit but he attributed the miraculous cure to God.

Vizcaíno's experience is instructive. People go about their lives not only in real and realizable ways but also imagining possible alternatives. Inventions enable possible worlds that were previously imaginary. Vizcaíno accidentally encountered a cure for scurvy in cactus fruit, but he failed to detect the relationship that would have allowed this possible world to be replicated. His embrace of God as father of mercy exemplifies the culture-specific logic that short-circuited innovation. Sailors and soldiers continued to die of scurvy for centuries after his discovery (Bollet 2004:173–186; Frankenburg 2009:71–95; Shectman 2003:51–54).

## Word Made Flesh

The structure of social systems consists of interlinked schemas and resources. Giddens defines resources as "anything that can serve as a source of power in social interactions" (quoted in Sewell 1992:9; see also Giddens 1979:92; 1984:258). He distinguishes between authoritative and allocative resources, or those capabilities that enable command over people and objects, respectively. Specifically, authoritative resources involve coordinating people and allocative resources monopolizing raw materials. Thus, resources are structures of domination that ensure the continuity of societies (Giddens 1984:258, 259). This definition proves of little utility when it comes to innovations: "Irrigation schemes and other technical innovations usually do not so much increase average productivity as regularize and co-ordinate production" (Giddens 1984:259). By ignoring their immediate effects, Giddens reduces innovations to practices that maintain social control and thus block social change. His definition fails to consider the agency necessary for innovation and its effect on space-time.

Resources point to the material conditions of life. Unlike schemas, they manifest in time and space. Giddens's distinction between authoritative and allocative resources becomes easier to understand in Sewell's (1992:9) reformulation of human versus nonhuman resources. Human resources encompass bodily capacities and abilities like endurance, physical strength, and dexterity; nonhuman resources are natural and manufactured, animate and inanimate objects. These resources are unequally distributed, particularly in complex societies, but all humans control some resources, if only their own bodies. "Part of what it means to conceive of human beings as agents," Sewell (1992:10) concludes, "is to conceive them as empowered by access to resources of one kind or another." Based on his critique of Giddens's definition, Sewell (1992, 2005) sees schemas as virtual and independent of context while resources are actual and context-dependent. Structure brings schemas and resources together. "The factory gate, the punching-in station, the design of the assembly line: all of these features of the factory teach and validate the rules of the capitalist labor contract" (Sewell 1992:13).

Translating imagination into invention requires materializing ideas. I rephrase this problem in religious terms: How can word be made flesh, as the Gospel of John (1:14) says? Christians struggle to comprehend how God materializes as a human being and ultimately is crucified. Official Catholic doctrine maintains that Jesus Christ is physically and ideally both human and god, suppressing alternative interpretations of John 1:14 as heretic. For example, docetists (from Greek *dokesis,* "apparition, phantom") argued that Christ did not have a physical but a phantom body while on earth (Ehrman 1993:181). Therefore, he only appeared to suffer death on the cross. Other religions grapple similarly with this problem. During rituals, Classic Maya elites turned into the *b'aah,* "images," of gods. During the accession of his king, the Palenque noble Janaab Ajaw impersonated Itzamnaaj (Figure 2.8). During intense meditation Tibetan Buddhist monks create *tulpas,* or "magic formations generated by a powerful concentration of thought" (David-Néel 1971:311). Spiritually enlightened leaders materialize their thoughts not merely as spiritual phantoms but also as *tulkus,* or incarnations. When Tashi Lama had to flee from Shigatze in 1924, he left behind a *tulku* who impersonated him so perfectly that even his enemies were deceived. The *tulku* vanished when Tashi Lama was safely out of reach (David-Néel 1971:121–122). Dokesis, *b'aah, tulku,* and other thought-forms mesh idea and matter.

Forms of impersonation epitomize the problem of representation. One can ask whether they are "like similes adrift without a string" (Nabokov 1992:77). In his phenomenology, Edmund Husserl (1950, 1960) employs representation in three general senses: as an ideal status (German, *Vorstellung*), as the placeholder for presentation (German, *Vergegenwärtigung*), and in reference to an ideal status (German, *Repräsentation*). Reality is factual while representations are, or stand in for, ideals. Jacques Derrida (2011:42) criticizes Husserl because in Husserl's model representations are byproducts of actual practices that are neither essential nor constitutive. Instead of framing them within the ideal-versus-fact dichotomy, Derrida (2011:71–75) emphasizes representations as pointers. Like signs in language (Derrida 2011:43), they presuppose comparison (that is, the existence of other impersonations) and repetition in the form of practices that reproduce them. Impersonations require a cultural system to be understandable while elucidating them with meaning. Therefore, representations refer to and reaffirm reality. In the practice called *thuic*, the Dinka of Sudan tie tufts of grass into knots when they hope to achieve a specific outcome (Lienhardt 1961:282–283). Enemies are "knotted in grass" to restrict their freedom of action; a grass-encased stone represents a lion to be killed; travelers leave knotted grass along their way to ensure food at the end of their journey. *Thuic* knots embody mental intentions while refining their formation. Thus, representations can combine indicative and expressive functions, contrary to Husserl's distinction (Derrida 2011:47).

Representations imply a dialectical process called *différance* that consists of differentiation and deferral (Derrida 2011:75). By differentiation, Derrida refers to the process that establishes dichotomies such as ideal versus fact in the case of representations. In a never-ending oscillation, *différance* swings pendulum-like back and forth between opposites. The repetition emphasizes the extremes: because it never reaches them, it defers finalizing their identity. *Différance* is the operation of differing and delaying (Derrida 2011:75). This analysis of representation moves from the categories of impersonation versus reality to the process of establishing them in time and space. My approach recalls Bernard Faure's (1996) analysis of Zen imagination, or the ways in which beliefs are rendered in images:

> The *imaginaire* can be conceived of as an intermediary modality between the truth and the false. It thus becomes the attitude, the domain, or the modality that allows us to keep together, and to mediate between, these two levels: belief and nonbelief, subitism and gradualism, form and formlessness. . . . *Imaginaire* is not really nominal, but rather adverbial, adjectival, or modal (a way of existing, in an imaginary way). We must guard against a tendency to substantivize, as we often do with the unconscious or the sacred, that which is only a modality of belief or perception. (Faure 1996:281; see also Meskell 2005:59; Taussig 1993:252)

Through *différance*, representations exteriorize categories and entangle them with reality. Objects represent ideas or structures not in a subordinating but a co-constitutive way (see Joyce 2005:142–143). My approach questions Giddens's (1984:25) definition of structures as autonomous. By defining structures as the "virtual order of differences," Giddens (1979:3) adopts Ferdinand de Saussure's (1966) concept of language (*langue*) as a system of elements whose meaning derives from being exchangeable or comparable to other elements. For Giddens, structure, like language, has different elements that imply only each other. It is closed, virtual, and autonomous from nonlinguistic aspects of the world. Therefore, structure is "out of time and space save its instantiations and co-ordination as memory traces" (Giddens 1984:25). Yet, the instantiations of structures are critical. Languages die if nobody speaks them, structures vanish if nobody enacts them. Derrida's (2011) *différance* stresses the process of becoming that establishes and intertwines structures and objects. The assumption of autonomy envisions stable structures. My critique replaces them with sticky structures, or structures that are valid only as long as they are being constituted.

Stickiness also applies to the objects within structures. Things have a social life only so long as they manifest socially relevant structures (for example, Appadurai 1986). "Any piece of writing, good or bad, always ends up appearing like a predetermined crystallization" (Saramago 1996:114; also Tambiah 1985:29). In his exploration of dirt as matter out of place and out of time, Hamann (2008a:830) suggests that "the contrasts of patina versus dirt and of heirloom continuity versus matter-out-of-time disjunction point to the ability of inanimate objects (when properly cared for and maintained) to have 'social lives' that resist decay and last far longer than the biological lives of human beings." Things serve as physical chronometers for religious conversion. "The relative malleability of objects made them attractive vehicles for the expression of ideas about time and chronological pollution in a context in which various human practices, also defined as 'of the past,' were much more recalcitrant" (Hamann 2008a:831).

### Animating the Inanimate

Objectification makes intangible ideas tangible and, in doing so, anchors them in a unique context. Classic Maya artists inhabited an animated universe (Monaghan 2000:25–26). Through their artistry, they gave life to things. On ceramic vessels, the so-called Primary Standard Sequence (PSS), a glyphic text, spells out the responsibility and challenge of artistic power. The vessel's maker lists how the vessel is decorated, what form it has, which liquid it contains, and who owns it (MacLeod 1990; Stuart 1989). This

Figure 4.1. The ensoulment of Maya ceramic vessels: *a*. Glyph D from vessel K791 (after photo in Kerr 1989:49); *b*. Glyph B from vessel K2914; note the conflation with the God N, or *t'ab*, glyph (after photo in Kerr 1990:297); *c*. Glyph B from vessel K4387 (after photo in Kerr 1992:487); *d*. Glyph A2 from vessel K6437 (after photo in Kerr 2000:967). (For additional examples see vessels K635, K1728, K2801, K4354, K4572, K5022, K5113, K5366, K5763.)

information seems superfluous since readers and viewers of the PSS hold the vessel itself in their hands. Yet, through the listing of all its attributes, the vessel becomes complete or, as expressed in the PSS, these traits "rise, climb up, or go up" to the viewer's attention (Wisdom 1950:683). The corresponding verb reads *t'ab*, and modern Ch'orti' use it to describe how the sun rises at dawn (and vanquishes the night) and how distilling a liquid removes its impurities (Wisdom 1950:683).

In some vessel texts, a different glyph replaces *t'ab* (Figure 4.1). This glyph captures a person's last breath: the T-shaped sign for "wind" emerges from the dying person's mouth, leaving behind the dead, rendered with closed eyes or as a skull. This moment captures the passage from alive to dead. The glyph possibly reads *uh* to spell *uhuy*, or "to sigh" (Grube 2006b:66; Wisdom 1950:746). Related verbs like *uhres*, "to make moral or good, to sacralize" identify breathing as one of the animating forces (Houston and Taube 2000:267). Thus, Maya artists breathed life into their vessels. For them, production meant not simply making things but creating life.

In Maya culture, creation resonates with ordering and completing the incomplete. Modern Ch'ol Maya attribute illnesses to soul loss (Josserand and Hopkins 2001). Earth powers that reside in caves and rivers can imprison human souls. In some cases, people make a pact with the earth lord to bewitch others. In other cases, fright, envy, or wrong thoughts create disharmony with the spirit world and result in soul loss (Josserand and Hopkins 2001:13). The affected person falls sick. Curing means making him or her complete again. The corresponding vocabulary is based on the root *tz'äk,* "medicine, remedy" (Josserand and Hopkins 2001:30). In Classic Maya inscriptions, the related term *tz'ak* indicates that something or somebody is put in order and made complete (Eberl 2015). From *tz'äk* derives *tz'äkan,* "to cure," and *tz'äkayaj,* "curer," but also *tz'äkäl,* "complete," and *tz'äktesäntel,* "to comply with an agreement" (literally "to be completed"). With ablutions, herbs, prayer, and other means, healers restore their patients' souls. Sometimes, they paint the sick person with bad-smelling weeds so that the soul reeks and the earth god says: "Get out of here; I don't want to smell you; you stink badly" (Whittaker and Warkentin 1965:144). The healer then snatches the soul and reunites it with the patient. The soulless human becomes ensouled again.

The life-giving power of Maya artisans expresses itself in highly ritualized production processes. Native Maya understandings of the human body, sicknesses, and healing converge in the creation of the Maya blue. This famous pigment resists corrosion and maintains its brilliance for hundreds of years. It is not based on lapis lazuli or azurite, common western sources for blue pigments. Instead, Maya artisans combined indigo, palygorskite clay, and incense to make Maya blue (Arnold 2005; Arnold et al. 2008). Yucatec Maya use all three ingredients medically and ritually. They cure epilepsy and convulsions with indigo, or what they call *ch'ooh* (Redfield and Redfield 1940:71; Roys 1931:80). They eat palygorskite, or *sak lú'um,* "white earth," to treat diarrhea (Arnold and Bohor 1975:27; Brady and Rissolo 2006:479; Folan 1969:183). Copal incense, or *pòom,* enjoys wide use for cleansing the bodies of patients and divining their sicknesses (Stross 1996). The artisans mixed the three ingredients. Kindling and burning the incense generated the sustained low heat that chemically bound indigo to palygorskite clay. Unlike industrial production, this process was part of a ritual. A three-legged bowl found at Chichen Itza contains a mixture of indigo, clay, and copal. Chemical analysis showed that the contents had been ignited (Arnold et al. 2008). While flames consumed the copal and smoke billowed skywards, Maya blue formed. In this case, instead of removing the specks of blue for use in painting or elsewhere, the artisans sacrificed the entire bowl into Chichen Itza's Sacred Cenote.

In inventions, ideas acquire phenomenological expression. They are linked to and embedded in their cultural context. In ancient and modern Maya cultures, objects come alive as artisans make them. Mopan Maya refer to imaginative or technological invention as *kux-kin-t-ik,* or "to bring something into being" (Danziger 2013:257). Artists participate in an animated universe in which life forces can be imbued as well as taken. Contrasts like old versus new and healthy versus sick are complementary opposites that are brought together in a ritualistic setting by specialists, be they healers or artisans.

## Obliging God and Family

Through innovation, humans transform structures that consist of virtual schemas and actual resources. I deliberately say structures—not structure—to avoid reducing society to a single set of rules and resources. Societies are complex, contingent, and fractured. "Forms of life differ. Ends, moral principles, are many," as Isaiah Berlin (2013:12) argues for pluralism. "We can discuss each other's point of view, we can try to reach common ground, but in the end what you pursue may not be reconcilable with the ends to which I find that I have dedicated my life." Societies have multiple structures, which can and will come into conflict with each other (competing obligations may have existed in Classic Maya society; see Houston and Inomata 2009:158–159). These conflicts play out not in an abstract social space but in human lives (Berlin 1997:239). Where Berlin laments humankind's tragedy, I locate the concrete action of innovations.

The Egyptian activist Zaynab al-Ghazali (1917–2005) was closely associated with the Muslim Brotherhood (Mahmood 2005:180–184). Publicly she urged women to abide by their traditional roles as mothers, wives, and daughters but privately she challenged these roles. She divorced her first husband because, as she argues in her autobiography, "if the interests of marriage conflict with the call to God [*al-da'wa 'ila allāh*], then marriage will come to an end and the call [to God] [*da'wa*] will prevail in my whole being/existence" (translated in Mahmood 2005:181). *Da'wa* comes from the root *da'ā,* or "to call, invite" (Canard 2012). In the religious sense, da'wa invites people "to the way of your lord with wisdom and with fair admonition, and dispute with them with what is better" (Jones 2007:260). Muslim missionaries are role models who proselytize through a dialogue in which they persuade others to accept Islam.

Zaynab al-Ghazali articulates two structures that define the lives of Muslim wives. In Islamic jurisprudence, a married woman owes duty to her family and to God, but her physical and moral obligations differ. Physical obligations are symmetrical: husband, wife, and children are bound to care for one another's physical well-being. Moral obligations are hierarchical: Within the family, the husband is responsible for the conduct of his wife, and his wife for the behavior of their children. But the wife is not responsible for her husband's behavior. Zaynab al-Ghazali took advantage of this small structural inconsistency to argue her case. "It was God's wisdom that He did not divert me from my [religious] activities by endowing me with a son, or blessing me with children" (Mahmood 2005:182). Infertility freed her from a wife's moral and physical obligations for her offspring and left her with the lesser physical duties to her husband. She undid the latter by calling herself mother to all Muslims. Her daʿwa, or call to God, was more than an ethical duty and became, literally, a marriage made in heaven that superseded her earthly marriage. This argument allowed al-Ghazali to do the unthinkable for an Egyptian woman. She divorced her husband and devoted herself to political activism in God's name.

I use Zaynab al-Ghazali's case to elaborate on Sewell's concept of complex structures. "Societies are based on practices," as Sewell (1992:17) says, "that derive from many distinct structures, which exist at different levels, operate in different modalities." Complex structures are multiple, and they coexist, interdepend, overlap, and compete. Egyptian women follow two obligations that reflect the religious and familial spheres of their lives and shape these spheres differently according to their distinctive moral and physical implications.[1] The two duties are distinct structures but they also overlap. While they are physically obliged to their husband and children, married women have moral obligations to their children and to God. Because Zaynab al-Ghazali had no children, her obligations were physically to her husband and morally to God. To make her case for divorce, she exposed the inherent structural conflict: Isn't her duty to God more important than her duty to her husband? Seen this way, the two duties compete.

Structures are polysemic in that their meaning is open to interpretation (Sewell 1992:18–19). Unlike most Egyptian wives who live their traditional roles, al-Ghazali sensed two coexisting structures that placed different demands on individuals. She also realized that these two structures were interdependent. As long as women stayed at home, they were able to reconcile the conflicting duties. The material conditions of their lives—their resources—then reinforced the schemas. Such reconciliation became difficult for al-Ghazali, however, when she turned into a public activist. The elements of structures—here, moral and physical obligations—are transposable; that is, "they can be applied to a wide and not fully predictable range of cases outside the context in which they are initially learned" (Sewell 1992:17).

Structures are embedded in daily life and form part of everybody's tacit knowledge. Egyptian women accepted their duties to God and family as normal. Zaynab al-Ghazali's argument exemplifies the process of *différance*. Structures simultaneously guide her life and clash. They are not however simply "embodied history, internalized as a second nature and so forgotten as history" (Bourdieu 1990:56). By exteriorizing the conflicting structures, al-Ghazali became aware of and was able to question them. She played her duty to God and to family off each other and created an innovative solution that allowed Egyptian women to divorce their husbands. Such an outsider mentality lets innovators like al-Ghazali perceive and exploit structural gaps and overlaps. Through inventions, innovators advance novel articulations of schemas and resources that compete with existing articulations.

Al-Ghazali's divorce polarized Egyptian society. As a public figure, Zaynab al-Ghazali exteriorized the inherent structural conflict for an entire society to see. Although few women have dared to follow in her footsteps, the previously accepted and understood role of women is now openly debated. Al-Ghazali enabled an alternative to what is normal and became a role model for change.

## Pebbles in the Garden of Forking Paths

Every day people decide how to behave in specific situations. They consider alternative courses of action and choose one over others. This means that they determine what their goal is and how they can best get there. Habit-based models of agency emphasize experience. Ordinarily, having accomplished something in the past enables people to repeat it again in the future. Nonetheless, they are not restricted to this course of action. People will also wonder what they *could* do; that is, they imagine possible but so far unrealized goals. Innovation is novel because it realizes previously impossible worlds. I contextualize it in a cognitive model of individual decision-making that I call the Garden of Forking Paths. In Jorge Borges's (1956) short story by that name, individuals consider possible outcomes of their actions. If Fang meets a stranger and resolves to kill him because he might uncover a secret, Fang might succeed, or the stranger might kill him, both might escape alive, or both might die. Each outcome becomes a point of departure for new forks. Individuals evaluate courses of action and eventually choose one over the alternatives. Events unfold in a fabric of divergent and parallel worlds. From an individual perspective, these worlds include not only those perceived as real but also those imagined to exist and those that could exist. "Action has to be understood in the light not of its real-world antecedents and consequences, but in the light of the fantasy-system which inspires it" (Gell 1992:184). Of course, fantasy can run wild. The question therefore becomes, if habit does not constrain human behavior, what does?

The answer is logic. Humans use commonsense to understand themselves and their world and to communicate intelligibly with others (Wilson 1970). They rely on three axioms (Hollis 1970:230–232). Through language and other means, humans express identity (p implies p), contradiction (not [p and not p]), and inference (p and [p implies q] implies q). These three axioms of standard logic are necessary for a system of logical reasoning.

I move now from states of existence to relationships. The concept of habit looks backward and invokes past experience to channel future action. In contrast, logic coherently aligns past, present, and future. From a phenomenological perspective, individuals continually modify their past experiences, thus allowing past experience to contribute to but not command current and future experience. For example, al-Ghazali broke with the traditional role of Egyptian women and defended her decision rationally. Her approach contrasts habit and logic, state of existence and coherent relationships.

Coherence requires assessing how close events, objects, and actions—in logic-speak, propositions—are to reality. Analytic propositions are true or false in all possible worlds; they are independent of human experience. Synthetic propositions are contingent; they are true in the world that is being described but in other worlds they are or might be false (Lyons 1977:787). Necessity and possibility are central to modal logic, the branch of formal logic concerned with modalities. In a system of fixed structures the statement "Zaynab al-Ghazali is married" means that her familial duties preclude divorce and that "she must obey her husband." How can the "must" be interpreted?

Philosophers and linguists identify various perspectives or modalities to answer this semantic question. The deontic, or "binding," modality assumes that structures are ultimate truths. It can be found in Émile Durkheim's (1982 [1894]) work, where collective consciousness and social fact override individuals. From this perspective, Egyptian women oblige because their duties are God-given and therefore unquestionable. Less extreme is an alethic, or truth-oriented, modality. In this perspective, al-Ghazali must oblige because she has no better alternatives. What is true in her current circumstances (or world) is also true in all other imaginable worlds. "She must obey" becomes an analytic proposition. Habit-based models of society take the alethic perspective and elevate habit to necessary truth. The third modality is epistemic and reflects the nature and source of knowledge (Lyons 1977:793). If someone who is acquainted with Egyptian society hears that Zaynab al-Ghazali is married, he or she applies knowledge of the traditional role of woman to this specific case and infers that Zaynab must obey her husband. However, this is no longer an analytic but a synthetic proposition. Epistemic logic arrives at the truthfulness of propositions by considering the conditions or possible worlds under which they are true. Zaynab al-Ghazali takes an epistemic position when she argues that she does not have to obey her husband because of her conflicting duty to God. Like sentences, structures are open to interpretation. "You must obey your husband" can be understood as an order, as resignation, or as advice. Deontic, alethic, and epistemic modalities describe the different ways in which individuals make sense of and adopt structures.

Innovation rests on the epistemic modality. Alfred Gell (1992:247) describes the implied mindset of individual innovators as "here we are obliged to think of possibilities as genuinely existing at certain times, in relation to certain possible worlds (worlds which we believe to be possible, anyway, even if they are not so in reality) but as not existing in relation to other possible worlds, at other times, in other circumstances (world in which that particular possibility has been foreclosed on, and has lost the feasibility it once may have possessed)." The epistemic modality results in a cognitive map of networked worlds (Figure 4.2). Each individual occupies the origin world, corresponding to what he or she perceives as the actual world in the present (Time 0). The origin world coexists with alternative worlds with various degrees of similarity. For example, Zaynab al-Ghazali might compare Egypt to contemporary western societies, where women have very different rights and duties. These coexisting worlds are inaccessible to each other. What is possible in one world might also be possible in a second but not in a third world. A similar plurality of possible worlds exists for the past and future. People can deliberate on what happened and how it might

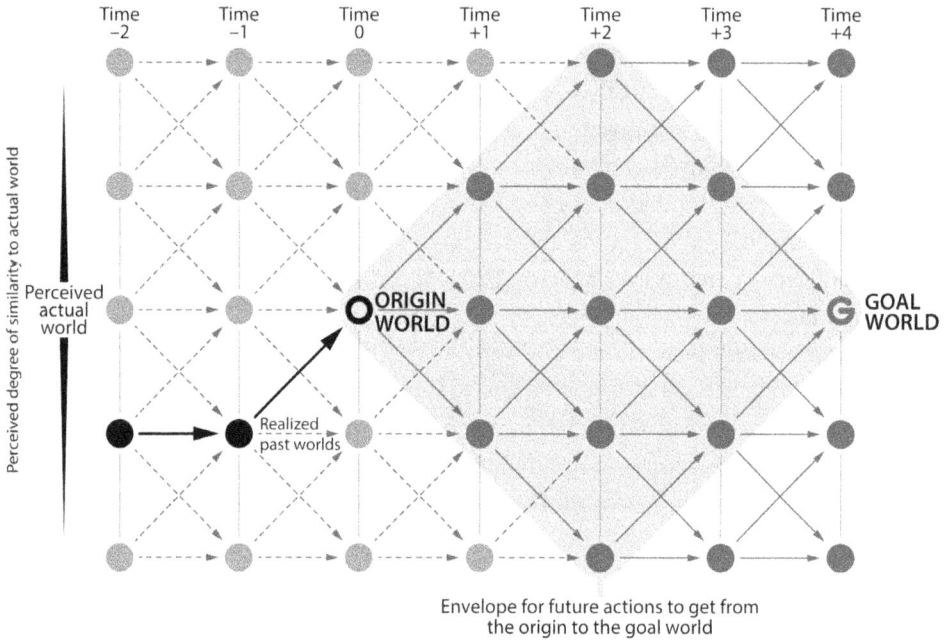

Figure 4.2. Cognitive map of individuals who plan the necessary actions to get from the present origin world to a future goal world. (Based in part on Gell 1992:257 Figure 25.3.)

have happened differently while imagining how things will or should look. In their mind, people create a patchwork of possible worlds in the past, present, and future. The development of women's rights during the twentieth century exemplifies how worlds that are impossible in the present may become possible in the future. Formally stated, relations between possible worlds are reflexive, transitive, and asymmetric. The result is a labyrinth of possible worlds connected by forking paths.

The Garden of Forking Paths manifests in culturally unique forms. In many traditional societies, dreams allow the articulation of alternative and novel forms of social interaction (Lohmann 2003:5). They serve as a source of information about external realities (Curley 1992; Shaw 1992; Tonkinson 2003). People dream to think about and even solve personal and social problems (Adler 1931:99; Bulkeley 1996; L. Graham 1995). "In dreaming, we are discovering the future—perhaps not the literal future, but ways we can move into it, ways it invites us forward—articulated in symbolic form" (Mageo 2003:35). For modern Tzotzil Maya, dreams form an alternative interpersonal sphere (Groark 2013). In it, life forces interact in ways that differ from the norms of physical interactions. Similar to navigating the

Garden of Forking Paths, Tzotzil Maya weave physical and dream realms of experience into a single experiential braid (Groark 2013:287).

Through logic individuals create relationships between past, present, and future. This implies that they are goal-oriented. From the here and now, they envision a goal world and plan the actions that are needed to get them there (Figure 4.2). Actions are directed to a goal (or *telos*), as Husserl (1987:275; 1995:117) observes, otherwise "I would be dead and not alive." Alfred Gell (1992:255) compares an individual's cognitive map to a road map: an interstate takes people straight to a goal, but if traffic jams are frequent, a side road might be preferable. Projecting future actions to reach the goal involves drawing out specific paths and linearizing the cognitive map, following a mental journey along different roads. However, not all of the roads are equally likely. Gell (1992:256) introduces the concept of modal distance between possible worlds to express that "the preferred route between O and G will be the one that has the least opportunity costs, while at the same time conforming to our estimates of the intrinsic likelihood of events, only a few of which are under our direct control." The optimal path minimizes opportunity costs, that is, the costs of not realizing alternative paths.

In the labyrinth of possible worlds, opportunity costs extend not only to feasible but also to imagined alternative worlds. We have a variety of options to commute to work. They range from the actual—walking, driving a car, or taking a bus—to the feasible—such as riding in a helicopter—and the impossible, like using a transporter à la *Star Trek*. The terms "actual," "feasible," and "impossible" reflect our past experience and consequent ability to calculate the costs of each alternative. Planning ahead introduces uncertainty however, not only because we have to extrapolate costs but also because we can envision innovations that could make the impossible possible. For example, Segways speed up pedestrians and bullet trains replace cars. Inherent additional benefits—such as mobility or time to read—minimize the modal distance and warrant adopting the invention.

## White Canoe to the Otherworld

Logic guides the making of traditional or innovative decisions. When we consider the costs and benefits of potential actions, we employ a practical logic that is based on rational and supposedly universal principles. At the same time, specific historical and cultural contexts shape the ways in which we perceive and evaluate our actions. Fischer (1999:474) defines cultural logic as "generative principles expressed through cognitive schemas that promote intersubjective continuity and are conditioned by social, political, and economic contingencies" (see also Hutson and Stanton 2007; Sahlins 1999; Stanton 2004). Cultural logic informs us about socially worthwhile goals of our actions. It contrasts with the assumption of a universal and time-transcending Popper-like logic (see Bloor 1991:55–83). In Classic Maya culture, sacrificing one's blood was deemed worthwhile (despite the self-inflicted pain) because it enabled communication with gods and ancestors in the otherworld. The distinction between practical and cultural logic is often lost in innovation research. Some scholars assume that inventions exemplify the rational *homo economicus* and correspondingly dismiss culture-specific ways as maladaptive (for example, Boyd and Richerson 2006:468).

Excavations at Comalcalco produced a cache of carved and inscribed bones and stingray spines. The glyphic texts juggle medium and message. On Stingray Spine 11, the inscription identifies the spine as *saak jukuub,* or "white canoe" (Zender 2004:256–257; for an alternative reading of T58 as *sǝk* see Bricker and Orie 2014:202). Then it links the carving of the stingray spine—the tool for blood sacrifice—to the impersonation of Saak Chin, an ancestor or deity. For ancient and modern Maya, canoes are containers for objects, people, and supernatural beings (Guernsey 2016:349; Stone 1995:35). Modern Ch'orti' Maya keep large bowls below their altars. They call these "canoes" and identify them as the center of the otherworld (Girard 1962:110, 154). Lacandon Maya celebrate balché rituals in their ritual hut (god house). "Set on the east side of the god house is the *balché chem,* a special dugout canoe in which balché is brewed" (McGee 1990:55; see also Davis 1978:84–112). Gods live in the *balché chem.* "It is covered with thatch when not in use (in essence, given a roof similar to that of the god house) and decorated with the same red circular designs as painted on the beams in the god house" (McGee 1990:55). The white canoe is the vehicle to the underworld.

Like the white canoe, the carved stingray spine simultaneously references material reality and sacred ideal. The sacred ideal is not self-evident. Every manifestation includes not only diverse but also opposite characteristics (Hegel 1986:282; 1991:217; see also Heidegger's [2006:142–148] concept of *Mannigfaltigkeit*). Whether something is possible or impossible depends on its actualization and the proper unfolding of its moments (Hegel 1991:217). Artists struggle to reveal the hidden ideal. In "On No Work of Words," Dylan Thomas laments writer's block: "The lovely gift of the gab bangs back on a blind shaft." For the ancient Maya, the artist revealed a preordained potential. Knappers produced eccentrics from obsidian. The shape of a flake corresponded to a specific god or goddess. For example, sun and moon deities were painted or incised on round flakes. Hruby (2007:80) suggests that these supernatural beings were inherent to the obsidian itself. Maya knappers had to follow the proper procedures—prayers, fasting, incensing, and so on—to re-create the mythological charter.

Achieving the ideal characterizes the agency of artists and craftspeople. It also becomes the essence of their identity. "All goals must connect in the unity of the *telos*" (Husserl 1995:117). Goal-oriented behavior manifests in a continual formulation of goals and the orientation of these goals toward a higher ideal. "The infinite chain of goals, purposes, and tasks cannot . . . be disconnected, otherwise the I would not be an I" (Husserl 1987:275; 1995:117). For Husserl, teleology "can only be the highest moral end" (Husserl 1995:117) and is an ongoing struggle for truth and authenticity (for example, Husserl 1970: 1:285–286; 1975–1984:19:50). In this respect I differ because I emphasize culture-specific goals.

In the sixteenth century, Yucatec Maya artisans who planned to carve new wooden god statues began by fasting (Tozzer 1941:160). During this fast, workmen went into the forest, cut a cedar (*k'uh che,'* "god tree," in Yucatec Maya), and brought it back. The artisans then built a straw hut where they isolated themselves from everybody, even their wives. They "began their work on the [god statues], often cutting their ears, and anointing those idols with their blood and burning their incense, and thus they continued until the work was ended" (Tozzer 1941:160). The blood sacrifices and fasting of colonial Maya artisans are at odds with the western principle of efficiency (Smith 1776:5). These seemingly unnecessary steps characterize ritualized production (Childs 1998:134; Hruby 2007:70). Three aspects stand out. First, a culture-specific logic explains production steps and purpose. For the colonial Yucatec Maya, the portrayed god inhabits the finished statue carved from wood; smearing blood on it animates the wooden block. Second, the production logic dictates specific settings and behaviors, such as the sacrifices and incense-burning of the woodcarvers. Third, the final product, in this case a god statue, materializes the logic (compare ritual craft specialization in Spielmann 1998:153–154; 2002). To understand ancient Maya production requires recognizing logic, practices, and products.

The production procedures of colonial Maya artisans reflect a distinct logic in which creation is vested in the supernatural and everything is or can be animated (Chapter 2). Dismissing the ritual steps as superfluous

Figure 4.3. The ancestral couple emerges from a cave and is greeted by elderly gods. (Drawing based on photo in Coe 1978:109–110.)

misses how myths describe the peculiar logic of western and non-western production (Hruby 2007; Reents-Budet 1998). In western societies, Thomas Edison and Steve Jobs command attention but the context in which they were working is ignored. For example, we credit Edison with the invention of the lightbulb in 1878; yet historians know of almost two dozen precursors (Friedel and Israel 1986). Edison created not the first but a technologically superior lightbulb. Western inventors are mythologized as maverick geniuses who transform industries single-handedly (Schiffer 2011:11, 16–17). In contrast, the ancient Maya situated innovation in the interaction between humans and gods. A painted vessel shows how the first human couple emerged on earth (Figure 4.3). Elderly gods greet them with the gifts of civilized life (Houston quoted in Inomata 2001b:437). The god offers a shell inkwell, the implement of writing, to the man, while the goddess bears an incense burner, the source of warmth and a tool for divination and healing. Instead of tracing these ingredients of civilized life to human insight, the Classic Maya saw them as gifts from gods. Alternatively, Itzamnaaj teaches human scribes how to calculate numbers and write glyphs (Figure 3.2). I discussed in Chapter 3 how Itzamnaaj and his court served as role models for human society. These mythological charters structured not only production but also society. Maya and western rationales delineate possible worlds and the ideal course of action in the Garden of Forking Paths (Figure 4.2).

Inventions emerge from individual creativity while satisfying culture-specific demands of space-time and logic. They attempt to connect individuals and society, personal visions and shared structures. What starts as the unique experience of an inventive individual (indexical context) becomes non-indexical and no longer tied to a unique here and now but instead accepted by many members of society. This process is automatic in daily life when individuals consider their circumstances and social norms to make decisions. On the other hand, inventions allow a tracing of the transition from indexical to non-indexical. Inventions change as one individual's dream becomes realized and widely adopted to fit structural constraints.

## Sticky Structures

So far I have discussed how creative individuals identify and take advantage of overlapping and competing structures. Now I flip the coin and show that these structures are not fixed but sticky. When Zaynab al-Ghazali justified her political activism as a call to God (da'wa), she took advantage of new scholarly interpretations of this concept. In the Qur'an, God urges prophets and humans to follow their calling, or da'wa, and to believe in Islam as the true religion (Mahmood 2005:57). Classic Islam paid little attention to da'wa and often used it interchangeably with terms for law and religion. Da'wa was interpreted as a vocation. Through a close study of the Qur'an, individuals became preachers or mosque teachers (Mahmood 2005:60). Da'wa was a collective duty that one member—preferably a scholar or a leader—fulfilled in the name of the community. This understanding of da'wa changed during the early twentieth century. Scholar Rashid Rida (1865–1935) wrote a commentary on the Qur'an in which he promoted a new way to undertake da'wa (Mahmood 2005:61–62). Rida argued that people would accept Islam through their profound understanding of history, sociology, politics, and other fields of knowledge. By linking *da'wa* to modern science, education, and organizational frameworks, Rida paved the way for a political interpretation and for proselytizing. Rida redefined *da'wa* as the duty of every individual, man or woman. His interpretation moved *da'wa* from a communal and religious concept to an individualized and political one.

Since the late 1920s, the Muslim Brotherhood has translated Rida's scholarship into public and political activism (Mahmood 2005:62–64). Hasan al-Banna, the Brotherhood's founder, promoted *da'wa* as a way to educate and reform all Egyptian Muslims. Tellingly, he understood *da'wa* in the sense of propaganda. Muslim Brothers used public spaces and mass media to promote *da'wa*. They transformed mosques from places of worship into universities where they offered education to the masses. Through these initiatives, women gained access to education and politics. Their literacy, social mobility, and public roles increased throughout the twentieth century (Mahmood 2005:64–70).

The *da'wa* is a structure in contemporary Egypt and other Muslim countries. Nonetheless, the call to God has been understood in different ways over time. In Egypt, Rashid Rida initiated a shift from communal to individual duty in his Qur'an commentary. Rida's scholarly work exemplifies a metadiscourse about structures and habits. In Chapter 2, I discussed Husserl's model of cognition in which past experiences are continuously modified in the present. This means that experiences are not simply "deposited in each organism in the form of schemes of perception, thought and action" (Bourdieu 1990:54). Distilling schemata from experiences is a cognitive act that makes some individuals aware of structures. Derrida conceptualizes *différance* as an open-ended process whose categories are in flux. Instead of "a present past that tends to perpetuate itself into the future" (Bourdieu 1990:54), I argue for an incomplete or contextualized doing.

Embedding social structures in individuals raises the question of power. Bourdieu (1990:291 n. 3) assumes that collective institutions use hegemonic domination and social sanctions to impose structures on individuals. For him, power relations are hierarchical and non-negotiable. The Muslim Brotherhood undercuts this top-down perspective. When Egypt was a British protectorate in 1928, six laborers who worked for the British Army approached Hasan al-Banna and, after thanking him for his teaching, complained that Arabs and Muslims "are not more than mere hirelings belonging to the foreigners" (Mitchell 1969:8). They pleaded with him to found the Muslim Brotherhood because "we are unable to perceive the

road to action as you perceive it, or to know the path to the service to the
fatherland [*watan*], the religion, and the nation [*'umma*] as you know it"
(Mitchell 1969:8). In subsequent decades, millions joined the Brotherhood.
The movement gained power in part by opposing the official government.
Its interpretation of *da'wa* coexisted with other interpretations in this factionalized environment and became dominant only with the Brotherhood's
social and political rise.

The case of Zaynab al-Ghazali demonstrates the complex power relations
in society. In the 1950s and 1960s, when most top leaders were in prison, she
became a leader in the Muslim Brotherhood (Mahmood 2005:181 n. 25); yet
she continued to live her life in ways that contradicted not only the official
policies of the Muslim Brotherhood but also her own public proclamations
(Ahmed 1992:199–200). Her life choices polarized the Egyptian public, yet
al-Ghazali never buckled under political or social pressure. She had the
power to lead her life her way. Structures can change because power is not
completely institutionalized, abstract, or anonymous. Individuals like Zaynab al-Ghazali occupy a nexus of power where they resist hegemony and
initiate change by serving as role models.

Applying their meta-awareness, individuals like Zaynab al-Ghazali
question what counts as normal. As a doxic experience, people perceive
the established order "not as arbitrary, i.e., as one possible order among
others, but as a self-evident and natural order which goes without saying
and therefore goes unquestioned" (Bourdieu 1977:166). Bourdieu (1990:54)
argues that structures are inculcated to such a degree that individuals exclude improbable practices as unthinkable. People submit themselves automatically to order and make a virtue of necessity by refusing what is already
denied them or by willing the inevitable. Norms force them to maintain
normality.

This perspective fails to explain Zaynab al-Ghazali's conscious rebellion
against prevailing norms. Her outsider mentality enabled her to unmask
norms and normality. Her leading role in the Muslim Brotherhood during
the 1950s and 1960s cut both ways. It shielded her from pressure within the
institution while providing her with a protective niche within society at
large. After World War II, the Egyptian state prosecuted the Muslim Brotherhood and jailed its leaders. Isolated from Egyptian society, the Brotherhood challenged the general understanding of what was normal. It formed
what Alissa Quart (2013) has called a counterpublic, a forum that hatches
alternative ideas.

Structures are sticky in the sense that they enable duality by serving as a model both of and for reality (Giddens 1984). At the same time, sticky structures are not permanent. Meta-awareness reveals how every established order naturalizes its own arbitrariness. Zaynab al-Ghazali stood at the public intersection of sweeping changes in twentieth-century Egypt. Sticky structures provide strategically placed individuals like her with opportunities to influence others.

## Standing Apart

Inventions become successful if they are widely adopted. To achieve success, their creators require extensive social networks and political influence. In the twentieth century, Zaynab al-Ghazali became a leader in Egypt's Muslim Brotherhood and an uncomfortable role model for other women while being shielded from social pressures. Comparable qualities distinguish ancient Maya artists. Similar to the byline *Goya fecit,* or "Goya made this," on western art, prominent Maya artists identified their works of art as *u tz'iib,* "his painting," or *y-u . . . l,* "his carving," followed by the artist's name and titles (Stuart 1989:156–158). Two stone carvers left their signatures on a monument from the kingdom of Pomoy (Figure 3.3). One of them apprenticed with a master craftsman who was not only *aj yul,* or "polisher," but also *aj k'uhuun,* "keeper or obeyer," and *itz'aat,* "sage." The latter titles suggest ritual roles, but in at least one case at Copan, the *aj k'uhuun* oversaw the production of featherwork, weaving, and ornaments (Jackson and Stuart 2003:224–225; Widmer 2009). At the Maya site of Xcalumkin, a house owner's name ends with *aj k'iin,* "priest," and *aj tz'iib,* "scribe" (Figure 4.4a). Another eighth-century resident of Xcalumkin identifies himself as *itz'aat* and *aj u[-?-]ul,* "carver" (Figure 4.4b; for more examples from this site see Grube 1994:317, 322).

Ancient Maya artists occupied socially, economically, and politically influential roles. This fact is especially evident for the *aj k'iinob,* or "priests," because they survived into colonial times and left ample testimony (Chuchiak 2001). These native priests dedicated themselves to the sciences by writing books, and teaching and examining children of priests and nobles. "The sciences which they taught were the computation of the years, months and days, the festivals and ceremonies, the administration of the sacraments, the fateful days and seasons, their methods of divination and their prophecies, events and the cures for diseases, and their antiquities and how to read and write with the letters and characters, with which they wrote, and drawings which illustrate the meaning of the writings" (Tozzer 1941:27–28).

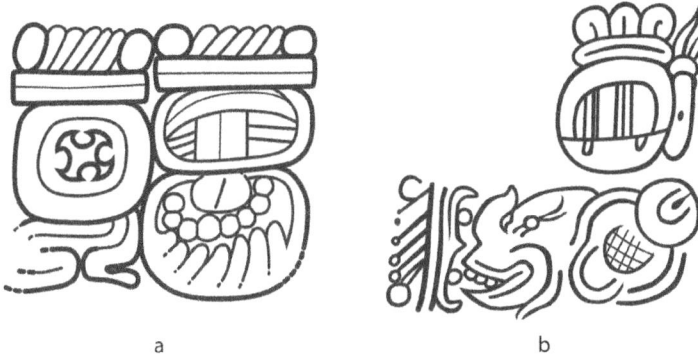

Figure 4.4. Titles of Classic Maya artisans at Xcalumkin: *a. aj k'iin,* "priest," and *aj tz'iib,* "scribe," on Xcalumkin Panel 4 (Glyph A1); *b. itz'aat,* "sage," and *aj u[-?-]ul,* "carver," on an incised vessel from the Xcalumkin area. (K8017, glyphs Q5a–Q6; drawings after, respectively, Graham and Von Euw 1992:182; Kerr 2000:1013.)

Their holistic knowledge included astronomy, astrology, mathematics, theology, medicine, and history. The *aj k'iinob* transcend western definitions of priests. Beyond their ritual roles, they were teachers and scientists.

Maya artists also distinguished themselves bodily. When the Pomoy Queen Yook Ahiin desired a new monument celebrating her likeness, she called upon two stone carvers (Figure 3.3). Ahkal, one of them, stood out because he identified himself as a dwarf (Glyph F4 in Figure 3.3). His queen presumably perceived him to have mystical powers (Houston 1992; Prager 2000a, 2000b). As conduits to the otherworld, dwarves assisted in the Maya ballgame and held the obsidian mirrors used in divination. Being physically different meant being exceptional for Ahkal and other Maya dwarves. Their bodies were symbols of unique, potent, and intangible qualities but also separated them from normal humans and regular norms (Helms 1993:56).

The physical separation of artists from the rest of society is also discernible in their workshops. Several craftspeople lived and worked in Copan's Group 9N-8, most notably in Patios B and H (Figures 1.7 and 5.1; Hendon, Fash, and Palma 1990:202, 239; Widmer 2009). Two workshops operated in Patio H's Structure 110B, where artifacts left behind in their place of use provide direct evidence for craft production (Figure 4.5). The building has four rooms, only two of which are directly accessible from the outside. One entrance leads into Room 4 on whose bench craftspeople produced shell ornaments, sharpened bone or wood artifacts, and cut hide (Widmer 2009:198). The second entrance opens into Room 1 where the bench and

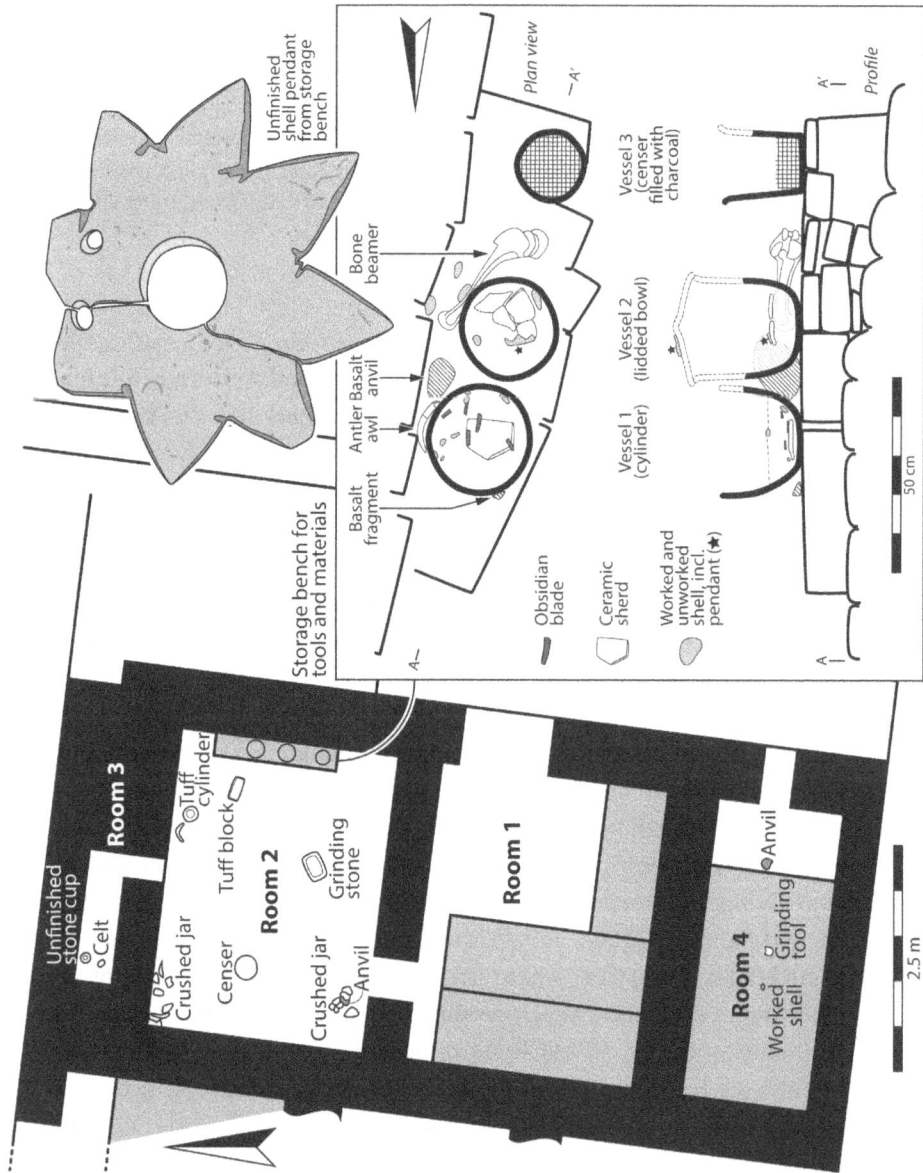

Figure 4.5. Workshop in Structure 110B, Patio H, of Copan's Group 9N-8; structure map on the left shows in situ artifacts. Contents of Room 2's storage bench are detailed in the lower right. The upper right shows the unfinished shell pendant from Room 2. (Drawings based on Widmer 2009:179, 181–182, 183–185; map from Figure 5.1.)

the absence of artifacts suggest a domestic use. A doorway links this room to Room 2, off which is Room 3, a closet-like space. Incense burners—one in the center and the other on a small bench—provided illumination for the artisans who cut shell with obsidian blades on basalt anvils. Alongside their tools on the bench, they stored unworked shell from freshwater and marine sources in two vessels. Their products included a shell bead and an unfinished star-shaped shell pendant. An unfinished stone cup and a celt in Room 3 point to stone-working. In addition to working shell, artisans carved stone cups, elaborated stone ornaments, ground pigment, and worked leather or wood (Widmer 2009:198).

Instead of focusing on a single product (and maximizing its production), the Copan artisans practiced multiple crafts in the same workshop. This type of situated learning erases boundaries that result from compartmentalizing knowledge, and facilitates the exchange of ideas (see Chapter 3). Widmer (2009:190–191) links the star-shaped shell pendant to Pawahtun and the Monkey Scribes, gods of writing and art, who are portrayed in Maya art wearing shell ornaments or holding shells as inkwells (inset in Figure 5.1; Schele and Miller 1986:54; Taube 1992:99). The pendant exemplifies that artisanal knowledge extended to the ideological underpinnings of Maya culture.

Ancient Maya artists set themselves apart not only through their esoteric knowledge but also literally. Based on the microdebitage they left behind, artisans practiced their craft inside Structure 110B (Widmer 2009:189). Those in Rooms 2 and 3 could not even be seen from outside. Their seclusion recalls the colonial Yucatec Maya woodcarvers who retreated into huts to make new god idols (Tozzer 1941:160). The workshops in Structure 110B differ in this regard from regular residential groups. Among the latter, rooms were used primarily for storing things, while activities took place outside in plazas, open platforms, or verandas (Johnston and Gonlin 1998:159). Residents of these groups were observable by others and thus integrated with the flow of social information. In contrast, artists shut themselves off. While they emphasized their special status in this way, they also ran the risk of being perceived as socially dangerous. For the modern Maya of Zinacantán, "staying indoors, or, even more unheard of, closing the house door is a gross and open admission of being up to no good" (Haviland and Haviland 1983:347).

## Structures and Inventions

Innovation transforms the unique into the common. The modern western world makes this process appear straightforward because its industrial processes simplify the mass production of inventions while most people confine themselves to consuming instead of tinkering. This top-down approach obscures the social dialogue inherent in innovation. A novel product has to transcend its inventor and speak to a wider audience to become adoptable. Its inventor faces the challenge of anticipating and materially expressing what groups of individuals unknowingly want and need. Inventions resonate with and correspondingly reveal structures. From the perspective of the Garden of Forking Paths, innovation requires reconstructing the possible worlds that are accessible to individuals in a given cultural context. Structural demands force specific decisions, while inventions enable new paths.

I illustrate my approach to innovation using petrified wood, a very rare material in Classic Maya culture. Two fragments were found in a Classic crypt at Tikal and a third in Copan Group 9M-27 (Moholy-Nagy 2003:56, 120f Figure B; Willey et al. 1994:261; cat. no. 1-156). The specimen from Copan is about finger-sized. These pieces of petrified wood are unsettling because it is unclear what they were used for. Wood becomes petrified when sediments or volcanic ash bury it and prevent its aerobic decomposition (Leo and Barghoorn 1976:5–9). Mineral-rich water permeates the wood and either fills open spaces in its cells or replaces cell walls with minerals. Silica is the most common mineral, especially in volcanic ash (Murata 1940). Petrified wood in ancient Maya contexts comes most likely from the volcanic highlands of Guatemala. Petrified wood deposits have been observed on the flanks of the Chingo and Ipala volcanoes (Gustavo Orellana, personal communication). A petrified wood trunk that is now exhibited in the central park of Jalapa comes from nearby the Jumay volcano.

During my excavations at Aguateca's Barranca Escondida, I discovered seventy-four fragments weighing approximately one kilogram in total (Figure 4.6; Inomata and Eberl 2014:115–117). The Barranca Escondida, "hidden chasm," is an isolated area south of Aguateca's Main Plaza where steep terrain makes access difficult and a rock conceals the entrance (Figure 4.7; Inomata and Eberl 2010). Several stelae and altars overlook a small plaza between the chasm and a rock outcrop. My excavations revealed an unusual artifact assemblage that included greenstone, petrified wood, and cave stones. These finds point to a public and likely ritually used space.

Figure 4.6. Petrified wood from the Barranca Escondida at Aguateca (scales in centimeters): *a.* Refitted stick (six pieces from 24A-2-2-1, 24A-4-1-1, and 24B-5-2-1); *b.* rounded edge (from 24A-10-2-1).

Monuments and artifacts date the Barranca Escondida to the seventh and eighth centuries A.D., and its main period of use likely predates that of the Main Plaza, the only other public space at Aguateca.

The seventy-four petrified wood fragments occur mostly on the rock outcrop. Since they consist mostly of silica and quartz, they are very hard (6.5–7 on Mohs hardness scale) and show no erosion. Laboratory analysis revealed use-wear, however; polishing or drilling likely caused the abrasions, while blackened and discolored spots point to selective exposure to fire. The tips of eight fragments are rounded and smoothed. Three of these fragments constituted a tip that broke apart when vertical pressure was exerted on it.

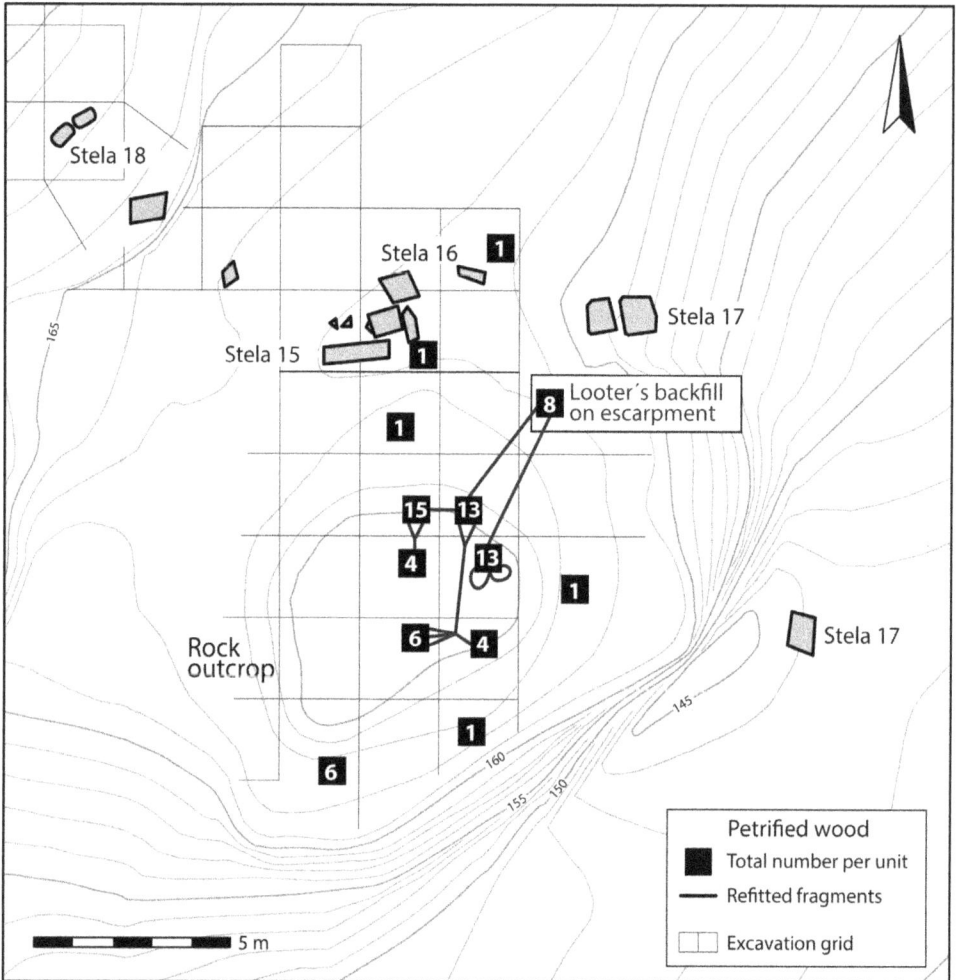

Figure 4.7. Map of Aguateca's Barranca Escondida, showing locations of the refitted petrified wood fragments.

Several of the petrified wood splinters fit to others. In addition to the three tip fragments, I matched fifteen more, or about one-quarter of all specimens. The refitted fragments come from six sticks that can be comfortably held in a hand (Figure 4.6). In most cases, the pieces were not found close to each other. In the case of the largest stick, two fragments (including the tip) came from the northern edge, three from the center, and the end fragment from the southeastern edge of the rock outcrop. Other refitting fragments distribute similarly widely over dozens of square meters (Figure 4.7). Cave stones show a similar pattern, with refits appearing randomly on the entire rock outcrop. The petrified wood sticks and cave stones were likely intentionally smashed and scattered as part of a termination ritual. Comparable cases have been observed elsewhere in the Maya Lowlands (for example, Ambrosino 2003:262–269; Andrews and Fash 1992; Freidel 1986; Inomata and Ponciano 2010:52; Inomata et al. 2001:296–297; Pendergast 1979–1990; Robertson 1983; Stanton et al. 2008; Suhler and Freidel 2003; Wagner 2006; Walker 1998). Termination rituals are intended "to ritually 'kill' an object, structure, person, or place" (Stanton et al. 2008:235). They often involve the dismantling of buildings and the rapid deposition of a dense artifact assemblage containing rare artifacts as well as broken and scattered pottery. Artifacts tend to be burned and sealed under white marl (237–238). Fire was a crucial component of termination rituals. In comparable ethnohistorical and modern ceremonies, a burning censer is placed in the entrance to a new building and the smoke that enters signals its transformation into a home (Stuart 1998:389–393).

The Barranca Escondida investigations allowed me to reconstruct how the ancient Aguatecans used petrified wood. They likely brought sticks of it to the rock outcrop. Abraded tips suggest that people used these sticks for polishing or drilling. Burn marks show that they were exposed to fire but were not burned entirely, a common feature in termination rituals. The petrified wood sticks are akin to fire drills. The ancient Maya drilled fire by twirling a wooden spindle between their hands (Figure 4.8). Alternatively, they spun the spindle with a bow while pressing it against a fireboard with a socket (for example, Eberl 2014a:311).

Fire-drilling bridges practical necessities and ritual obligations among the Classic Maya. A lintel from the Usumacinta region portrays a Yaxchilan king drilling fire on the maw into the otherworld. The accompanying text identifies the otherworld as Matwiil, a subterranean and aquatic place where gods are born (Stuart and Houston 1994:77; Tokovinine 2013:72–73). Nobles kindled and maintained sacred fires to various deities as part of their observance of time (Grube 2000). Drilling also relates to divination. A Dresden Codex almanac shows four deities drilling into the glyph *chi* or *chich* (Figure 4.8). The accompanying text reads *u jooch'-[ow] u chich,* or "he drills/reveals the discourse of" the four gods.[2]

The petrified wood sticks from the Barranca Escondida are and at the same time are not wooden fire drills. They are heavier and thicker than their wooden counterparts. It is unclear whether they could have been rotated fast enough to kindle a fire. Their tree rings are clearly visible and in most fragments curve tightly. The preserved cambium of some fragments

Figure 4.8. Image of drilling from the Dresden Codex. (Page 6b; omitted are Tzolk'iin coefficient and distance number; drawing based on facsimile in Förstemann 1880.)

suggests that they came from tree branches rather than the trunk or roots. The petrified wood sticks combine the characteristics of wood and stone. They are intermaterial through referencing two materials that contrast in appearance, pliability, and touch. The abraded tips demonstrate that the petrified wood sticks embody actual practices, while leaving the question open whether they were real or symbolic fire drills. Classic Maya artists excelled in intermaterial plays by, for example, making ceramic vessels that look like woven baskets (Houston 2014). The petrified wood from the Barranca Escondida recalls the use of fossilized materials at Palenque and other Maya sites (for example, Cuevas García 2007, 2008; Joyce 1992; Riquelme et al. 2012:632–634; Ruz Lhuillier 1959:70). These fossilized examples resemble but are materially different from their modern equivalents. Their liminal status may explain why they were found in caches.

The ancient inhabitants of Aguateca employed petrified wood in a novel yet recognizable way, when seen in the context of Classic Maya culture. Likely due to its ritual significance, people did not simply abandon the Barranca Escondida but decided on a termination ritual. This required burning, breaking, spreading, and burying artifacts, as well as dismantling associated buildings (Stanton et al. 2008:237–238). These activities took place in a sequence that linked the origin world through several steps to the end goal (Figure 4.2). Variations and alternatives are available for each step and reflect different structural demands. For example, only some termination ritual deposits include human bone fragments, possibly to reflect specifically the desecratory nature of this event (Lamoureux-St-Hilaire et al. 2015:553). Earlier I discussed how the Classic Maya employed fire not simply to annihilate existing matter but to transform it into something new. The petrified wood sticks/fire drills are novel in the context of termination rituals, but they resonate with structures elsewhere in Classic Maya society.

Inventions are approximations and not endpoints. Waves of invention and adoption respond to social issues that are not static but interfere with and build on each other. As material expressions, inventions recursively affect social issues. The challenge is to identify the different versions and modifications that adjust inventions to shifting social desires and needs. Innovation is an open-ended process of becoming. Missteps and errors are as informative as successes for reconstructing why and how innovation works in a given context.

## Opening the Garden of Forking Paths

The ability to invent is sometimes perceived as uniquely modern. In *Das Kunstwerk im Zeitalter seiner technischen Reproduzierbarkeit* (The Artwork in the Age of Its Technological Reproducibility), Walter Benjamin (2006) bemoans how modern art has lost its authenticity. He defines authenticity as "the essence of all that is transmissible from its beginning, ranging from its substantive duration to its testimony to the history which it has experienced" (Benjamin 1968:221). In Benjamin's perspective, preindustrial artists are traditionalists who answer to context and history. By hitching authentic art to tradition, Benjamin implicitly dismisses innovation as a modern fad and reduces premodern art to its unique tie to the here and now.

I argue that innovation and tradition are not contradictory. The potter Àbátàn produced ceramics for the worship of the Yorùbá deity Eyinle while also serving as a senior member of Eyinle's cult (Thompson 1969). Her vessels embodied kingship and divinity, but Àbátàn did not feel restricted by expectations. To the contrary, she believed that art "must not only honor the expression of myth and moral truth; it must embody experiments and innovation, or else lose all aliveness and emotional flavor" (Thompson 1969:181). Her work is embedded in cultural traditions and at the same time autonomous. Tradition and innovation are for premodern artists not antithetical but dynamically unified (Thompson 1969:121; also see McAnany 2010:205). Doing enough is not enough, otherwise everything would stay the way it was (Grönemeyer 1998). The interplay of the limits and the possibilities of structures characterizes novel solutions. Zaynab al-Ghazali became aware of the structures that restrained her life choices and found a way to play off conflicting structures to her advantage. I model her mental map as the Garden of Forking Paths. Real and realizable worlds coexist with possible yet so-far imaginary worlds. Both alternate and find their expresssion in make-believe or fantasy play (Lancy 2015:178–180). While many people may dream about living in an alternative universe, it falls to the inventor to come up with a solution that enables a previously unrealized world. Yet an invention may never gain traction due to power imbalances and differential adoption. I mentioned that Zaynab al-Ghazali would very likely not have been able to divorce her husband if she had not been a Muslim leader. In Chapter 5, I discuss more fully how individuals wield power to shape innovation. A successful innovation bridges individual and society through the process of adoption. I say "bridge" instead of "join" because the individual and society are like the poles of a magnet: codependent yet separate. The Garden of Forking Paths expresses the possibilities for and likelihood of action. An invention enables new paths, and it becomes socially relevant if many adopt it.

People experience heterogeneous structures that overlap and even contradict each other. In their daily lives, they take these structures into account and, in most situations, follow them habitually. Nonetheless, structures are not fixed but sticky. In the 1960s, the Guatemalan weaver Juliana dreamed one night of oversized cloth designs (Blum Schevill 1997:138). On waking up, she started to enlarge the animals, flowers, and geometric motifs on her weavings. Other weavers noticed Juliana's work and soon not only followed suit but also came up with their own variations. Nonetheless, oversized motifs spread only to everyday clothing whereas the ceremonial style remained more traditional. Previously, one structure dictated the design of all clothes. Juliana and her fellow weavers explored the limits of this structure by separating daily clothing from Sunday dresses (for young Maya weavers as innovators see also Greenfield [2004] and, more generally, Lancy [2015:317–322]). In Chapter 6, I discuss adoption as a discursive process that defines and redefines evolving structures.

The Garden of Forking Paths is a cognitive model with quantifiable consequences. Inventions like Àbátàn's pottery and Juliana's weaving materialize possible worlds. The archaeological record preserves humankind's inventions across time and space. They often escape scholarly attention because they defy expectations and customs. Earlier I suggested that the petrified wood sticks from Aguateca may have served as symbolic or actual fire drills. This interpretation is preliminary due to the dearth of comparative cases. A similar argument can be made for ancient Maya metalworking. Metal objects appear in the Maya Lowlands for the first time around A.D. 500 (Pendergast 1970) and especially after A.D. 800 (Bray 1977). Most items were imported as finished products. The tantalizing find of a specialized hammer suggests, though, that the ancient Maya may have worked metal as well (Bruhns and Hammond 1982, 1983). Ancient creativity remains arcane as long as its unique material expressions remain overlooked.

# 5

## A Ruler Just Like Me

### Status, Power, and Innovation

Every K'atun, or roughly every twenty years, the Yucatec Maya head chief examined all chiefs under his authority to find out whether they were worthy leaders. This did not involve physical competition or documents. Instead, the head chief challenged the nobles with riddles and expected them to find the correct answers. For example, he might ask a chief, "Son, bring me a very beautiful woman with a very white countenance. I greatly desire her. I will cast down her skirt and her loose dress before me" (Roys 1967:97). The chief would respond, "Caybacac be, yume" (It is well, father). To pass the test, he had to find a turkey-hen, pluck her feathers, and roast her for eating. Such interrogation went on for several rounds. Known as the Language of Zuyua, it tested the cultural knowledge and poise of the candidates (Stross 1983). Those who failed were punished harshly: "They shall be hung by the neck; the tips of their tongues shall be cut off; their eyes shall be torn out" (Roys 1967:92). Those who passed received a mat and a throne, the symbols of authority. The head chief told them to rule their towns and made their wisdom widely known.

Riddles and puns forced contestants to interweave their cultural knowledge. When the head chief asked to see the brains of the sky, he expected to receive copal gum, presumably associated with brains for its grayish color, gummy consistency, and billowing smoke when burned (Roys 1967:90). Satisfactory answers link idea and matter. The Language of Zuyua exemplifies the play of symbols as basis for creativity (Chapter 2).

For the Yucatec Maya, knowledge separated true leaders from mere pretenders. Knowledge and creativity are unequally distributed resources that involve power. Following Max Weber (1991:180), powerful individuals and institutions realize their interests at the expense of others. Yucatec Maya yielded to their leaders only if they passed the periodic interrogation. Power extends beyond imposing one's will and encompasses "the capacity to constitute interests and determine their significance within the management of existing conditions" (Smith 2003:108). In the Language of Zuyua, the head chief would remind a contestant, "You are a ruler, too," and ask him for green prayer beads (Roys 1967:94). Nobles who brought him the expected beads, made of precious and rare jade, demonstrated both their cultural knowledge and how to express it properly. Like others in power, they formulated their interests in such a way that their actions aligned seamlessly with cultural conceptions and values. Instead of demonstrating their power, they allowed it to be revealed.

I relate the direct and indirect aspects of power to the Garden of Forking Paths. The agency to transform structures varies. Case studies have identified facilitating as well as impeding factors (for example, Aldenderfer 1993; Kohler et al. 2004; Schachner 2001; Wiessner 2002). In the following, I discuss how powerful individuals shape choice architecture, that is, the framework that guides decision-making (Thaler and Sunstein 2008). As choice architects they promote or inhibit innovation.

## Status and Innovative Spirit

Innovation takes place within socially differentiated settings. Gender, age, skills, and other factors influence the status of individuals and their ability and willingness to innovate. For example, when missionaries gifted steel axes to Australia's Yir-Yoront, they found eager adopters among the women. The stone axes with which older men had previously expressed their status lost appeal and the traditional social hierarchy disintegrated (Sharp 1952). Eighteenth-century philosopher David Hume was among the first to contemplate the social effects of inequality. He observed that "too great disproportion among the citizens weakens any state" and argued that "every person, if possible, ought to enjoy the fruits of his labour, in a full possession of all the necessaries, and many of the conveniences of life" (Hume 1987:265). "Where the riches are in few hands, these must enjoy all the power, and will readily conspire to lay the whole burthen on the poor, and oppress them still farther, to the discouragement of all industry" (265). Frank Cancian (1979) has proposed a model for the relationship between status and innovativeness. He assumes that people want at least to maintain their status and, if possible, climb the social ladder (Cancian 1979:11).

In innovation, inhibiting effects counteract facilitating ones (Cancian 1967). On the one hand, innovation is risky. As the case of the steel axes among the Yir-Yoront illustrates, inventions create uncertain social outcomes and people therefore shy away from developing or adopting them. Those on top have nowhere to go but down, and therefore they shun experimenting with innovation (Cancian 1979:15; Dittes and Kelley 1956). In his novel *Quesadillas*, Juan Pablo Villalobos fictionalizes this experience: "I had supposed that rich people's days were devoted to surprise, to experiencing continually the euphoria of discoveries, the frisson of first times, the optimism of new beginnings. I hadn't imagined the force of attraction imposed by the need to feel safe: a second law of gravity, the power of inertia calling its children to the warm bosom of boredom" (Villalobos 2013:51). On the other hand, people at the bottom see innovation as a means to advance their status. Yet, they lack wealth and gamble with their survival by innovating.

Cancian (1979) deals with perfectly divisible innovations, such as whether one does or does not have a tractor. If the tractor fails to perform adequately, penniless farmers who adopted that tractor face hunger and worse. Yet, innovations can often be integrated more subtly, as the marked contrast between traditional Hopi agriculture and western monocropping shows (Soleri and Cleveland 1993; for a comparable study from the Soconusco region see Gasco 2017). Instead of one highly profitable crop, Hopi farmers plant more than a dozen crops, and variants of the same crop, at one time. Most common are corn, lima beans, string beans, field beans, and squash (Soleri and Cleveland 1993:213). For example, the Hopi language differentiates between twelve major corn varieties, mostly by color (Table 5.1). Farmers plant between two and eleven corn varieties (on average 6.3 varieties) at the same time (Soleri and Cleveland 1993:214). The casual observer sees a chaotic agricultural field that seems neither economically nor rationally organized (Annis 1987:31–39 discusses comparable milpa agriculture among Highland Maya). Contrary to popular perception, even poor Hopi farmers will try any seed once (Whiting 1939:10). For them, each variety has the potential to succeed or fail and therefore represents an alternative world in the cognitive model I developed in the previous chapter. By planting different varieties at the same time, they minimize the risk that an individual variety will fail and maximize the potential for at least one variety to succeed. The Hopi example resonates with other studies, thereby challenging Cancian's argument that innovations are risky due to their newness (Morrison et al. 1976:918).

Table 5.1. Corn varieties grown by fifty Hopi farmers, with native names

| Variety | Pct. of Farmers Growing |
|---|---|
| Blue corn | 100 (grown by all) |
| "Standard" blue (*sakwaqaö*) | 82 |
| Hard blue (*huruskwapu*) | 10 |
| Gray blue (*maasiqaö*) | 24 |
| Pueblo blue[a] (*nenengqaö, Hopoqaö?*) | 4 |
| Blue/*kokoma* mixture | 12 |
| White corn (*qötsaqaö*) | 96 |
| Yellow corn (*takuri*) | 70 |
| Hopi sweet corn (*tawaktsi*) | 64 |
| Red corn (*palaqaö*) | 62 |
| Commercial sweet corn[a] (*pahaana tawaktsi*) | 52 |
| *Supai*/chinmark corn (*koninquaö*) | 44 |
| Greasy hair corn (*wiqtö*) | 36 |
| *Kokoma* corn | 24 |
| Speckled/owl corn (*avatsa*) | 12 |
| Pink corn (*palatspipi*) | 6 |
| Commercial popcorn[a] | 4 |
| Miscellaneous corn varieties | 12 |

*Source:* Based on Soleri and Cleveland (1993:214 Table 2).
*Note:* a. Non-Hopi variety

Traditional Hopi agriculture simplifies innovation because new plant varieties are easily planted alongside established varieties. If innovation is seen as part of active risk management, individual knowledge and skills are crucial. Wealth confers the advantage of cognitive freedom. Money buys education. Wealthier people tend to be better informed about the potential for and effectiveness of an invention (Cancian 1979:16). In Panama, low-income entrepreneurs have many creative business ideas, but they generally fail to generate revenue from them (Doering 2016). Poverty impedes them from waiting long enough for consumers to become familiar with their new products and services. It also limits their ability to develop and optimize their inventions.

Status influences the innovative spirit. Some scholars argue for a linear relationship: the wealthy adopt innovations quickly while the poor lag behind (Morrison et al. 1976; Rogers 1995). Cancian (1979), however, sees a S-shaped relationship. The inhibiting and facilitating effects play out differently in a society with high, middle, and low classes. While high-ranked people have few social incentives for innovation, their wealth allows them to innovate more than everybody else in society. Lower-class people, on the other hand, want to rise socially but they lack the necessary economic resources. The middle class combines social ambition with economic strength. In Cancian's model, the lower middle class gambles on innovation while the upper middle class is conservative because it lacks the abundant resources of the upper class and can gain little socially through innovation. Both models correlate status with innovativeness.

## Innovation Interfering with Structures

Models of innovation tend to classify people into distinct categories. Everett Rogers (1995) famously separates innovators from laggards with three adopter types in between. Instead of accepting his or comparable typologies as a starting point, I argue that they represent post hoc assessments that ignore the dynamics of the adoption process. Specifically, I discuss individuals as knowledgeable agents who make social assessments. In the French village of Pellaport, farmers rely on a tripartite scheme to assess each other's actions (Layton 1989:45). Those whose acts are inexplicable are called *fou*, "irrational"; accountable acts point to either deliberately antisocial, *"fier,"* or sociable, *"gentil"* personalities. Individuals may classify a specific person differently. For example, some see a farmer who frequently purchases expensive equipment as a fool, while others see him as someone who cares for his farm and deserves to be respected. The tripartite classification exemplifies the framing and classification inherent in schemas (see Chapter 1).

People monitor each other reflexively. They observe the behavior of others, reconstruct the underlying motivations, and adjust their own behavior accordingly. Of course, they cannot read each other's minds and therefore take behaviors as proxies; yet, behaviors are fallible proxies because humans are sarcastic and even liars. In social interaction, they face that "I know that you know that I know that you know . . . ," or what Aristotle identified as infinite regress in his *Metaphysics*. The truth of a proposition rests on a second proposition that in turn rests on a third, and so forth like Russian dolls. Innovation breaks this vicious cycle. Developing and adopting an invention involves choosing an alternative world and exhibiting it publicly through changes to material reality or behavior. Social interaction quickly identifies those who deviate from customary ways.

At Pellaport, each farmer's land was divided into strips that interlaced with the lands of neighbors; therefore, everybody could observe others and quickly learn of new agricultural techniques and equipment (Layton 1989). Quite predictably, innovators initially drew public scorn for deviating from custom. For example, when César Maitrugue upgraded to a more powerful tractor, everyone called him crazy because parcels in Pellaport were generally so small that nobody could envision a need for a large tractor (Layton 1989:46). César stood his ground and his tractor proved valuable, so valuable in fact that many of his critics bought more powerful tractors themselves. The peer effect—working in close proximity to each other and learning from word-of-mouth—propelled innovation. César became an opinion leader whom his neighbors watched closely and often, albeit hesitantly, imitated. Over time, César's status shifted from ridiculed to respected.

Individuals are aware of social and economic conditions. For example, Pellaport farmers complain that "there are poor farmers who have many better ideas than those who own all the equipment" (Layton 1989:44). Nonetheless, their awareness does not translate into a conflict between poor and rich farmers. Instead, they act within a normative environment that emphasizes equality. Many Pellaport farmers produce milk for the same dairy (Layton 1989:46). They are aware that everyone, poor or rich, has to get up early to milk cows. They are also members of a dairy cooperative and therefore bound to each other in order to sell their milk and to succeed economically. The Pellaport farmers share similar practices and form an economic community. Their egalitarian ideology differs from the tangled social and economic reality of their lives. The normative order suggests consensus but masks conflict and divergent interpretations. Modern peasants "do not simply react to the objective conditions per se but rather to the interpretation they place on those conditions as mediated by values embedded in concrete practices" (Scott 1985:305).

The tension between objective conditions and norms manifests in innovations. Depending on the model, those who have at least relatively greater means innovate, while others lag behind. These two groups form the opposite ends of Everett Rogers's (1995) typology of five adopter types, ranging from innovators to early adopters to early and late majority to laggards. The problem with these roles is that they have no intrinsic meaning and are "situation-specific and entirely contextual" (McGlade and McGlade 1989:287). This typology of adopters overlooks that people change their stance over time and often in response to the ways others assess them (Layton 1989:45). At Pellaport, Maurice Genre started out as an innovator after World War II, but twenty years later he had become a laggard (Layton 1989:49–50).

Instead of participating in the communal hire of a combine, Maurice harvested with a scythe. He justified his decision by pointing out that he did not have to wait for the machine to arrive but could harvest when the grain was ripe and dry. He also felt that his old-fashioned threshing machine did a better job than the combine. Yet, his self-defense only heightened his social isolation and he was commonly judged *fou,* or "crazy." The evaluation of César Maitrugue evolved in reverse. Most villagers resented him when he bought the village's first tractor in 1952; yet, they highly respected him a decade later. The public opinion in Pellaport was never homogeneous, though. For example, young farmers admired Nicholas Jouffroy for experimenting with rotary mowers while older villagers mocked him (Layton 1989:45).

Social structures are complex. They can overlap, crisscross, and even contradict each other, as my discussion of status and social norms shows. More importantly, structures are not simply objective conditions that influence innovation from the top down. Instead, innovation interferes with social structures. Modern peasants often hesitate to innovate, as Ruben Reina's (1963) experience in Chinautla exemplifies. Instead of being conservative by nature, peasants are often forced to behave this way. If demand for different products is weak or absent, innovation stalls, as case studies of Iranian weavers (Tehrani and Collard 2009:289) and prehistoric Huron potters (Smith 2005:71) show.

Dick Papousek (1981) studied pottery production in central Mexico. In the 1960s and '70s, Mazahua potters were in an uneasy relationship with mestizo middlemen. The latter controlled the pottery trade and not only bought the potters' wares but also lent them money for glaze and firewood. Whenever a potter produced more to pay off his debt, his middleman paid him less to keep him indebted (Papousek 1989:147). Due to their lack of power, potters preferred to produce little and resigned themselves to poverty. Since then, however, at least some of them have improved their lot considerably. They took advantage of the increasing demand for ceramic piñatas that Mexicans fill with candies, fruits, and other goodies and then smash at a party. Since a piñata bowl is fired only once and needs fewer finishing touches, potters saved fuel and time and paid off their debt (Papousek 1989:142). The social framework for individual action provided constraints (the mestizo middlemen) and opportunities (the piñata bowls). When the framework changed during the mid-twentieth century, innovative potters profited. Structures can inhibit innovation through conservative customs, values, and rules, or they can stimulate it by providing education and enabling competition. Powerful individuals influence how structures and innovation interact.

## Choice Architecture

Innovation is a novel choice among the possible worlds that an individual can choose. An invention opens a new path in the Garden of Forking Paths (Figure 4.2). As individuals select their course of action among these possible worlds, they recognize that not all the paths are equally feasible. In part, their considerations reflect what Richard Thaler and Cass Sunstein call choice architecture. Power enables individuals to organize the context in which others make their decisions (Thaler and Sunstein 2008:3). A building exemplifies this basic idea. Its design is never neutral; architects select which features to include and how to arrange them relative to each other. The final design greatly influences how the building will be used. These influences range from the mandatory—for example, where to enter or how to move around inside—to subtle details like lighting and seating arrangements. Choice architects shape the Garden of Forking Paths.

Six principles characterize choice architecture (Thaler and Sunstein 2008:81–100). First, choice architects understand the garden's layout and the path of least resistance that leads from the origin to the goal world. Second, they know that most people will follow the default yet some carve their own paths and introduce variation. Third, choice architects provide feedback, whether by outright force or subtle suggestion, to steer people to the preferred path. Fourth, they map possibilities and behavior in response to given feedback; that is, they consider why people choose one possible world over others. Fifth, their position of power allows choice architects to shape or even eliminate possible worlds. Sixth, they structure the incentives—for example, by promoting an invention—and facilitate choosing the possible worlds that they prefer.

These six principles describe how choice architects steer others. They outline the possible as well as preferred courses of action in a given cultural and historical context. For example, lack of money impedes substantial behavioral changes among the poor in modern societies (for example, Baird et al. 2016; Baird et al. 2015; Loibl et al. 2016). Thaler and Sunstein (2008:100) call the six principles "nudges" and envision them as positive forces. Their rose-colored view of power has to be critically examined, however. They disregard the threat or use of coercion. Evil nudging or phishing exposes less savory possibilities (Akerlof and Shiller 2015). Innovative behaviors have to be studied for their potential to upend not only the status quo but also the framework of social action. In addition, power is not abstract. Choice architects are not omnipotent puppeteers but have to legitimize their power as members of society.

### Empowering Maya Rulers and Commoners

Divine Maya kings and queens claimed absolute power, stressing their control over time and cosmos (Demarest 1989, 1992a, 1992b; Freidel 1981; Lucero 2003; A. G. Miller 1986; Rice 2004, 2007, 2008; Sharer and Golden 2004; Stuart 1996; 2005:186–189). Their power extended to innovation, as Daron Acemoglu and James Robinson (2012:143–149) believe. These authors distinguish between extractive and inclusive states (73–76). In extractive states, elites govern an obedient populace and use their pervasive powers to enrich themselves. In contrast, inclusive states have democratic institutions that create economic opportunity for everyone, foster innovation, and increase wealth sustainably. Acemoglu and Robinson (2012:149) classify Classic Maya kingdoms as extractive states whose rulers wrested as much wealth as possible from their subjects. Nobles glorified themselves in arts and architecture but failed to promote general technological progress. Inequality rose over the course of the Classic period and an increasing number of elites fought for the spoils. Ultimately, extraction became unstable and caused the Maya collapse.

By assigning absolute power to Maya rulers, Acemoglu and Robinson (2012) revert to a Lévi-Straussian model of agency. In *The Elementary Structures of Kinship*, Lévi-Strauss weds rule-based structures to individual choice. "A preferential system is prescriptive when envisaged at the model level; a prescriptive system must be preferential when envisaged on the level of reality" (Lévi-Strauss 1969:xxxiii). He then goes on to construct from this premise a probabilistic model of society. The "awareness of the rule inflicts choices ever so little in the prescribed direction" (xxxiii) and, instead of being random, the outcome is biased toward the underlying structure. By linking structure and action directly, Lévi-Strauss remains indifferent to the impact of social interaction and the warping effects of power on individual decision-making. If Maya rulers dominated their subordinates completely (Acemoglu and Robinson 2012), nonroyals would have re-created the unequal structures of Classic Maya society automatically and without dissent.

The myth of Itzamnaaj's court reinforces the narrative of absolute royal power. The ancient Maya ascribed creativity to the supreme god Itzamnaaj, who dispensed it to the artisans and clients who gathered in his court (Figures 2.4 and 2.7). In Figure 2.7 the hummingbird approaches Itzamnaaj with offerings and obtains wings in return. While the god rests comfortably on a pillow, the bird lingers submissively at his feet. Their spatial relationship mirrors the power differential. Maya rulers and nobles replicated this arrangement. Through impersonation, they transformed themselves into gods. Royal courts instantiated Itzamnaaj's heavenly court (Miller and Martin 2004:51–65).

The myth of Itzamnaaj's court has to be understood as a self-serving narrative. A closer look reveals chips and chinks. As elsewhere, political ritual and public performances are not always effective mechanisms to naturalize ideological discourses (Comaroff and Comaroff 1993; Inomata 2006; Kelly and Kaplan 1990; Kertzer 1988). When Palenque King K'inich Ahkal Mo' Nahb III acceded to the throne in A.D. 721, he took the royal headband from Janaab Ajaw, watched by five court officials (Figure 3.4). He embodied one of Palenque's patron gods while Janaab Ajaw impersonated Itzamnaaj (Figure 2.8). The accompanying text explains this tableau as a replay of the creation of the universe when Itzamnaaj installed the patron god. The edifying if warped replication of Itzamnaaj's celestial court masked shrewd political calculation. Unlike earlier Maya rulers, who focused their art and writing exclusively on themselves, Ahkal Mo' Nahb granted lesser nobles unprecedented privileges. Court officials appear on carved monuments and are mentioned in hieroglyphic texts. Like Palenque's Ahkal Mo' Nahb, rulers at Copan and Yaxchilan faced the same dilemma and reacted similarly (Figure 1.9; Fash et al. 1992; Schele and Freidel 1990:262–345). In fact, nonroyal elites multiplied all over the Maya Lowlands during the eighth century A.D. (Figure 3.5).

The power of ancient Maya rulers was neither absolute nor unquestioned. In the past, little was known about the ways in which elites and commoners related to each other (Canuto and Fash 2004; Demarest 2009; Demarest and Foias 1993:174; Webster 2000:88). More recent studies of commoners, households, communities, and gender roles have contributed to a better understanding (Robin 2001, 2002, 2003, 2006; Yaeger and Canuto 2000). Classic-period elite rituals arguably emerged from ordinary ritual practices (Lucero 2003, 2010; McAnany 1995; Walker and Lucero 2000). Links between elites and commoners are visible in the quadripartite layout of caches and settlements (Lohse 2007:18–22; McAnany 1995:104; Robin 2001:21; 2002); architectural style (Wauchope 1938:150–151); cache layers as cosmograms (Bozarth and Guderjan 2004; Guderjan 2004); rituals (Hutson and Terry 2006); and a solar observatory (Zaro and Lohse 2005).

Ideologies are discursive concepts whose contents individuals are able to articulate and therefore to respond to, at least to a certain degree. To remain viable, a social system must allow individuals to make free choices and to manipulate the system to their own advantage. Instead of assuming that commoners accept an ideology, one has to ask why individuals (who belong to but may not act as a social group) accept it and what alternatives they have (Abercrombie et al. 1980). Commoners no longer follow their leaders' instructions blindly but rather counter domination with strategies that range from resistance and avoidance to engagement (Joyce et al. 2001; Scott 1985). Systems of power require social negotiation among all members of society (Bourgois 1995; Butler 1993; Comaroff 1985; Comaroff and Comaroff 1993; Fargher et al. 2010; Scott 1985, 1990; Willis 1977). In this understanding, domination and social control form only one aspect of power. Equally important is the ability to use knowledge, skills, and social relationships to advance one's interests. All individuals, to different degrees, have transformative capacity ("power to" in Miller and Tilley 1984).

## Yearning to Play Ball

Copan's nobles (like many of their contemporaries) strove to be heard during the eighth century A.D. They paved their path to power with the emblems of divine rulership. Or, to borrow the terms of Thaler and Sunstein's (2008) model, the divine rulers of Copan provided the role model or default for power in Classic Maya society. I exemplify this point with Copan's Group 9N-8. This group is the largest residential group outside of the royal precinct and is connected to it via a *sacbe*, or road (Figure 1.7). Group 9N-8 contains about fifty buildings in eleven courtyards (Figure 5.1). Its original extent is unknown because the Copan River has washed away its eastern and southern sides. At its center is the "House of the Bacabs," or Structure 9N-82 (Figure 1.8; Webster 1989a). Stone sculptures of scribes emerging from the underworld and possible portraits of the house occupants adorn the facade of this vaulted building. A bench with a hieroglyphic text fills the structure's center room. According to the inscription, Mak'an Chanal,

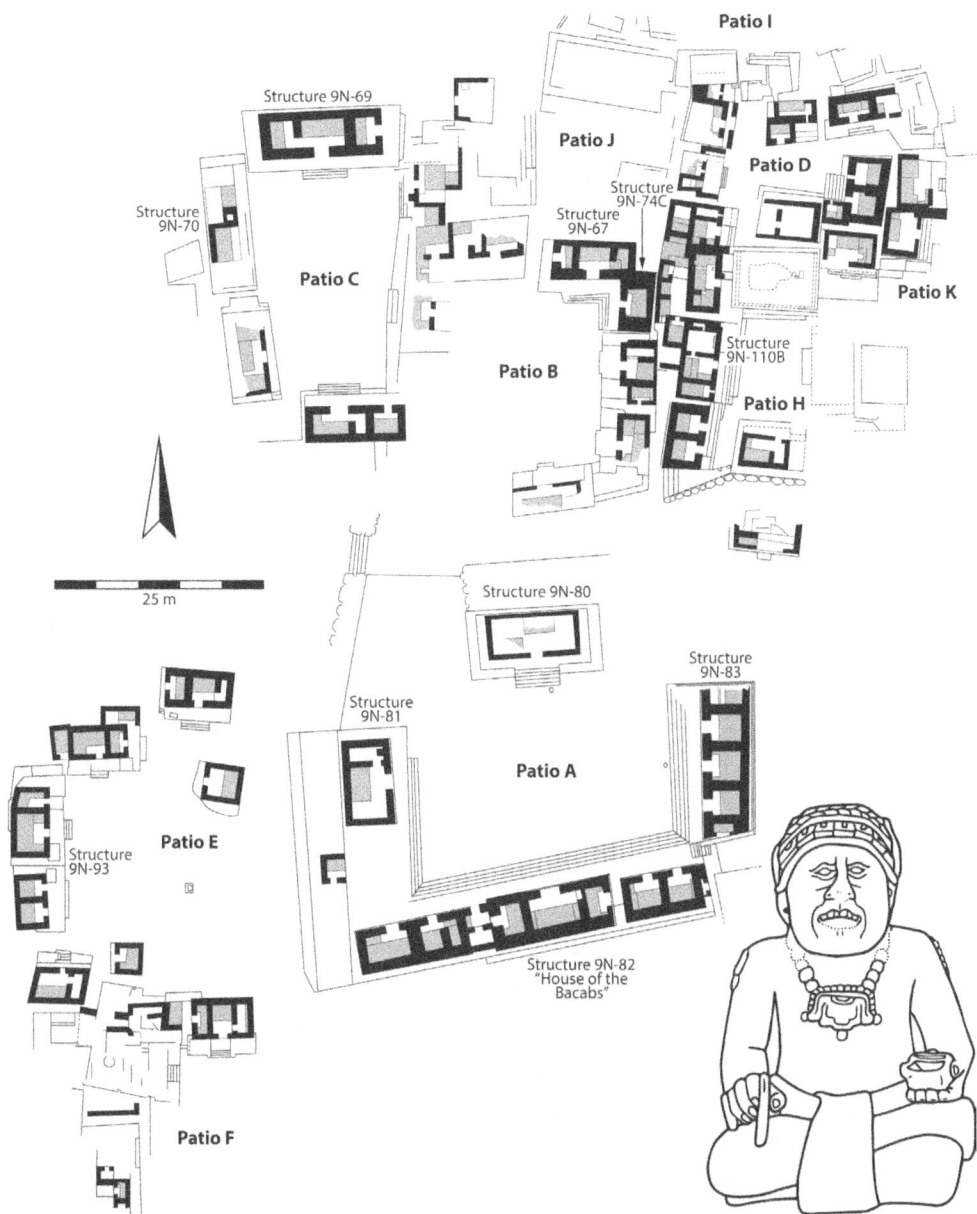

Figure 5.1. Group 9N-8 in the Las Sepulturas neighborhood of Copan; *inset*: stone sculpture of a supernatural scribe from the construction fill of the House of the Bacabs. (Map modified after Fash 1991:154 with additions from Gerstle and Webster 1990:245 and Hendon, Fash, et al. 1990:202, 239; sculpture drawing based on Fash 1989:55 Figure 45.)

a court official of Copan's last grand king, dedicated Structure 9N-82 as his residence in A.D. 781 (Figure 1.9).

Mak'an Chanal imitated Copan's divine rulers to express his own status. His vaulted residence is raised on the center of a C-shaped platform, directly facing a freestanding shrine (Structure 9N-80). Flanking the House of the Bacabs on the platform is another residence (Structure 9N-83) on the western wing, and Structure 9N-81 on the eastern wing (detailed in Figure 5.2). Unlike its vaulted neighbor, Structure 9N-81 had a low cobble wall that supported a perishable roof. Its stuccoed wall was painted brown and not red like the buildings elsewhere (Webster et al. 1986:207). Jaguar heads flanked its doorway. Inside, excavators recovered three smashed ceramic vessels, an effigy incense burner with a mustachioed human face; seven plain yokes; and two *hachas* in the form of a skull and a macaw. (*Hacha* translates as "axe" but refers to a thin roughly head-sized sculpture, often with a hole in the back that allowed it to be worn). The yokes and *hachas* (or equivalents in leather) were part of the ballgame attire. Ballplayers wore yokes to protect their hips and torso from the impact of the rubber ball while they attached *hachas* to their clothing (Scott 2001). The ceramic vessels sitting on the floor were smashed to pieces then the building was burned down, leaving a layer of dark soil mixed with carbon (Webster et al. 1986:209). Since the ballgame equipment was embedded in the carbonized layer and splintered over a wide area, it probably originally hung from the roof or was stored on the wall.

The ballcourt in Copan's Principal Group provides the reference point for Structure 9N-81 and its artifacts. The macaw-shaped *hacha* imitates the macaw heads that serve as ballcourt markers at Copan's Great Ballcourt (Figure 5.3). The macaw plays a special role at Copan because its founder is K'inich Yax K'uk' Mo' (Sun-Eyed First Quetzal Macaw). Later Copan kings invoke macaws in stuccoed panels and in different versions of the ballcourt. The macaw-shaped *hacha* at Structure 9N-81 aligns Mak'an Chanal and his family with the ruling dynasty. On Altar W', Mak'an Chanal refers to himself or a family member as a *pitzil ch'ok,* "ballplayer [and] prince." The macaw served as a powerful symbol beyond the Copan Valley. The site of La Unión, a few dozen kilometers east of Copan, has a ballcourt whose parrot-shaped markers are remarkably similar to the markers of Copan's Ballcourt III (Strömsvik 1952).

The ballgame equipment and reference to a ballplayer in Copan's Group 9N-8 are puzzling in the absence of an actual ballcourt nearby. Yet, its Patio A was likely conceived as a symbolic ballcourt similar to Copan's

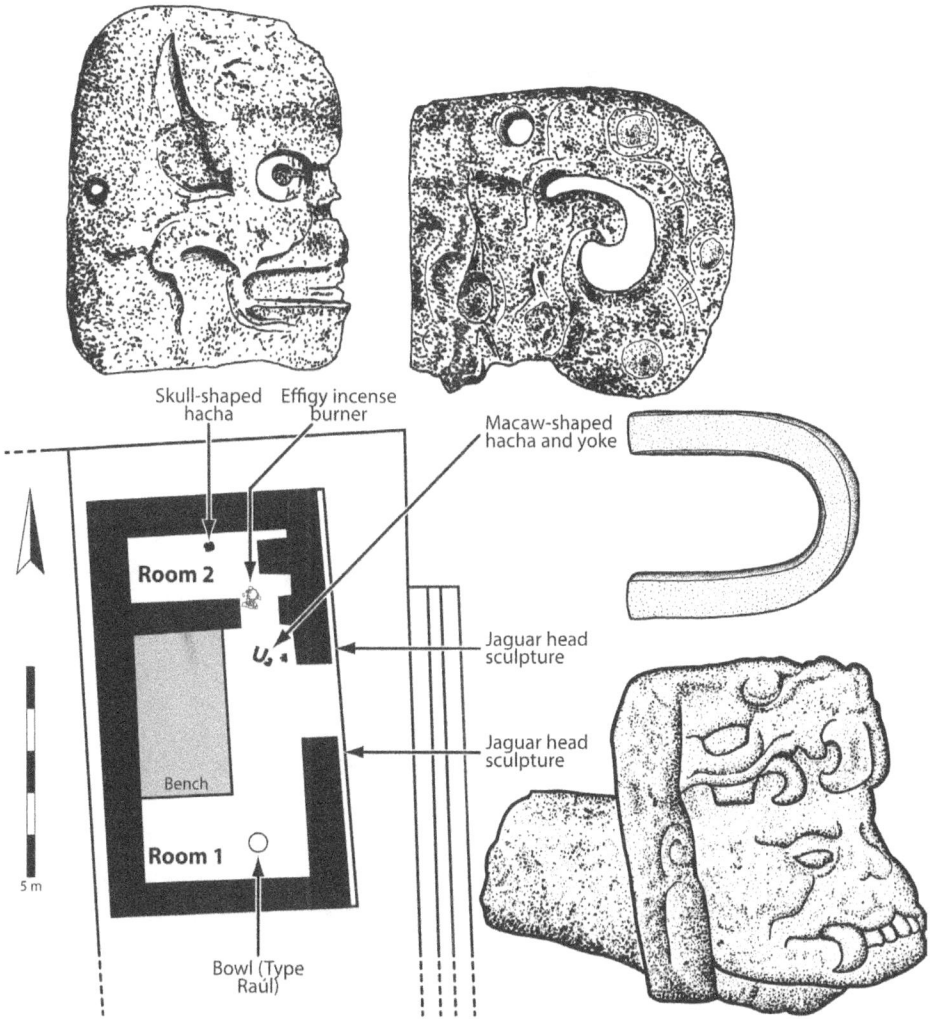

Figure 5.2. Structure 9N-81 in Copan's Group 9N-8 with a selection of associated sculptures and artifacts. (Ground plan and artifact distribution after Webster 1989b:10, 20; Webster et al. 1986:282 Figure 46; artifact drawings after photos in Webster et al. 1986:311, 314–315.)

East Court. Three ballcourt markers line up along the latter's central axis. The Jaguar Stairs on the courtyard's west side and corresponding stairs on the east side re-create a ballcourt alley (Figure 5.4; Miller and Houston 1987:58–59). Two jaguar sculptures flank the image of the Jaguar God of the Underworld on the Jaguar Stairs. The jaguar is the most dangerous animal of the Maya Lowlands and a creature of the night. Similar to counterparts at

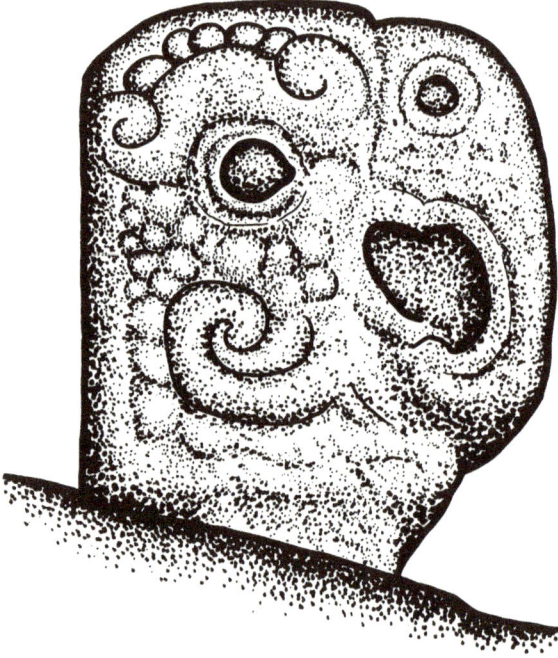

Figure 5.3. Ballcourt marker in the shape of a macaw head from Copan's Great Ballcourt. (Drawn after photo in Heyden and Gendrop 1988:118.)

La Amelia and Seibal, Copan's jaguar imagery reinforces sacrifice, torture, and death as aspects of the ballgame. Incense burners were likely placed on top of the Jaguar Stairway block and lighted during fire offerings (Taube 1998:450). Patio A in Group 9N-8 replicates the East Court and alludes to a ballcourt. The House of the Bacabs and the presumed shrine (Structure 9N-80) form the ends of the ballcourt, paralleling Structure 10L-22 and Temple 10L-16 in the East Court (compare Figures 5.1 and 5.4). Stairways in front of Structures 9N-81 and 9N-83 form the ballcourt alley. A symbolic ballcourt is called *wak ehb-nal,* or "six step-place," in glyphic texts (Stuart and Houston 1994:58). Fittingly, six steps lead to the entrance of Structure 9N-81. The jaguar heads on both sides of its doorway and the smashed incense burner inside cite the Jaguar Stairs. Mak'an Chanal employed the Maya ballgame in its diverse facets to manifest his close associations with his king Yax Pasaj and with divine rulership.[1]

During the Late Classic, and especially the eighth century A.D., Maya nobles like Copan's Mak'an Chanal wrested public voice and space from the divine rulers (Figure 3.5). Their path to power followed the template established by Maya kings and queens and appropriated the symbols of rulership. To employ Thaler and Sunstein's (2008) choice architecture, the nobles

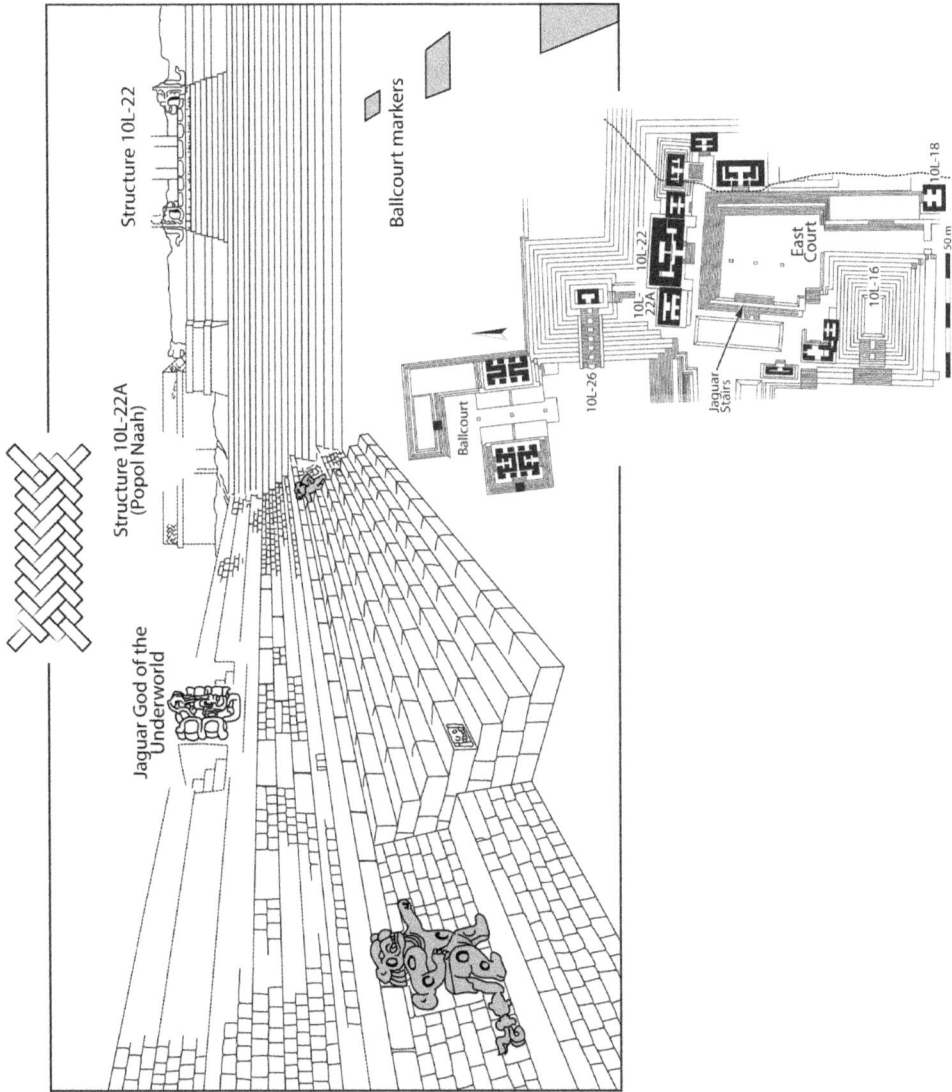

Figure 5.4. Reconstruction drawing of the East Court of Copán's Acropolis; insets show the map of the eastern part of the Acropolis and a mat sculpture from Structure 10L-22A. (Reconstruction drawing modified after Proskouriakoff 1963:44; map after Fash et al. 1992:431; Fash and Long 1983: Mapa 12; Hohmann and Vogrin 1982: Abbildung 44; mat design based on Fash et al. 1992:436.)

took the path of least resistance to get from the origin to the goal world. By reinforcing the established model, the nobles legitimized the royal leadership. They allowed the rulers to "perpetuate the existing political order within a discursive framework that generates the allegiance of subjects" (Smith 2003:108).

## Seizing the Mat

According to Thaler and Sunstein's (2008) choice architecture, decisions and behaviors that deviate from the default path provoke the powerful to respond. Then the questions become, Do leaders understand why people choose to deviate? Can they steer the mavericks? Ancient Maya rulers exhibited their power in diverse ways, and their followers exploited this rich symbolism to express their aspirations.

Among the Maya, the mat is one of the longest-enduring symbols of authority (Sharer 2006:272; also Robicsek 1975; Tozzer 1941:63). When a colonial noble mastered the Language of Zuyua, the head chief applauded him: "I will deliver your mat and your throne and your authority to you, son; yours is the government, yours is the authority" (Roys 1967:95). Mats covered thrones and rulers seated themselves on top of those mats when they took power (Robicsek 1975; Sharer 2006:218, 232, 273). *Pop Tz'am,* "mat (and) throne," form the diphrastic kenning meaning "authority" (Knowlton 2002).

Maya rulers appropriated the mat as a symbol of authority (for example, Yax Pasaj holds a ceremonial bar with a mat design in Figure 7.3). At Copan, the image on Stela J's east side weaves the strands of time into a mat. The glyphic text interweaves Waxaklajuun Ubaah K'awiil, Copan's thirteenth ruler, with founding king K'inich Yax K'uk' Mo' and goes back and forth between the eighth and fifth centuries A.D. Stela J celebrates time as much as divine rulers. Knowing the calendar and the attached history brought authority. Colonial Yucatec leaders still "counted the mat of the K'atun in its order" (*u tzolahob u pop katun;* Roys 1967:72). They seated each new year on its mat in the proper order of the twenty years of a K'atun. Classic Maya rulers emphasized how they were seated like time periods on mats and how they repeated events similar to how time's wheel turned (A. G. Miller 1986; Rice 2004, 2007, 2008; Stuart 2005:186–189). The kings and queens appropriated the mat of the K'atun as their mat.

The weight of time conveys not only authority but also a burden. During the eighth century the mat slipped out of royal hands. The spread of mat iconography in Maya structures reflects the decline of royal authority after a neighboring king defeated Copan's King Waxaklajuun Ubaah K'awiil in A.D. 738. His successor, K'ahk' Joplaj Chan K'awiil (A.D. 738–749), adopted a new political strategy and embraced lesser nobles. He directed the construction of Structure 10L-22A at the northern edge of Copan's Acropolis (Figure 5.4). Likely completed in A.D. 746, the building overlooks the East Court and attaches to several throne houses where Copan's rulers acceded to the throne. Ten mat designs adorn its facade, leading Structure 10L-22A to be called a "mat house" (Cheek 2003; Fash et al. 1992; Looper 2003:114–115; Wagner 2000). Eight human sculptures sit between the mats. They represent ancestors or impersonators of otherworldly deities. They encircle a much larger sculpture—presumably of K'ahk' Joplaj Chan K'awiil—on the roof crest.

A glyph below each human sculpture refers to an otherworldly place, including the Five-Flower Mountain, the Fish-Place, and the Black Sea-Place. Taken together, these toponyms detail the ancient Maya otherworld as a watery and dark region accessible through mountain clefts and caves. The dangerous journey to the otherworld is a crucial aspect of Maya theology: obligatory for the dead and a challenge for the privileged few who undertook this journey in their lifetime during rituals. The latter left the world of the living, entered the otherworld, and finally returned from the dead. Their journey was like a dream-filled sleep, so not accidentally does a glyphic inscription inside Structure 10L-22A call the building a *wahyib*, or "that which facilitates sleep."

Structure 10L-22A provides the cosmological blueprint for the journey into the otherworld and, at the same time, the space for its ritual recreation. The building conflates myth and reality (see also Fash and Fash 1994). Its mythic place glyphs may have had real-world pendants, and nobles possibly led processions from one locale to the next as they traveled into the otherworld (for example, the Fish-Place reference resonates with a fish sculpture from Group 10L-2 south of the East Court; Andrews and Fash 1992:69). Divine rulers enjoy privileged access to the otherworld. K'ahk' Joplaj Chan K'awiil surmounts eight other nobles on Structure 10L-22A. Yet, the mere presence of the other thrones indicates how the ritual and political dynamic had shifted by the eighth century.

K'ahk' Joplaj Chan K'awiil reconfigured the mat design in response to the new uses of this symbol of authority. As a choice architect, he grasped the rationales on which his lesser nobles made their decisions and mapped their choices to behavior, as Thaler and Sunstein's (2008) model outlines.

a

b

Figure 5.5. Structure 9N-67 and its mat motif in Patio B of Copan Group 9N-8: *a*. South facade of Structure 9N-67; *b*. Mat motif next to the doorway of Structure 9N-67.

By offering them access to royal symbols, he enabled dialogue about their status and directed the mavericks back into the royal fold. However, the price of elevating their status by negotiating previously untouchable royal symbols proved to be steep for his royal successors.

Earlier, I discussed how the ballgame theme suffuses Patio A—Mak'an Chanal's residence—in Copan Group 9N-8. I look now at other patios in the same group (Figure 5.1). Members of Mak'an Chanal's extended family, clients, artisans, and others (including even non-Maya people) lived in them (Sanders 1989). Immediately north of Mak'an Chanal's compound is Patio B. It lacks the low platform of Patio A and is instead easily accessible from all sides. A short cobblestoned *sacbe* leads into the courtyard, and openings between buildings lead to neighboring patios. Vaulted buildings—Structures 9N-67 and 9N-74C—form the northwest corner of Patio B (Figure 5.5a). Structure 67 is a small building with three rooms. On each side of its doorway is a recessed panel with stone blocks that form a simplified mat (Figure 5.5b). Contrasting with the ballgame-themed Patio A in Group 9N-8, the inhabitants of Patio B chose the mat to express their aspirations. The two patios exemplify different paths that individuals chose to achieve their goals.

## Scepters Out of Royal Hands

Maya rulers, like other choice architects, shape the possible worlds that are available to choose from. They structure incentives and promote practices to suit their interests. Out of the large repertoire of royal symbols, Maya rulers made only some available to nobles. Scepters played a unique role because they were handed over at ascension. Here, I use "scepter" in a broad sense. Classic Maya used the corresponding objects in a variety of ritualized contexts that included combat, hunting, and dance (Krempel 2014; Taube and Zender 2009:207–209).

Scepters marked, and still mark, status in Maya society. *Cargo* officials (officeholders) in modern Maya communities hold staffs. In Zinacantán, *regidores* have plain wooden clubs while the *alcaldes viejos,* the highest officers, carry black batons with silver heads and ribboned tips (Vogt 1969:98, 254, 283–284). Hundreds of years earlier, in colonial Yucatan, the head chief gave nobles who passed their interrogations not only a mat and throne but also a wand of office (Roys 1967:92). During the Postclassic, leaders from all over northern Yucatan maintained houses in the then-capital of Mayapan, and they charged a steward to maintain order while they were absent. The steward "bore for his office a short and thick stick, and they called him *caluac*" (Tozzer 1941:26; italics in the original). Classic Maya rulers took scepters when they acceded to the throne. On Piedras Negras Stela 3, Lady K'atun Ajaw "grasped the staff (?)" (*u ch'amaw loom*).

Some scepters were shaped like K'awiil, the god of rulership, (for example, on stelae from Machaquila) and actual examples have survived (see, for example, Miller and Martin 2004:32). Other scepters had simpler forms that include P-shapes and so-called wrenches (Figure 5.6). The accession iconography of the former and the glyphic reference to the lordship of a Naranjo king in the latter attest to these examples as royal scepters.

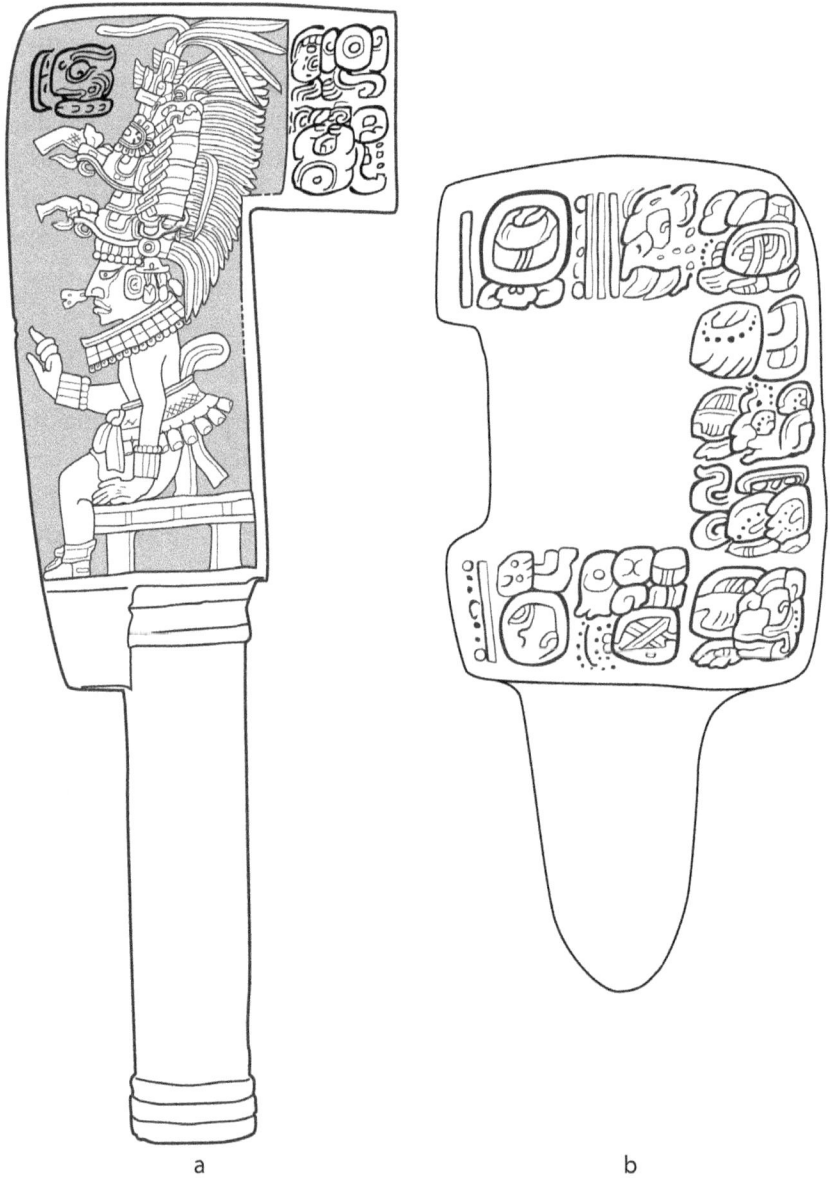

Figure 5.6. Royal scepters from the Maya Lowlands; *a.* P-shaped slate scepter (after photo in Deletaille and Deletaille 1992:226 Figure 180B); *b.* Wrench-shaped scepter of Naranjo ruler K'ahk' Ukalaw Chan Chaak (after photo in Helmke and Awe 2008:83 Figura 16a).

Comparable scepters were found in the Copan Valley (Table 5.2). Two complete examples from Group 9N-8 share the P-shape (Figure 5.7). Like other scepters, they are plain and show no wear from use (Willey et al. 1994:258). A cord was presumably threaded through the hole at the handle base. On an unprovenanced ceramic vessel (K8731), seven people who hold P-shaped scepters surround a lord on a bench. This representation of

Table 5.2. Complete and fragmented scepters from residential groups outside the royal Principal Group in the Copan Valley

| Provenience[a] | Form | Material | Dimensions (L × W × Th, in cm) | Reference |
|---|---|---|---|---|
| **COMPLETE** | | | | |
| 8N-11 (Type 4 group), Structure 51C, Feature 35[b] | Mace head with incised armadillo | ? | ? | Webster et al. 1998:335 |
| 9M-18, side patio (Type 3 group), cat. no. 1-966 | P-shaped | Fine-grained stone | 21.0 × 6.9 × 3.5 | Willey et al. 1994:258–259 |
| 9N-8 (Type 4 group), Patio C, cat. no. CPN-47[b] | P-shaped | Slate | 25.5 × 7 × 2 | Hendon, Fash, et al. 1990:52 |
| 9N-8 (Type 4 group), Structure 93 in Patio E, Feature 85[b] | P-shaped | Schist | 25 × 8 × 2.5 | Diamanti 2000:111, 238 |
| 9N-8 (Type 4 group), Patio C, cat. no. CPN-50[b] | P-shaped | Slate | 28.8 × 11.3 × ? | Eggebrecht et al. 1994:444 no. 119c[c] |
| **FRAGMENTED** | | | | |
| 9M-18, side patio (Type 3 group), cat. nos. 1-901 and 1-922 | Handle fragment | Schist | >20.5 × >4.5 × >3 | Willey et al. 1994:258 |
| 9M-18, main patio (Type 3 group), cat. no. 1–617 | Blade fragment | Schist | >9.0 × >8.0 × 1.2 | Willey et al. 1994:259 |
| 9M-27 (Type 2 group), cat. no. 1-206 | Handle fragment | ? | >14.4 × >5.4 × ? | Willey et al. 1994:259 |

*Notes:* Figure 1.7 locates the groups where these scepters were found.

a. The Copan Valley survey classified all residential groups, by mound size and number of mounds, into eight categories that range from nonmound to Type 5, the royal precinct (Leventhal 1979; Willey and Leventhal 1979). Types 1–4 range from the smallest (Type 1) to the largest nonroyal residential groups (Type 4).

b. Scepter dates to the Late Classic Coner phase (A.D. 700–900).

c. According to the catalog text, this scepter comes from Patio C in Group 9N-8, but it is not attested in the excavation report.

hierarchy, alongside the striking difference between the elaborate and the plain examples, suggest that these various scepters indicate status or rank.

The scepters at Copan distribute in spatially and temporally telling ways. All dated scepters come from Coner-phase contexts and date to the eighth or ninth century A.D., that is, toward the end of Copan's royal dynasty. During the survey of the valley, archaeological features were grouped into eight categories (Freter 1988; Leventhal 1979; Willey and Leventhal 1979). These range from artifact scatters ("Nonmound") to Type 5, in Copan's Main Group and ceremonial center. The classification takes into account the number of mounds, structure height, and structure construction quality. Simple farmers presumably inhabited Type 1 groups, with three to five low structures made of cobble or masonry, while nonroyal nobles like Mak'an Chanal presided over Type 4 groups with 8–100 mounds in multiple courtyards. Some of these structures are higher than five meters, have vaults, and include sculpture. Excavations confirmed that the survey typology correlates with ancient social hierarchies (Webster 1989b:11; 1992:140).

With one exception, the scepters occur in high-ranking Type 3 and Type 4 residential groups (Table 5.2). Few scepters were found in the main patios of these groups, however. Group 9N-8 is centered around Mak'an Chanal's Patio A, and its three known scepters come from Patios C and E. Two of the three scepters from Group 9M-18, whose main patio housed an *aj k'uhuun* like Mak'an Chanal, are from side buildings. The nobles, members of their extended family, or associates adopted scepters as wands of office. Their situation is comparable to that of the *caluacs* in Postclassic Mayapan (Tozzer 1941:26).

Earlier, I discussed the relationship between status and innovation. Everett Rogers (1995) proposes a linear model according to which high status correlates with innovative spirit, whereas Frank Cancian (1979) argues for an S-shaped relationship and sees the upper and lower middle classes as the most willing innovators. Since the inhabitants of Copan's groups were linked to each other, it remains unclear whether clients or kin could have adopted innovations independent of the influence of Mak'an Chanal and other nobles. Therefore, the spatial and temporal distribution of Copan scepters resonates only with the general idea that high status promotes innovation but fails to support Rogers's or Cancian's model specifically.

Ballgames, mats, and scepters illustrate the different ways in which Copan's nobles expressed power. From the perspective of choice architecture, they illustrate individual variation and unique paths to a goal. The

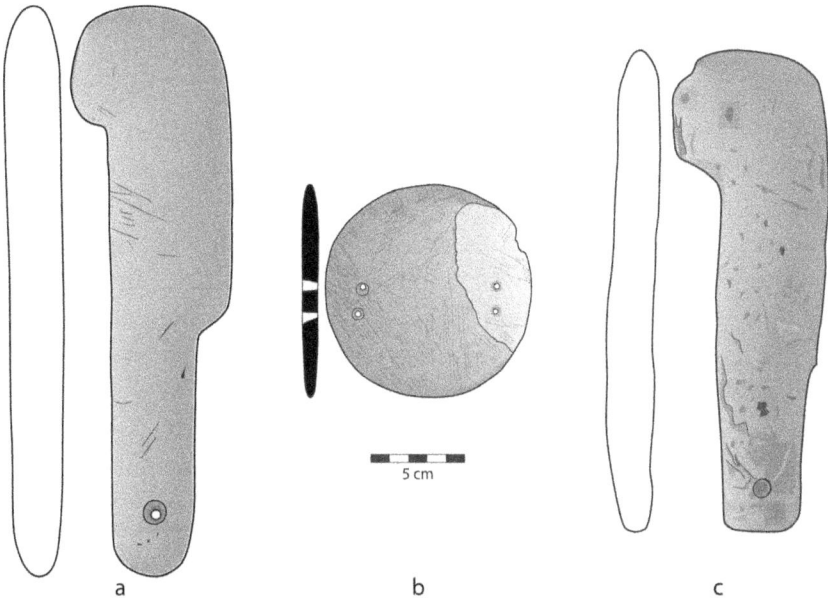

Figure 5.7. Scepters and a mirror back from Copan's Group 9N-8: *a.* Scepter found in Structure 9N-70 of Patio C (drawn after Hendon, Agurcia Fasquelle, et al. 1990:65 Figura 12); *b.* Stone mirror back found in Structure 9N-70 of Patio C (drawn after Hendon, Agurcia Fasquelle, et al. 1990:65 Figura 11); c. Scepter from Structure 9N-93 in Patio E (drawn after Diamanti 2000:238 Figura 72).

nobles operated in a social framework in which rulers controlled symbols of power while also relying on them. Accessions exemplified these mutual dependencies. For example, the Palenque noble Janaab Ajaw handed king K'inich Ahkal Mo' Nahb the royal headband (Figure 2.8). Instead of wielding absolute power, Classic Maya rulers channeled social and political processes. The ballgame, mat, and scepter originated as royal symbols but were appropriated by Copan's nobles. From Structure 9N-70 in Patio C of Group 9N-8 comes not only a scepter but also a stone disk with four perforations, flat surfaces, and beveled edges (Figure 5.7b; see Figure 5.8 for location). Similar disks have been found in the Copan Valley (Willey et al. 1994:251–252) and elsewhere (for example, Willey 1972:141–143). Associated pyrite pieces identify these disks as mirror backs. Maya rulers gazed into them, presumably for divination, or wore them as part of their attire (Miller and Martin 2004:43–45). If the Patio C disk was originally a mirror, it was another royal symbol that nonroyals adopted.

## Crumbling Ideological Support

Charismatic leaders not only demonstrate their power but also let it be revealed (Anderson 1990:74). These two forms of power differ in causality (Keane 1997:11). To demonstrate power, leaders act intentionally and impose their will even against the resistance of others. Power is revealed but not by the leaders themselves; an exterior force with which they are associated is seen as the cause. For example, Frank Sinatra casually observed that his Jeep seemed in need of a new paint job. "The word was swiftly passed down through the channels, becoming ever more urgent as it went, until finally it was a command that this Jeep be painted now, immediately, yesterday" (Talese 1966). Since doing so would require that special painters work overtime, approval had to be sought back up the line until the order landed on Sinatra's desk again. With a tired look on his face, Sinatra confessed that he did not care when his Jeep was painted. He did not have to order (or even request) that his Jeep be painted; instead, his people tried to read his mind.

Power is similarly revealed in Classic Maya society. When rulers defeated enemies in war, they celebrated the success as *hubuy u took' u pakal*, "it got downed [their enemies'] flint [and] shield." Instead of attributing the victory to their strength, they invoked an impersonal force by literally saying "it got downed." Similar passive and antipassive phrasings are much more common in Maya writing than active "he did it" sentences. Exteriorizing the cause of actions is the source and Achilles' heel of revealed power. The cause must appear apart from but still closely associated with the leader.

During the eighth century, Copan's kings became divorced from the symbols of rulership. The ballgame, mat, and scepter all underwent resignification and negotiation. In addition, Maya nobles increasingly appeared in glyphic texts (Figure 3.5) and even dedicated their own inscriptions. Copan mirrored this development (Figure 1.9). For example, at Copan Mak'an Chanal adorned his residence, the House of the Bacabs, with an elaborate glyphic bench. Parallel to these developments runs the reuse of glyphic texts. Carved monuments were reused throughout the Classic period.[2] At Copan Altars J' and K' were cached in the foundation of the Late Classic Stela 10 while Altar A' was resculpted into a block of the Hieroglyphic Stairway (Marcus 1976:125–126). Many more examples attest to the resetting and modification of monuments. Yet, such reuse remains limited to the royal precinct until the eighth century A.D., when it spreads throughout the Copan Valley.

When Mak'an Chanal built the House of the Bacabs in A.D. 781, four blocks with glyphs were reused as steps of the main stairway (Figure 5.8a shows the three best preserved ones). The blocks came from different monuments, were reset without regard for reading order, and were then stuccoed over (Webster et al. 1986:168). The central block commemorates the death of K'ahk' Uti' Witz' K'awiil, one of Copan's greatest kings, on 9.13.3.5.7 12 Manik' 0 Yaxk'iin, or June 15, 695. Sometime between A.D. 695 and 781, Mak'an Chanal or one of his predecessors carved up a royal monument, brought the blocks to their residence, and reused them as a step of a stairway. That this happened under the eyes of Copan's kings attests to the growing power of nonroyal elites.

Within a few decades, Mak'an Chanal's family members or associates followed suit. Several glyph blocks were found in Patio C (Figure 5.8b). Structure 9N-69, the only vaulted building in Patio C, dates to about A.D. 800 or somewhat later (Webster 1989b:15). Glyphs adorned both sides of its doorway. The numbers and glyphs on the left side form a nonsensical text while the day sign 8 Ajaw was found on the right side of the doorway and on an isolated block south of Structure 9N-70. The sign 8 Ajaw possibly refers to the period ending 9.13.0.0.0, or the year A.D. 692. The crescent-shaped eyes and mouth date the second 8 Ajaw block stylistically to A.D. 730–760 (compare Stela H [dedicated in A.D. 730], Altar S [A.D. 731], Stela M [A.D. 756], and Stela N [A.D. 761]). The glyphic texts from Patio C likely predate their reuse by two or three generations.

King Yax Pasaj, whom Mak'an Chanal served as *aj k'uhuun,* turned out to be Copan's last official ruler. He dedicated his last building—Structure 10L-18 near the East Court (Figure 5.4)—in A.D. 801 and Stela 11, his last carved monument, about twenty years later (Figure 7.3). Copan's dynasty ended but the symbols of rulership retained their appeal. Structure 10L-18 and its tomb, which may have been Yax Pasaj's resting place, were looted (Becker and Cheek 1983). The building's sculpture was reused as a bench in Structure 11L-77, which dates to about A.D. 900 (Manahan 2004:112–113). Similar scavenging occurred throughout the Maya Lowlands after the collapse of divine rulership (Joyce et al. 2001:371). By then, divine ruler and supportive symbolism had divorced.

Power includes "the capacity to constitute interests and determine their significance within the management of existing conditions" (Smith

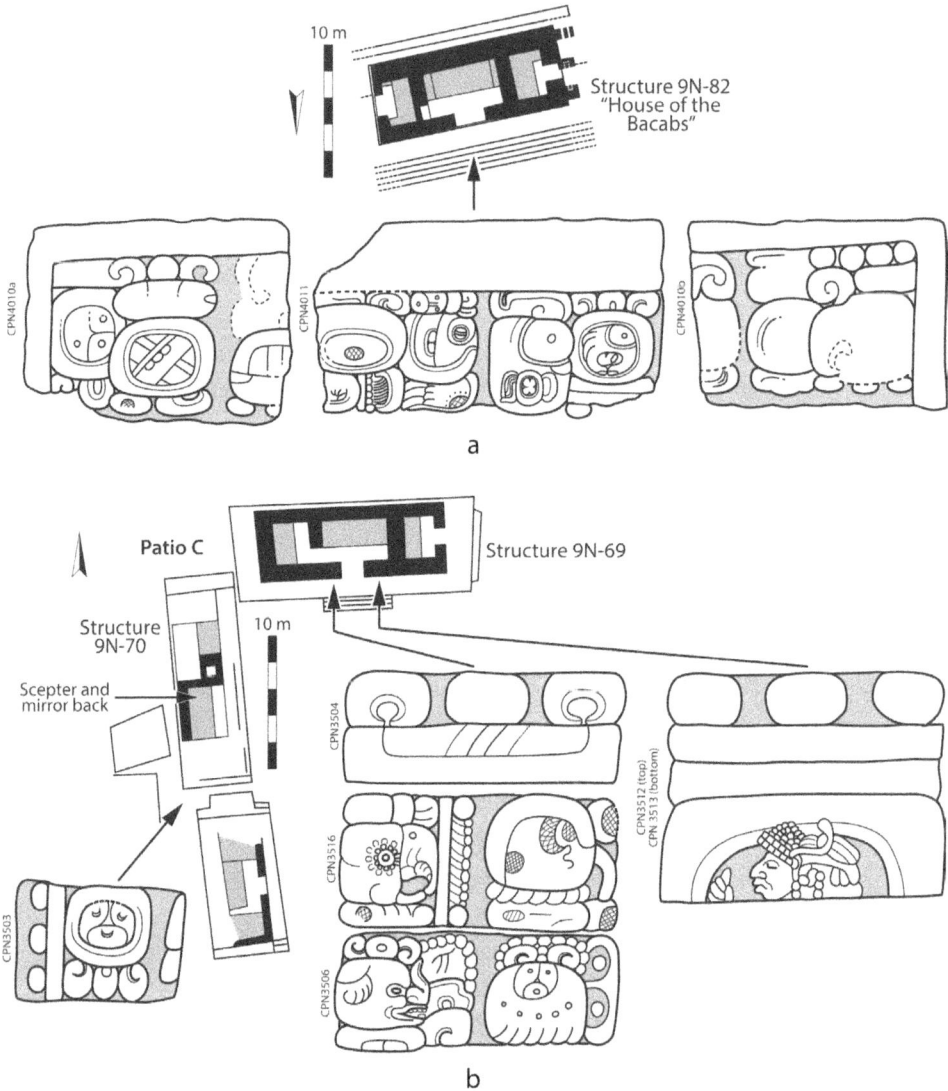

Figure 5.8. Reused glyphic inscriptions in Copan's Group 9N-8: *a.* Reused glyph blocks from the stairway of Structure 9N-82; they are shown as mounted, with the middle block upside-down; *b.* Reused glyph blocks from Patio C; the glyph blocks from Structure 9N-69 were presumably mounted on both sides of the doorway. (Maps after Fash 1991:154 with additions from Gerstle and Webster 1990:245 and Hendon, Fash, et al. 1990:202, 239. Fig. 5.8a after Webster et al. 1986:241 Figura 3 [glyph blocks] and 292–293 [position and location]. Glyphs in Fig. 5.8b after Hendon, Agurcia Fasquelle, et al. 1990: 61 Figura 6.)

2003:108). The powerful strive to maintain the status quo by channeling everybody's behavior through the appropriate choice architecture. Ideally, their hands are invisible and others reveal their power. Eighth-century Copan nobles dedicated their own glyphic texts while subordinating themselves to the king. Their participation, which was necessary for choice architecture to work, entailed at least partial understanding of the choice architecture and some options to negotiate it. Late Classic glyphic texts outside Copan's Principal Group manifest this discourse. Starting in the eighth century, Copan nobles appropriated royal material culture and employed it as steps, doorways, and benches for their residences. Partial and upside-down glyph blocks suggest that they not only transferred but also transposed these objects, likely creating their own meanings. Their reuse of glyphs and sculptures illustrates how the royal ideology became disassociated from the divine rulers. The structures that maintained the status quo eventually helped to upend it.

## Politics of Innovation

Power skews the ability of agents to achieve desired outcomes. A modern notion of structure has to consider the asymmetries of power (Sewell 1992:9). Anthony Giddens adds this dimension by defining resources as sources of power (Giddens 1979:92; Sewell 1992:9). I discuss the Maya ballgame, scepter, mat, and glyphic writing as the resources through which the ancient Copanecos negotiated power. Only some of these resources serve similar purposes in other cultures. Equating resources with power sources ignores, on the one hand, how they are culturally embedded and, on the other hand, how they come to represent power (also Walker and Schiffer 2006). Following Sewell (1992), I differentiate between resources as (human or nonhuman) forms and resources as symbols. To become sources of power, resources undergo the process of signification that I discuss in Chapter 2. In the case of the Maya symbols discussed previously, these processes started in the first centuries B.C.—visible, for example, in the murals of San Bartolo (see Chapter 1 and Figure 1.1)—and continued for more than a thousand years. The developments during the eighth century A.D. exemplify how the meanings of power symbols shifted in response to social negotiation.

Structures provide the framework for social action. Cancian's (1979) model correlates status with innovativeness and elucidates the influence of education, wealth, and other factors. Yet, the model interprets the correlation as a causal relationship in which status determines innovation (Cancian 1967:4). I argue against the objectification of status or other social structures. In the French village of Pellaport, structures (be they norms or wealth) cannot be abstracted from the individual. Close social interaction puts the individual before the category and allows the often belated appreciation of innovators, even if they run afoul of expectations. Social dynamics redefine roles and norms. Status and innovation influence each other mutually.

Technologies (in the ancient Greek sense of idea *and* matter) order human activities. They enable culture-specific ways to work, to communicate, or to express one's status. Individuals decide how technologies engage with social structures. "In the processes by which structuring decisions are made, different people are situated differently and possess unequal degrees of power as well as unequal levels of awareness" (Winner 1986:28). I captured these processes by applying Thaler and Sunstein's (2008) concept of choice architecture to the Garden of Forking Paths. At eighth-century Copan, King Yax Pasaj and Aj K'uhuun Mak'an Chanal exemplify the power differential between individuals. The different case studies—ball game, mat, scepters, inscriptions—illustrate how nonroyal Copanecos wrested control over these royal symbols from the kings.

Divine Maya rulers like Copan's kings set themselves apart from the rest of society. Their narrative of absolute power tempts us to peg them as extractive leaders who were concerned only about their wealth and well-being (Acemoglu and Robinson 2012:143–149). Classic Maya rulers are convenient straw men: dominant, male, and eventual losers. History seems to lead from them to inclusive states where opportunity and innovation await. The Late Classic reality was more complex however. Maya rulers claimed power as part of a totalizing discourse (Keane 2003:420). They succeeded in establishing a choice architecture to their liking but at the price of negotiation. Copan's Late Classic kings and their growing inclusion of nonroyals exemplify the limits of royal power. Nobles and commoners underwrote Classic Maya society. Yet, their submission implies awareness and agency. The developments at Copan show how participation fostered innovation and eventually upheaval.

# 6

## Stillman Wanders, Babel Rises

### Innovation's Impact on Structures

According to a medieval legend, Roman Emperor Constantine ordered the construction of a basilica dedicated to the Virgin Mary during the fourth century A.D. (Gregory of Tours 1988:28; Krusch 1885:493). Workers dragged thick stone columns to the church but were unable to erect them because they were too heavy. Days of futile struggles went by. One night, the architect had a dream in which the Virgin Mary appeared and told him: "Noli maestus esse [Don't despair], for I will show you how to raise these columns." She then explained him what scaffolding was appropriate and how to arrange the pulleys and ropes. She added that he should ask three boys for assistance. After waking up, the architect prepared everything as ordered and summoned three boys from school. To the astonishment of onlookers, the three boys raised what many strong men could not lift. With the columns in place, the architect and the workers soon finished the basilica. This legend describes the invention of the rope-and-pulley system but veils the technological achievement in magic and supernatural intervention. By pointing to the Virgin Mary, the architect invokes established structures to legitimize change.

As I have pointed out, structures are complex and leave room to imagine alternative worlds. The Latin original for "what scaffolding was appropriate" is *quae apparentur machinae. Machina* translates not only as "scaffolding" but also as "machine" and "contrivance." Similar to the ancient Greek term *tekhnología* (Chapter 1), the Latin *machina* refers to the tool and the idea, to the material and immaterial aspects of technology. Innovators understand the frame of reference and align structures in novel but logical ways. In the following, I link invention to its adoption and its impact on structures. The three boys who magically lifted heavy stone columns mark the transition from individual vision—the architect's dream—to a changing collective perception. Innovation invokes public discourse, as the architect's astonished audience shows.

## Diacritical Consumption

The transition from invention to adoption places novel products in a public discourse. As they acquire a social life, inventions potentially impact society. They exemplify how commodities are a "nonverbal medium for the human creative faculty" (Douglas and Isherwood 1996:41). Three propositions stand out (Brumfiel 1987:676). First, the consumption of goods has the "capacity to make sense" (Douglas and Isherwood 1996:40). Access to goods differentiates and classifies people. Second, consumption is competitive. Those who can control access may erect barriers against entry and consolidate control of opportunities. "For those excluded, the only two strategies are to withdraw and consolidate around the remaining opportunities, or to seek to infiltrate the monopolistic barrier" (Douglas and Isherwood 1996:62). Third, consumption reflects the openness of social structures. It "should flourish in fluid, competitive political situations, and it should languish in structured contexts where rights are rigidly ascribed" (Brumfiel 1987:676).

Diacritical consumption characterizes Classic Maya society. The possession of artifacts manifests status differences and the dynamic struggle to maintain or change status. The villagers of Nacimiento and Dos Ceibas expressed their wealth at least partially through the size of their homes, a measure based on production (Figures 3.7 and 3.9). The inhabitants of Aguateca (Figure 1.5), an eighth-century royal capital, similarly displayed their status through the consumption of animal remains. Since they were recovered from rapidly abandoned buildings, these animal bones and shells elucidate ancient consumption patterns particularly well (Inomata and Triadan 2010). Based on Kitty Emery's study (2003), I grouped the animal remains into eight classes (Table 6.1; see also Sharpe and Emery 2015). Marine mollusks are by far the most dominant species despite the inland location of Aguateca. Like wildcats, these mollusks likely served mostly ornamental purposes. The river and lagoon that the site overlooks provided freshwater mollusks, fishes, turtles, and crocodiles. Hunting added deer and smaller mammals like peccaries or armadillos. Domesticated dogs and turkeys account for a small portion of the diet, likely because Aguateca's crowded center had little room for raising domesticated animals.

Table 6.1. Consumption of animal species by royal elites, nobles, and low-status crafts-people at the royal Maya capital of Aguateca

| | Palace | Structure M8-8 | Structure M8-4 | Structure M8-10 | Structure M8-13 | Aguateca Total |
|---|---|---|---|---|---|---|
| | King | Noble | Noble | Noble | Low status | |
| Marine mollusks | 800 | 300 | 200 | 0 | 11 | 1,311 (79.3%) |
| Freshwater mollusks and river snails | 8 | 51 | 30 | 108 | 11 | 208 (12.6%) |
| Deer | 26 | 5 | 7 | 8 | 9 | 55 (3.3%) |
| Domestic dogs and galliform birds | 2 | 8 | 4 | 12 | 2 | 28 (1.7%) |
| Fishes, turtles, crocodiles | 2 | 4 | 4 | 8 | 1 | 19 (1.1%) |
| Small wild animals[a] | 3 | 3 | 2 | 5 | 1 | 14 (0.8%) |
| Wildcats | 4 | 2 | 2 | 2 | 1 | 11 (0.7%) |
| Other[b] | 2 | 2 | 2 | 1 | 1 | 8 (0.5%) |
| **Total MNI** | **847** | **375** | **251** | **144** | **37** | **1,654 (100.0%)** |
| Goodness of fit test: chi-square value | 136.66 | 5.39 | 1.33 | 637.36 | 80.55 | |
| Probability[c] | < 0.001 | 0.145 | 0.722 | < 0.001 | < 0.001 | |

Notes: Minimum number of individuals (MNI) after Emery (2003:506, Table 2).
a. Small wild mammals include peccaries, armadillos, agouties, and pacas.
b. Other includes opossums, lizards, frogs, toads, and bats.
c. The chi-square value for three classes of freedom and a significance level of 5 percent is 7.815 (since expected frequencies were estimated from observed frequencies, a second degree of freedom was removed).

A goodness-of-fit analysis comparing the consumption of animals by rulers, nobles, and low-status craftspeople shows that rulers and their families monopolized imported marine mollusks while nobles had at best average access and the craftspeople notably little access to them (Table 6.1). Shells of Spondylus and other marine shellfish mostly adorned elaborate costumes, and their distribution at Aguateca correlates with status. The royal family used (in this case, likely ate) local species like domestic dogs, turkeys, and freshwater mollusks much more rarely than nobles or craftspeople did. The unusually high number of deer remains among the craftspeople likely relates to the working of bone (Emery and Aoyama 2007:81–83). Aguateca's animal remains reflect a wide variety of uses that include food, ornaments, tools, and artifacts. The rulers, nobles, and craftspeople who were living within a few hundred meters of each other had noticeably different access to these faunal remains and likely employed them to differentiate themselves in appearance and behavior.

Classic Maya nobles also competed through their clothing (Corson 1976; Schele and Miller 1986:66). On the south side of Palenque's Temple XIX platform, six court officials surround the eighth-century king K'inich Ahkal Mo' Nahb at his accession (Figure 3.4). The highest-ranking noble sits to the ruler's right and hands him the royal headband (Houston 1998:342–343; Palka 2002). The three attendants on the left side of the panel occupy the banded bird office, as the accompanying glyphic texts attest, whereas only the first of the three attendants on the right side has a title. Their costumes vary accordingly. The higher-ranking attendants on the left side wear ear flares whereas the ones on the right side have ear plugs (Stuart 2005:113). Similar contrasts existed at other royal courts. On carved monuments at Yaxchilan, the ear flares and sandals of lower-ranked *sajals* are smaller and less elaborate than those worn by divine rulers (Parmington 2003:50). K'awiil Chan K'inich, the fourth king of Dos Pilas, wears an ear spool while the nobles who sit in front of him have ear plugs (Figure 1.3).

Clothing was similarly important outside of the royal courts. At the villages of Nacimiento and Dos Ceibas south of Aguateca, I found greenstone ornaments only in prestigious contexts (Eberl 2014a:297–299). For example, a disk fragment came from a burial in the only pyramid in Dos Ceibas, and a complete bead from the community's largest residence (Figure 6.1a). These ornaments have simpler designs, are smaller, and consist of cheaper minerals—that is, not jade—than the ones worn by Maya rulers and nobles. They manifest the status differences between royal courts and villages but also the mutual dependency. Jade had to be imported into the Maya Lowlands, and regional elites controlled its trade and manufacture (Demarest et al. 2014). They may have given ornaments to followers to attract and reward them (Freidel 1993; Freidel et al. 2002). While local gentry enjoyed access to these greenstone ornaments, other villagers came up with alternatives. They decorated themselves with stone beads, a conch replica of a jaguar tooth, and pendants made from reused ceramic sherds (Figure 6.1b–e).

Classic Maya society constructed identity at least partially through material remains (see Joyce 2005:142–143; Veblen 2007). Now as then, wealthy people engage in conspicuous consumption not only to demonstrate their wealth but also to build and enhance their social and political standing (see Bell 2002; D'Altroy and Earle 1985; DeMarrais et al. 1996; Douglas and Isherwood 1979; Helms 1993; Miller 1985, 1987; Treherne 1995; Walker

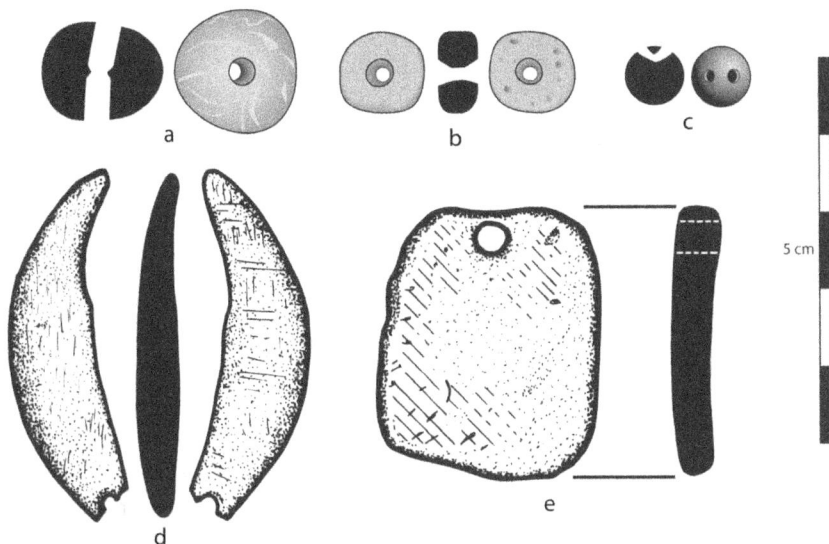

Figure 6.1. Ornaments from the Petexbatún villages of Dos Ceibas and Nacimiento: *a.* Greenstone bead from Dos Ceibas Structure R27-83; *b.* Stone bead from the midden next to Nacimiento Structure M4-3; *c.* Hematite bead from Nacimiento Structure M4-3; *d.* Shell pendant in the form of a jaguar canine from Nacimiento Structure M4-2; *e.* Ceramic pendant made from a Tinaja Red sherd from Nacimiento Structure N5-1.

and Schiffer 2006).[1] Food and clothing served as highly visible symbols to mark status among ancient Maya. Palace scenes on polychrome vessels portrayed tamales stacked high on plates, atole overflowing from jars, and cacao frothing out of cylinders (Figure 1.3). Classic Maya defined their status through greenstone ornaments as well as other rare accessories like jaguar furs and marine shells. The differential access of nobles to these valuable goods manifested in their size and likely extended to their material and artistic quality. Competitive consumption extended beyond the royal courts, though. Hinterland villagers wore cheap imitations of greenstone ornaments. The negative consumption of imitations identifies greenstone ornaments as positional goods that were socially scarce (Hirsch 1976). Sumptuary rules may have distinguished nobles from non-elites. Nonetheless, exclusion implies that non-elites participated in and at least partially understood the socially shared value system. The consumption of greenstone ornaments varies over the course of the Classic period. Innovation in the form of alternative materials and forms seems to have peaked during the Late Classic.

## Capitalizing on Knowledge

In a complex society, the unequal distribution of knowledge reflects both inborn talent and happenstance. From Pierre Bourdieu's perspective, people like ancient Maya dwarves and *aj k'iinob* differ in socially constructed cultural capital. He identifies three types of cultural capital: embodied, objectified, and institutionalized (Bourdieu 1983:185–190). Individuals acquire cultural capital in its embodied form through education and socialization. They have to invest their own time and cannot delegate the acquisition of cultural capital to others. In exchange, they hone socially useful skills and attributes like food connoisseurship and high-status dialects. Objectified cultural knowledge refers to the media of cultural knowledge and the ability to identify their significance. Examples in western cultures are paintings and wine; and in ancient Maya culture, glyphic writing, scepters, and the ballgame (Chapter 5). These objects require embodied cultural knowledge to be appreciated properly. Institutionalized cultural knowledge comes in the form of titles. In this way, society differentiates between autodidacts and graduates. Titles like *aj k'iin, itz'aat,* and *aj tz'iib* provide public recognition, while schools, government, and other institutions funnel individual talent among the ancient Maya.

Bourdieu's concept of cultural capital ignores unique individual talents and emphasizes education. Years spent in school indicate knowledge accumulated and the amount of cultural capital one possesses. Through this acquisition process, knowledge becomes internalized and part of an individual's habitus (Bourdieu 1983:187). Social expectations are similarly normative. In western societies, artists can and even should look and behave differently from the rest of society. The ancient Maya ascribed mythical powers to a dwarf like Ahkal. They traced writing to supernatural origins and may have regarded scribes as superhuman (Houston in Inomata 2001b:337). Ideally, unique talents meet and match social ideals of creativity. Artists' exalted status then allows them to become role models or to actively promote novel ideas. The risk arises, however, that appearance may trump merit. A dwarf may be short on artistic brilliance or an *aj k'iin* merely entitled. Climbing a career ladder with multiple rungs, or acquiring multiple titles, calibrates rank and knowledge throughout an individual's life. Institutionalizing knowledge implies not only recognizing and rewarding knowledge but also correcting gaps between ideal and reality.

Cultural capital lends itself to social manipulation. Control over its institutional framework—schools, patrimony, titles—influences the access to knowledge. Trade secrets manifest this process. Families and communities with craft specialists often protect their knowledge (for example, Nicklin 1971:33–34; Skeaping 1953:138–141). A Mexican potter "who hits upon a new technique in colouring or glazing jealously guards his secret, so that pottery-making knowledge is no longer universally shared" (Foster 1965:58). Cultural capital and social structure were entangled in colonial Yucatec Maya society (Tozzer 1941:27). The *aj k'iinob* gendered and gentrified access to education by teaching only the sons of nobles and priests. In turn, Maya leaders gave them presents and consulted them on important decisions. As privileged children grew up to assume the roles of their parents and reproduce the mutual dependency, elites eventually monopolized education.

By all appearances, colonial Yucatec Maya segregated knowledge. To study whether the situation was similar in Classic Maya society, I examine textile production. Classic Maya wore astonishing clothes that rival acclaimed modern Maya textiles (see, for example, Figure 1.3). Bales of textiles are often depicted as gifts or tributes in palace scenes.

Art and artifacts entangle knowledge and social status by placing the spinning and weaving of textiles in the hands of Classic elites (Chase et al. 2008; Houston and Stuart 2001; McAnany and Plank 2001). Textile-making tools and spindle whorls are concentrated in elite residences. However, spindle whorls are attested among the villagers at Nacimiento and Dos Ceibas in the form of centrally perforated sherd disks (Table 6.2; for the identification of these disks as spindle whorls see Halperin 2008:116). Since these disks are lightweight and small, they could only be used for spinning fine fibers like cotton. Coarser fibers like henequen require much heavier spindle whorls (Feinman et al. 2002:267 Figure 12). In addition, the village whorls are in their dimensions indistinguishable from elite specimens elsewhere, which suggests that they were used for spinning cotton.

At Motul de San José (see Figure 1.3), Halperin (2008) correlated the density of spinning tools with social status. About one spinning tool occurs for every 1,000 ceramic sherds in elite and high-status households. Noticeably fewer spinning tools—about one per 1,500 sherds—are present in lower-class households. The residential groups at Nacimiento and Dos Ceibas compare in size to Halperin's lower-class households. In Group Chispa at Nacimiento, about one spinning tool occurs per 6,000 sherds, a density well below that of lower-class groups at Motul de San José. The low frequency of spinning in the Petexbatún villages supports Halperin's (2008) conclusion that the spinning and weaving of textiles differ in scale

Table 6.2. Comparisons of presumed spindle whorls from the villages of Nacimiento and Dos Ceibas with specimens from Caracol, Copan, and Motul de San José

| Site | Group | Construction volume (m³) | Diameter (mm) | Height (mm) | Hole diameter (mm) | Weight (g) |
|------|-------|------------------|----------|--------|---------------|-----------|
| Nacimiento | Chispa | 102.0 | 43.0 | 6.0 | 6.4 | 6.4 |
| Nacimiento | Chispa | 102.0 | 30.0 | 16.0 | 5.0 | 3.5 |
| Nacimiento | Caña de Azúcar West | 31.0 | 20.0 | 8.3 | 5.1 | 13.5 |
| Nacimiento | Chiltepe | 93.7 | 44.0 | 5.8 | 2.6 | 12.6 |
| Dos Ceibas | MP12 | 186.8 | 35.0 | 8.7 | 4.1 | 4.0 |
| **MEANS AND STANDARD DEVIATIONS** | | | | | | |
| Nacimiento and Dos Ceibas | $N = 5$ | 103.1 ± 55.4 | 34.4 ± 9.9 | 9.0 ± 4.2 | 4.6 ± 1.4 | 8.0 ± 4.8 |
| Caracol | $N = 59$[a] | – | 25.7 ± 4.9 | – | 5.6 ± 1.4 | 10.8 ± 4.7 |
| Copan | Sepulturas $N = 66$[b] | – | 38.8 ± 9.4 | 4.8 ± 1.6 | 5.4 ± 1.7 | – |
| Motul de San José | Small whorls $N = 33$ | – | 36.5 | 6.6 | 5.7 | 6.9 |

*Notes:* Halperin (2008:116) identifies sherd disks with central perforations as spindle whorls; Nacimiento and Dos Ceibas residential groups with spindle whorls are marked in Figure 3.7 to illustrate their standing within each village. Caracol data based on Chase et al. (2008:132); Copan data from Hendon (1987:375); Motul de San José data from Halperin (2008:114).
a. At Caracol, most spindle whorls ($N = 48$) are made of stone; nine are ceramic and two are shell.
b. Copan data for sixty-six spindle whorl disks with central perforations. Measurement was not possible for all specimens.

and intensity but not in kind between elite and non-elite households. At Copan's Group 9N-8, spinning and weaving tools occur mostly in lower-ranking patios (Hendon 1997:43). The latter's residents likely produced textiles for noble Mak'an Chanal and his family, who resided in the group's largest patio (Figure 5.1; Jackson and Stuart 2003:224–225). Knowledge of spinning and weaving was concentrated among but not exclusive to Classic Maya elites.

Status and power splinter knowledge. On the surface, this is the outcome of an unequal society. Digging deeper, though, reveals a problem. Esoteric knowledge must be limited to a select few in order to be exclusive, and those not in the know have to be aware of its existence so that it can serve as cultural capital. Modern suits illustrate the conundrum (Kuchta 2002). Their cuff buttons stem from military uniforms on which pips indicate rank (Suitably Dressed 2010). Unlike the merely decorative buttons on most suits, the jacket sleeves of bespoke suits can be unbuttoned. By leaving one button undone or rolling back the sleeve, wearers of bespoke suits can signal their wealth so subtly that most people will miss it. At the same time, people can learn the attributes of bespoke suits without owning one. Acquiring embodied knowledge requires investing time but not material resources. The few spinning tools at Nacimiento and Dos Ceibas are less interesting as evidence for the meager production of textiles than for the way they document how these villagers held esoteric knowledge and how spinning and weaving served as cultural capital through which status distinctions played out in Classic Maya society. The Nacimiento and Dos Ceibas villagers were in a position to develop a meta-awareness of their social structures. Thus, they turned an unknown unknown into a known unknown.

## Dog Tooth Turns Relic

Structures intertwine with individual lives. Whereas William Sewell (1996:842) insists that "social relations are profoundly governed by underlying social and cultural structures," I argue against prioritizing structure. The case of Zaynab al-Ghazali shows how structures and individuals mutually influence each other (Chapter 4). I now link the decision-making of individuals to structural change. The key component is the socially visible commitment. By adopting the same course of action or the same invention, individuals signal shared decisions. In turn, these overlapping decisions accumulate and cohere into structural changes.

A Tibetan fable illustrates the process (David-Néel 1971:301). A trader traveled each year to India. At one point his aging mother asked him to bring back a relic since India was Buddhism's Holy Land. Her son promised to do so, but as soon as he left Tibet he forgot his promise and came back empty-handed. His mother felt sad and repeated her request when he traveled the following year. Again her son promised a relic, and again he forgot it. In the third year, the mother asked again for a relic. Her son forgot about her request until he had returned from India and was close to home. Should he disappoint his mother yet again? At this moment he glimpsed the decaying corpse of a dog next to the road. The bleached bones inspired him to break off a tooth. When he reached home, he wrapped the tooth in silk and offered it to his mother as the tooth of the great god Sariputra. The woman welcomed the tooth, placed it in the family shrine, and prayed to it daily. Other people soon joined her and eventually the tooth began to

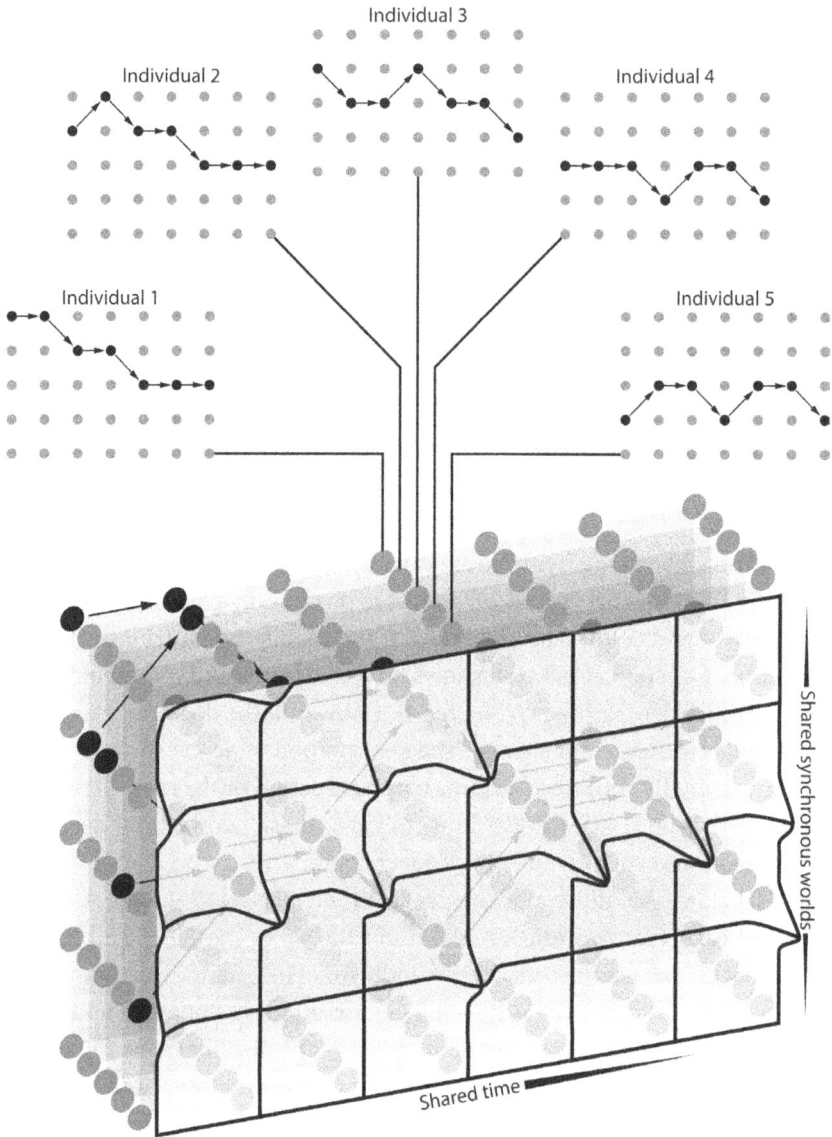

Figure 6.2. Accumulated social responses from individual cognitive maps and actions (see Figure 4.2 for the cognitive maps of individuals).

shine. Collective faith transformed a feeble invention into a shared holy relic, giving rise to the Tibetan proverb, "If there is veneration, even a dog's tooth emits light" (David-Néel 1971:301). The shared veneration of the dog's tooth induced commitment (see also Nickerson and Rogers 2010).

On the individual level, people recognize the possible worlds for future action, identify obstacles associated with either world, and consider the concrete actions necessary to realize their choice. Instead of getting lost, people orient themselves in the labyrinth of possible worlds (Figure 4.2). They implement their intentions and commit to a path to get from the origin to the goal world. On the structural level, social interaction around a specific case encourages commitment. By participating in the veneration of a dog's tooth, individuals discern the intentions of others and signal their own intentions. They evaluate and adjust their actions to the social context and structural demands. Prosocial behaviors that otherwise remain diffuse become salient. In terms of possible worlds, social interaction demarcates possible courses of action and their associated costs.

Commitment bridges individual and structure. The two depend on each other for meaning and to remain meaningful. The dog's tooth shines only if a Tibetan perceives it as a relic. A folly thus becomes meaningful while veneration is confirmed as a guiding structure. Venerating the dog's tooth epitomizes the generation and maintenance of structure; structure is not possible in the mind of a single individual but requires the commitment of a group of people, or more broadly speaking, social consent. Social interaction allows structure and individual to resonate. I visualize this process as the overlapping of individual decisions. Each of the five individuals shown in Figure 6.2 undertakes a different course of action. When all five paths are layered on top of each other, similar individual actions overlap and form bumps on the surface. They result in a map of social action. Based on social interaction and mutual observation, individuals take actions that resonate with the actions of others. Actions cohere around possible worlds and harmonize individual and social logic. While the number of possible worlds is countless, structural constraints and preferences limit the number of worlds that are realized.

Inventions enable possible worlds that were previously seen as improbable or even impossible. As individuals acquire knowledge about an invention, they gauge its acceptability and its potential, evaluating it by comparing it with existing objects or services. For example, Leonardo Da Vinci's aerial screw was out of touch with fifteenth-century Italian society and predated the helicopter by four centuries. An invention's overlap with what exists promotes subjective continuity; that is, individuals feel the invention fits logically with existing structures. I deliberately say "feel" because the evaluation of an invention is seldom completely conscious, rational, and transparent (for a case study see Papousek 1989:159–160). This is particularly relevant to an invention's potential; individuals have to estimate the impact of adopting an invention, an action that can have unintended consequences. By using comparisons, individuals decide whether or not to adopt an invention.

Individual choices fuse into a landscape of shared decisions. At the same time, individual courses of action fail to overlap consistently or perfectly. Figure 6.2 portrays this diversity as two or more vertically aligned bumps or synchronous worlds. This does not mean that everybody agrees. Instead, overlaps result when some people act in unison and in accordance with specific structures. Elections in democratic societies provide an apt analogy. Only a limited number of political parties exist; they represent the possible worlds and are defined by a society's power structures. Voters select among these parties. Each vote is unique and reflects individual concerns; yet, taken together with thousands or millions of other votes, the vote count elevates one party to power and makes this choice socially relevant.

## Pottery as Material Discourse

To create culture, an individual experience "must be attached to material forms through which people can perceptually access it" (Urban 1996:245). These material forms, or what I call resources, can be myths or objects. They are shared across space among members, and across time between generations, of a society (Gell 1998; Hodder 2012; Strathern 1988). The objectification of unique personal experiences links individuals to broader social, political, and ideological orders. It asserts them as members of the collective. Nonetheless, the complex structures of society provide individuals with different ways to objectify their experiences. The fault lines of society—different status, unequal power, and splintered knowledge—steer personal decisions (Chapter 5). As innovation reveals, the aspiration to unity and the inherent complexity of society clash in a tension-filled public discourse.

The transformation from individual to collective experience requires replication. Individuals have to adopt the invention and spread it in space-time. During the Late Classic, the Maya in the southern lowlands shared similar pottery belonging to the Tepeu 1 and 2 ceramic spheres (Figure 1.4). The Tepeu 1–2 spheres were first recognized at Uaxactun, where they divided the Late Classic into an early (c. A.D. 550–700) and a late phase (c. A.D. 700–830; Smith 1955). Many sites in the southern lowlands turned out to have similar pottery and the Tepeu 1–2 distinction was adopted widely, albeit with different local names (Willey et al. 1967:299–300). To avoid confusion, I use Tepeu 1 and Tepeu 2 to describe this pottery type throughout the lowlands instead of defining all the corresponding local terms (for these terms see Figure 1.4). I discuss the changes in more detail elsewhere (Eberl 2014a:47–66) and restrict myself here to the basic aspect: Maya pottery underwent two waves of innovation during the Late Classic.

Late Classic Maya pottery comes in four basic shapes—bowls, jars, plates, and cylinders—that are generally either slipped and painted, or left unslipped and incised or stamped (Figure 6.3). Tepeu 1 and 2 vessels differ primarily in shape details and decoration motifs. At Tikal, Late Classic pottery "changed completely in character from curving and rounded graceful forms with fine linear designs executed in subtle gradations of orange [Tepeu 1] to an emphatic, virile and simplified vocabulary of forms with a radically reduced iconography, executed in clear intense color [Tepeu 2]" (Coggins 1975:406–407). The other noticeable change occurred in decoration motifs.

On slipped pottery polychrome painting predominates, and geometric fillers like lines and dots frame main motifs. During Tepeu 1, the motifs are often naturalistic, portraying animals and plants while humans are rare (see, for example, Coggins 1975:258–262; Culbert 1993; Smith 1955:5–6, 25). Glyphs are executed in a cursive style where heavy exteriors contrast with finely executed interiors and rounded contours are preferred (Coggins 1975:285–286). During Tepeu 2, humans take the center stage. Painted vessels show seated Maya lords, palace scenes, and episodes like the capture of prisoners or ceremonies (500–501). Other motifs include the *ajaw* (lord) and other glyphs, owls, and the Mexican year symbol (Coggins 1975:280–282; Culbert 1993; Smith 1955:25). Unlike the closely keyed Tepeu 1 palette, Tepeu 2 colors are more intense and more contrastive (Coggins 1975:406). Glyphs become blocky carved inscriptions, and their interior and exterior lines are similar in width. Overly large central motifs, especially day signs and other isolated glyphs, exemplify the overall sense of boldness and contrast (Coggins 1975:408).

Ceramic typologies and the resulting chronologies (like the ones shown in Figure 1.4) ascribe immutability to ancient cultures. New pottery types

Figure 6.3. Profile views of Late Classic Maya ceramic vessels *a*. Tepeu 1, or Early Nacimiento, round bowl (vessel number 310504); *b*. Early Tepeu 2, or Middle Nacimiento, angled bowl (vessel number 310492); *c*. Early Tepeu 2, or Middle Nacimiento, tripod plate (vessel number 310493). (All are Saxche-Palmar Orange Polychromes from the village of Nacimiento; scales in centimeters; see also Eberl 2014a:377–392.)

are seemingly rare and change not within years or decades but across centuries. Tikal's pottery offers a rare glimpse into a more dynamic reality (discussed in Eberl 2014a:47–66). The ancient Maya were not simply consumers of pottery, but many households produced their own vessels and had the means and skills to tinker with new ideas (Ball 1993; Fry 1979, 1980; Fry and Cox 1974; McAnany 2010; Rands and Bishop 1980; Rice 2009). The Tikal sample consists of almost thirty burials dating from A.D. 630 to A.D. 760 and containing more than one hundred ceramic vessels as grave goods.[2] Tikal's Late Classic burials and caches are rather accurately dated. Stratigraphy and associated hieroglyphic inscriptions with dates or personal names narrow them to tight time frames of a few years (Coggins 1975). Therefore, they preserve ceramic developments very well. They cover two waves of ceramic innovation: the rounded Tepeu 1 pottery of the seventh century A.D. and the angled Tepeu 2 pottery of the eighth century A.D. Most of the ceramic vessels come in three shapes: plates and dishes, cylinders, and bowls. The interior angles of plates and bowls capture the differences among vessels and the shape changes (Figure 6.4). Tepeu 1 plates have rim-base angles of almost 160°; a century later, rim-base angles average 135°, halfway between a straight line and a right angle. Tepeu 1 bowls are rounded while Tepeu 2 bowls are angled. Rim-base angles of plates plummet, and center-body angles of bowls rise, around A.D. 700, when Tepeu 1 transitions into Tepeu 2.

Culture rests on transforming individual experience into material forms that can be publicly perceived. Tikal's ceramic vessels preserve the decisions that potters made centuries ago. While their overall shape is similar, they vary in the details. For example, only two Tepeu 2 bowls have exactly the same interior angle (Figure 6.4). Tikal's Tepeu 1 or Ik plates and dishes vary by 8.4° from the average rim-base angle of 156.8°; during Tepeu 2 or early Imix, the average and standard deviation fall to 134.9° ± 4.5°. The center-rim angle of bowls averages 75.8° ± 3.6° during Tepeu 1 and 87.1° ± 2.6° during Tepeu 2. The standard deviations within each time period vary from 2.6 to 8.4 degrees. These differences persist yet the frequency distributions show that around A.D. 700 individual potters move to popularize novel pottery, but in different ways. They replace open Saxche plates and dishes with angled Palmar Orange Polychromes. The form change accompanies decoration changes from fine linear designs in subtle shades of orange to blocky iconography in more contrastive red-orange hues (Coggins 1975:406–407).

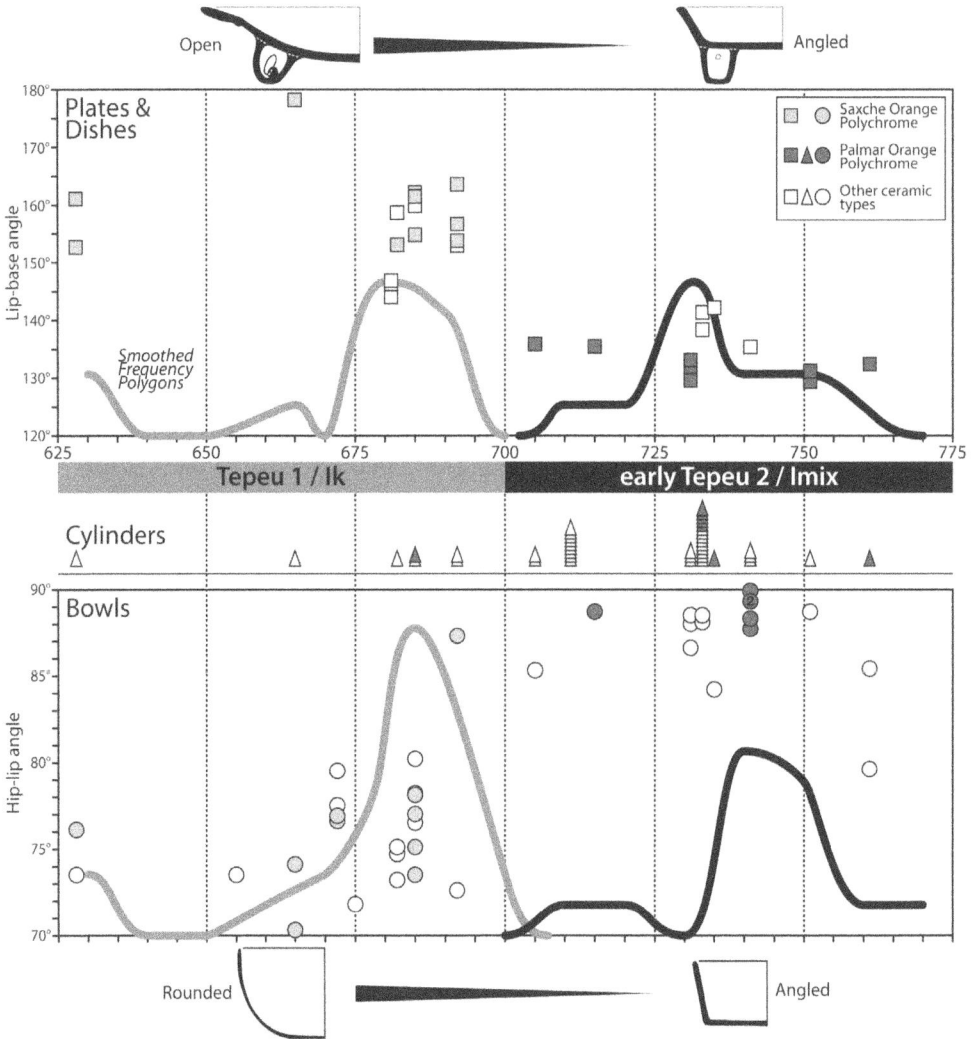

Figure 6.4. Tikal's inhabitants adopted new ceramic types over the course of the seventh and eighth centuries A.D. Each data point represents a vessel found in a burial (burial dates after Coggins [1975]; Eberl [2014a:52]). I measured the angles of ceramic vessels by superimposing a triangle over their profiles in Culbert (1993); the triangle corners correspond to the lip, the base, and the hip, or the point where base and body meet (Eberl 2014a: Figure 3.9); the hip corresponds to the position of the flange in the cases of plates and dishes and to the intersection of a 45° line with the vessel body in the case of bowls. The lip-base angle $\gamma$ for plates and dishes changes from open to angled during the sixth and seventh centuries A.D. For bowls, the hip-lip angle $\beta$ indicates their roundedness; angle changes are highly significant for plates and bowls ($t_S = 8.20$ and $t_S = 10.77$, respectively, with $p < 0.001$).

These changes are less obvious among bowls. For example, a late Saxche bowl from Burial 81 prefigures the angled shape of Palmar bowls. Potters start to produce cylinders (which are typical eighth-century forms) decades before A.D. 700. A Palmar Orange Polychrome cylinder already appears by A.D. 685, decades before this type becomes popular. Ancient Maya potters continuously invent new forms, new decorations, and new types. Their individual decisions eventually aggregate to form the distinctive Tepeu 2 ceramic assemblage.

Tikal's Late Classic pottery exhibits dynamic innovation. While some of the Tikal vessels are high-end products with elaborate iconography and glyphic texts, many are much simpler and indistinguishable from pottery found in non-elite contexts. The latter are comparable to the plates and bowls found at Nacimiento and Dos Ceibas (Eberl 2014a:377–392). Complete utilitarian vessels are rare in Tikal's ceramic assemblage but likely changed as well (see discussion in Eberl 2014a:65, 415 n. 11). Even traditional pottery is much less stable than often assumed (McAnany 2010:223; Reina and Hill 1978:231). Emulation and conformity based on the notion of *costumbre,* "tradition," explain these developments only partially.

Objectification forms the basis for a public discourse through replication and delimitation. The dated burials reveal when Tikal's inhabitants adopted novel pottery. The frequency curves are roughly bell-shaped (Figure 6.4; compare Robinson 1951). People switched from Tepeu 1 to Tepeu 2 forms at the beginning of the eighth century A.D. The change from open to angled was swift for plates and dishes. Bowls similarly evolved from rounded to angled, but the A.D. 685 bowl with an eighth-century form points to an overlap of Tepeu 1 and Tepeu 2 shapes. Cylinders appear infrequently during the seventh century, become a staple in the first half of the eighth century A.D., then fade in popularity. Inventions like the novel pottery forms and types at Tikal enable courses of action that were not previously feasible. Innovators coalesce around one form over time and the resulting adoption pattern is bell-shaped. Nonetheless, not everybody makes the same decision, as grave goods demonstrate. Ancient Maya selected different ceramic vessels—likely filled with food for the way into the otherworld—to bury with their deceased. During Tepeu 1, two-fifths of all burials contain only bowls while half (53.3 percent) pair a plate with a bowl and a cylinder. During Tepeu 2, two-thirds of all burials combine a plate with a bowl and a cylinder.

The adoption of an invention, like Tikal's altered pottery shapes, makes a new material form widely available. The invention links adopters into a

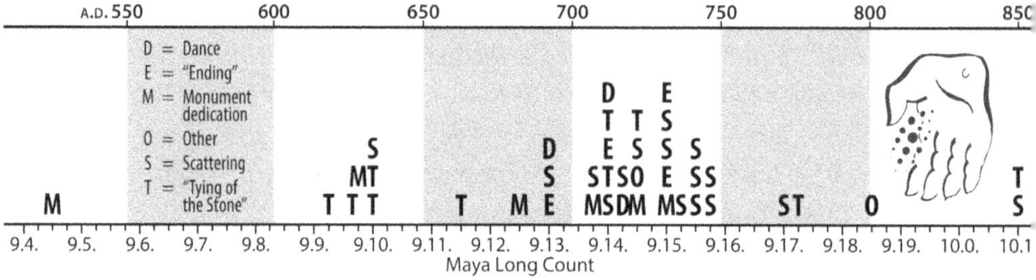

Figure 6.5. Temporal distribution of period-ending rituals in the Petexbatún and Pasión regions. (Each letter represents a dated event mentioned in hieroglyphic texts; based on Eberl 2014a:44 Table 3.2; inset shows the glyph for *chok*, "to scatter.")

network of shared material forms. However, this process is neither homogeneous nor pervasive in space-time. People differ in whether and when they adopt inventions. A similar argument can be made for the complex spatial adoption of Late Classic pottery inventions across the Maya Lowlands (Figure 6.10; discussed in Eberl 2014a:47–66). The replication of material forms is bounded in time and space. Their differential distributions illustrate the heterogeneous and complex nature of the public discourse about culture.

## Apprising War Owls

Innovation creates a new public discourse. It converts an individual experience—the vision of the inventor—into a material form or resource (the invention) that is perceptually accessible and replicable for society at large. The transformation also touches on the second aspect of culture: collectively shared meanings or schemas. This entails a dilemma best illustrated by an example from Lewis Carroll's *Through the Looking-Glass*. Alice asks Humpty Dumpty what he means by *glory* and he defines it as "there's a nice knock-down argument for you!" When Alice objects, Humpty Dumpty responds scornfully: "When I use a word, it means just what I choose it to mean—neither more nor less" (Carroll 2009:190). Individuals may use the same material forms but sometimes understand their meanings differently. "The replicability of perceptible substance cannot guarantee equivalence of meaning" (Urban 1996:248). Because the material forms require shared meaning to be understood in public discourse, the question becomes how they transmit meaning.

To discuss meaning in public discourse, I select two key symbols of Classic Maya culture: the glyph for *ajaw*, "lord," and the sign for the owl.

My analysis of iconographic motifs on Classic Maya pottery calls attention to the relationship between pottery design and social structures (Conkey 1982; Hodder 1984; Washburn 1983, 1999). Hegmon and Kulow (2005:314) argue that "the act of painting a design on a vessel is a form of agency, and the overall style of that design in part can be conceptualized as a kind of structure." For them, design structures fail to reproduce social systems but instead are analogous because they encompass "the rules and resources that are central to some conceptualization of structure" (317). In Maya glyphic inscriptions, scribes tend to write the word-sign for *ajaw* with a stylized face whose features are reduced to round eyes and mouth, and a triangular nose (Figure 6.6a). The symbol predates Maya glyphic writing and

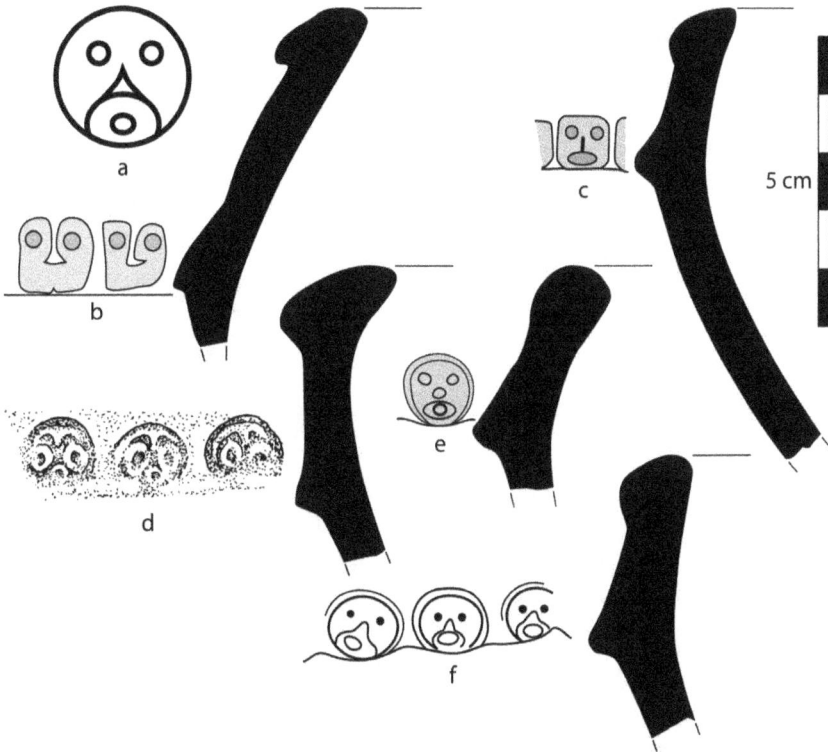

Figure 6.6. Different examples of the glyph for *ajaw*, "lord" (all except *a* from Chaquiste Impressed sherds at Nacimiento and shown at the same scale): *a*. Standard glyph for *ajaw* (T533 in Thompson 1962:452); *b*. Examples from Structure M4-6 in Group Chispa (NC1H-1-3-1; no. 822328); *c*. Example from Structure M4-6 in Group Chispa (NC1H-7-4-1; no. 822260a); *d*. Examples from Chochi's Rockshelter (AG108C-4-1-1; no. 809421a); *e*. Example from Structure M4-2 in Group Chispa (NC1E-5-2-1; no. 810719); *f*. Examples from Structure M4-2 in Group Chispa (NC1E-1-1-2; no. 810371).

Figure 6.7. *Ajaw* pendants worn by Maya rulers (see also Figure 2.7 for god Itzamnaaj wearing an *ajaw* pendant): *a.* Palenque King K'inich Ahkal Mo' Nahb on the south face of the Temple XIX platform; *b.* Dos Pilas King K'awiil Chan K'inich on polychrome vessel K1599.

is first attested around 650 B.C. in Olmec writing (Pohl et al. 2002). The term *ajaw* designates elites in Classic Maya society (when enclosed in a cartouche, though, the glyph for *ajaw* designates the twentieth day sign of the Tzolk'iin, the ritual calendar of 260 days). The glyph appears frequently in texts, and Maya nobles and lords wore pendants in its shape (Figure 6.7). *Ajaw* also substitutes for the Jester God, the symbol of Maya rulership (Stuart 2012:135).

Owls are the other prominent motif in the eighth-century villages. Ceramic figurines highlight their large forward-facing eyes and raptor beaks (Figure 6.8e and insets in Figure 1.6). Owls appear in various forms in Maya art and writing, including *way* characters (González Cruz and Bernal Romero 2012:96–97; Grube and Nahm 1994:703–704). Maya artists tend to depict the features of the ferruginous pygmy-owl (Grube and Schele 1994). This species has a feather horn, a feather on its forehead, a feather-fringed jaw, dark eye shades, and black-tipped feathers (Figure 6.8a). Owl feathers often adorn painted vessels (a.k.a. Muwan feathers; Figure 6.8f). Stamps on

Chaquiste Impressed bowls reduce pygmy owls to *kuy* symbols with eyes and the feather horn (Figures 6.8b–d).

Owls are birds of the night. In Classic Maya thought, owls evoke the otherworld, war, and exchange. God L, the lord of the otherworld, bears a *kuy* owl on his headdress (Taube 1992:79–88). Since this god oversees

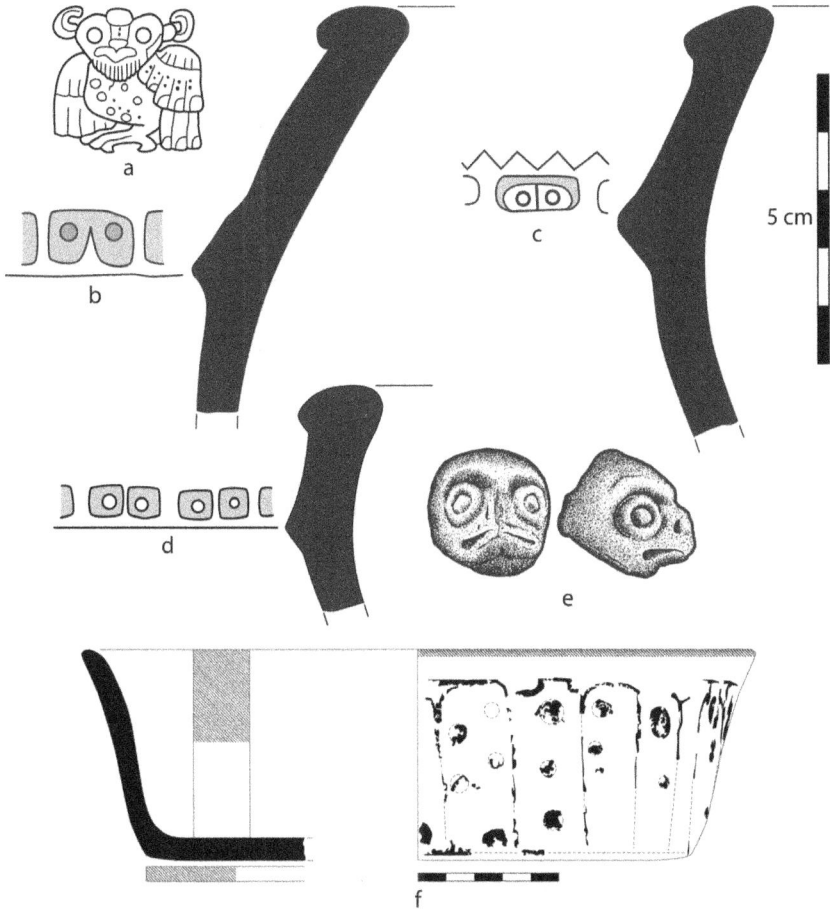

Figure 6.8. Different examples of owls from Nacimiento and Dos Ceibas: *a.* Glyph C3 from Tikal's Ballcourt Marker; *b.* Stamped Chaquiste Impressed sherd from Structure M4-6 in Nacimiento Group Chispa (NC1H-3-2-1; no. 822298); *c.* Stamped Chaquiste Impressed sherd from Dos Ceibas Group MP9 (ST4B-1-2-2; no. 821099a); *d.* Stamped Chaquiste Impressed sherd from Structure M4-1 in Nacimiento Group Chispa (NC1C-12-2-1; no. 805269); *e.* Figurine fragment from Structure M4-1 in Nacimiento Group Chispa (NC1C-12-3-2; no. 283); *f.* Saxche-Palmar Orange Polychrome (Palmar variety) bowl from Structure M4-2 in Nacimiento Group Chispa (NC1E-2-4-2; no. 310507). (Right scale applies to *b–e*; insets in Figure 1.6 show more owl figurines from Dos Ceibas.)

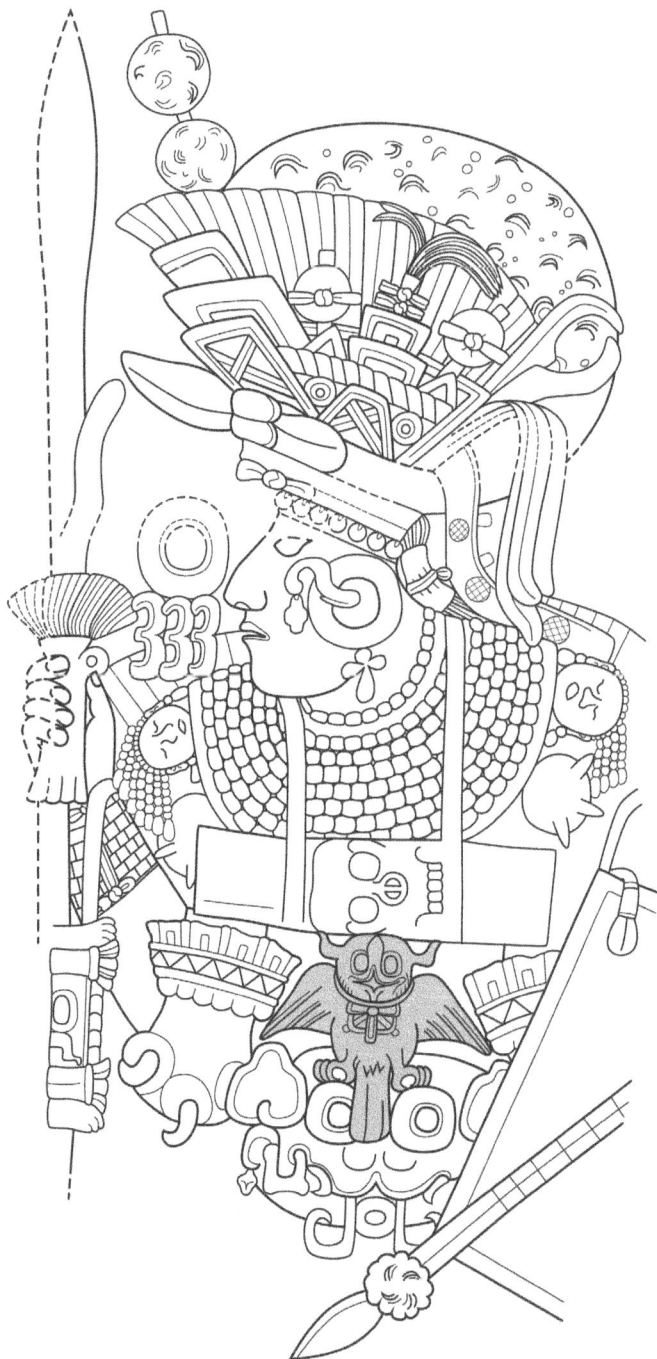

Figure 6.9. The owl as part of the warrior costume of Late Classic Maya rulers. (Detail from Dos Pilas Stela 2; based on Graham 1967:12.)

merchants, owls are also associated with trade and exchange (Akkeren 2012:158–163). In the colonial Popol Vuh, the lords of the otherworld employ owls as messengers to communicate with humans (Tedlock 1985). They are omens of illness and death among colonial and modern Yucatec Maya (for example, Redfield and Villa Rojas 1934:210–211; Tozzer 1941:202). Owls are also part of the Tlaloc-Venus costume of warriors (Schele and Freidel 1990:146–148). This costume originated during the fourth century A.D. when Maya elites came into contact with Highland Mexico and were influenced by the weaponry and symbolism in use there (Braswell 2003; Stuart 2000; Taube 2000). On Dos Pilas Stela 2, the third ruler of the Dos Pilas dynasty celebrates his defeat of Seibal's king (Figure 6.9). His weapons include a lance, spear-thrower darts, and a rectangular shield. He wears a balloon-shaped headdress with Mexican Year signs, Tlaloc goggles, and a skull-shaped chest pendant from which the owl dangles.

In Maya art and writing, the meanings of *ajaw* and owl emerge from comparison and entanglement. Both symbols are embedded in the glyphic and iconographic vocabulary as bounded systems. Substitutions with comparable elements circumscribe these symbols' meaning within Maya writing and art. Name phrases with multiple titles contextualize *ajaw*. Maya nobles identify themselves as *ajaw* combined with their courtly title—*aj k'uhuun, sajal,* and so on—and thus flesh out what it means to be a lord in Classic Maya society (an example appears on Site R Lintel 1). The owl appears in the attire of the lord of the otherworld as well as of successful warriors.

*Ajaw* and owl also entangle with elite life. As part of public discourse, these symbols encode information about the world (Urban 1996:246). Classic Maya nobles wear *ajaw* and owl pendants (Figure 6.7). Palace scenes convey the meaning of *ajaw* spatially. Seated on a throne-bench, a Maya noble occupied the top of the social hierarchy while his subordinates stood, kneeled, or sat below and arranged around him (Figures 1.3 and 3.4). Judging from the layout of actual palaces, these scenes reflect lived reality (Inomata 2001a). When Dos Pilas Ruler 3 captured Seibal's king, he "exhibited" him, as the text on Dos Pilas Stela 2 puts it, likely in a public victory parade. His owl-adorned warrior costume formed a highly visible aspect of celebrating conquest and prowess (Figure 6.9). In other cases, rulers wore owl or owl feather headdresses (Bassie-Sweet and Hopkins 2015:139–142). The close association of *ajaw* and owl with elite culture and the person of the lord must have been obvious to anyone who interacted with nobles, saw their likenesses on the carved monuments of plazas, or attended public rituals. Palaces and public rituals—space-time and practices—reinforce each other to create environments in which observers identify individual components as part and parcel of a larger message. Until the eighth century A.D., comparison and entanglement constrain the meanings of *ajaw* and owl and tie them to Maya elites.

## From Rulers to Rulership

Relationships enable generalization. Comparison and entanglement link individual elements to the larger system. They move from the indexical and context-dependent instance to the non-indexical and abstract. Webb Keane (2005) argues for the contingent co-presence of attributes. For example, the red color of an apple coincides with a specific shape, weight, and flavor. "Redness cannot be manifest without some embodiment that inescapably binds it to some other qualities as well, which can become contingent but real factors in its social life" (Keane 2005:188). Not all coinciding attributes are equal, however. Greenstone *ajaw* or owl pendants combine a specific material, color, and shape with the decoration. On one hand, these attributes enhance each other: the rare material and the prized color reinforce the status of the pendant's wearer. On the other hand, these attributes refer to nonmaterial structures. The shape of the *ajaw* glyph and the owl only becomes meaningful in the context of Classic Maya society. In Chapter 5, I discuss ballgame, mat, scepter, and glyphic writing. These and other symbols are linked into the Maya idea of rulership. Their comparison and entanglement entail the transition from ruler to rulership. The more symbols are linked to each other, the more important is the general idea that they represent. Classic Maya rulership is what Dan Sperber (1996:106–112) calls an attractor, or a higher-level schema that influences how other structures are perceived, transmitted, and distributed.

An attractor's influence on other ideas makes it crucial to the reproduction of society. At the same time, attractors threaten to confuse labels with things. Classifying Maya rulership as an institution risks overlooking the bundled relationships and rectifying processes from which the attractors were abstracted. Attractors depend on other structures to become manifest. No ruler without rulership; no rulership without ruler. Label and thing depend on and fuse with each other. Nonetheless the two need to be kept apart conceptually. Saul Kripke (1981) critiques description theory for conflating label and thing. From Kripke's perspective, a label fixes but does not determine a referent. A chain of communication attaches labels to things in the world. Kripke (1981:91) gives the example of someone who is called by a name from birth. People will talk about him to their friends and other people will meet him. "Through various sorts of talk the name is spread from link to link as if by a chain" (Kripke 1981:91). In the case of a famous person like physicist Richard Feynman, a speaker may have heard the name but not know from whom or why Feynman is famous. "So [the speaker] doesn't have to know these things, but, instead, a chain of communication going back to Feynman himself has been established, by virtue of [the speaker's] membership in a community which passed the name on from link to link, not by a ceremony that [the speaker] makes in private in his study: "By 'Feynman' I shall mean the man who did such and such and such and such" (Kripke 1981:91–92). Kripke's historical theory of reference calls for contextualizing the relationships bundled into attractors like the ancient Maya concept of rulership.

The sustaining structures of Maya rulership are dynamically linked and historically situated. The entangled structures of warfare, ballgames, regalia, and so on, changed over the course of the Classic period (for Copan see Chapter 5). Maya nobles became more prominent and forced a clearer delineation of elite status (Figure 3.5). Early Classic rulers tended to call themselves simply *ajaw*, "lord," while their Late Classic counterparts set themselves apart from regular nobles by calling themselves *k'uhul ajaw*, "divine lord" (Graña-Behrens 2006; Houston 1986; Houston and Stuart 2001). This differentiation among elites coincided with the increasing public exposure of Maya rulers. Plazas grew in size to allow thousands of people to participate in public ceremonies (Inomata 2006). Maya rulers celebrated the end of major time periods, especially of the K'atun (approximately twenty years), by erecting new monuments on plazas, dancing, or scattering incense or blood (Figure 6.5). In the southwestern lowlands, period-ending rituals were rare until the late seventh century A.D. They peaked in number and regularity during the early eighth century A.D. before disappearing together with the divine kings and queens. From the perspective of Kripke's historical theory of reference, the chain of communication changed for Maya rulership during the Late Classic. Including the general populace enlarged the community that passed concepts from link to link.

## Shared Inventions, Contested Meanings

Meaning arises from the ways in which elements relate to each other and to the world. Comparison and entanglement elucidate these interior and exterior relationships. Replacing *ajaw* with *sajal* asserts that both words mean something similar—a Maya noble—but not that they mean exactly the same thing. These substitutions imply equivalence but they also hide "shadows of differences" (Nabokov 1992:202). Through public discourse, people contest meanings. They employ their power "to formulate a genuine experience of the world and to resist others" (see Chapter 5; also Robb 1998:338; Robin 2016). The negotiation of meaning is, as inventions show, a continuous process in society.

During the Late Classic, the Petexbatún Maya used large and heavy ceramic bowls, often to store food. They lifted these vessels with the help of a horizontal flange. In one popular type called Chaquiste Impressed, the flange was decorated (lower right inset in Figure 6.10; Foias and Bishop 2013:190–194). The manner of decoration and the type of motifs change over the course of the Late Classic, mirroring the developments at Tikal (Figure 6.4; also Eberl 2014a:325–327). This evolution started in the seventh century A.D. with hand-modeled motifs. Local potters pressed a finger or a simple tool into the flange to create a round or other geometric indentation. They repeated the same motif over and over again around the entire flange. Since they incised motifs individually, each indentation varied from the next. At the beginning of the eighth century A.D., potters started to use stamps like the one found at Nacimiento (inset in Figure 6.10). Made of fired ceramic, this stamp is slightly thicker than and less than half the length of a pencil. It has a star-shaped decoration on one end. Actual ceramic vessels with similar motifs are attested in the Petexbatún region (for example, motif 229 in Foias and Bishop 2013:401–410). With the stamps, local potters could standardize the appearance of a motif and create strings of identical impressions.

The motifs themselves changed during the Late Classic. During the seventh century, Chaquiste Impressed motifs were geometric with a preponderance of round impressions and meandering swirls (Figure 6.10). A century later, the stamped motifs were often recognizable by the standards of Maya writing and iconography. They included the *ajaw* glyph and the owl symbol.[3] The motifs on Chaquiste Impressed bowls reflected wider iconographic changes because they also appeared on other media and in other forms of decoration; for example, on painted ceramic plates and as modeled figurines. After A.D. 700, Tikal vessels began to show palace scenes with nobles seated on throne-benches (Coggins 1975:500–501). In the more elaborate examples, paraphernalia like pillows, mirrors, and food containers surround the noble who is receiving visitors or being

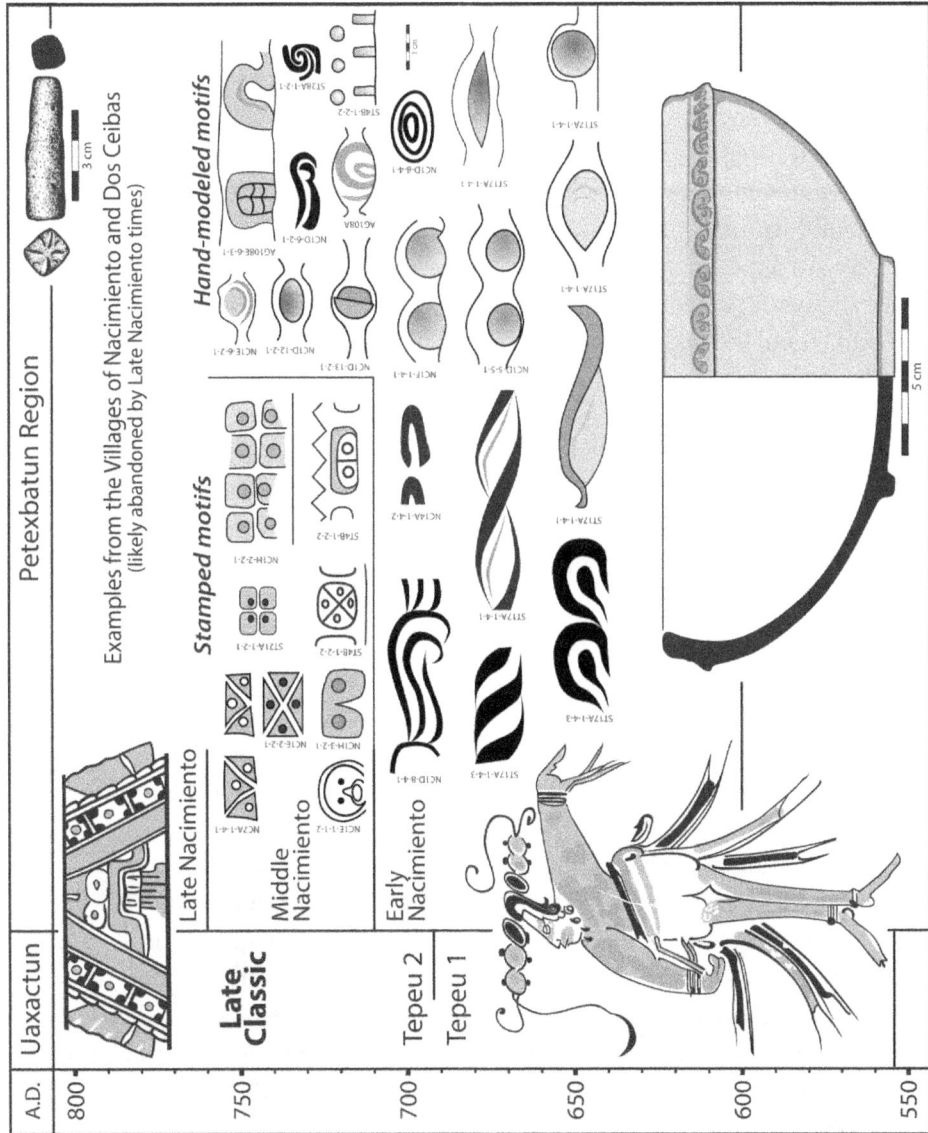

Figure 6.10. Chronological change in ceramic motifs on Chaquiste Impressed bowls from the Petexbatún region. *Insets: Lower right* shows a complete Chaquiste Impressed bowl with owl stamps on its flange (based on Foias and Bishop 2013:191 Figure 7.31b). *Upper right* is a ceramic stamp from Nacimiento. *Upper left* is a Tlaloc motif flanked by oblique bands of K'an crosses and a winglike element from a Tepeu 2 bowl from Uaxactun (based on Smith 1955:Figure 63a7). *Lower left* is a dancer from a Tepeu 1 polychrome tripod plate from Uaxactun (based on Smith 1932:Plate 2).

entertained by dwarves, musicians, and courtiers (for example, Figures 1.3 and 3.4). Painted throne scenes adorn eighth-century polychrome plates at Nacimiento and Dos Ceibas (Eberl 2014a:327 Figure 11.4).

Chaquiste Impressed bowls occur widely in the Petexbatún region, including at Nacimiento and Dos Ceibas (Figure 1.5; Foias and Bishop 2013:401–410). The ancient villagers very likely produced the bowls themselves. In addition to the stamp, I found a potential pottery workshop in Group Chispa at Nacimiento (Eberl 2014a:158–159, 292–296). The paste of Chaquiste Impressed vessels is very similar to local clays. INAA analysis of samples from the entire Petexbatún region revealed a diverse chemical composition consistent with local production (Foias and Bishop 2013:343–344). Representations of *ajaw* and owl vary stylistically but maintain the characteristics of examples found in Maya writing and iconography (Figures 6.6–6.9). *Ajaw* is rendered as a stylized face with circles for eyes and mouth, while the nose is reduced to a vertical stroke or dot (Figure 6.6). The owl appears on Chaquiste Impressed bowls as a rounded rectangular frame with two round eyes separated by a stylized feather horn (Figure 6.8). These stylistic variations demonstrate that local potters were well acquainted with ajaw and owl in Maya art and writing. They chose not to copy them exactly but to modify them and presumably to attach their own meanings to them.

Ajaw and owl denote the social hierarchy and divine ruler-centric ideology of Classic Maya culture. These underlying structures emerged with the first divine rulers in the first centuries A.D. (Chapter 1). Even though they persisted for centuries their material expressions appeared in the rural villages of Nacimiento and Dos Ceibas only during the eighth century A.D. Potters adorned local Chaquiste Impressed bowls with geometric motifs during the earlier part of the Late Classic and added the *ajaw* and owl only toward the end of the Late Classic. This late adoption suggests that royal elites and villagers interacted to varying degrees and intensities over the course of the Late Classic.

Inventions are vehicles for negotiating meaning in society. For the Petexbatún Maya, the new material forms alter the previous standards for comparison and entanglement. *Ajaw* and owl are no longer embedded in complex texts or scenes but are repeated in endless identical strings. Now, same compares with same. Instead of being legible, these symbols become logos and their effectiveness rests on repetition. Their entanglement similarly changes. Maya rulers, their practices, and their symbols become more accessible during the Late Classic. The villagers of Nacimiento and Dos

Ceibas begin to build palace-like three-room structures that encourage self-presentation (Figure 3.8) and to replicate royal symbols in their ornaments (Figure 6.1). At the same time, stratification increases in Nacimiento and Dos Ceibas, and local leaders emerge (Figure 3.7). The circulation of *ajaw* and owl on Chaquiste Impressed bowls and other objects make these symbols accessible to the collective. Their novelty initiates and requires an awareness of where these symbols appeared before and where they appear now. By changing comparison and entanglement, the new material forms propel public discourse about their meaning.

## Rulership and Authority

Maya rulership is an attractor, a defining structure, of Classic Maya society. In Chapters 5 and 6, I have outlined both its importance and also how it changed at the end of the Late Classic. Over the course of several generations, royal dynasties ended, some like Dos Pilas abruptly with the exile of the last king, others like Tikal petering out with short-lived kinglets. Popularly labeled a mystery, the Maya Collapse has attracted wide attention and diverse explanations (Webster 2002). In the preceding chapters I linked my discussion of innovation to the downfall of Maya rulers or, more properly speaking, of Maya rulership as the defining structure of Classic Maya society. My data came principally from the Copan Valley and the Petexbatún region (Figures 1.7 and 1.5, respectively). Therefore, I cannot claim the comprehensive coverage required to explain the Maya Collapse on a broader level. Instead, I outline how innovation can explain this structural change. Three aspects come into play: invention, physical adoption, and discourse about meaning.

The material culture of Classic Maya society changed over the course of the seventh and eighth centuries A.D. I have discussed various inventions, ranging from new pottery forms with novel designs (for example, angled tripod plates showing enthroned rulers) to simplified versions of royal scepters (Figure 5.7) and ceramic bowls with new motifs (Figure 6.10). Comparable changes have been noted for eccentrics at Piedras Negras. From A.D. 550 to 620 (Balché phase), eccentrics have unidentifiable shapes, while in the Yaxche phase (A.D. 620–750) eccentrics relate to known Maya symbols and reproduce deities (Hruby 2007:81–82). Inventions likely arose throughout the Maya Lowlands but remain difficult to recognize in the archaeological record because chronologies often lack sufficient resolution (discussion in Demarest 2009). For the inventors, novelties fuse idea and matter, or schema and resource; they carry meaning and relate to key aspects of Classic Maya rulership. From the perspective of the Garden of Forking Paths (Figure 4.2), inventions realize previously impossible worlds.

Some of these inventions were adopted widely. For example, ceramics showing rulers and owls appeared in the central and southwestern lowlands during the eighth century A.D. Nonroyal Copanecos living throughout the Copan Valley adopted plain scepters, an adoption pattern that in many cases may have been obscured by the localized nature of archaeological investigations. Inventions spread in time and space and the key questions are, where did they originate, how fast did they spread, and how did they change along the way? Individuals evaluate inventions and integrate them into their lives at different times and in different ways (Figure 6.2). The *ajaw* glyph possibly transformed similarly after the end of the Classic period. Comparable faces—now reduced to three simple dots—appear on Post-classic incense burners from the Maya Highlands and on modern Lacandon god pots as well as rubber figures (see Wauchope 1948 for the former, and Davis 1978:72–84, 132–159; McGee 1990:49–53; and Palka 2014:188–189 for the latter). These examples suggest the Classic Maya glyph might have come to signal the authority of gods and ancestors in later times.

Adoption varies with economic, social, and political structures. The different manifestations of Maya rulership remain restricted to royal elites until the eighth century A.D., when nobles and commoners start to use them. In the Petexbatún hinterland, Nacimiento and Dos Ceibas villagers possibly adopted Chaquiste Impressed bowls differently (Figure 6.10). Chaquiste Impressed sherds with geometric motifs ($N = 51$) are found in seventeen residential groups with an average construction volume of 166.6 $m^3 \pm 284.1$ $m^3$. Sherds with recognizable motifs like *ajaw* and owl ($N = 27$) come from ten larger residential groups (average construction volume of 207.7 $m^3 \pm 363.6$ $m^3$). Geometric motifs occur in a larger number of small residential groups than do *ajaw*, owl, and other recognizable motifs.

Innovation initiates a new public discourse. In the eye of the inventor, a novelty carries meanings and manifests structures, but these meanings are not obvious to others. Instead, inventions create new signifying and organizing practices. Their meaning for a society arises from a set of internal and external relationships, or what I call comparison and entanglement. I argue that these sets of relationships changed in Maya society. Over the course of the Late Classic, the structures bundled together into Maya rulership unraveled and various competing discourses emerged. According to Coggins (1975:397), Tikal's rulers created a new iconographic pottery style—including *ajaw* and owl—to express their shift toward a more militaristic and egocentric ideology (see Stone 1989:164). They and other rulers may have given this pottery to lesser nobles and even commoners to form alliances and attract followers (sensu LeCount 1999). Alternatively, non-elites like the Petexbatún villagers could have reworked previously royal ideologies to express diversification (sensu Brumfiel 2011) or to resist domination (sensu Joyce et al. 2001; Lohse 2007). In all these scenarios the underlying question is, how did Maya rulers lose control over the discourse that authorized their rulership? To simplify the collapse, how did royal rulership generalize to nonroyal authority? How, in the end, did the war owls detach themselves and swoop in?

## Footsteps Reveal Babel

In "City of Glass," novelist Paul Auster (2008) portrays a disguised detective who stalks Peter Stillman. Years earlier, Stillman had been convicted of confining his only son to a closet and depriving him of all human contact, in order to find out what words his son would utter and which language he would speak intrinsically. Stillman assumed that his son would manifest the original language of innocence, the language spoken in the Garden of Eden. Then, and only then, would a new age dawn: by casting all linguistic differences aside, humankind would re-create paradise and finish the Tower of Babel. Stillman hoped to recapture this language by imprisoning his son, but his experiment failed horribly. He was discovered and sent to jail. Upon Stillman's release, the detective trails him, trying to figure out his intentions. Every day, the old man wanders through the city, haltingly and without discernible purpose. He picks up flotsam that he inspects and sometimes bags. The detective discerns a pattern only when he traces Stillman's daily route on a map. Each day's wandering outlines a letter that constitutes a phrase: "The Tower of Babel."

Paul Auster's allegory captures how material forms enable a public discourse. To transmit and negotiate meaning, people employ words, gestures, and things. *Ajaw* and owl were stamped in textlike linear arrangements on vessel flanges. Other motifs may also have acquired meaning through the ways individuals interacted with the ceramic vessels. For example, a zigzag line often runs around the neck of Pantano Impressed jars (see, for example, Foias and Bishop 2013:184–187; Inomata et al. 2010:211, 267, 358–359).

When viewed from above (for example, when scooping water out of the jar), the zigzag line surrounding the round opening of the jar resembles the rays of the sun or of stars.

More so than words—after all, one can ask whether one understood this or that utterance correctly—material objects illustrate the problem of meaning. The motifs on Chaquiste Impressed vessels have counterparts in modern Maya textiles. Many scholars treat the modern serial motifs as interpretable symbols or even readable texts (as discussed in Holsbeke 2003; Chacón de Willemsen 2011; Knoke de Arathoon 2005; Morris 1987a:105–152, 1987b; Prechtel and Carlsen 1988; Rodas and Rodas Corzo 1938). Nonetheless, some argue that descriptive names like the Kaqchiquel *Xajol qol,* "dancing turkey," are misleading because "textile designs are not associated with any conventional symbolic or iconographic meaning" (Looper 2004:5; also Delgado 1963:114). The designs become meaningful only in specific contexts; for example, when they refer to folktales or myths.

Tangible forms convey intangible ideas in publicly visible ways. This is an ongoing process given that structures are complex rather than hardwired universals (sensu Lévi-Straussian binary opposites or Sperber's [1996] modules). Structures overlap and even contradict each other. In unique and ever-changing contexts, people must continually ask themselves which structures apply and how. Their interpretations differ but become partially deducible to others through the adoption of inventions. In this way, innovation offers vicarious transcendence.

# 7

## Names of the Owl

### Exploring Creativity and Innovation

Just like spoken words, music vanishes easily. Musicians grow feeble, and singers become hoarse. The origins of blues would be lost by now were it not for the efforts of Robert "Mack" McCormick after World War II. Mack drove endless miles across the American South and asked countless people about their songs, their music, their stories, and their customs. Over the course of decades, he surveyed 888 counties from the Atlantic coast deep into Texas. Based on his copious notes, Mack McCormick "realized that the county itself, as an organizing geographical principle, had some reality beyond a shape on the map, that it retained in some much-dismissed but not quite extinguished sense, the old contours of the premodern world, the world of the commons, how in one county you would have dozens of fiddle players, but in the very next county, none—there everyone played banjo" (Sullivan 2014:28).

The culture of each county emanates "outward from vortices where craft-making and art-making suddenly rise, under a confluence of various pressures, to higher levels" (Sullivan 2014:28). For the outsider, invisible structures collide tornado-like and shape human action into visible culture. Structures are ambient: ever-present and ingrained. Nonetheless, habits fail to capture how the very creation of culture demands constant innovation. Tornadoes blow away the sad, noxious particles that befoul the everydayness of ordinary life and urge humans to embark on a search for causes and cures (Percy 1966:25). In Houston's Fourth Ward, a black neighborhood, Mack McCormick found piano players practicing a particular style of rollicking barrelhouse called the Santa Fe style (after the Santa Fe Railroad whose tracks cut through the ward). A man called Peg Leg Will, who regularly played for passersby on the porch of an Italian grocery store, invented the style in the early 1900s (Hall 2002:117). Other musicians would listen, hop on their pianos, and imitate Peg Leg Will. In short order they invented their own variations, which piano players elsewhere picked up and used to define the barrelhouse style of a different neighborhood.

Peg Leg Will exemplifies the challenge of habit-based models of society to explain change. Ingrained daily practices—Bourdieu's (1977, 1990) habitus and Giddens's (1984) routinization—tie structures to individual behavior but leave unanswered the question of how humans shake up their habits. I argue that culture resembles less a tornado than the game Twister, in which players connect colored circles—structures—with their limbs in unusual ways. I introduce change from two perspectives. Subjectively, humans are aware of their own behavior and their own habits. I model their ability to change and be creative on a symbolic approach that involves metaphor and metonymy. Objectively, the spatial and temporal context— space-time, in short—constrains and enables daily practices. Innovations not only manifest human creativity but also are ways in which humans modify space-time.

## Bedeviled Tasmanians

For humans, social learning occurs by observing the most skilled individuals in their group. Their learning opportunities depend on the available pool of social learners. For Henrich, culture evolves due to incomplete copying. Individuals can never copy something perfectly: "Even if the inferential machinery of human minds were perfect, the transmission process would still result in a range of errors because behavioral (phenotypic) displays provide learners with incomplete information from which to mentally reconstruct the underlying skill, strategies, and abilities" (Henrich 2004:200). Henrich then adapts the Price equation to model selective transmission and incomplete inference among Tasmanians, the people with the simplest known set of tools.

Humans arrived in Tasmania between thirty-four thousand and twelve thousand years ago. Rising sea levels cut them off until the Dutch explorer Abel Tasman arrived in A.D. 1642 (Robson 1983). By then, the Tasmanians (or Parlevars) were down to twenty-four tools, including spears, rocks, and throwing clubs (Henrich 2004:198). They had fewer tools than did their Late Pleistocene ancestors or their contemporary Australian neighbors. Henrich explains the maladaptive loss of technologies as defective transmission, or what has become known as the Tasmanian effect (see for example, Boyd and Richerson 2005:272; Marquet et al. 2012; Vaesen et al. 2016). For Henrich (2004), social learning can be reduced to the incomplete copying of observable behaviors (see also Allen 1989; Henrich's approach ignores the possibility that societies might give up practices and associated technologies voluntarily; for this perspective see Jones 1977; Politis 2007:339). He assumes that behaviors flow from intangible cognitive capacities, much like phenotypes originate with genotypes. Imitation of behaviors therefore provides only indirect clues about mental skills, strategies, and abilities. The Tasmanian effect comes from incomplete and uncompletable information.

Is social learning among humans incomplete? Henrich (2004) assumes that skills determine behavior in the same way genes determine characteristics and features, and that they are therefore inaccessible to an observer. This hypothesis is flawed, as language illustrates. Speech and writing express the vocabulary and grammar of language (Chapter 2). The former are observable while the latter are inaccessibly memorized. When humans speak and write, they often slur words, talk fast, or scribble. Does this mean that listeners or readers are unable to understand them? No, because information is presented redundantly. In a noisy environment, individuals can read lips or ask people to repeat themselves. More importantly, they know the language and can reconstruct garbled pieces from their knowledge of vocabulary and grammar. Language depends on communication; speaking and writing realize and reinforce linguistic rules. I assume a similar mutuality between cognitive abilities and behavior. Cognition is not a prerequisite to behavior. Within the structuralist framework of society, structure and practice are mutually dependent. In the case of the Tasmanians, toolmaking expresses and reproduces tool-related skills.

For westerners imitating or copying reeks of plagiarism not innovation, but a closer look reveals underlying complexity (for example, Lethem 2007; Meskell 2005:53). The Chinese phrase *lín mó* refers to the copying of masters. *Lín* (临) means "faithful reproduction" and *mó* (摹) "tracing" (Sirén 1963:151). Through observation and imitation, artists capture the spirit (*lín*) and structure (*mó*) of a master's original work (Yuedi 2011:100). Novices learn by imitating and they continue to call their expert work imitation out of respect for the master who guided or inspired them (Sirén 1963:151). *Lín mó* also implies a search for aesthetic ideals. "Tai Wên-chin of the present [Ming] dynasty copied famous works by painters of the Sung period, he grasped their secrets and came really very close to the truth. He imitated Huang Tzǔ-chiu and Wang Shu-ming and surpassed them both" (sixteenth-century writer and poet Tu Lung quoted in Sirén 1963:151). The seventeenth-century artist T'ang Chih-ch'i maintained that "copying and tracing is very easy, while it is very difficult to transmit the soul and life (of a picture)" (Sirén 1963:151–152).

The Maya concept of *costumbre* similarly entails faithful imitation. It refers to local customs about how things should be done. Among Mopan Maya, ancestors—*ti mam, ti chich;* or "our grandfathers, our grandmothers"—established these laws, and everybody is expected to show respect (*tzik*) and to obey *costumbre* (*tz'okes*; Danziger 2013). The verb *tz'okes,* "to obey, believe," relates to ancient Maya *tz'ak,* "to put in order" (Eberl 2015) and literally means "to make complete." *Costumbre* requires enacting an ancestrally given order. In my view this does not mean mindless imitation or unquestioned acceptance (contra Danziger 2013). As a causative, *tz'okes* requires agency. It allows for innovation as long as people couch their argument as an extension of *costumbre* (for examples see Danziger 2013:258; Shoaps 2009). The challenge is to balance structural maintenance with novel ideas.

Is social learning among humans incompletable? Henrich (2004:201) sees social learning as noisy and biased because copiers never accurately replicate skills and because they tend to be less skilled than the master they are imitating. Errors inevitably accumulate and knowledge can never be fully transmitted. In fact, however, so-called autonomous learning is surprisingly efficient (Lancy 2015:210, 283–292). Maya novices learn to operate on their own simply by observing experienced weavers (Nash 1958:26–27; also Lancy 2015:267–278). Imitation plays a crucial role in children's learning (Lancy 2015:171, 180). Child psychologists have observed that "children accompanied their assistance [to adults] by relevant verbalizations and by evidence that they knew the goals of the tasks, even adding appropriate behaviors not modeled by the adults" (Rheingold 1982:114). Infant cognition studies point to a "child-initiated acquisition of culture rather than an adult-directed 'transfer of cultural knowledge'" (Lancy 2015:209).

Learning is a symbolic process that encourages not only repetition but also creativity. The rabbit-duck illusion (Figure 2.1) illustrates how individuals perceive only one animal (epitomizing a world of meaning) in a given moment. Instead of being stuck in that interpretation, however, most are capable of switching to the other animal. Toggling back and forth requires meta-awareness of different animals or worlds. Through metonymy and metaphor, humans create structured relationships for incomplete or even incoherent assemblages or bricolage. In other words, humans organize chaos and thus complete the inherently incomplete. This is a process that leads toward but never arrives at finality. Even very specific schemata, like those for making tools, are cognitively not unique. Organizational principles apply to different schemata and are socially shared (see Chapter 2). The culture-specific organization of knowledge and social interaction allows students to fully apprehend skills and associated behaviors. My model of social learning inverts Henrich's (2004) and envisions not a falling short of unattainable perfection but instead an incessant movement toward order (see also Sperber 1996:100–106). Instead of falling from Eden, individuals struggle like Prometheus.

## The Curious Case of Humankind's First Tooth Implants

Innovation distinguishes western industrial societies. Its promise of ever-growing material abundance has elevated progress to a global paradigm. From the western perspective, the technological inferiority of premodern and nonwestern societies calls into question whether they are even capable of innovating. Correspondingly, nonwestern Others are often understood as driven by traditions and habits. *Costumbre,* or ancestral and unchangeable customs, supposedly impeded Maya from accepting novel agricultural practices or new craft products (Reina 1963). From a nonwestern perspective, many societies have felt the need to modernize "and become more secular and rational, relegating their premodern past to museums, or, in the case of religion, to private life" (Mishra 2014:vii). Achievements of past civilizations are not recognized as showing evolution but are downplayed as involution, or "progressive complication, variety within uniformity, virtuosity within monotony" (Goldenweiser 1936:103). Their inventions are assumed only to rearrange elements—repeating, combining, and recombining them however artfully—within unchanging overall schemas.

Progress as a conceptual framework distorts the study of nonwestern and premodern innovation. It focuses on inventions that are recognizable to western eyes while discarding everything else as mysteries or superstitions. It motivates upstreaming by declaring ancient cases as forerunners of modern inventions. Humankind's first tooth implants exemplify these two biases. Modern orthodontists claim that the ancient Maya were the first people to extract teeth and replace them with replicas that successfully bonded with the patient's bone (for example, Abraham 2014:50; Anusavice et al. 2013:7; Babbush et al. 2011:5; Balaji 2007:302; Misch 2007:26; Ratner 2013:xli; Ring 1985:17). The challenges of this procedure are considerable. Dentists require skills and proper equipment (in the case of the Classic

Maya this meant no metal tools). The patient has to manage high levels of pain and overcome infections. Western dentists started to tackle these obstacles in the nineteenth century and implanted teeth successfully only in the second half of the twentieth century. The ancient Maya are said to have preceded them by at least a millennium.

The Classic Maya are well known for their dental skills. They modified teeth by filing them or by inserting inlays made of jade and other materials (Cifuentes Aguirre 1963; Danforth et al. 1997; López Olivares 1997; Tiesler Blos 1999). Instead of preventing tooth decay or re-enabling tooth use, these modifications were decorative and motivated by aesthetic appeal and embodiment of gods. For example, the Sun God is shown with one T-shaped tooth protruding from his mouth (Houston et al. 2006:147). Presumably desiring to look like him, some Maya had their incisors filed into a T-shape (for example, Uaxactun Burial A34; Cifuentes Aguirre 1963:156 Figura 5c). Tooth implants go beyond ornamental dentistry, though.

At the end of the nineteenth century, John G. Owen excavated several burials at the Classic Maya capital of Copan (Gordon 1896:26–28). Dentist R. R. Andrews (1893) studied the skeletons and noted various filed and inlaid teeth. The lower jaw of skeleton no. 8 stood out for a lower incisor made from some dark stone. The accompanying drawing shows a slightly curved cylinder with a rounded bottom (916). Calculus had built up on the stone tooth, showing "that it had been worn for some time during life" (917). The presence of calculus would be compelling evidence for a successful implant except it is not clear that tartar would form on a stone tooth (Janice Jun, personal communication, March 8, 2016). Unfortunately, the tooth was lost during the twentieth century and is no longer available for study (Bobbio 1972:2). Skeleton no. 8 had no grave goods to enable dating, but all surrounding burials date to the Late Classic (Longyear 1952:35–37).

The second case comes from Playa de los Muertos in Honduras (Figure 1.2). Dorothy Popenoe (1934) excavated a number of burials there. In 1931, she found the fragment of a human jaw with three false teeth, triangular shell replicas replacing three incisors (Figure 7.1). The shells have horizontal furrows that imitate the enamel hypoplasia of adjacent teeth. Dentist Amadeo Bobbio (1972) studied the jaw and reported that the shell teeth are extremely firmly anchored in the bone. X-rays allowed him to observe that "the bone surrounding all implants was radiographically similar to that which would surround a blade implant of today" (Bobbio 1972:4). The shell implants align beautifully with the wall of the root socket. The contiguous interface suggested to Bobbio that the implants fused with the bone.

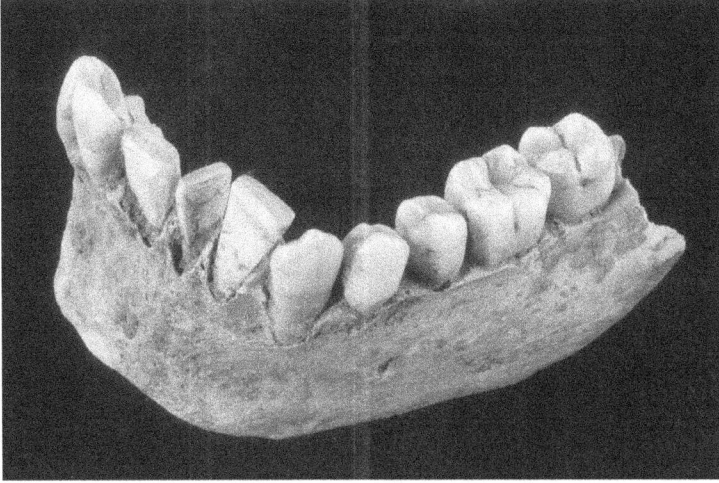

Figure 7.1. Lower jaw with three shell teeth implants, found at Playa de los Muertos. (© President and Fellows of Harvard College, Peabody Museum of Archaeology and Ethnology, PM# 33-19-20/254.0 [digital file #80110075].)

The jaw fragment is assumed to date to the seventh century A.D. (Bobbio 1972:4), which led Bobbio to conclude that these shell implants are "the earliest authentic endosseous alloplastic implants which have yet been discovered" (5).

Though dentists cite it widely, Bobbio's conclusion remains tenuous. Tooth extraction and implantation carry a high risk of infection and it is unclear whether the ancient Maya could have kept such wounds sterile (Janice Jun, personal communication). Osseointegration and remodeling of bone could occur only in patients who survived the procedure. Bobbio's X-rays show a space between the tip of the implants and the bottom of the tooth sockets. Bone would fill this space in approximately six months (Janice Jun, personal communication). If the shell teeth were implanted during life, the patient must have died shortly after. During her examination of the jaw, physical anthropologist Vera Tiesler noted unusually large gaps between the shell teeth (personal communication, March 12, 2016). Close-up photos show a red powdery substance between the roots of the shell teeth and the cortical bone. Because this substance would wear off in a living patient, its presence suggests that the teeth were implanted after death.

The Playa de los Muertos jaw is comparable to a skull mask from Xuenkal (Tiesler Blos et al. 2010:372). A robust young or middle-aged male was buried wearing this mask on his chest. The nonlocal strontium signature of the skull suggests a sacrificed war captive (375). Holes in the mandible and the skull allowed the mask to be tied onto the body and worn as an ornament. Just as this mask was fitted after death, "During its use-life, some of the original teeth must have fallen out of their sockets and at least two incisors were replaced with teeth of other individuals, whose roots were filed to fit into the bony tooth sockets" (372).

Ancient Maya dentistry was highly developed. Beyond the filing of teeth and insertion of inlays during life, fake and real teeth were implanted—probably not during life but definitely after death. These Maya implants attest to considerable medical knowledge and skill but also expose the limits of innovation. They were unique at their find locations and were found widely apart. The lack of continuity within Classic Maya culture suggests implants might have been unique inventions that failed to catch on with society at large ("isolated anomalies" in Hegmon and Kulow 2005:329).

Evolutionary approaches to innovation assume that inventions are transmitted across time and space. Tooth implants were known outside the Maya area. At Teotihuacan, sacrificial victims were found with necklaces made of artificial human teeth (Cabrera Castro et al. 1991:80; Sugiyama and López Luján 2007:130, 144). The recently excavated "Woman from Tlailotlacan" had an incisor made of greenstone that likely came from the Maya area (Instituto Nacional de Antropología 2016). It remains unclear whether only the raw greenstone or the finished tooth was exported to Teotihuacan. Since the burial dates to A.D. 350–400, its implant is hundreds of years earlier than the previously discussed examples. The cases from Teotihuacan assert the transcendence of tooth implants within Mesoamerica. Different cultures seem to have adopted or independently invented them over the course of several centuries.

The medical literature goes beyond precolumbian Mesoamerica by claiming the Maya examples as forerunners of modern western achievements. Their evolutionary framework remains unproven as long as a link to the present is missing (compare the curing of scurvy with *jucoystle* cactus fruits described in Chapter 4; Frankenburg 2009:73–75). De-othering coerces the nonwestern and premodern pasts into the western discourse on progress. Ancient people like the Classic Maya are transformed into forbears who (unbeknownst to themselves) were modern and revolutionary. Progress is no longer a recent trend but is traced back hundreds and thousands of years. In extending the idea of progress to the past, its forward momentum is intensified (Tanpınar 2014:314).

I argue that innovation has to be decoupled from progress. Ancient societies invented new products and services according to their individual cultural logics. Maya tooth implants were likely not functional but part of elaborate funerary rituals. Inventions can also die out without cross-fertilizing and without feeding into western traditions. Archaeology offers the spatial and temporal coverage to reconstruct waves of innovation. Premodern and nonwestern cultures should not be funneled into the western narrative, but should remain as others. Their failed inventions are as important as their successful ones for elucidating their cultural logic and social wants.

## Grabbing Souls from the Earth God

For a person to have free will, he or she must be able to act against external constraints. "If we choose to remain at rest, we may; if we choose to move, we also may" (Hume 1894:95). Phrased in the terms of structuralism, the question becomes, How can agents act against structures while preserving their ability to maintain structures? Previous structuralist models of society have left little room for free will. In his model of society, Lévi-Strauss (1969:xxxiii) equates prescriptions with preferences. For him, individuals are unable to distinguish between rule and personal choice, thus (con)fusing the model of reality with the reality of the model (Bourdieu 1990:38–39). The "awareness of the rule inflicts choices ever so little in the prescribed direction" (Lévi-Strauss 1969:xxxiii). Lévi-Strauss's model of society is probabilistic, which leaves his concept of agency undertheorized: Individuals make free choices but the cumulative choices of all members of society confirm existing structures. Poststructuralist models assume that individuals unconsciously and automatically replicate structures by invoking habits and routines. Nonetheless, if knowledge were entirely tacit, individuals would find it difficult to act against structures in the way Hume's statement demands.

Structure-based models of society differentiate socially shared structures from individual agency. Bourdieu's habitus (1977) and Giddens's structure (1984) are both internalized as tacit knowledge that guides the behavior of individuals and, external to the individual, as knowledge shared by a society. A key problem is the autonomy of structures. Language, in Ferdinand de Saussure's sense of *langue,* exemplifies how structure internalizes externalities. Unlike Saussure (1966:19), who saw language as both instrument and product of speech, Bourdieu and Giddens see structure as preceding agency. "'Communciation [*sic*] of consciousnesses' presupposes community of 'unconsciouses' (that is, linguistic and cultural competences)" (Bourdieu 1990:58). Structure is marked by the "absence of the subject" (Giddens 1984:25), a concept that comes from literary theory (Barthes 2007:35–36; Carroll 1978; Derrida 1976:69; 2011:79). To explain it, Jacques Derrida (2011:79) writes, "I see a particular person by the window." Readers of this sentence are removed in time and space from the event. Without actually witnessing someone by a window, they imagine Derrida seeing this person and understand what he intends to say. Discourse tolerates the absence of shared perceptions and correspondingly the absence of a perceiving subject. For Giddens (1984) this absence implies an autonomous structure. While I agree with the separation of individual and structure, I do not think that these structures are necessarily tacit. In my dialectical model (Chapter 2), individuals became aware of structures by switching back and forth between them.

Modern Maya healers occupy the liminal space between individuals and social structures. Throughout the Maya area and Mesoamerica, traditional medicine interweaves with moral norms, religious rituals, and social concepts. Healers address not only physical well-being but also emotions, soul(s), and social relations. Bodily symptoms reflect the quality of the patient's social relations. Sicknesses are traced to witches who leave their signatures in the blood of their victims until a healer is called to hear them (Nash 1967:133). In highland Chiapas, curers read the pulse of their patients and are confident that the blood tells them everything: "If you strike your wife, it says so" (Groark 2008:442). Curers have unusual insight into physical and social processes. Modern Ch'ol Maya attribute to their healers and other powerful people two souls that allow them to speak to God and to heal the sick (Whittaker and Warkentin 1965:139). Soul loss causes sickness, the Ch'ol believe. Health returns only when the soul is freed from the earth gods who captured it. When a patient calls an old female healer, the healer responds: "Now I will go to the lord" (*wʌle mi kaj k majlel ba'an ajaw*) and asks for liquor to warm up (Whittaker and Warkentin 1965:143). After drinking it, she falls asleep and the patient soon sees her struggling. She fights with the earth lord to grab the soul and bring it back to the patient. For the Ch'ol, healers are able "to understand a little" (*i ts'ita' ña'tan*) and they know how to care for the world (*i kʌñʌtan pañimil*; Whittaker and Warkentin 1965:92). Ch'ol healers boast to their patients: "Because now there is no one who will guard you well. . . . I alone take good care of you" (93). Their ability to leave the known world and fight the earth god manifests the dialectical movement through which individuals form meta-awareness (Chapter 2).

Knowledge about knowledge reveals the fallacy of habits. Bourdieu (1990:53) argues that individuals plan future action "without any calculation" and in relation to an objective potentiality that "excludes all deliberation." His habitus is a world of already realized ends or (borrowing here from Husserl) a world with a permanent teleological character. Bourdieu (1990:53–54) justifies this assumption: "The regularities inherent in an arbitrary condition ('arbitrary' in Saussure's and Mauss' sense) tend to appear as necessary, even natural, since they are the basis of the schemes of perception and appreciation through which they are apprehended." Language (for Saussure 1966) and magic (for Mauss 1972) are arbitrary. From the perspective of formal logic, Bourdieu argues that arbitrary classification systems are necessary and sufficient for schemes of perception, thus linking both and making classifications appear natural or autonomous. In Chapter 4, I discuss the three basic modalities—deontic, alethic, and epistemic—and the corresponding understanding of structures as ultimate truths, rules without alternatives, or conditional statements, respectively. Bourdieu's interpretation follows the alethic or even deontic modality. I differ by pointing to the epistemic perspective. My dialectical approach links structure and individual in necessary but not sufficient relationships. A language provides the classification system to order perception, but it does not have to be the only source of classification because individuals can learn other languages or use nonlinguistic systems. In other words, the teleological character of structures is not permanent but context-dependent.

These three modalities describe different ways to analyze the relationship between structures and individuals. I assume that all individuals apply them to their personal decision-making. An Egyptian woman who must obey her husband can interpret this statement as an order, as a fact of life, or as commonsense. Her future decisions are correspondingly affected. If her husband is abusive, she can stay married either because she sees her union as God-given or because she depends on him, or she can seek a divorce. The three modalities outline the spectrum of her possible behaviors. These are not human categories. Individuals are not conformists nor creatures of habit nor innovators by nature. How they interpret and react to structures depends on the specific context in which they exist and may involve any one of the three modalities.

My critique of habit-based models of society does not lead me to contrast habit with innovation. Instead, I widen the understanding of agency

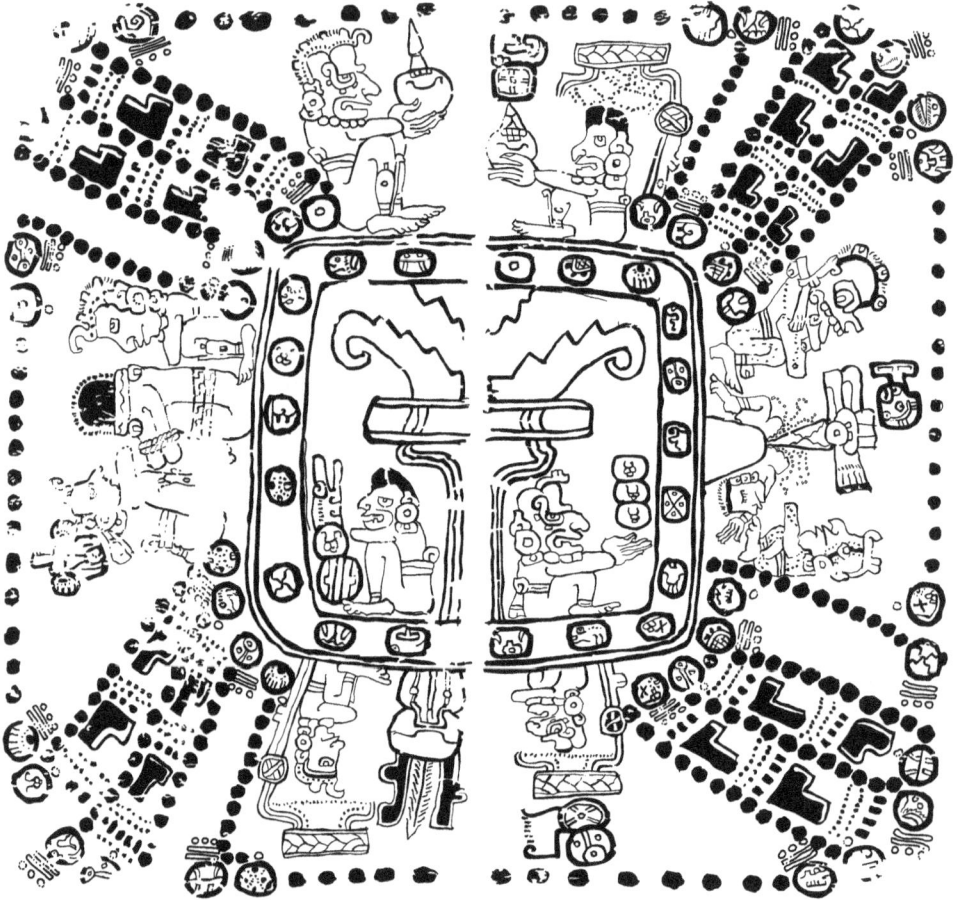

Figure 7.2. The Maya creation of space-time in the Madrid Codex (pp. 75–76). In the center, the twenty day signs of the Tzolk'iin encircle a creator couple with Itzamnaaj on the right. As the glyphs indicate, pairs of deities with sacrifices and offerings occupy the four sides that correspond to the cardinal directions. Black dots and numbered day signs weave the Tzolk'iin's 260 days around the gods in the shape of a Formé cross; in the corners, footsteps trace the Tzolk'iin and situate humankind in space and time.

and see habit as an important but not exclusive aspect thereof (Bargh et al. 1996). Social scientists estimate that up to 80 percent of all behaviors are habit-driven. For example, U.S. Americans who move between states continue to buy 40 percent of the same goods they knew from their earlier residences (Bronnenberg et al. 2012). Among Russian men, drinking vodka versus beer during their teenage years largely determines their preferred drink during their adult lives (Kueng and Yakovlev 2014). Some people do break their habits, though. They have an epistemic mindset and develop meta-awareness of the structures they are embedded in. Depending on their power relationships, they may become innovators like Zaynab al-Ghazali. My modality-based model of agency acknowledges their free will and ability to act against external constraints.

## Twelve Feet in Space-Time

Space-time is for Giddens (1979, 1984) a fixed backdrop for social practices. He defines structure as the "virtual order of differences" (Giddens 1979:3). In doing so, he adopts Ferdinand de Saussure's (1966) concept of language (*langue*) as a system of elements whose meaning derives from being exchangeable with or comparable to other elements. For Giddens, structure, like language, has different elements that entail only each other. It is closed, virtual, and autonomous from nonlinguistic aspects of the world. Therefore, structure is "out of time and space save its instantiations and co-ordination as memory traces" (Giddens 1984:25). Social practices are, as Nancy Munn (1992:106) counters Giddens, meaning-forming and meaningful processes "in which people ongoingly produce both themselves as spatiotemporal beings and the space-time of their wider world" (see also Munn 1983:280; 1986:10–11; Urry 1991). Giddens's shortsightedness stems in part from equating resources with sources of power (see Giddens 1979:92). This definition obscures the fact that resources are both context for and outcome of social practices. For example, a factory is the physical setting for economic production and a representation of the imbalance of power between factory owner and worker. Technological innovations show that Giddens's definition conflates two aspects. When Copan's Mak'an Chanal adopted the ballgame, he modified the material setting of his residential group and also made a statement about power in the Copan Valley. Therefore, I separate resource as form from resource as symbol. The latter elucidates power through the process of signification while the former leads to the context of social practices, that is, space-time.

The *winal*, or basic calendrical unit of twenty days, is attached to a Maya creation myth in which humans and gods create space-time (Figure 7.2). *Ti ma to ahac cab cuchie*, "Before the world had awakened" begins the myth, which continues: *ca hopi u ximbal t u ba, t u hunal* "then (s)he began to travel by him-/herself, alone" (modified after Bricker 2002:14). The Maya scribe Chilam Balam of Chumayel (*chilam*, "seer"; balam, "jaguar") wrote down these lines in the eighteenth century, wrestling to explain how time and space came into being (glyphic passages in the Dresden Codex 61 and 69 suggest that the preconquest Maya struggled similarly; Calloway 2009; Knowlton 2010:156). His story influenced by his forced conversion to Christianity, Chilam Balam conflates native beliefs with biblical dogma. In the beginning the world is chaotic, until a wanderer who turns out to be God, begins walking. Ancestors then arrive in the east, where the sun rises, and see God's footprint. They ask themselves who passed by and size up the footprint with their own feet. "This is the beginning," one of them says, steps into the print, and starts tracing God's journey. *Xoc lah cab oc lae, lahca oc,* "It counts the entire world, this footprint here [as does the] 12 Ok."

This enigmatic sentence holds the key to the Maya understanding of space-time. In it, the word *oc* appears twice. The first occurrence means "foot, footprint" and refers to the physical impression that the wandering God left behind. The second instance—*oc,* "foot"—is also a day in the ritual calendar of 260 days and combines here with the number 12 to form the date 12 Ok (colonial Yucatec Maya *oc* corresponds to "ok" in my translation). Every *winal* contains a total of twenty day signs. The numbers 1 through 13 attach consecutively to the day signs—11 Muluk comes before 12 Ok and then 13 Chuwen—for a total of 260 days (13 sets of 20 day signs). The entire sentence parallels space and time by making them sound almost identical. Only a *b* separates *lah cab oc* from *lahca oc*; that is, "the entire world's footprint" from "12 Ok." The two meanings of *oc* resonate with the verb *xoc* at the beginning of the sentence; *xoc* means both "to study, to read" a physical footprint and "to count" the day 12 Ok, or "Twelve Feet." God's footprint is the starting point for the spatial and temporal order of the world.

As part of the twenty days of the *winal,* Ok provides spatiotemporal orientation (see also Monaghan 1998). The Creation of the Winal myth aligns the twenty day signs in their proper order and explains their meaning, often based on puns and synonyms. For example, God creates light on day 6 Kib (*kib* means "candle") and animating breath on day 12 Ik' (*ik'* means "wind, breath"). Ritual specialists called *aj k'iin,* or "(s)he of the day," used explanations like this to divine the future (see Figure 4.4 for an *aj k'iin* at Xcalumkin). A Spanish report from 1579 mentions that the Maya consulted books to declare "the times when to plant and to harvest, to hunt and go to war" (translated after Garza 1983:86). Ok and the other days of the *winal* are not merely abstract calendrical concepts that allow humans to locate events. Knowing that something took place on day 12 Ok also enabled the *aj k'iin* to predict the character of the event and even its future consequences. The *aj k'iin* forecasted human destiny.

Human activities unfold in a specific spatial and temporal context, be it the seven-day week for westerners or the *winal* for the Maya. For most people, the spatiotemporal setting orders their activities. For example, westerners generally take it for granted that they work from Monday through Friday and have the weekend off. Whether the alarm clock rings on a Sunday or a Monday elicits very different reactions. Still half-asleep, most people don't have to consult the calendar to know whether they can turn over and continue to sleep or they have to get up. They are unconsciously aware of space-time and employ it to routinize their behavior. In this sense, space-time is fixed, as Giddens (1979, 1984) argues, and is a part of social practices.

The Creation of the Winal relates the habitual aspect of space-time to its constitution. Sociocultural practices "do not simply go on in or through time and space, but [they also] . . . constitute (create) the spacetime . . . in which they 'go on'" (Munn 1983:280). The myth tells of the human ancestors who stumble across God's footprint. After wondering whose footprint it could be, they step into the footprint and follow God. Instead of simply admiring God's order, the Maya ancestors trace God's journey and re-create space-time for themselves. As these wanderers journey, each step and each day reveals its meaning to them. That is, actors generate in and through their practices the meaning relations of space-time (Munn 1992:106).

The Maya Creation of the Winal makes it clear that not everybody has knowledge of space-time. Only sages like the *aj k'iin* have access to the hidden meaning of the twenty days of the *winal.* They are the ones who know the past, understand the present, and predict the future. Their meta-awareness reflects the unequal distribution of knowledge in society. Power relations influence access to knowledge, just as they do other resources. My argument circles back to Giddens's (1979:92) definition of resources as sources of power. I link the creation of space-time to knowledge, and knowledge to power. Unlike Giddens, who links resources and power directly, I argue that resources are filtered through human awareness and that power partially influences awareness.

## An Origin House Ends

This book opened with the emergence of Maya rulership around 100 B.C., and it closes with the downfall of Maya kings and queens a thousand years later. Myths frame this process. In the San Bartolo murals, the Maya ancestral couple emerges from a cave with food and water, the ingredients of civilized life (Figures 1.1 and 4.3). On Copan Stela 11, the last official king returns to the *way* portal and disappears into the otherworld (Figure 7.3). This event happened, as the accompanying text informs us, on the day 8 Ajaw, presumably in the year A.D. 820. Looking back at a reign that lasted several decades, King Yax Pasaj laments his fate: *jomoy Wiin-Te'-Naah,* "it ended the 'Origin House,'" where he and other Copan rulers obtained their authority and acceded to the throne. K'inich Yax K'uk' Mo', the founding father, and Yax Pasaj, the last in the lineage, depart. An ominous reference in the text to the obsidian-eyed, flint-eyed war deity Waxaklajuun Ubaaj Chan conjures dark times, unrest, and war. The San Bartolo murals and Copan Stela 11 offer stories not only of the rise and fall of Maya rulership, but also of the ways in which the ancient Maya made sense of their world. They highlight aspects like maize agriculture, writing, and weapons that become understandable for modern readers only if explained in the culture-specific classification of their world.

It is easy to overlook the vital importance of the Origin House's ending and other mythic stories because strange and droll facets abound. The San Bartolo cave rendering has a snake as tongue and stalactites as teeth, while cute hummingbirds flutter near its mouth. "The myth does not exist that is not the ever-renewed revelation of a reality, which so imbues the being, that he makes his behavior conform to it" (Leenhardt 1979:192). Myths enable inner speech. When people "think through" behavior and plan actions, they tend to translate amorphous possibilities into clear-cut positions and converse with these voices in their head (Luria 1961, 1966; Vygotsky 1962). In doing so, they draw on a culture-specific reservoir of characters and stories. These might be Disney characters and movies—what would Buzz Lightyear do in this situation?—or ancient Maya gods and their myths (Suskind 2014:221). Classic Maya nobles reenacted both consciously (see Chapter 2, Figure 2.8).

Myths express a cultural logic (Fischer 1999, 2001). At the same time, they remain stories, as many ethnographers learn: "One of my initial frustrations in working with [Yucatec Maya] midwives was that it was almost impossible to get them to talk about how they would handle cases other than the ones we were engaged in dealing with at just that time" (Jordan 1989:934). When pressed to reveal their schema or logic, midwives often misunderstood the question or retorted, "Pues, quién sabe?" (Well, who knows?) Sometimes the context aligned with the question. Walking by a

Figure 7.3. The downfall of Maya rulership: Yax Pasaj, the last official king of Copan, disappears into the otherworld on Copan Stela 11. (Based on private photos and Becker and Cheek 1983:492 Fig. M-27.)

house where a patient lived or remembering the case of a relative triggered a story. An inquiry into ruptured uteruses elicited a story about a woman—in the house over there—who almost died after oxytocin injections caused her uterus to rupture (Jordan 1989:935). These examples demonstrate that abstract knowledge is embedded contextually, which leads to the problem of representation (Chapter 4). I argue for the process of *différance* (Derrida 2011): instead of distilling the schema from the story, people oscillate continuously between the generalization and its unique manifestations.

The ongoing tension between story and schema offers a different perspective on culture change. Change is an integral part of the model of cultural logic, "but such change must be reconciled with preexisting cognitive schemas in a manner that allows for an intersubjective sense of cultural continuity, even—perhaps especially—in the face of dramatic externally induced modification" (Fischer 1999:479). In this perspective, change happens on the surface while the underlying logic remains the same. I maintain that structures change because the link between story and schema, reality and structure, remains continually contested.

Stories must be probed for meaning and their exegesis is never final. Creator god Itzamnaaj exemplifies changing interpretations. Classic Maya elites appropriated him as supreme god and god of rulers (Taube 1992:31–41). They show him just like a Maya ruler, seated on a throne-bench with petitioners kneeling in front of him (Figure 2.7). After the collapse of Maya rulership, Itzamnaaj survived, but with a twist. During a ceremony in the sixteenth century, an *aj k'iin,* "daykeeper," reportedly took a maize tamale, held it up to the sky, and addressed Itzamnaaj as *ki ahtepale, u yumi ka'ane, yan ti muyal, yan ti ka'ane,* or "our supreme god, lord of the sky, [who] is in the clouds, [who] is in the sky" (my translation based on Garza 1983:II:322 n. 1). The daykeeper then asked Itzamnaaj to provide his community with a good year of maize harvests. Clearly, early colonial Maya still revered Itzamnaaj as supreme god; however, they now saw him as supreme priest (Taube 1992:35). For example, Itzamnaaj served as patron of Ak'bal years, and a priest disguised himself as the god to conduct the corresponding new year's ceremony (Figure 7.4). After dedicating the New Eagle Tree in the north, the priest decapitated a turkey, scattered fifteen kernels of maize or incense, and placed offerings of deer meat as well as tamales with turkey meat in front of it (for a description of the colonial rituals see Tozzer 1941:139–149). Within the overall discourse of Itzamnaaj as high god, the emphasis shifted from supreme ruler in the Classic to supreme priest in the Postclassic.

Figure 7.4. Reinvented as the supreme priest during Postclassic times, the god Itzamnaaj offers a decapitated turkey alongside other gifts as part of the new year ceremony (bottom of Dresden Codex 28; based on photo in Förstemann 1880).

People search for order and look for conclusions as well as final accounts. Their daily realities however are messy and often at odds with their logical principles. Ever-oscillating *différance* explains not with periods and full stops but with commas, dashes, and ellipses.

## Imagining and Materializing Culture

Every September 14, the Catholic Church celebrates the Exaltation of the Holy Cross. The feast commemorates the finding of the cross on which Jesus Christ was supposedly crucified. Saint Helena, the mother of Roman Emperor Constantine, made the miraculous discovery in A.D. 326. For centuries, the feast was known as the Invention of the True Cross. Here, "invention" refers to Latin *invenire,* or "to find," in the sense of discovering something new as well as revealing something hidden. This wider definition of invention fits my structuralist approach to innovation. Instead of reducing it to a creative activity, I link invention to structures. I situate it in the tension between discovering and revealing a desired vision of society.

Innovation addresses the contingency of culture. Similar to terms like *community* or *fairness, culture* is an empty or floating signifier (Lévi-Strauss 1987:63). It means anything and everything. Dan Sperber argues that communication involves transformation of information. "The degree of transformation may vary between two extremes: duplication and total loss of information. Only those representations which are repeatedly communicated *and* minimally transformed in the process will end up belonging to the culture" (Sperber 1996:83; emphasis in the original).

Different people will understand innovation in different ways—not out of desperation but out of necessity. As social animals, humans require a shared culture (at a minimum, mutually understood norms of behavior) to reproduce themselves literally and metaphorically. They will never be identical and they remain unique individuals with divergent attitudes and expectations. Humans share names for things but differ in their interpretations of those things. These names are empty and *nomina nuda tenemos,* or "naked names are all we have" (Bernard of Cluny 1557:279; my translation). The term *culture* lubricates social interaction by appealing to transcendent commonalities while remaining vague about details. Culture materializes in discourses and is often taken for granted. Novel words and novel items implicitly ask listeners and onlookers to define where they stand. Innovation stimulates meta-awareness about the underlying issue of culture.

Culture also implies an abstract ideal, or what Niklas Luhmann (1981:378–379) calls a *Perfektionsbegriff.* People congregate under a believable image of a socially shared whole. Despite and because of their uniqueness, they imagine themselves to be similar. Due to the gap between a diverse reality and a harmonious image, people's vision of society is always a desired ideal to be fulfilled in the future. These visions are, as Giddens (1984:19) defines them, models of reality and provide the categories for understanding the world. At the same time, structures are likewise models for reality and serve as blueprints for individual behavior. To appropriate Geertz's (1966:8) phrase, structures give meaning to reality "by shaping themselves to it and by shaping it to themselves." This dialectical tendency toward isomorphism rules out change and assumes that structures are external to social conditions and states of self (Asad 1993:32). I argue that imagination intervenes between structures and reality. People interpret structures and behave according to their desired vision of reality. In Chapter 4, I visualize desire, structures, and reality as the Garden of Forking Paths (Figure 4.2). Social realities are complex and at any given moment multiple worlds coexist. People enact their desired vision of society and plan their actions to reach a specific goal world. Social structures go beyond models of and for reality.

To create culture, individual experiences "must be attached to material forms through which people can perceptually access" them (Urban 1996:245). These material forms may be myths or objects. They are shared across space among members of society and across time between generations, or at least they are believed to bridge space-time. They are imagined to be collectively shared in the past, present, and future. Culture requires the illusion of permanence and continuity. The reality is more complex. Structures overlap and contradict each other. Different status, unequal power, and splintered knowledge warp individuals' access to the material forms that underlie the public discourse. The process of innovation mirrors this social complexity. Inventions manifest alternative visions of culture (or what I call possible worlds), and by adopting them differently, members of society shape the public discourse. Innovation bridges social realities and desires.

## The Traps of Knowledge

Culture represents a continual struggle for meaning. Individuals rely on culture to understand and interpret their perceptions. Dreams exemplify intimate and unique experiences that nonetheless build on shared cultural frameworks (Hunt 1977; Urban 1996). In Chapter 6, I discussed the owl in ancient Maya culture and its associations with darkness, the otherworld, and war. I juxtapose these conceptions with medieval western ones. Writing at the end of the seventeenth century, Sor Juana Inés de la Cruz alludes to owls in her poem "The First Dream." Sor Juana describes her soul's voyage during a dream. Appropriate for the nightly setting, the owl appears "with sluggish flight and song, jarring on ear and even more on spirit" (Juana Inés de la Cruz 1988:172). As the bird of darkness, the owl poaches temples, hoping to "desecrate the brightly shining holy lamps perpetually lit, extinguishing, even defiling them" by drinking their oil (172). Sor Juana calls the owl Nyctimene, alluding to the daughter of the king of Lesbos. The king desired his ravishingly beautiful daughter so much that he raped her. Out of shame, Nyctimene fled into a forest. The goddess Minerva took pity on her and turned her into an owl, "which because of shame does not come out into the light but appears at night" (Apollodorus 2007:166). Repeating ancient Greek and Roman beliefs, Sor Juana perceives the ghostly owl in a way comparable to yet distinct from ancient Maya beliefs. Specific cultural references make her dream images intelligible to a European audience. At work is the process of enframing and classifying. Sor Juana selects identifiable elements from the bottomless dream imagery and puts owls into culturally relevant categories.

In their kaleidoscopic diversity, dreams exemplify the myriad perceptions humans have to make sense of. Culture simplifies the complex reality into categories and generalizes individual experiences. Humans' knowledge of culture allows them to leap from perception to category and to provide meaning. Yet, just as individual and society always remain separate, experiences cannot be reduced to a cultural category. The gap between perception and culture enables creativity and novel solutions; that is, inventions. Innovation exposes the limits and opportunities of cultural knowledge. The inherent tension between idea and reality materializes in an ongoing process. For Hegel (1821:xxiv, my translation), the traps of knowledge become obvious only in hindsight: "Only when dusk falls does Minerva's owl spread its wings and rise."

# Notes

Chapter 1. Flower Mountain Revealed: Innovation and Social Change in
Ancient Societies

1. V. Gordon Childe's "revolutions" have been debated with regard to their sequence, impact, and other characteristics (see Binford 1968; M. E. Smith 2009). For example, the transition from foraging to farming was complex and material culture like pottery and food processing predated the domestication of plants (e.g., Piperno et al. 2004; Wu et al. 2012). In the conclusion, I discuss how evolutionary frameworks distort the understanding of innovations in ancient societies.

2. The recent publication of his *Schwarze Hefte* (Black Notebooks) reveals Heidegger's profound disdain for modern technology (Heidegger 2014a, 2014b, 2014c).

3. The apostrophe in *aj tz'iib* refers to a glottalized *tz*. Glottalized consonants are a distinguishing feature of Classic and modern Mayan languages, and I indicate them with an apostrophe. A regular stop blocks the vocal tract until air from the lungs releases it. In glottalized stops, the glottis is closed; the larynx moves upward and pushes air into the vocal tract to release the stop. Throughout this book I use the apostrophe and other spelling conventions of Maya epigraphers (e.g., Coe and Van Stone 2005) instead of alternative colonial and linguistic conventions.

Chapter 2. Wings for Hummingbirds to Fly With: Creativity as a Play of Symbols

1. The rabbit-duck illusion goes back to an 1892 illustration in the German satire magazine *Fliegende Blätter*. The American psychologist Joseph Jastrow (1899:312) was the first scientist to point to the visual confusion. His article inspired Wittgenstein (2001:165); for an archaeological application see Hodder and Hutson (2003:18).

2. Husserl (1988:164–181) discusses the relationship between phenomenology and anthropology critically. He is especially concerned with presupposing an existing world or a world that could be in existence and calls for examining anthropology's a priori, transcendental foundations (Duranti 2010). "Once the inadequacy of the naïve attitude has been realized, this is the only possible way of establishing science in its genuine radicality—more precisely, the way to the only possible, radically grounded philosophy" (Husserl 1981:322).

3. The Classic Maya name of the god whom I call Itzamnaaj is debated. He is sometimes still identified as "God D" according to Schellhas's (1897, 1904) initial classification. The name glyph conflates various elements, including God N and the Principal Bird Deity (Boot 2008:17–20; Stone and Zender 2011:46–47). Early colonial sources attest to God D as Itzamna (Fewkes 1895; Seler 1887:227). Phonetic complements in the form of initial *'i* on

page 80 of the Codex Madrid and final *ma* on the Hauberg Stela support the *Itzam* reading. The T23 -*na* suffix in Itzamna first appears at the end of the Late Classic at Xcalumkin and recurs consistently in the Postclassic codices. Classic texts prefix T4 *naah*- and suffix T136 -*ji* (the relevant texts are Palenque Temple XIX Platform, south side, glyphs D7 and V1, and Quirigua Stela C, glyph B12). Some epigraphers interpret the -*ji* suffix as a phonetic complement for *Itzamnaaj,* while others see it as a reference to the Principal Bird Deity.

## Chapter 3. Itzamnaaj's Court: Creativity Embedded in Social Opportunity Structures

1. Scholars still debate the meaning of the *anaab* title (see, for example, Jackson 2013:31, 100; Stone 1995:183). I use the translation "stone carver" because of its recurrence in artists' signatures on carved monuments and the colonial Tzotzil word *'an,* "to hew, carve" (Laughlin 1988:136; compare colonial Tzeltal *anaghon,* "to carve wood"; Ara 1986:244).

2. Warfare, rituals, and other practices destroyed, fragmented, or mutilated many monuments (see, for example, Baker 1962; Marcus 1976:125–126; Martin 2000). Most hieroglyphic texts come from the Late Classic period. Therefore, nonroyal elites possibly were more numerous and more diverse during the Early Classic (Scott Hutson, personal communication, June 27, 2015), and Figure 3.5 may overestimate their Late Classic surge. Apart from the archaeologically attested growth of elites, text-internal reasons lead me to believe that the overall picture is valid. Maya rulers left numerous king lists cataloging the lords of a royal dynasty (for example, Copan Altar Q; also Eberl 2014b; Martin 1997). Comparable lists are absent among nonroyal Maya elites, with very few exceptions like Palenque's K'an Tok' Panel (Bernal Romero 2009). Nobles also lack anything equivalent to the count of rulers that expresses the position of rulers in their dynasty (Grube 1988; Riese 1984; Schele 1992). Instead, Late Classic texts of nonroyal elites provide parentage statements and lists of officeholders that are at best a few generations deep.

3. The architectural volume of residential architecture is a production-based measure of wealth (see, for example, Cheek 1986; Ringle and Andrews V 1988; Tourtellot 1988; Turner et al. 1981). Differential access to raw construction materials is less important among the Classic Maya than in many other societies because builders generally used locally available limestone (different varieties of limestone may have been emically important, however; Carmean et al. 2011). This leaves labor as the crucial differentiating factor. Energetic assessments of architecture serve to translate construction volumes into labor equivalents (Abrams 1994; Erasmus 1965; Morris et al. 1931). Wealthier households generally tend to be larger (that is, more people live in them) than less fortunate ones (Hayden and Cannon 1982; Netting 1982; Wilk 1983, 1991). The size differential occurs in part because family members wish to inherit land (Wilk and Rathje 1982) and because non-family members are added to the household as clients (Hendon 1991; McAnany 1993, 1995; Wilk and Rathje 1982). Wealthier people also tend to have better access to building materials.

## Chapter 4. Bleibt Alles Anders: Modeling Invention

1. A similar structural conflict characterizes medieval Christian Crusade songs (Hölzle 1980; Lewent 1905; Ortmann 1996; Ortmann and Ragotzky 1993; Wentzlaff-Eggebert 1960). In some of these lyric poems and songs troubadours ask whether a knight can at the same time court a lady and fight far away to liberate the Holy Land. In *Ich vant si âne huote* (I found her without a guard), a knight pleads with his lady to love him (Bekker

1978:25–32). She however rejects him: *got der wer iuch anderswâ, des ir an mich dâ gert,* "God may grant you in some other way what you desire from me" (my translation). Instead of seeking consummation, he should keep loving, *daz ir dest werder sint,* "that you are thereby of greater value" (Hasty 2006:146). For troubadour Albrecht von Johansdorf, serving lady and God are not contradictory goals. Instead, they imply a never-ending quest for self-improvement and thus complement each other.

2. I translate *chich* as "discourse" based on colonial Yucatec Maya. The Motul dictionary translates *chiich* as "theme, motto" of a sermon or a war cry (Arzápalo Marín 1995:240). It can be a narrative (*chiichtah,* "to tell tales") or a tacit rule (*chiich betah,* "to guide, to direct"; *chiichna,* "mode, order, manner"; dictionary entries from Arzápalo Marín 1995:240–241).

### Chapter 5. A Ruler Just Like Me: Status, Power, and Innovation

1. Palenque provides an interesting comparison to Copan. Many Gulf Coast *hachas* and yokes were found in late rooms and subdivisions of Palenque's Palace (Ruz Lhuillier 1952:50, 58, 65–66).

2. Carved monuments were reused not only at Copan but at many other Maya sites as well (see, for example, Martin 2000). At Tikal, a Preclassic sculpture was refitted with another fragment and placed in Late Classic fill while Early Classic Stela 31 was cached under the floor of Late Classic Structure 5D-33-2nd (Coe 1965:14; 1990:512–513). El Zacatal Stela 1 was resculpted, apparently in order to reuse its parts as round altars (Šprajc and Flores Esquivel 2010:3).

### Chapter 6. Stillman Wanders, Babel Rises: Innovation's Impact on Structures

1. Inequality possibly correlates with conspicuous consumption (Bricker et al. 2014). Personal ornaments from Nacimiento and Dos Ceibas are too rare to statistically prove a similar shift among Classic Maya non-elites. At stake is fungibility. In modern industrial societies, money serves as the universal medium of exchange and buys better education, better health, and political influence among other things (see, for example, Chetty, Hendren, Kline, and Saez 2014; Chetty, Hendren, Kline, Saez, and Turner 2014; Hagan and Peterson 1995; Wilson 1999). The use of money was much more limited in the Maya Lowlands (see, for example, Reents-Budet 2006). Therefore, it remains unclear how easily one good could be exchanged for another good or service (Papadopoulos and Urton 2012; Renfrew 2012).

2. New ceramic developments around A.D. 760 warrant splitting Tepeu 2 into two or more phases. While early and late Tepeu 2 have been recognized elsewhere (Foias 1996; Foias and Bishop 1997; Inomata 2010), the ceramic chronology of the central lowlands still awaits a comparable update. Therefore, I exclude Tikal vessels from the late Tepeu 2 period here.

3. Antonia Foias's catalog of Chaquiste Impressed stamps documents the graphic variability of the *ajaw* glyph and the owl symbol (Foias and Bishop 2013:401–410). Motifs 12, 56, 110, 136, 141, 146, 168, 172, 173, 175, 188, 189, 223, and 224 replicate *ajaw* faces; and motifs 34, 131, and 190 replicate owls.

# References Cited

Abercrombie, N., S. Hill, and B. S. Turner
1980     *The Dominant Ideology Thesis.* G. Allen & Unwin, London.

Abraham, C. M.
2014     A Brief Historical Perspective on Dental Implants, Their Surface Coatings and Treatments. *Open Dentistry Journal* 8 (Supplement 1):50–55.

Abrams, E. M.
1994     *How the Maya Built Their World: Energetics and Ancient Architecture.* University of Texas Press, Austin.

Abul-Magd, A. Y.
2002     Wealth Distribution in an Ancient Egyptian Society. *Physical Review E* 66:057104.

Acemoglu, D., and J. A. Robinson
2012     *Why Nations Fail: The Origins of Power, Prosperity, and Poverty.* Crown, New York.

Adler, A.
1931     . . . *What life Should Mean to You.* Little, Brown, Boston.

Ahmed, L.
1992     *Women and Gender in Islam: Historical Roots of a Modern Debate.* Yale University Press, New Haven, Connecticut.

Akerlof, G. A., and R. J. Shiller
2015     *Phishing for Phools: The Economics of Manipulation and Deception.* Princeton University Press, Princeton, New Jersey.

Akkeren, R. v.
2012     *Xibalba y el nacimiento del nuevo sol: una visión posclásica del colapso maya.* Editorial Piedra Santa, El Pedregal, Guatemala.

Aldenderfer, M.
1993     Ritual, Hierarchy, and Change in Foraging Societies. *Journal of Anthropological Archaeology* 12(1):1–40.

Allen, P. M.
1989     Modelling Innovation and Change. In *What's New? A Closer Look at the Process of Innovation,* edited by S. E. v. d. Leeuw and R. Torrence, pp. 258–280. One World Archaeology 14. Unwin Hyman, London.

Ambrosino, J. N.
2003     The Function of a Maya Palace at Yaxuna: A Contextual Approach. In *Maya Palaces and Elite Residences: An Interdisciplinary Approach,* edited by J. J. Christie, pp. 253–273. University of Texas Press, Austin.

Anderson, B. R.
1990     The Idea of Power in Javanese Culture. In *Language and Power: Exploring Political Cultures in Indonesia*, edited by B. R. Anderson, pp. 17–77. Cornell University Press, Ithaca, New York.

Anderson, J. R., and G. H. Bower
1973     *Human Associative Memory*. V. H. Winston, Washington, D.C.

Andres, C. R., C. Helmke, S. G. Morton, G. D. Wrobel, and J. J. González
2014     Contextualizing the Glyphic Texts of Tipan Chen Uitz, Cayo District, Belize. *Latin American Antiquity* 25(1):46–64.

Andrews, E. W., V
1990     The Early Ceramic History of the Lowland Maya. In *Vision and Revision in Maya Studies*, edited by F. S. Clancy and P. D. Harrison, pp. 1–19. University of New Mexico Press, Albuquerque.

Andrews, E. W., V, and B. W. Fash
1992     Continuity and Change in a Royal Maya Residential Complex at Copan. *Ancient Mesoamerica* 3:63–88.

Andrews, R. R.
1893     Prehistoric Crania from Central America. *International Dental Journal* 14(12):914–917.

Annis, M. B.
1985     Resistance and Change: Pottery Manufacture in Sardinia. *World Archaeology* 17(2):240–255.

Annis, S.
1987     *God and Production in a Guatemalan Town*. University of Texas Press, Austin.

Anusavice, K. J., C. Shen, and H. R. Rawls
2013     *Phillips' Science of Dental Materials*. 12th ed. Saunders, St. Louis, Missouri.

Aoyama, K.
2007     Elite Artists and Craft Producers in Classic Maya Society: Lithic Evidence from Aguateca, Guatemala. *Latin American Antiquity* 18(1):3–26.

Apollodorus
2007     *Apollodorus' Library and Hyginus' Fabulae: Two Handbooks of Greek mythology*. Translated by R. S. Smith and S. M. Trzaskoma. Hackett, Indianapolis, Indiana.

Appadurai, A. (editor)
1986     *The Social Life of Things: Commodities in Cultural Perspective*. Cambridge University Press, New York.
1990     Disjuncture and Difference in the Global Cultural Economy. *Public Culture* 2(2):1–24.

Ara, D. de
1986     *Vocabulario de lengua tzeldal según el orden de Copanabastla*. Universidad Nacional Autónoma de México, México, Méxicom D.F.

Arnold, D. E.
2005     Maya Blue and Palygorskite: A Second Possible Pre-Columbian Source. *Ancient Mesoamerica* 16(1):51–62.

Arnold, D. E., and B. F. Bohor

1975      Attapulgite and Maya Blue: An Ancient Mine Comes to Light. *Archaeology* 28(1):23–29.

Arnold, D. E., J. R. Branden, P. R. Williams, G. M. Feinman, and J. P. Brown

2008      The First Direct Evidence for the Production of Maya Blue: Rediscovery of a Technology. *Antiquity* 82(315):151–164.

Arzápalo Marín, R. (editor)

1987      *El ritual de los bacabes*. Instituto de Investigaciones Filológicas, Centro de Estudios Mayas, Universidad Nacional Autónoma de México, México, D.F.

1995      *Calepino de Motul: Diccionario maya–español*. Universidad Nacional Autónoma de México, Dirección General de Asuntos del Personal Académico e Instituto de Investigaciones Antropológicas, México, D.F.

Asad, T.

1993      *Genealogies of Religion: Disciplines and Reasons of Power in Christianity and Islam*. John Hopkins University Press, Baltimore, Maryland.

Ashmore, W., J. Yaeger, and C. Robin

2004      Commoner Sense: Late and Terminal Classic Social Strategies in the Xunantunich Area. In *The Terminal Classic in the Maya Lowlands: Collapse, Transition, and Transformation*, edited by A. A. Demarest, P. M. Rice, and D. S. Rice, pp. 302–323. University Press of Colorado, Boulder.

Auster, P.

2008      *The New York Trilogy*. Green Integer, Los Angeles.

Babbush, C. A., J. A. Hahn, J. T. Krauser, and J. L. Rosenlicht (editors)

2011      *Dental Implants: The Art and Science*. 2nd ed. Saunders, Maryland Heights, Missouri.

Baird, P., D. Cullinan, P. Landers, and L. Reardon

2016      Nudges for Child Support: Applying Behavioral Insights to Increase Collections. Electronic document, http://www.acf.hhs.gov/programs/opre/resource/nudges-for-child-support-applying-behavioral-insights-to-increase-collections, accessed February 24, 2016.

Baird, P., L. Reardon, D. Cullinan, D. McDermott, and P. Landers

2015      Reminders to Pay: Using Behavioral Economics to Increase Child Support Payments. Electronic document, http://www.acf.hhs.gov/programs/opre/resource/reminders-to-pay-using-behavioral-economics-to-increase-child-support-payments, accessed February 24, 2016.

Baker, R. G.

1962      Recarving and Alteration of Maya Monuments. *American Antiquity* 27(3):281–302.

Balaji, S. M.

2007      *Textbook of Oral and Maxillofacial Surgery*. Elsevier India, New Delhi.

Ball, J. W.

1993      Pottery, Potters, Palaces, and Polities: Some Socioeconomic and Political Implications of Late Classic Maya Ceramic Industries. In *Lowland Maya Civilization in the Eighth Century A.D.*, edited by J. A. Sabloff and J. S. Henderson, pp. 243–272. Dumbarton Oaks, Washington, D.C.

Baranowski, E.
2011        Documents from the 1602–1603 Sebastián Vizcaíno Expedition up the Califor-
            nia Coast. Electronic document, http://escholarship.org/uc/item/38295559,
            accessed January 14, 2014.
Bargh, J. A., M. Chen, and L. Burrows
1996        Automaticity of Social Behavior: Direct Effects of Trait Construct and Ste-
            reotype Activation on Action. *Journal of Personality and Social Psychology*
            71(2):230–244.
Barnett, H. G.
1953        *Innovation: The Basis of Cultural Change*. McGraw-Hill, New York.
Barrera Vásquez, A., and S. Rendón (editors)
1948        *El libro de los libros de Chilam Balam*. Fondo de Cultura Económica, México,
            D.F.
Barth, F.
1975        *Ritual and Knowledge among the Baktaman of New Guinea*. Yale University
            Press, New Haven, Connecticut.
Barthes, R.
2007        *Criticism and Truth*. Translated by K. Pilcher Keuneman. Continuum, Lon-
            don.
Bassie-Sweet, K., and N. A. Hopkins
2015        Ancient Thunderbolt and Meteor Deities. In *The Ch'ol Maya of Chiapas*, edited
            by K. Bassie-Sweet, pp. 123–144. University of Oklahoma Press, Norman.
Bateson, G.
1955        A Theory of Play and Fantasy: A Report on Theoretical Aspects of the Project
            of Study of the Role of the Paradoxes of Abstraction in Communication. *Psy-
            chiatric Research Reports* 2:39–51.
Baudez, C. F. (editor)
1983        *Introducción a la Arqueología e historia de Copán, Honduras*. Proyecto Arque-
            ológico Copán, Secretaría del Estado en el Despacho de Cultura y Turismo,
            Tegucigalpa, Honduras.
Baudez, C. F., and P. L. Mathews
1980        Capture and Sacrifice at Palenque. In *Tercera Mesa Redonda de Palenque, 1978
            (Part 1)*, edited by M. Greene Robertson and D. C. Jeffers, pp. 31–40. Palenque
            Round Table Series IV. Pre-Columbian Art Research Center, Palenque, Méxi-
            co.
Becker, M. J., and C. D. Cheek
1983        La estructura 10L-18. In *Introducción a la arqueología e historia de Copán,
            Honduras*, Vol. 2, edited by C. F. Baudez, pp. 381–500. Proyecto Arqueológico
            Copán, Secretaría del Estado en el Despacho de Cultura y Turismo, Teguci-
            galpa, Honduras.
Bekker, H.
1978        *The Poetry of Albrecht von Johansdorf*. Davis Medieval Texts and Studies 1. E.
            J. Brill, Leiden, The Netherlands.
Bell, A.
2002        Emulation and Empowerment: Material, Social, and Economic Dynamics in

Eighteenth- and Nineteenth-Century Virginia. *International Journal of Historical Archaeology* 6(4):253–298.

Bender Jørgensen, L.
2012        Writing Craftsmanship? Vocabularies and Notation Systems in the Transmission of Craft Knowledge. In *Archaeology and Apprenticeship: Body Knowledge, Identity, and Communities of Practice*, edited by W. Wendrich, pp. 240–254. University of Arizona Press, Tucson.

Benjamin, W.
1968        *Illuminations: Essays and Reflections*. Translated by H. Zohn. Harcourt, Brace & World, New York.
2006        *Das Kunstwerk im Zeitalter seiner technischen Reproduzierbarkeit*. Suhrkamp, Frankfurt am Main.

Berlin, H.
1963        The Palenque Triad. *Journal de la Société des Américanistes* 52(1):91–99.

Berlin, I.
1997        *The Proper Study of Mankind: An Anthology of Essays*. Chatto & Windus, London.
2013        *The Crooked Timber of Humanity: Chapters in the History of Ideas*. 2nd ed. Princeton University Press, Princeton, New Jersey.

Bernal Romero, G.
2009        *El tablero de K'an Tok. Una inscripción glífica maya del Grupo XVI de Palenque, Chiapas*. Serie Testimonios y Materiales Arqueológicos para el Estudio de la Cultura Maya 2. Universidad Nacional Autónoma de México, México, D.F.

Bernard of Cluny
1557        De Contemptu Mundi. In *Varia doctorum piorumque virorum, De corrupto Ecclesiæ statu, Poemata, Ante nostrum ætatem conscripta: ex quibus multa historica quoque utiliter, ac summa cum uoluptate cognosci possunt*, edited by M. Flacius, pp. 247–349. Ludouicus Lucius, Basle.

Bestor, T. C.
2006        *Kaiten-Zushi* and *Konbini*: Japanese Food Culture in the Age of Mechanical Reproduction. In *Fast Food/Slow Food: The Cultural Economy of the Global Food System*, edited by R. R. Wilk, pp. 115–130. Society for Economic Anthropology Monograph 24. AltaMira Press, Lanham. Maryland.

Bharati, Agehananda
1970        The Hindu Renaissance and Its Apologetic Patterns. *Journal of Asian Studies* 29(2):267–287.

Biceaga, V.
2010        *The Concept of Passivity in Husserl's Phenomenology*. Contributions to Phenomenology 60. Springer, Dordrecht, Germany.

Binford, L. R.
1968        Post-Pleistocene Adaptations. In *New Perspectives in Archeology*, edited by S. R. Binford and L. R. Binford, pp. 313–341. Aldine, Chicago.
1971        Mortuary Practices: Their Study and Their Potential. In *Approaches to the Social Dimensions of Mortuary Practices*, edited by J. A. Brown, pp. 6–29. Memoir 25. Society for American Archaeology, Washington, D.C.

Blanton, R. E.

1994    *Houses and Households: A Comparative Study*. Plenum Press, New York.

Bloch, M.

1991    Language, Anthropology, and Cognitive Science. *Man* 26(2):183–198.

Bloor, D.

1991    *Knowledge and Social Imagery*. 2nd ed. University of Chicago Press, Chicago.

Blum Schevill, M.

1997    Innovation and Change in Maya Cloth and Clothing. In *The Maya Textile Tradition*, edited by M. Blum Schevill, pp. 129–175. Harry N. Abrams, New York.

Bobbio, A.

1972    The First Endosseous Alloplastic Implant in the History of Man. *Bulletin of the History of Dentistry* 20:1–6.

Bollet, A. J.

2004    *Plagues & Poxes: The Impact of Human History on Epidemic Disease*. 2nd ed. Demos, New York.

Bolton, H. E. (editor)

1916    *Spanish Exploration in the Southwest, 1542–1706*. C. Scribner's Sons, New York.

Boot, E.

2008    At the Court of Itzam Nah Yax Kokaj Mut. Preliminary Iconographic and Epigraphic Analysis of a Late Classic Vessel. Electronic document, http://www.mayavase.com/God-D-Court-Vessel.pdf, accessed September 18, 2012.

Borges, J. L.

1956    El jardín de senderos que se bifurcan. In *Ficciones*, edited by J. L. Borges, pp. 97–111. Emecé Editores, Buenos Aires.

Bourdieu, P.

1977    *Outline of a Theory of Practice*. Cambridge University Press, Cambridge.

1983    Ökonomisches Kapital, kulturelles Kapital, soziales Kapital. In *Soziale Ungleichheiten*, edited by R. Kreckel, pp. 183–198. Soziale Welt Sonderheft 2. Otto Schartz & Co., Göttingen. Germany.

1990    *The Logic of Practice*. Translated by R. Nice. Stanford University Press, Stanford, California.

Bourgois, P.

1995    From Jíbaro to Crack Dealer: Confronting the Restructuring of Capitalism in El Barrio. In *Articulating Hidden Histories: Exploring the Influence of Eric R. Wolf*, edited by J. Schneider and R. Rapp, pp. 125–141. University of California Press, Berkeley.

Boyd, R., and P. J. Richerson

2005    *The Origin and Evolution of Cultures*. Oxford University Press, New York.

2006    Culture and the Evolution of the Human Social Instincts. In *Roots of Human Socialization: Culture, Cognition and Interaction*, edited by N. J. Einfield and S. C. Levinson, pp. 453–477. Berg, Oxford.

Boyd, R., P. J. Richerson, and J. Henrich
2011    The Cultural Niche: Why Social Learning Is Essential for Human Adaptation. *Proceedings of the National Academy of Sciences of the United States of America* 108(Supplement 2):10918–10925.

Bozarth, S. R., and T. H. Guderjan
2004    Biosilicate Analysis of Residue in Maya Dedicatory Cache Vessels from Blue Creek, Belize. *Journal of Archaeological Science* 31(2):205–215.

Brady, J. E., and D. Rissolo
2006    A Reappraisal of Ancient Maya Cave Mining. *Journal of Anthropological Research* 62(4):471–490.

Braswell, G. E. (editor)
2003    *The Maya and Teotihuacan: Reinterpreting Early Classic Interaction.* University of Texas Press, Austin.

Bray, W. M.
1977    Maya Metalwork and Its External Connections. In *Social Process in Maya Prehistory: Essays in Honour of Sir Eric Thompson*, edited by N. Hammond, pp. 365–403. Academic Press, London.

Bricker, J., R. Ramcharan, and J. Krimmel
2014    Signaling Status: The Impact of Relative Income on Household Consumption and Financial Decisions. Electronic document, http://www.federalreserve. gov/econresdata/feds/2014/files/201476pap.pdf, accessed September 25, 2014.

Bricker, V. R.
1995    Advances in Maya Epigraphy. *Annual Review of Anthropology* 24:215–235.
2002    The Mayan *Uinal* and the Garden of Eden. *Latin American Indian Literatures Journal* 18(1):1–20.

Bricker, V. R., and O. O. Orie
2014    Schwa in the Modern Yucatecan Languages and Orthographic Evidence of Its Presence in Colonial Yucatecan Maya, Colonial Chontal, and Precolumbian Maya Hieroglyphic Texts. *International Journal of American Linguistics* 80(2):175–207.

Broca, P.
1861    Remarques sur le siège de la faculté du langage articulé; suivies d'une observation d'aphémie (perte de la parole). *Bulletin de la Société Anatomique* 6:330–357.

Bronnenberg, B., J.-P. Dubé, and M. Gentzkow
2012    The Evolution of Brand Preferences: Evidence from Consumer Migration. *American Economic Review* 102(6):2472–2508.

Bruhns, K. O., and N. Hammond
1982    A Maya Metal-Worker's Tool from Belize. *Antiquity* 56(218):175–180.
1983    The Moho Cay Hammer: A Revised Opinion. *Antiquity* 57(220):136–137.

Brumfiel, E. M.
1987    Consumption and Politics at Aztec Huexotla. *American Anthropologist* 89(3):676–686.
2011    Technologies of Time: Calendrics and Commoners in Postclassic Mexico. *Ancient Mesoamerica* 22(1):53–70.

Bulkeley, K. (editor)
1996      *Among All These Dreamers: Essays on Dreaming and Modern Society*. State University of New York Press, Albany.

Butler, J.
1993      *Bodies That Matter: On the Discursive Limits of "Sex."* Routledge, New York.

Cabrera Castro, R., S. Sugiyama, and G. L. Cowgill
1991      Templo de Quetzalcoatl Project at Teotihuacan: A Preliminary Report. *Ancient Mesoamerica* 2(1):77–92.

Calloway, C.
2009      The Birth of the Number Twenty as Recorded in the Dresden Codex. Electronic document, http://www.ajchich1.blogspot.com/2009/05/birth-of-number-twenty-as-recorded-in.html, accessed January 26, 2014.

Canard, M.
2012      Da'wa. In *The Encyclopaedia of Islam*, edited by P. J. Bearman, T. Bianquis, C. E. Bosworth, E. J. v. Donzel, and W. P. Heinrichs. 2nd ed. Brill, Leiden, The Netherlands.

Cancian, F.
1967      Stratification and Risk-Taking: A Theory Tested on Agricultural Innovation. *American Sociological Review* 32(6):912–927.
1979      *The Innovator's Situation: Upper-Middle-Class Conservatism in Agricultural Communities*. Stanford University Press, Stanford, California.

Canuto, M. A., and W. L. Fash
2004      The Blind Spot: Where the Elite and Non-Elite Meet. In *Continuities and Changes in Maya Archaeology: Perspectives at the Millennium*, edited by C. W. Golden and G. Borgstede, pp. 51–75. Routledge, New York.

Canuto, M. A., and J. Yaeger (editors)
2000      *The Archaeology of Communities: A New World Perspective*. Routledge, London.

Carlsen, R. S., and M. Prechtel
1991      Flowering of the Dead: An Interpretation of Highland Maya Culture. *Man* 26(1):23–42.

Carmean, K., P. A. McAnany, and J. A. Sabloff
2011      People Who Lived in Stone Houses: Local Knowledge and Social Difference in the Classic Maya Puuc Region of Yucatan, Mexico. *Latin American Antiquity* 22(2):143–158.

Carraher, T. N., D. W. Carraher, and A. D. Schliemann
1985      Mathematics in the Streets and in Schools. *British Journal of Developmental Psychology* 3(1):21–29.

Carrasco Vargas, R., and M. Colón González
2005      El reino de Kaan y la antigua ciudad maya de Calakmul. *Arqueología Mexicana* 13(75):40–47.

Carrasco Vargas, R., and M. Cordeiro Baqueiro
2012      The Murals of Chiik Nahb Structure Sub1-4, Calakmul, Mexico. In *Maya Archaeology 2*, edited by C. W. Golden, S. D. Houston, and J. Skidmore, pp. 8–59. Precolumbia Mesoweb Press, San Francisco, California.

Carrasco Vargas, R., V. A. Vázquez López, and S. Martin
2009        Daily Life of the Ancient Maya Recorded on Murals at Calakmul, Mexico. *Proceedings of the National Academy of Sciences of the United States of America* 106(46):19245-19249.

Carroll, D.
1978        The Subject of Archeology or the Sovereignty of the Episteme. *Modern Language Notes* 93(4):695–722.

Carroll, L.
2009        *Alice's Adventures in Wonderland and Through the Looking-Glass and What Alice Found There.* Oxford University Press, New York.

Carter, N. P.
2014        Space, Time, and Text: A Landscape Approach to the Maya Hieroglyphic Record. In *Archaeologies of Text: Archaeology, Technology and Ethics*, edited by M. T. Rutz and M. M. Kersel, pp. 31–58. Joukowsky Institute Publication 6. Oxbow Books, Oxford.

Caso Barrera, L., and M. Aliphat Fernández
2012        Mejores son huertos de cacao y achiote que minas de oro y plata: Huertos especializados de los choles del Manché y de los k'ekchi'es. *Latin American Antiquity* 23(2):282–299.

Casson, R. W.
1983        Schemata in Cognitive Anthropology. *Annual Review of Anthropology* 12:429–462.

Cervantes Saavedra, M. d.
2004 [1605] *Don Quijote de la Mancha.* Real Academia Española, Madrid.

Chacón de Willemsen, T.
2011        *Hilos mayas de Guatemala: el lenguaje de los símbolos.* PROTEJE, Guatemala.

Chapman, R.
1987        Mortuary Practices: Society, Theory Building and Archaeology. In *Death, Decay, and Reconstruction: Approaches to Archaeology and Forensic Science*, edited by A. Boddington, A. N. Garland, and R. C. Janaway, pp. 198–213. Manchester University Press, Manchester, UK.

Chase, A. F.
1992        Elites and the Changing Organization of Classic Maya Society. In *Mesoamerican Elites: An Archaeological Assessment*, edited by D. Z. Chase and A. F. Chase, pp. 30–49. University of Oklahoma Press, Norman.

Chase, A. F., and D. Z. Chase
1992        Mesoamerican Elites: Assumptions, Definitions, and Models. In *Mesoamerican Elites: An Archaeological Assessment*, edited by D. Z. Chase and A. F. Chase, pp. 3–17. University of Oklahoma Press, Norman.
1996a       A Mighty Maya Nation: How Caracol Built an Empire by Cultivating Its "Middle Class." *Archaeology* 49(5):66–72.
1996b       The Organization and Composition of Classic Lowland Maya Society: The View from Caracol, Belize. In *Eighth Palenque Round Table, 1993*, edited by M. Macri and J. McHargue, pp. 213–222. Palenque Round Table Series 10, M.

Greene Robertson, general editor. Pre-Columbian Art Research Institute, San Francisco, California.

1998 Scale and Intensity in Classic Period Maya Agriculture: Terracing and Settlement at the "Garden City" of Caracol, Belize. *Culture and Agriculture* 20(2):60–77.

Chase, A. F., D. Z. Chase, E. Zorn, and W. Teeter

2008 Textiles and the Maya Archaeological Record. *Ancient Mesoamerica* 19(1):127–142.

Chavajay, P.

2006 How Mayan Mothers with Different Amounts of Schooling Organize a Problem-Solving Discussion with Children. *International Journal of Behavioral Development* 30(4):371–382.

Cheek, C. D.

1986 Construction Activity as a Measurement of Change at Copan, Honduras. In *The Southeast Maya Periphery*, edited by P. A. Urban and E. M. Schortman, pp. 50–71. University of Texas Press, Austin.

2003 Maya Community Buildings: Two Late Classic *popal nahs* at Copan, Honduras. *Ancient Mesoamerica* 14(1):131–138.

Chetty, R., N. Hendren, P. Kline, and E. Saez

2014 Where Is the Land of Opportunity? The Geography of Intergenerational Mobility in the United States. *Quarterly Journal of Economics* 129(4):1553–1623.

Chetty, R., N. Hendren, P. Kline, E. Saez, and N. Turner

2014 Is the United States Still a Land of Opportunity? Recent Trends in Intergenerational Mobility. *American Economic Review Papers and Proceedings* 104(5):141–147.

Childe, V. G.

1936 *Man Makes Himself*. Library of Science and Culture 5. Watts, London.

Childs, S. T.

1998 Social Identity and Craft Specialization among Toro Iron Workers in Western Uganda. In *Craft and Social Identity*, edited by C. L. Costin and R. P. Wright, pp. 109–121. Archeological Papers of the American Anthropological Association 8. American Anthropological Association, Arlington, Virginia.

Chuchiak, J. F.

2001 Pre-Conquest *Ah Kinob* in a Colonial World: The Extirpation of Idolatry and the Survival of the Maya Priesthood in Colonial Yucatan, 1563–1697. In *Maya Survivalism*, edited by U. Hostettler and M. Restall, pp. 135–157. Acta Mesoamericana 12. Verlag Anton Saurwein, Markt Schwaben, Germany.

Cifuentes Aguirre, O.

1963 *Odontología y mutilaciones dentarias mayas*. Colección Editorial Universitaria 46. Editorial Universitaria, Guatemala.

Coe, M. D.

1977 Supernatural Patrons of Maya Scribes and Artists. In *Social Process in Maya Prehistory: Essays in Honour of Sir Eric Thompson*, edited by N. Hammond, pp. 327–349. Academic Press, London.

1978      *Lords of the Underworld: Masterpieces of Classic Maya Ceramics.* Art Museum, Princeton University, Princeton, New Jersey.

1992      *Breaking the Maya Code.* Thames & Hudson, New York.

Coe, M. D., and S. D. Houston

2015      *The Maya.* 9th ed. Thames & Hudson, London.

Coe, M. D., and M. Van Stone

2005      *Reading the Maya Glyphs.* 2nd ed. Thames & Hudson, London.

Coe, W. R.

1965      Tikal: Ten Years of Study of a Maya Ruin in the Lowlands of Guatemala. *Expedition* 8(1):5–56.

1990      *Excavations in the Great Plaza, North Terrace and North Acropolis of Tikal.* Tikal Report 14. University of Pennsylvania, Philadelphia.

Coggins, C. C.

1975      Painting and Drawing Styles at Tikal: An Historical and Iconographic Reconstruction. Unpublished Ph.D. dissertation, Department of Art History, Harvard University, Cambridge, Massachusetts.

Collard, M., B. Buchanan, and M. J. O'Brien

2013      Population Size as an Explanation for Patterns in the Paleolithic Archaeological Record: More Caution Is Needed. *Current Anthropology* 54(S8):S388–S396.

Collard, M., B. Buchanan, M. J. O'Brien, and J. Scholnick

2013      Risk, Mobility or Population Size? Drivers of Technological Richness among Contact-Period Western North American Hunter–Gatherers. *Philosophical Transactions of the Royal Society B: Biological Sciences* 368(1630):20120412.

Collier, G. A.

1994      *Basta! Land and the Zapatista Rebellion in Chiapas.* Food First Books, Oakland, California.

Comaroff, J.

1985      *Body of Power, Spirit of Resistance: The Culture and History of a South African People.* University of Chicago Press, Chicago.

Comaroff, J., and J. L. Comaroff

1993      Introduction to *Modernity and Its Malcontents: Ritual and Power in Postcolonial Africa,* edited by J. Comaroff and J. L. Comaroff, pp. xi–xxxvii. University of Chicago Press, Chicago.

Conkey, M. W.

1982      Boundedness in Art and Society. In *Symbolic and Structural Archaeology,* edited by I. Hodder, pp. 115–128. Cambridge University Press, Cambridge.

Corak, M.

2006      Do Poor Children Become Poor Adults? Lessons for Public Policy from a Cross-Country Comparison of Generational Earnings Mobility. *Research on Economic Inequality* 13:143–188.

2013      Inequality from Generation to Generation: The United States in Comparison. In *The Economics of Inequality, Poverty, and Discrimination in the 21st Century,* edited by R. S. Rycroft, pp. 107–123. ABC-CLIO, Santa Barbara, California.

Correa-Chávez, M., and B. Rogoff

2005     Cultural Research Has Transformed Our Ideas of Cognitive Development. *International Journal of Behavioral Development* 29(3):7–10.

Corson, C.

1976     *Maya Anthropomorphic Figurines from Jaina Island, Campeche*. Ballena Press Studies in Mesoamerican Art, Archaeology and Ethnohistory 1. Ballena Press, Ramona, California.

Costin, C. L.

1991     Craft Specialization: Issues in Defining, Documenting, and Explaining the Organization of Production. In *Archaeological Method and Theory*, Vol. 3, edited by M. B. Schiffer, pp. 1–56. University of Arizona Press, Tucson.

Crapanzano, V.

1980     *Tuhami, Portrait of a Moroccan*. University of Chicago Press, Chicago.

Csordas, T. J.

1994     Introduction: The Body as Representation and Being-in-the-World. In *Embodiment and Experience: The Existential Ground of Culture and Self*, edited by T. J. Csordas, pp. 1–24. Cambridge Studies in Medical Anthropology 2. Cambridge University Press, Cambridge.

Cuevas García, M.

2007     Restos fósiles en Palenque y su relación con los mitos de la creación. *Los Investigadores de la Cultura Maya* 15(2):613–624.

2008     Paisaje paleontológico en Palenque. In *XXI Simposio de Investigaciones Arqueológicas en Guatemala, 2007*, edited by J. P. Laporte, B. Arroyo, and H. E. Mejía, pp. 669–685. Museo Nacional de Arqueología y Etnología, Guatemala.

Culbert, T. P. (editor)

1973     *The Classic Maya Collapse*. University of New Mexico Press, Albuquerque.

1993     *The Ceramics of Tikal: Vessels from the Burials, Caches, and Problematical Deposits*. Tikal Report 25 Part A. University Museum, University of Pennsylvania, Philadelphia.

Culbert, T. P., and D. S. Rice (editors)

1990     *Precolumbian Population History in the Maya Lowlands*. University of New Mexico Press, Albuquerque.

Curley, R. T.

1992     Private Dreams and Public Knowledge in a Camerounian Independent Church. In *Dreaming, Religion and Society in Africa*, edited by M. C. Jꞵdrej and R. Shaw, pp. 135–152. Studies on Religion in Africa 7. E. J. Brill, Leiden, The Netherlands.

Dahlin, B. H., C. T. Jensen, R. E. Terry, D. R. Wright, and T. Beach

2007     In Search of an Ancient Maya Market. *Latin American Antiquity* 18(4):363–384.

D'Altroy, T. N., and T. K. Earle

1985     Staple Finance, Wealth Finance, and Storage in the Inka Political Economy. *Current Anthropology* 26(2):187–206.

D'Andrade, R. G.
1995    *The Development of Cognitive Anthropology.* Cambridge University Press, Cambridge.

Danforth, M. E., S. L. Whittington, and K. P. Jacobi
1997    An Indexed Bibliography of Prehistoric and Early Historic Maya Human Osteology: 1839–1994. In *Bones of the Maya: Studies of Ancient Skeletons,* edited by S. L. Whittington and D. M. Reed. Smithsonian Institution Press, Washington, D.C.

Danziger, E.
2013    Conventional Wisdom: Imagination, Obedience and Intersubjectivity. *Language & Communication* 33(3):251–262.

David-Néel, A.
1971    *Magic and Mystery in Tibet.* Dover, New York.

Davies, J. B., S. Sandström, A. Shorrocks, and E. N. Wolff
2008    *The World Distribution of Household Wealth.* WIDER Discussion Paper 2008/03. UNU-WIDER, Helsinki.

Davis, V. D.
1978    Ritual of the Northern Lacandon Maya. Unpublished Ph.D. dissertation, Department of Anthropology, Tulane University, New Orleans, Louisiana.

Deletaille, L., and E. Deletaille
1992    *Trésors du Nouveau Monde. Catalogue de l'exposition aux Musées Royaux d'Art et d'Histoire, 15 septembre–27 décembre 1992.* Musées Royaux d'Art et d'Histoire, Brussels.

Delgado, H. S. d.
1963    Aboriginal Guatemalan Handweaving and Costume. Unpublished Ph.D. dissertation, Department of Anthropology, Indiana University, Bloomington.

Demarest, A. A.
1989    Ideology and Evolutionism in American Archaeology: Looking beyond the Economic Base. In *Archaeological Thought in America,* edited by C. C. Lamberg-Karlovsky, pp. 89–102. Cambridge University Press, Cambridge.
1992a   Archaeology, Ideology, and Pre-Columbian Cultural Evolution: The Search for an Approach. In *Ideology and Pre-Columbian Civilizations,* edited by A. A. Demarest and G. W. Conrad, pp. 1–13. School of American Research Press, Santa Fe, New Mexico.
1992b   Ideology in Ancient Maya Cultural Evolution: The Dynamics of Galactic Polities. In *Ideology and Pre-Columbian Civilizations,* edited by A. A. Demarest and G. W. Conrad, pp. 135–157. School of American Research Press, Santa Fe, New Mexico.
1997    The Vanderbilt Petexbatun Archaeological Project, 1989–1994. Overview, History and Major Results of a Multidisciplinary Study of the Classic Maya Collapse. *Ancient Mesoamerica* 8(2):209–227.
2006    *The Petexbatun Regional Archaeological Project: A Multidisciplinary Study of the Maya Collapse.* Vanderbilt Institute of Mesoamerican Archaeology Monograph 1. Vanderbilt University Press, Nashville, Tennessee.

2009 Maya Archaeology for the Twenty-First Century: The Progress, the Perils, and the Promise. *Ancient Mesoamerica* 20(2):253–263.

Demarest, A. A., C. Andrieu, P. Torres, M. Forné, T. Barrientos, and M. Wolf
2014 Economy, Exchange, and Power: New Evidence from the Late Classic Maya Port City of Cancuen. *Ancient Mesoamerica* 25(1):187–219.

Demarest, A. A., and A. E. Foias
1993 Mesoamerican Horizons and the Cultural Transformations of Maya Civilization. In *Latin American Horizons*, edited by D. S. Rice, pp. 147–191. Dumbarton Oaks, Washington, D.C.

Demarest, A. A., M. O'Mansky, C. Wolley, D. Van Tuerenhout, T. Inomata, J. Palka, and H. L. Escobedo
1997 Classic Maya Defensive Systems and Warfare in the Petexbatun Region: Archaeological Evidence and Interpretations. *Ancient Mesoamerica* 8(2):229–253.

Demarest, A. A., P. M. Rice, and D. S. Rice (editors)
2004 *The Terminal Classic in the Maya Lowlands: Collapse, Transition, and Transformation.* University Press of Colorado, Boulder.

DeMarrais, E., L. J. Castillo, and T. K. Earle
1996 Ideology, Materialization, and Power Strategies. *Current Anthropology* 37(1):15–31.

Derex, M., M.-P. Beugin, B. Godelle, and M. Raymond
2013 Experimental Evidence for the Influence of Group Size on Cultural Complexity. *Nature* 503(7476):389–391.

Derex, M., and R. Boyd
2016 Partial Connectivity Increases Cultural Accumulation within Groups. *Proceedings of the National Academy of Sciences of the United States of America* 113(11):2982–2987.

Derrida, J.
1976 *Of Grammatology.* Translated by G. Chakravorty Spivak. Johns Hopkins University Press, Baltimore, Maryland.
2011 *Voice and Phenomenon: Introduction to the Problem of the Sign in Husserl's Phenomenology.* Translated by L. Lawlor. Northwestern University Press, Evanston, Illinois.

Devisch, R.
1993 *Weaving the Threads of Life: The Khita Gyn-eco-logical Healing Cult among the Yaka.* University of Chicago Press, Chicago.

Diamanti, M.
2000 Excavaciones en el conjunto de los patios E, F y M, Grupo 9N-8 (Operación XV). In *Excavaciones en el área urbana de Copán*, Vol. 4, edited by W. T. Sanders. Instituto Hondureño de Antropología e Historia, Tegucigalpa, Honduras.

Dirven, R.
1999 Conversion as a Conceptual Metonymy of Basic Event Schemata. In *Metonymy in Language and Thought*, edited by K.-U. Panther and G. Radden, pp. 275–287. Human Cognitive Processing 4. J. Benjamins, Amsterdam.

Dittes, J. E., and H. H. Kelley
1956      Effects of Different Conditions of Acceptance upon Conformity to Group Norms. *Journal of Abnormal and Social Psychology* 53(1):100–107.

Dobres, M.-A., and C. R. Hoffman
1994      Social Agency and the Dynamics of Prehistoric Technology. *Journal of Archaeological Method and Theory* 1(3):211–258.

Doering, L.
2016      Necessity Is the Mother of Isomorphism: Poverty and Market Creativity in Panama. *Sociology of Development* 2(3):235–264.

Douglas, M.
1996      *Natural Symbols: Explorations in Cosmology.* Routledge, New York.

Douglas, M., and B. Isherwood
1979      *The World of Goods.* Basic Books, New York.
1996      *The World of Goods: Towards an Anthropology of Consumption.* 2nd ed. Routledge, London.

Duranti, A.
2010      Husserl, Intersubjectivity and Anthropology. *Anthropological Theory* 10(1–2):16–35.

Durkheim, É.
1982 [1894]      *The Rules of Sociological Method and Selected Texts on Sociology and Its Method.* Translated by W. D. Halls. Macmillan, New York.
1995      *The Elementary Forms of Religious Life.* Translated by K. E. Fields. Free Press, New York.

Ebbinghaus, H.
1885      *Über das Gedächtnis. Untersuchungen zur experimentellen Psychologie.* Duncker & Humblot, Leipzig, Germany.
1964      *Memory: A Contribution to Experimental Psychology.* Translated by H. A. Ruger and C. E. Bussenius. Dover, New York.

Eberl, M.
2013      Nourishing Gods: Birth and Personhood in Highland Mexican Codices. *Cambridge Archaeological Journal* 23(3):453–476.
2014a      *Community and Difference: Change in Late Classic Maya Villages of the Petexbatun Region.* Vanderbilt Institute of Mesoamerican Archaeology Studies Series 8. Vanderbilt University Press, Nashville, Tennessee.
2014b      Real/Fictive Lords/Vessels: A List of M.A.R.I. Lords on the Newly Discovered Andrews Coffee Mug. In *The Maya and Their Central American Neighbors: Settlement Patterns, Architecture, Hieroglyphic Texts and Ceramics,* edited by G. E. Braswell, pp. 223–242. Routledge, London.
2015      "To Put in Order": Classic Maya Concepts of Time and Space. In *The Measure and Meaning of Time in the Americas,* edited by A. Aveni, pp. 79–104. Dumbarton Oaks, Washington, D.C.

Eberl, M., M. d. l. Á. Corado, C. M. Vela González, T. Inomata, D. Triadan, J. Guerra Ruiz, and A. Seijas
2009      El asentamiento Preclásico del sitio arqueológico Dos Ceibas en la región del Petexbatún, Guatemala. *Mexicon* 31(6):134–141.

Eberl, M., and D. Graña-Behrens

2004       Proper Names and Throne Names: On the Naming Practice of Classic Maya Rulers. In *Continuity and Change: Maya Religious Practices in Temporal Perspective. Fifth European Maya Conference at the University of Bonn, December 2000*, edited by D. Graña-Behrens, N. K. Grube, C. M. Prager, F. Sachse, S. Teufel, and E. Wagner, pp. 101–120. Acta Mesoamericana 14. Verlag Anton Saurwein, Markt Schwaben, Germany.

Edmonson, M. S.

1985       Quiche Literature. In *Literatures*, edited by M. S. Edmonson, pp. 107–132. Supplement to the Handbook of Middle American Indians, Vol. 3, V. R. Bricker, general editor. University of Texas Press, Austin.

Edmonson, M. S., and V. R. Bricker

1985       Yucatecan Mayan Literature. In *Literatures*, edited by M. S. Edmonson, pp. 44–63. Supplement to the Handbook of Middle American Indians, Vol. 3, V. R. Bricker, general editor. University of Texas Press, Austin.

Eggebrecht, A., E. Eggebrecht, and N. K. Grube

1994       *Die Welt der Maya. Archäologische Schätze aus drei Jahrtausenden (with additional artifacts for the exhibit in Cologne)*. Von Zabern, Mainz, Germany.

Ehrman, B. D.

1993       *The Orthodox Corruption of Scripture: The Effect of Early Christological Controversies on the Text of the New Testament*. Oxford University Press, New York.

Emery, K. F.

2003       The Noble Beast: Status and Differential Access to Animals in the Maya World. *World Archaeology* 34(3):498–515.

Emery, K. F., and K. Aoyama

2007       Bone, Shell, and Lithic Evidence for Crafting in Elite Maya Households at Aguateca, Guatemala. *Ancient Mesoamerica* 18(1):69–89.

Erasmus, C. J.

1965       Monument Building: Some Field Experiments. *Southwestern Journal of Anthropology* 21(4):277–301.

Fargher, L. F., R. E. Blanton, and V. Y. Heredia Espinoza

2010       Egalitarian Ideology and Political Power in Prehispanic Central Mexico: The Case of Tlaxcallan. *Latin American Antiquity* 21(3):227–251.

Fash, B. W., and W. L. Fash

1994       Copán Temple 20 and the House of Bats. In *Seventh Palenque Round Table, 1989*, edited by V. M. Fields, pp. 61–68. Palenque Round Table Series IX. Pre-Columbian Art Research Institute, San Francisco, California.

Fash, B. W., W. L. Fash, Jr., S. Lane, R. Larios, L. Schele, J. Stomper, and D. Stuart

1992       Investigations of a Classic Maya Council House at Copán, Honduras. *Journal of Field Archaeology* 19(4):419–442.

Fash, W. L., Jr.

1983       Reconocimiento y excavaciones en el valle. In *Introducción a la arqueología e historia de Copán, Honduras*, Vol. 1, edited by C. F. Baudez, pp. 229–469.

Proyecto Arqueológico Copán; Secretaría del Estado en el Despacho de Cultura y Turismo, Tegucigalpa, Honduras.

1989 The Sculptural Façade of Structure 9N-82: Content, Form, and Significance. In *The House of the Bacabs, Copan, Honduras*, edited by D. L. Webster, pp. 41–72. Studies in Pre-Columbian Art & Archaeology 29. Dumbarton Oaks, Washington, D.C.

1991 *Scribes, Warriors, and Kings: The City of Copán and the Ancient Maya*. Thames & Hudson, London.

Fash, W. L., Jr., and K. Z. Long

1983 Mapa arqueológico del valle de Copán. In *Introducción a la arqueología e historia de Copán, Honduras*, Vol. 3, edited by C. F. Baudez. Proyecto Arqueológico Copán; Secretaría del Estado en el Despacho de Cultura y Turismo, Tegucigalpa, Honduras.

Fash, W. L., Jr., and D. Stuart

1991 Dynastic History and Cultural Evolution at Copan, Honduras. In *Classic Maya Political History: Hieroglyphic and Archaeological Evidence*, edited by T. P. Culbert, pp. 147–180. Cambridge University Press, New York.

Faure, B.

1996 *Visions of Power: Imagining Medieval Japanese Buddhism*. Translated by P. Brooks. Princeton University Press, Princeton, New Jersey.

Feinman, G. M., L. M. Nicholas, and H. R. Haines

2002 Houses on a Hill: Classic Period Life at El Palmillo, Oaxaca, Mexico. *Latin American Antiquity* 13(3):251–277.

Fernandez, J. W.

1986 *Persuasions and Performances: The Play of Tropes in Culture*. Indiana University Press, Bloomington.

Fewkes, J. W.

1895 The God "D" in the Codex Cortesianus. *American Anthropologist* 8(3):205–222.

Fischer, E. F.

1999 Cultural Logic and Maya Identity. Rethinking Constructivism and Essentialism. *Current Anthropology* 40(4):473–499.

2001 *Cultural Logics and Global Economics: Maya Identity in Thought and Practice*. University of Texas Press, Austin.

Fischer, E. F., and P. Benson

2006 *Broccoli and Desire: Global Connections and Maya Struggles in Postwar Guatemala*. Stanford University Press, Stanford, California.

Fiske, A. P.

1992 The Four Elementary Forms of Sociality: Framework for a Unified Theory of Social Relations. *Psychological Review* 99(4):689–723.

Foias, A. E.

1996 Changing Ceramic Production and Exchange and the Classic Maya Collapse in the Petexbatun Region. Unpublished Ph.D. dissertation, Department of Anthropology, Vanderbilt University, Nashville, Tennessee.

Foias, A. E., and R. L. Bishop

1997   Changing Ceramic Production and Exchange in the Petexbatun Region, Guatemala: Reconsidering the Classic Maya Collapse. *Ancient Mesoamerica* 8(2):275–291.

2013   *Ceramics, Production, and Exchange in the Petexbatun Region: The Economic Parameters of the Classic Maya Collapse*. Vanderbilt Institute of Mesoamerican Archaeology Series 7. Vanderbilt University Press, Nashville, Tennessee.

Folan, W. J.

1969   Sacalum, Yucatán: A Pre-Hispanic and Contemporary Source of Attapulgite. *American Antiquity* 34(2):182–183.

Förstemann, E. W.

1880   *Die Mayahandschrift der königlichen öffentlichen Bibliothek zu Dresden*. Verlag der A. Naumann'schen Lichtdruckerei, Leipzig, Germany.

Foster, G. M.

1965   The Sociology of Pottery: Questions and Hypotheses Arising from Contemporary Mexican Work. In *Ceramics and Man*, edited by F. R. Matson, pp. 43–61. Viking Fund Publications in Anthropology 41. Wenner-Gren Foundation for Anthropological Research, New York.

Foucault, M.

1997   *Ethics: Subjectivity and Truth*. Translated by R. Hurley. Essential Works of Foucault (1954–1984) 1. New Press, New York.

Frankenburg, F. R.

2009   *Vitamin Discoveries and Disasters: History, Science, and Controversies*. Praeger/ABC-CLIO, Santa Barbara, California.

Frazer, J. G.

1905   *Lectures on the Early History of the Kingship*. Macmillan, London.

Freidel, D. A.

1981   Civilization as a State of Mind: The Cultural Evolution of the Lowland Maya. In *The Transition to Statehood in the New World*, edited by G. D. Jones and R. R. Kautz, pp. 188–248. Cambridge University Press, Cambridge.

1986   Introduction to *Archaeology at Cerros, Belize, Central America*. Vol. 1: An *Interim Report,* edited by R. A. Robertson and D. A. Freidel, pp. xiii–xxiii. Southern Methodist University Press, Dallas, Texas.

1993   The Jade Ahau: Toward a Theory of Commodity Value in the Maya Civilization. In *Precolumbian Jade: New Geological and Cultural Interpretations*, edited by F. W. Lange, pp. 149–165. University of Utah, Salt Lake City.

Freidel, D. A., K. Reese-Taylor, and D. F. Mora-Marín

2002   The Origins of Maya Civilization: The Old Shell Game; Commodity, Treasure and Kingship. In *Ancient Maya Political Economies*, edited by M. A. Masson and D. A. Freidel, pp. 41–86. AltaMira Press, Walnut Creek, California.

Freidel, D. A., L. Schele, and J. Parker

1993   *Maya Cosmos: Three Thousand Years on the Shaman's Path*. William Morrow, New York.

Freter, A.

1988   The Classic Maya Collapse at Copan, Honduras: A Regional Settlement

Perspective. Unpublished Ph.D. dissertation, Department of Anthropology, Pennsylvania State University, University Park.

1992    Chronological Research at Copan: Methods and Implications. *Ancient Mesoamerica* 3:117–133.

Friedel, R. D., and P. Israel

1986    *Edison's Electric Light: Biography of an Invention.* Rutgers University Press, New Brunswick, New Jersey.

Fry, R. E.

1979    The Economics of Pottery at Tikal, Guatemala: Models of Exchange for Serving Vessels. *American Antiquity* 44(3):494–512.

1980    Models of Exchange for Major Shape Classes of Lowland Maya Pottery. In *Models and Methods in Regional Exchange*, edited by R. E. Fry, pp. 3–18. SAA Paper 1. Society for American Archaeology, Washington, D.C.

Fry, R. E., and S. C. Cox

1974    The Structure of Ceramic Exchange at Tikal, Guatemala. *World Archaeology* 6(2):209–225.

Gadamer, H.-G.

1990    *Hermeneutik 1: Wahrheit und Methode. Grundzüge einer philosophischen Hermeneutik.* Gesammelte Werke 1. J.C.B. Mohr (Paul Siebeck), Tübingen, Germany.

García de León, A.

1988    *Resistencia y utopía: memorial de agravios y crónica de revueltas y profecías acaecidas en la provincia de Chiapas durante los últimos quinientos años de su historia.* 2nd ed. Ediciones Era, México, D.F.

García Márquez, G.

1970    *One Hundred Years of Solitude.* Harper and Row, New York.

Garibay Kintana, Á. M.

1953–1954 *Historia de la literatura náhuatl.* Biblioteca Porrúa 1. Editorial Porrúa, México, D.F.

Garza, M. d. l.

1983    *Relaciones histórico-geográficas de la gobernación de Yucatán (Mérida, Valladolid y Tabasco).* Fuentes para el Estudio de la Cultura Maya Vols. 1–2. Universidad Nacional Autónoma de México, Instituto de Investigaciones Filológicas, Centro de Estudios Mayas, México, D.F.

Gasco, J.

2017    Anthropogenic Landscapes of Soconusco Past and Present. In *Colonial and Postcolonial Change in Mesoamerica*, edited by R. T. Alexander and S. Kepecs. University of New Mexico Press, Albuquerque.

Geertz, C.

1966    Religion as a Cultural System. In *Anthropological Approaches to the Study of Religion*, edited by M. Banton, pp. 1–46. Tavistock, London.

Gell, A.

1992    *The Anthropology of Time: Cultural Constructions of Temporal Maps and Images.* Berg, Oxford.

1998    *Art and Agency: An Anthropological Theory.* Clarendon Press, Oxford.

Gerstle, A. I., and D. L. Webster

1990    Excavaciones en 9N-8, conjunto del patio D. In *Excavaciones en el Área Urbana de Copán*, Vol. 3, edited by W. T. Sanders. Instituto Hondureño de Antropología e Historia, Tegucigalpa, Honduras.

Giddens, A.

1979    *Central Problems in Social Theory: Action, Structure, and Contradiction in Social Analysis.* University of California Press, Berkeley.

1984    *The Constitution of Society: Outline of the Theory of Structuration.* University of California Press, Berkeley.

Gini, C.

1912    *Variabilità e mutabilità: Contributo allo studio delle distribuzioni e delle relazioni statistiche.* C. Cuppini, Bologna.

Girard, R.

1962    *Los mayas eternos.* Antigua Librería Robredo, México, D.F.

Godzinski, R., Jr.

2005    (En)Framing Heidegger's Philosophy of Technology. *Essays in Philosophy* 6(1):Article 9.

Goffman, E.

1974    *Frame Analysis: An Essay on the Organization of Experience.* Harvard University Press, Cambridge, Massachusetts.

Golden, C. W., and A. K. Scherer

2013    Territory, Trust, Growth, and Collapse in Classic Period Maya Kingdoms. *Current Anthropology* 54(4):397–435.

Goldenweiser, A.

1936    Loose Ends of Theory on the Individual Pattern, and Involution in Primitive Society. In *Essays in Anthropology Presented to A. L. Kroeber in Celebration of His Sixtieth Birthday, June 11, 1936*, edited by R. H. Lowie, pp. 99–104. University of California Press, Berkeley.

Göncü, A., J. Mistry, and C. Mosier

2000    Cultural Variations in the Play of Toddlers. *International Journal of Behavioral Development* 24(3):321–329.

González Cruz, A., and G. Bernal Romero

2012    The Discovery of the Temple XXI Monument at Palenque: The Kingdom of Baakal during the Reign of K'inich Ahkal Mo' Nahb. In *Maya Archaeology 2*, edited by C. W. Golden, S. D. Houston, and J. Skidmore, pp. 82–103. Precolumbia Mesoweb Press, San Francisco, California.

Goody, E. N.

1978    Toward a Theory of Questions. In *Questions and Politeness: Strategies in Social Interaction*, edited by E. N. Goody, pp. 17–43. Cambridge Papers in Social Anthropology 8. Cambridge University Press, Cambridge.

Gordon, G. B.

1896    *Prehistoric Ruins of Copan, Honduras: A Preliminary Report of the Explorations by the Museum, 1891–1895.* Memoirs of the Peabody Museum of American Archaeology and Ethnology, Harvard University 1, 1. Peabody Museum of American Archaeology and Ethnology, Harvard University, Cambridge, Massachusetts.

Graham, I.
1967 *Archaeological Explorations in El Peten, Guatemala.* Middle American Research Institute Publication 33. Tulane University, New Orleans, Louisiana.

Graham, I., and E. Von Euw
1992 *Uxmal, Xcalumkin.* Corpus of Maya Hieroglyphic Inscriptions 4, Part 3. Peabody Museum of Archaeology and Ethnology, Harvard University, Cambridge, Massachusetts.

Graham, L. R.
1995 *Performing Dreams: Discourses of Immortality among the Xavante of Central Brazil.* University of Texas Press, Austin.

Graña-Behrens, D.
2006 Emblem Glyphs and Political Organization in Northwestern Yucatan in the Classic Period (A.D. 300–1000). *Ancient Mesoamerica* 17(1):105–123.

Greenfield, P. M.
2004 *Weaving Generations Together: Evolving Creativity among the Mayas of Chiapas.* School of American Research Press, Santa Fe, New Mexico.

Gregory of Tours
1988 *Glory of the Martyrs.* Translated by R. Van Dam. Translated Texts for Historians. Latin Series 3. Liverpool University Press, Liverpool, UK.

Grigg, R.
2008 *Lacan, Language, and Philosophy.* State University of New York Press, Albany.

Groark, K. P.
2008 Social Opacity and the Dynamics of Empathic In-Sight among the Tzotzil Maya of Chiapas, Mexico. *Ethos* 36(4):427–448.
2013 Toward a Cultural Phenomenology of Intersubjectivity: The Extended Relational Field of the Tzotzil Maya of Highland Chiapas, Mexico. *Language & Communication* 33(3):278–291.

Grönemeyer, H.
1998 *Bleibt alles anders.* Grönland Records, London.

Grube, N. K.
1988 Städtegründer und "Erste Herrscher" in Hieroglyphentexten der klassischen Mayakultur. *Archiv für Völkerkunde* 42:69–90.
1994 Hieroglyphic Sources for the History of Northwest Yucatan. In *Hidden among the Hills: Maya Archaeology of the Northwest Yucatan Peninsula,* edited by H. J. Prem, pp. 316–358. Acta Mesoamericana 7. Verlag von Flemming, Möckmühl, Germany.
2000 Fire Rituals in the Context of Classic Maya Initial Series. In *The Sacred and the Profane: Architecture and Identity in the Maya Lowlands,* edited by P. R. Colas, K. Delvendahl, M. Kuhnert, and A. Schubart, pp. 93–109. Acta Mesoamericana 10. Verlag Anton Saurwein, Markt Schwaben, Germany.
2006a Ancient Maya Royal Biographies in a Comparative Perspective. In *Janaab' Pakal of Palenque: Reconstructing the Life and Death of a Maya Ruler,* edited

by V. Tiesler Blos and A. Cucina, pp. 146–166. University of Arizona Press, Tucson.

2006b      Die Hieroglyphentexte auf den Keramiken. In *Die Maya. Schrift und Kunst*, edited by N. K. Grube and M. Gaida, pp. 58–81. SMB-DuMont, Berlin.

Grube, N. K., and W. Nahm

1994      The Census of Xibalba: A Complete Inventory of *Way* Characters on Maya Ceramics. In *The Maya Vase Book. A Corpus of Rollout Photographs of Maya Vessels*, Vol. 4, edited by J. Kerr, pp. 686–715. Kerr Associates, New York.

Grube, N. K., and L. Schele

1994      Kuy, the Owl of Omen and War. *Mexicon* 16(1):10–17.

Guderjan, T. H.

2004      Recreating the Cosmos: Early Classic Dedicatory Caches at Blue Creek. In *Continuity and Change: Maya Religious Practices in Temporal Perspective. Fifth European Maya Conference at the University of Bonn, December 2000*, edited by D. Graña Behrens, N. K. Grube, C. M. Prager, F. Sachse, S. Teufel, and E. Wagner, pp. 33–40. Acta Mesoamericana 14. Verlag Anton Saurwein, Markt Schwaben, Germany.

Guenther, L.

2011      Subjects without a World? An Husserlian Analysis of Solitary Confinement. *Human Studies* 34(3):257–276.

2012      The Living Death of Solitary Confinement. *New York Times*, August 26, 2012.

Guernsey, J.

2016      Water, Maize, Salt, and Canoes: An Iconography of Economics at Late Preclassic Izapa Chiapas, Mexico. *Latin American Antiquity* 27(3):340–356.

Hagan, J., and R. D. Peterson (editors)

1995      *Crime and Inequality*. Stanford University Press, Stanford, California.

Hall, M.

2002      Mack McCormick Still Has the Blues. *Texas Monthly* (April):112–117, 165–168.

Halperin, C. T.

2008      Classic Maya Textile Production: Insights from Motul de San José, Peten, Guatemala. *Ancient Mesoamerica* 19(1):111–125.

Hamann, B. E.

2008a      Chronological Pollution: Potsherds, Mosques, and Broken Gods before and after the Conquest of Mexico. *Current Anthropology* 49(5):803–836.

2008b      How Maya Hieroglyphs Got Their Name: Egypt, Mexico, and China in Western Grammatology since the Fifteenth Century. *Proceedings of the American Philosophical Society* 152(1):1–68.

Hanks, W. F.

1990      *Referential Practice: Language and Lived Space among the Maya*. University of Chicago Press, Chicago.

Hanson, A.

1989      The Making of the Maori: Culture Invention and Its Logic. *American Anthropologist* 91(4):890–902.

Hasaki, E.

2012      Craft Apprenticeship in Ancient Greece: Reaching beyond the Masters. In

*Archaeology and Apprenticeship: Body Knowledge, Identity, and Communities of Practice*, edited by W. Wendrich, pp. 171–202. University of Arizona Press, Tucson.

Hastie, R.
1981    Schematic Principles in Human Memory. In *Social Cognition*, edited by E. T. Higgins, C. P. Herman, and M. P. Zanna, pp. 39–88. Ontario Symposium 1. L. Erlbaum Associates, Hillsdale, New Jersey.

Hasty, W.
2006    *Minnesang*—The Medieval German Love Lyrics. In *German Literature of the High Middle Ages*, edited by W. Hasty, pp. 141–160. Camden House History of German Literature 3. Camden House, Rochester, New York.

Haviland, L. K., and J. B. Haviland
1983    Privacy in a Mexican Indian Village. In *Public and Private in Social Life*, edited by S. I. Benn and G. F. Gaus, pp. 341–361. St. Martin's Press, New York.

Hayden, B. D., and A. Cannon
1982    The Corporate Group as an Archaeological Unit. *Journal of Anthropological Archaeology* 1(2):132–158.
1984    Interaction Inferences in Archaeology and Learning Frameworks of the Maya. *Journal of Anthropological Archaeology* 3(4):325–367.

Heaney, Seamus
1966    *Death of a Naturalist*. Oxford University Press, New York.

Hegel, G. W. F.
1821    *Grundlinien der Philosophie des Rechts*. Nicolaische Buchhandlung, Berlin.
1986    *Enzyklopädie der philosophischen Wissenschaften im Grundrisse 1830. Erster Teil: Die Wissenschaft der Logik. Mit den mündlichen Zusätzen*. Werke 8. Suhrkamp, Frankfurt am Main.
1991    *The Encyclopaedia Logic. Part I of the Encyclopaedia of Philosophical Sciences with the Zusätze*. Translated by T. F. Geraets, W. A. Suchting, and H. S. Harris. Hackett, Indianapolis, Indiana.

Hegmon, M., and S. Kulow
2005    Painting as Agency, Style as Structure: Innovations in Mimbres Pottery Designs from Southwest New Mexico. *Journal of Archaeological Method and Theory* 12(4):313–334.

Heidegger, M.
1957    *Der Satz vom Grund*. G. Neske, Pfullingen, Germany.
1962    *Being and Time*. Translated by J. Macquarrie and E. Robinson. Harper San Francisco, San Francisco, California.
1977    *The Question Concerning Technology, and Other Essays*. Translated by W. Lovitt. Harper and Row, New York.
2006    *Sein und Zeit*. Max Niemeyer Verlag, Tübingen, Germany.
2014a   *Überlegungen II–VI (Schwarze Hefte 1931–1938)*. Gesamtausgabe IV. Abteilung: Hinweise und Aufzeichnungen, Band 94. Vittorio Klostermann, Frankfurt am Main.
2014b   *Überlegungen VII–XI (Schwarze Hefte 1938–1939)*. Gesamtausgabe IV. Abteilung: Hinweise und Aufzeichnungen, Band 95. Vittorio Klostermann, Frankfurt am Main.

2014c    *Überlegungen XII–XV (Schwarze Hefte 1939–1941)*. Gesamtausgabe IV. Abteilung: Hinweise und Aufzeichnungen, Band 96. Vittorio Klostermann, Frankfurt am Main.

Helmke, C., and J. Awe

2008    Organización territorial de los antiguos mayas de Belice Central: Confluencia de datos arqueológicos y epigráficos. *Mayab* 20:65–91.

Helms, M. W.

1993    *Craft and the Kingly Ideal: Art, Trade, and Power*. University of Texas Press, Austin.

Hendon, J. A.

1987    The Uses of Maya Structures: A Study of Architecture and Artifact Distribution at Sepulturas, Copan, Honduras. Unpublished Ph.D. dissertation, Department of Anthropology, Harvard University, Cambridge, Massachusetts.

1991    Status and Power in Classic Maya Society: An Archaeological Study. *American Anthropologist* 93(4):894–918.

1997    Women's Work, Women's Space and Women's Status among the Classic Period Maya Elite of the Copan Valley, Honduras. In *Women in Prehistory: North America and Mesoamerica*, edited by C. Claassen and R. A. Joyce, pp. 33–46. University of Pennsylvania Press, Philadelphia.

Hendon, J. A., R. Agurcia Fasquelle, W. L. Fash, and E. Aguilar Palma

1990    Excavaciones en 9N-8, conjunto del patio C. In *Excavaciones en el área urbana de Copán*, Vol. 2, edited by W. T. Sanders, pp. 11–109. Instituto Hondureño de Antropología e Historia, Tegucigalpa, Honduras.

Hendon, J. A., W. L. Fash, and E. Aguilar Palma

1990    Excavaciones en 9N-8, conjunto del patio B. In *Excavaciones en el área urbana de Copán*, Vol. 2, edited by W. T. Sanders, pp. 111–293. Instituto Hondureño de Antropología e Historia, Tegucigalpa, Honduras.

Henrich, J.

2004    Demography and Cultural Evolution: How Adaptive Cultural Processes Can Produce Maladaptive Losses—The Tasmanian Case. *American Antiquity* 69(2):197–214.

Heyden, D., and P. Gendrop

1988    *Mittelamerika: Die alten Kulturen*. Deutsche Verlags-Anstalt, Stuttgart.

Hill, R. M., II

1992    *Colonial Cakchiquels: Highland Maya Adaptations to Spanish Rule, 1600–1700*. Harcourt Brace Jovanovich, Fort Worth, Texas.

Hirsch, F.

1976    *Social Limits to Growth*. Harvard University Press, Cambridge, Massachusetts.

Hodder, I.

1984    Burials, Houses, Women, and Men in the European Neolithic. In *Ideology, Power, and Prehistory*, edited by D. Miller and C. Y. Tilley, pp. 51–68. Cambridge University Press, Cambridge.

2012    *Entangled: An Archaeology of the Relationships between Humans and Things*. Wiley-Blackwell, Malden, Massachusetts.

Hodder, I., and S. R. Hutson
2003    *Reading the Past: Current Approaches to Interpretation in Archaeology.* 3rd ed. Cambridge University Press, Cambridge.

Hohmann, H., and A. Vogrin
1982    *Die Architektur von Copan (Honduras): Vermessung, Plandarstellung, Untersuchung der baulichen Elemente und des räumlichen Konzepts.* Akademische Druck- und Verlagsanstalt, Graz.

Hollis, M.
1970    Reason and Ritual. In *Rationality,* edited by B. R. Wilson, pp. 221–239. Blackwell, Oxford.

Holsbeke, M.
2003    Textile as Text. Maya Traditional Dress and the Messages It Conveys. In *With Their Hands and Their Eyes: Maya Textiles, Mirrors of a Worldview,* edited by M. Holsbeke and J. Montoya, pp. 16–45. Etnografisch Museum Antwerpen, Antwerp.

Hölzle, P.
1980    *Die Kreuzzüge in der okzitanischen und deutschen Lyrik des 12. Jahrhunderts: Das Gattungsproblem 'Kreuzlied' im historischen Kontext.* Göppinger Arbeiten zur Germanistik 278. Kümmerle, Göppingen, Germany.

Houston, S. D.
1986    *Problematic Emblem Glyphs: Examples from Altar de Sacrificios, El Chorro, Río Azul, and Xultun* Research Reports on Ancient Maya Writing 3. Center for Maya Research, Washington, D.C.
1989    *Reading the Past: Maya Glyphs.* University of California, Berkeley.
1992    A Name Glyph for Classic Maya Dwarfs. In *The Maya Vase Book: A Corpus of Rollout Photographs of Maya Vessels,* Vol. 3, edited by J. Kerr, pp. 526–531. Kerr Associates, New York.
1993    *Hieroglyphs and History at Dos Pilas: Dynastic Politics of the Classic Maya.* University of Texas, Austin.
1998    Classic Maya Depictions of the Built Environment. In *Function and Meaning in Classic Maya Architecture,* edited by S. D. Houston, pp. 333–372. Dumbarton Oaks, Washington, D.C.
2000    Into the Minds of the Ancients: Advances in Maya Glyph Studies. *Journal of World Prehistory* 14(2):121–201.
2014    *The Life Within: Classic Maya and the Matter of Permanence.* Yale University Press, New Haven, Connecticut.

Houston, S. D., and T. Inomata
2009    *The Classic Maya.* Cambridge University Press, New York.

Houston, S. D., J. Robertson, and D. Stuart
2000    The Language of Classic Maya Inscriptions. *Current Anthropology* 41(3):321–356.

Houston, S. D., and D. Stuart
1989    *The Way Glyph: Evidence for "Co-Essence" among the Classic Maya.* Research Reports on Ancient Maya Writing 30. Center for Maya Research, Washington, D.C.

1996        Of Gods, Glyphs and Kings: Divinity and Rulership among the Classic Maya. *Antiquity* 70:289–312.

1998        The Ancient Maya Self: Personhood and Portraiture in the Classic Period. *Res: Anthropology and Aesthetics* 33:73–101.

2001        Peopling the Classic Maya Court. In *The Royal Courts of the Ancient Maya*. Vol. 1: *Theory Comparison, and Synthesis*, edited by T. Inomata and S. D. Houston, pp. 55–83. Westview Press, Boulder, Colorado.

Houston, S. D., D. Stuart, and K. A. Taube

2006        *The Memory of Bones: Body, Being, and Experience among the Classic Maya.* University of Texas Press, Austin.

Houston, S. D., and K. A. Taube

2000        An Archaeology of the Senses: Perception and Cultural Expression in Ancient Mesoamerica. *Cambridge Archaeological Journal* 10(2):261–294.

Hruby, Z. X.

2007        Ritualized Chipped-Stone Production at Piedras Negras, Guatemala. *Archaeological Papers of the American Anthropological Association* 17:68–87.

Hubert, H., and M. Mauss

1902–1903   Esquisse d'une théorie générale de la magie. *L'Année Sociologique* 7:1–146.

Hume, D.

1894        *Enquiries Concerning the Human Understanding and Concerning the Principles of Morals.* Clarendon Press, Oxford.

1987        *Essays, Moral, Political, and Literary.* Liberty Classics, Indianapolis, Indiana.

Hunt, E.

1977        *The Transformation of the Hummingbird: Cultural Roots of a Zinacantecan Mythical Poem.* Cornell University Press, Ithaca, New York.

Husserl, E.

1950        *Cartesianische Meditationen und Pariser Vorträge.* Husserliana 1. Martinus Nijhoff, The Hague.

1960        *Cartesian Meditations: An Introduction to Phenomenology.* Translated by D. Cairns. Martinus Nijhoff, The Hague.

1966        *Zur Phänomenologie des inneren Zeitbewusstseins (1893–1917).* Husserliana 10. Martinus Nijhoff, The Hague.

1970        *Logical Investigations.* Translated by J. N. Findlay. 2 Vols. Routledge, London.

1975–1984   *Logische Untersuchungen.* Husserliana Vols. 18–19. Martinus Nijhoff, The Hague.

1981        *Husserl, Shorter Works.* University of Notre Dame Press, Notre Dame, Indiana.

1987        *Aufsätze und Vorträge, 1911–1921.* Husserliana 25. Martinus Nijhoff, Dordrecht.

1988        *Aufsätze und Vorträge (1922–1937).* Husserliana 27. Kluwer Academic Publishers, The Hague.

1995        Fichte's Ideal of Humanity. *Husserl Studies* 12:111–133.

Hutchins, E.

1990        The Technology of Team Navigation. In *Intellectual Teamwork: Social and Technological Foundations of Cooperative Work*, edited by J. R. Galegher, R.

E. Kraut, and C. Egido, pp. 191–220. L. Erlbaum Associates, Hillsdale, New Jersey.

Hutson, S. R.
2010   *Dwelling, Identity, and the Maya: Relational Archaeology at Chunchucmil.* AltaMira Press, Lanham, Maryland.
2011   The Art of Becoming: The Graffiti of Tikal, Guatemala. *Latin American Antiquity* 22(4):403–426.
2016   *The Ancient Urban Maya: Neighborhoods, Inequality and Built Form.* University Press of Florida, Gainesville.

Hutson, S. R., D. R. Hixson, A. Magnoni, D. Mazeau, and B. Dahlin
2008   Site and Community at Chunchucmil and Ancient Maya Centers. *Journal of Field Archaeology* 33(1):19–40.

Hutson, S. R., and T. W. Stanton
2007   Cultural Logic and Practical Reason: The Structure of Discard in Ancient Maya Houselots. *Cambridge Archaeological Journal* 17:123–144.

Hutson, S. R., and R. E. Terry
2006   Recovering Social and Cultural Dynamics from Plaster Floors: Chemical Analyses at Ancient Chunchucmil, Yucatan, Mexico. *Journal of Archaeological Science* 33(3):391–404.

Iannone, G.
2005   The Rise and Fall of an Ancient Maya Petty Royal Court. *Latin American Antiquity* 16(1):26–44.

Ingold, T.
1993   Technology, Language, Intelligence: A Reconsideration of Basic Concepts. In *Tools, Language, and Cognition in Human Evolution*, edited by K. R. Gibson and T. Ingold, pp. 449–472. Cambridge University Press, Cambridge.
2000   *The Perception of the Environment: Essays on Livelihood, Dwelling and Skill.* Routledge, London.
2001   From the Transmission of Representations to the Education of Attention. In *The Debated Mind: Evolutionary Psychology versus Ethnography*, edited by H. Whitehouse, pp. 113–153. Berg, Oxford.

Inomata, T.
1995   Archaeological Investigations at the Fortified Center of Aguateca, El Peten, Guatemala: Implications for the Study of the Classic Maya Collapse. Unpublished Ph.D. dissertation, Department of Anthropology, Vanderbilt University, Nashville, Tennessee.
2001a  The Classic Maya Royal Palace as a Political Theater. In *Reconstruyendo la ciudad maya: El urbanismo en las sociedades antiguas*, edited by A. Ciudad Ruiz, M. J. Iglesias Ponce de León, and M. d. C. Martínez y Martínez, pp. 341–362. Publicaciones de la S.E.E.M. 6. Sociedad Española de Estudios Mayas, Madrid.
2001b  The Power and Ideology of Artistic Creation. Elite Craft Specialists in Classic Maya Society. *Current Anthropology* 42(3):321–349.
2004   The Spatial Mobility of Non-Elite Populations in Classic Maya Society and Its

Political Implications. In *Ancient Maya Commoners*, edited by J. C. Lohse and F. Valdez, Jr., pp. 175–196. University of Texas Press, Austin.

2006      Plazas, Performers, and Spectators. Political Theaters of the Classic Maya. *Current Anthropology* 47(5):805–842.

2010      The Temporal and Spatial Distribution of Ceramics. In *Burned Palaces and Elite Residences of Aguateca: Excavations and Ceramics*, edited by T. Inomata and D. Triadan, pp. 163–179. Monograph of the Aguateca Archaeological Project First Phase 1, T. Inomata and D. Triadan, general editors. University of Utah Press, Salt Lake City.

Inomata, T., and K. Aoyama

1996      Central-Place Analyses in the La Entrada Region, Honduras: Implications for Understanding the Classic Maya Political and Economic Systems. *Latin American Antiquity* 7(4):291–312.

Inomata, T., and M. Eberl

2010      The Barranca Escondida. In *Burned Palaces and Elite Residences of Aguateca: Excavations and Ceramics*, edited by T. Inomata and D. Triadan, pp. 138–148. Monograph of the Aguateca Archaeological Project First Phase 1, T. Inomata and D. Triadan, general editors. University of Utah Press, Salt Lake City.

2014      Stone Ornaments and Other Stone Artifacts. In *Life and Politics at the Royal Court of Aguateca. Artifacts, Analytical Data, and Synthesis*, edited by T. Inomata and D. Triadan, pp. 84–117. Monographs of the Aguateca Archaeological Project First Phase 3, T. Inomata and D. Triadan, general editors. University of Utah Press, Salt Lake City.

Inomata, T., and E. Ponciano

2010      The Palace Group. In *Burned Palaces and Elite Residences of Aguateca: Excavations and Ceramics*, edited by T. Inomata and D. Triadan, pp. 23–52. Monograph of the Aguateca Archaeological Project First Phase 1, T. Inomata and D. Triadan, general editors. University of Utah Press, Salt Lake City.

Inomata, T., E. M. Ponciano, O. Chinchilla, O. Román, V. Breuil-Martínez, and O. Santos

2004      An Unfinished Temple at the Classic Maya Center of Aguateca, Guatemala. *Antiquity* 78(302):798–811.

Inomata, T., and D. Triadan (editors)

2010      *Burned Palaces and Elite Residences of Aguateca: Excavations and Ceramics*. University of Utah Press, Salt Lake City.

2014      *Life and Politics at the Royal Court of Aguateca: Artifacts, Analytical Data, and Synthesis*. University of Utah Press, Salt Lake City.

Inomata, T., D. Triadan, K. Aoyama, V. Castillo, and H. Yonenobu

2013      Early Ceremonial Constructions at Ceibal, Guatemala, and the Origins of Lowland Maya Civilization. *Science* 340(6131):467–471.

Inomata, T., D. Triadan, and E. Pinto

2010      Complete, Reconstructible, and Partial Vessels. In *Burned Palaces and Elite Residences of Aguateca: Excavations and Ceramics*, edited by T. Inomata and D. Triadan, pp. 180–361. Monograph of the Aguateca Archaeological Project First Phase 1. University of Utah Press, Salt Lake City.

Inomata, T., D. Triadan, E. Ponciano, E. Pinto, R. E. Terry and M. Eberl

2002        Domestic and Political Lives of Classic Maya Elites: The Excavation of Rapidly Abandoned Structures at Aguateca, Guatemala. *Latin American Antiquity* 13(3):305–330.

Inomata, T., D. Triadan, E. Ponciano, R. E. Terry, and H. F. Beaubien

2001        In the Palace of the Fallen King: The Royal Residential Complex at Aguateca, Guatemala. *Journal of Field Archaeology* 28(3–4):287–306.

Instituto Nacional de Antropología

2016        Estudian entierro de mujer de élite descubierta en Teotihuacan. Electronic document, http://www.inah.gob.mx/es/boletines/5386-estudian-entierro-de-mujer-de-elite-descubierta-en-teotihuacan, accessed October 10, 2016.

Jackson, M.

1998        *Minima Ethnographica: Intersubjectivity and the Anthropological Project.* University of Chicago Press, Chicago.

Jackson, S. E.

2013        *Politics of the Maya Court: Hierarchy and Change in the Late Classic Period.* University of Oklahoma Press, Norman.

Jackson, S. E., and D. Stuart

2003        The *Aj K'uhun* Title: Deciphering a Classic Maya Term of Rank. *Ancient Mesoamerica* 12(2):217–228.

Jakobson, R., and M. Halle

1956        *Fundamentals of Language.* Janua Linguarum Minor Series Vol. 1. Mouton, The Hague.

Jastrow, J.

1899        The Mind's Eye. *Popular Science Monthly* 54:299–312.

Johnson, M.

1987        *The Body in the Mind: The Bodily Basis of Meaning, Imagination, and Reason.* University of Chicago Press, Chicago.

Johnston, K. J., and N. Gonlin

1998        What Do Houses Mean? Approaches to the Analysis of Classic Maya Commoner Residences. In *Function and Meaning in Classic Maya Architecture*, edited by S. D. Houston, pp. 141–185. Dumbarton Oaks, Washington, D.C.

Jones, A.

2007        *The Qur'ān.* Translated by A. Jones. Gibb Memorial Trust, Cambridge.

Jones, A. H.

1980        *Wealth of a Nation to Be: The American Colonies on the Eve of the Revolution.* Columbia University Press, New York.

Jones, G. D.

1982        Agriculture and Trade in the Colonial-Period Southern Maya Lowlands. In *Maya Subsistence: Studies in Memory of Dennis E. Puleston*, edited by K. V. Flannery, pp. 275–293. Academic Press, New York.

Jones, R.

1977        The Tasmanian Paradox. In *Stone Tools As Cultural Markers: Change, Evolution and Complexity*, edited by R.V.S. Wright, pp. 189–204. Prehistory and Material Culture Series 12. Humanities Press, Atlantic Highlands, New Jersey.

Jordan, B.

1989        Cosmopolitical Obstetrics: Some Insights from the Training of Traditional Midwives. *Social Science & Medicine* 28(9):925–944.

Josserand, J. K., and N. A. Hopkins

2001        Chol Ritual Language. Electronic document, http://www.famsi.org/reports/94017/index.html, accessed September 6, 2012.

Joyce, A. A., L. A. Bustamante, and M. N. Levine

2001        Commoner Power: A Case Study from the Classic Period Collapse on the Oaxaca Coast. *Journal of Archaeological Method and Theory* 8(4):343–385.

Joyce, R. A.

1992        Ideology in Action: Classic Maya Ritual Practice. In *Ancient Images, Ancient Thought: The Archaeology of Ideology. Proceedings of the Twenty-Third Annual Conference of the Archaeological Association of the University of Calgary*, edited by A. S. Goldsmith, S. Garvie, D. Selin, and J. Smith, pp. 497–505. University of Calgary Archaeological Association, Calgary, Alberta.

2005        Archaeology of the Body. *Annual Review of Anthropology* 34:139–158.

Joyce, R. A., and J. Lopiparo

2005        Postscript: Doing Agency in Archaeology. *Journal of Archaeological Method and Theory* 12(4):365–374.

Juana Inés de la Cruz

1988        *A Sor Juana Anthology*. Translated by A. S. Trueblood. Harvard University Press, Cambridge, Massachusetts.

Kamp, K. A.

2001        Prehistoric Children Working and Playing: A Southwestern Case Study in Learning Ceramics. *Journal of Anthropological Research* 57(4):427–450.

Kaufman, T. S.

1976        Archaeological and Linguistic Correlations in Mayaland and Associated Areas of Meso-America. *World Archaeology* 8(1):101–118.

Kaufman, T. S., and W. M. Norman

1984        An Outline of Proto-Cholan Phonology, Morphology, and Vocabulary. In *Phoneticism in Mayan Hieroglyphic Writing*, edited by J. S. Justeson and L. Campbell, pp. 77–166. Institute for Mesoamerican Studies Publication 9. University of Albany, State University of New York, Albany.

Keane, W.

1997        *Signs of Recognition: Powers and Hazards of Representation in an Indonesian Society*. University of California Press, Berkeley.

2003        Semiotics and the Social Analysis of Material Things. *Language & Communication* 23:409–425.

2005        Signs Are Not the Garb of Meaning: On the Social Analysis of Material Things. In *Materiality*, edited by D. Miller, pp. 182–205. Duke University Press, Durham, North Carolina.

Kelly, J. D., and M. Kaplan

1990        History, Structure, and Ritual. *Annual Review of Anthropology* 19:119–150.

Kelly-Buccellati, M.

2012        Apprenticeship and Learning from the Ancestors: The Case of Ancient

Urkesh. In *Archaeology and Apprenticeship: Body Knowledge, Identity, and Communities of Practice*, edited by W. Wendrich, pp. 203–223. University of Arizona Press, Tucson.

Kempe, M., and A. Mesoudi

2014    An Experimental Demonstration of the Effect of Group Size on Cultural Accumulation. *Evolution and Human Behavior* 35(4):285–290.

Kerr, J.

1989    *The Maya Vase Book: A Corpus of Rollout Photographs of Maya Vessels*. Vol. 1. Kerr Associates, New York.

1990    *The Maya Vase Book: A Corpus of Rollout Photographs of Maya Vessels*. Vol. 2. Kerr Associates, New York.

1992    *The Maya Vase Book: A Corpus of Rollout Photographs of Maya Vessels*. Vol. 3. Kerr Associates, New York.

2000    *The Maya Vase Book: A Corpus of Rollout Photographs of Maya Vessels*. Vol. 6. Kerr Associates, New York.

Kertzer, D. I.

1988    *Ritual, Politics, and Power*. Yale University Press, New Haven, Connecticut.

King, E. M. (editor)

2015    *The Ancient Maya Marketplace: The Archaeology of Transient Space*. University of Arizona Press, Tucson.

Klepper, M. M., and R. Gunther

1996    *The Wealthy 100: From Benjamin Franklin to Bill Gates—A Ranking of the Richest Americans, Past and Present*. Carol, Secaucus, New Jersey.

Kline, M. A., and R. Boyd

2010    Population Size Predicts Technological Complexity in Oceania. *Proceedings of the Royal Society B: Biological Sciences* 277(1693):2559–2564.

Knoke de Arathoon, B.

2005    *Símbolos que se siembran*. Museo Ixchel del Traje Indígena, Guatemala City.

Knowlton, T. W.

2002    Diphrastic Kennings in Mayan Hieroglyphic Literature. *Mexicon* 24(1):9–14.

2010    *Maya Creation Myths: Words and Worlds of the Chilam Balam*. University Press of Colorado, Boulder.

Kohler, T. A., S. Van Buskirk, and S. Ruscavage-Barz

2004    Vessels and Villages: Evidence for Conformist Transmission in Early Village Aggregations on the Pajarito Plateau, New Mexico. *Journal of Anthropological Archaeology* 23(1):100–118.

Krempel, G.

2014    A Unique Carved Greenstone Artifact in the Chocolate Museum, Cologne. *Mexicon* 36(5):125–130.

Kripke, S. A.

1981    *Naming and Necessity*. Blackwell, Malden, Massachusetts.

Krusch, B. (editor)

1885    *Gregorii Turonensis opera 2: Miracula et opera minora*. Hahnsche Buchhandlung, Hannovera.

Kuchta, D.

2002 *The Three-Piece Suit and Modern Masculinity: England, 1550–1850*. Studies on the History of Society and Culture 47. University of California Press, Berkeley.

Kueng, L., and E. Yakovlev

2014 How Persistent Are Consumption Habits? Micro-Evidence from Russia's Alcohol Market. Electronic document, http://www.nber.org/papers/w20298.pdf, accessed October 7, 2014.

Kuhn, T. S.

1996 *The Structure of Scientific Revolutions*. 3rd ed. University of Chicago Press, Chicago.

Lacadena, A.

1997 Bilingüismo en el Códice de Madrid. *Los Investigadores de la Cultura Maya* 5(1):184–204.

2008 El título *lakam*: evidencia epigráfica sobre la organización tributaria y militar interna de los reinos mayas del Clásico. *Mayab* 20:23–43.

Lacadena, A., and S. Wichmann

2004 On the Representation of the Glottal Stop in Maya Writing. In *The Linguistics of Maya Writing*, edited by S. Wichmann, pp. 103–162. University of Utah, Salt Lake City.

Lamoureux-St-Hilaire, M., S. Macrae, C. A. McCane, E. A. Parker, and G. Iannone

2015 The Last Groups Standing: Living Abandonment at the Ancient Maya Center of Minanha, Belize. *Latin American Antiquity* 26(4):550–569.

Lancy, D. F.

2015 *The Anthropology of Childhood. Cherubs, Chattel, Changelings*. 2nd ed. Cambridge University Press, Cambridge.

Lane, F. C.

1973 *Venice, a Maritime Republic*. Johns Hopkins University Press, Baltimore, Maryland.

Laughlin, R. M.

1988 *The Great Tzotzil Dictionary of Santo Domingo Zinacantán*. Smithsonian Contributions to Anthropology 31. Smithsonian Institution Press, Washington, D.C.

Lave, J.

1977 Tailor-Made Experiments and Evaluating the Intellectual Consequences of Apprenticeship Training. *Quarterly Newsletter of the Institute for Comparative Human Development* 1(2):1–3.

Lave, J., and E. Wenger

1991 *Situated Learning: Legitimate Peripheral Participation*. Cambridge University Press, Cambridge.

Layton, R.

1989 Pellaport. In *What's New? A Closer Look at the Process of Innovation*, edited by S. E. v. d. Leeuw and R. Torrence, pp. 33–53. One World Archaeology 14. Unwin Hyman, London.

Leach, E. R.
1962        On Certain Unconsidered Aspects of Double Descent Systems. *Man* 62:130–134.
LeCount, L. J.
1999        Polychrome Pottery and Political Strategies in Late and Terminal Classic Lowland Maya Society. *Latin American Antiquity* 10(3):239–258.
Lee, T. A.
1985        *Los códices mayas.* Universidad Autónoma de Chiapas, Tuxtla Gutiérrez, México.
Leenhardt, M.
1979        *Do Kamo: Person and Myth in the Melanesian World.* Translated by B. M. Gulati. University of Chicago Press, Chicago.
Leibowitz, E.
1999        Bar Codes: Reading between the Lines. *Smithsonian* 29(11):130–146.
Lemonnier, P.
1986        The Study of Material Culture Today: Towards an Anthropology of Technical Systems. *Journal of Anthropological Archaeology* 5(2):147–186.
1993        *Technological Choices: Transformation in Material Cultures since the Neolithic.* Routledge, London.
Leo, R. F., and E. S. Barghoorn
1976        Silicification of Wood. *Botanical Museum Leaflets, Harvard University* 25(1):1–47.
León-Portilla, M.
1963        *Aztec Thought and Culture: A Study of the Ancient Nahuatl Mind.* Translated by J. E. Davis. University of Oklahoma Press, Norman.
1985        Nahuatl Literature. In *Literatures*, edited by M. S. Edmonson, pp. 7–43. Supplement to the Handbook of Middle American Indians 3, V. R. Bricker, general editor. University of Texas Press, Austin.
Lethem, J.
2007        The Ecstasy of Influence: A Plagiarism. *Harper's Magazine* 314(1881):59–71.
Leventhal, R. M.
1979        Settlement Patterns at Copan, Honduras. Unpublished Ph.D. dissertation, Department of Anthropology, Harvard University, Cambridge, Massachusetts.
Lévi-Strauss, C.
1960        Four Winnebago Myths: A Structural Sketch. In *Culture in History: Essays in Honor of Paul Radin*, edited by S. Diamond, pp. 351–362. Columbia University Press, New York.
1966        *The Savage Mind.* Translated by G. Weidenfeld. University of Chicago Press, Chicago.
1969        *The Elementary Structures of Kinship.* Translated by J. H. Bell, J. R. v. Sturmer, and R. Needham. Beacon Press, Boston.
1987        *Introduction to the Work of Marcel Mauss.* Translated by F. Baker. Routledge & Kegan Paul, London.

Lewent, K.
1905    *Das altprovenzalische Kreuzlied.* Druck von Junge und Sohn, Erlangen, Germany.

Lewis, O.
1951    *Life in a Mexican Village: Tepoztlán Restudied.* University of Illinois Press, Urbana.

Liddell, H. G., and R. Scott
1996    *A Greek-English Lexicon.* Clarendon Press, Oxford.

Lienhardt, R. G.
1961    *Divinity and Experience: The Religion of the Dinka.* Oxford University Press, London.

Lincoln, A.
1920    *Abraham Lincoln; Complete Works, Comprising His Speeches, Letters, State Papers, and Miscellaneous Writings.* Century Co., New York.

Linton, R.
1936    *The Study of Man: An Introduction.* D. Appleton-Century, New York.

Lohmann, R. I.
2003    Dream Travels and Anthropology. In *Dream Travelers: Sleep Experiences and Culture in the Western Pacific,* edited by R. I. Lohmann, pp. 1–17. Palgrave Macmillan, New York.

Lohse, J. C.
2007    Commoner Ritual, Commoner Ideology: (Sub)Alternate Views of Social Complexity in Prehispanic Mesoamerica. In *Commoner Ritual and Ideology in Ancient Mesoamerica,* edited by N. Gonlin and J. C. Lohse, pp. 1–32. University Press of Colorado, Boulder.
2010    Archaic Origins of the Lowland Maya. *Latin American Antiquity* 21(3):312–352.

Loibl, C., L. E. Jones, E. Haisley, and G. Loewenstein
2016    Testing Strategies to Increase Saving and Retention in Individual Development Account Programs. Electronic document, http://ssrn.com/abstract=2735625, accessed February 24, 2016.

Longyear, J. M., III
1952    *Copan Ceramics: A Study of Southeastern Maya Pottery.* Carnegie Institution of Washington Publication 597. Carnegie Institution of Washington, Washington, D.C.

Looper, M. G.
2003    *Lightning Warrior: Maya Art and Kingship at Quirigua.* University of Texas Press, Austin.
2004    *Birds and Thorns: Textile Designs of San Martín Sacatepéquez.* Editorial Antigua, Guatemala City.
2009    *To Be Like Gods: Dance in Ancient Maya Civilization.* University of Texas Press, Austin.

López Austin, A.
1980    *Cuerpo humano e ideología: las concepciones de los antiguos nahuas.* Serie

Antropológica 39. Instituto de Investigaciones Antropológicas, Universidad Nacional Autónoma de México, México, D.F.

López Cogolludo, D., and F. d. Ayeta
1685        *Historia de Yucathan*. Juan García Infanzon, Madrid.

López Olivares, N. M.
1997        Cultural Odontology: Dental Alterations from Petén, Guatemala. In *Bones of the Maya: Studies of Ancient Skeletons*, edited by S. L. Whittington and D. M. Reed, pp. 105–115. Smithsonian Institution Press, Washington, D.C.

Lounsbury, F. G.
1976        A Rationale for the Initial Date of the Temple of the Cross at Palenque. In *The Art, Iconography, and Dynastic History of Palenque*. Part III: *Proceedings of the Segunda Mesa Redonda de Palenque*, edited by M. Greene Robertson, pp. 211–224. Robert Louis Stevenson School, Pebble Beach, Florida.

Lucero, L. J.
2003        The Politics of Ritual. The Emergence of Classic Maya Rulers. *Current Anthropology* 44(4):523–558.
2010        Materialized Cosmology among Ancient Maya Commoners. *Journal of Social Archaeology* 10(1):138–167.

Luhmann, N.
1981        Gerechtigkeit in den Rechtssystemen der modernen Gesellschaft. In *Ausdifferenzierung des Rechts: Beiträge zur Rechtssoziologie und Rechtstheorie*, edited by N. Luhmann, pp. 374–418. Suhrkamp, Frankfurt am Main.

Luria, A. R.
1961        *The Role of Speech in the Regulation of Normal and Abnormal Behavior*. Liveright, New York.
1966        *Higher Cortical Functions in Man*. Translated by B. Haigh. Basic Books, New York.

Lyons, J.
1977        *Semantics*. Cambridge University Press, Cambridge.

MacLeod, B.
1990        Deciphering the Primary Standard Sequence. Unpublished Ph.D. dissertation, Department of Art History, University of Texas, Austin.

Mageo, J. M.
2003        Subjectivity and Identity in Dreams. In *Dreaming and the Self: New Perspectives on Subjectivity, Identity, and Emotion*, edited by J. M. Mageo, pp. 23–40. State University of New York Press, Albany.

Mahmood, S.
2005        *Politics of Piety: The Islamic Revival and the Feminist Subject*. Princeton University Press, Princeton, New Jersey.

Malinowski, B.
1948        *Magic, Science and Religion, and Other Essays*. Beacon Press, Boston.

Manahan, T. K.
2004        The Way Things Fall Apart: Social Organization and the Classic Maya Collapse of Copan. *Ancient Mesoamerica* 15(1):107–125.

Marcus, J.

1976        *Emblem and State in the Classic Maya Lowlands: An Epigraphic Approach to Territorial Organization.* Dumbarton Oaks, Trustees for Harvard University, Washington, D.C.

Marquet, P. A., C. M. Santoro, C. Latorre, V. G. Standen, S. R. Abades, M. M. Rivadeneira, B. Arriaza, and M. E. Hochberg

2012        Emergence of Social Complexity among Coastal Hunter-Gatherers in the Atacama Desert of Northern Chile. *Proceedings of the National Academy of Sciences of the United States of America* 109(37):14754–14760.

Martin, S.

1997        The Painted King List: A Commentary on Codex-Style Dynastic Vessels. In *The Maya Vase Book: A Corpus of Rollout Photographs of Maya Vases,* Vol. 5, edited by B. Kerr and J. Kerr, pp. 847–867. Kerr Associates, New York.

2000        At the Periphery: The Movement, Modification, and Re-Use of Early Monuments in the Environs of Tikal. In *The Sacred and the Profane: Architecture and Identity in the Maya Lowlands. (3rd European Maya Conference, University of Hamburg, November 1998)*, edited by P. R. Colas, K. Delvendahl, M. Kuhnert and A. Schubart, pp. 51–61. Acta Mesoamericana 10. Saurwein, Markt Schwaben, Germany.

2006        On Pre-Columbian Narrative: Representation across the Word-Image Divide. In *A Pre-Columbian World*, edited by J. Quilter and M. E. Miller, pp. 55–105. Dumbarton Oaks, Washington, D.C.

2012        Hieroglyphs from the Painted Pyramid: The Epigraphy of Chiik Nahb Structure Sub 1-4, Calakmul, Mexico. In *Maya Archaeology 2*, edited by C. W. Golden, S. D. Houston, and J. Skidmore, pp. 60–81. Precolumbia Mesoweb Press, San Francisco, California.

Martin, S., and N. K. Grube

2008        *Chronicle of the Maya Kings and Queens. Deciphering the Dynasties of the Ancient Maya.* 2nd ed. Thames & Hudson, London.

Marx, K., and F. Engels

1998 [1846] *The German Ideology, including Theses on Feuerbach and Introduction to the Critique of Political Economy.* Prometheus Books, New York.

Mathews, P. L.

1991        Classic Maya Emblem Glyphs. In *Classic Maya Political History: Hieroglyphic and Archaeological Evidence*, edited by P. T. Culbert, pp. 19–29. Cambridge University Press, Cambridge.

Mauss, M.

1972        *A General Theory of Magic.* Translated by R. Brain. Routledge and Kegan Paul, London.

1990        *The Gift: The Form and Reason for Exchange in Archaic Societies.* Translated by W. D. Halls. W. W. Norton, New York.

Mayer, K. H.

1995        *Maya Monuments: Sculptures of Unknown Provenance, Supplement 4.* Maya Monuments 7. Academic, Graz, Austria.

Maynard, A. E.
2004    Cultures of Teaching in Childhood: Formal Schooling and Maya Sibling Teaching at Home. *Cognitive Development* 19:517–535.

McAnany, P. A.
1993    The Economics of Social Power and Wealth among Eighth-Century Maya Households. In *Lowland Maya Civilization in the Eighth Century A.D.*, edited by J. A. Sabloff and J. S. Henderson, pp. 65–89. Dumbarton Oaks, Washington, D.C.
1995    *Living with the Ancestors: Kinship and Kingship in Ancient Maya Society.* University of Texas Press, Austin.
2010    *Ancestral Maya Economies in Archaeological Perspective.* Cambridge University Press, Cambridge.

McAnany, P. A., and S. E. Plank
2001    Perspectives on Actors, Gender Roles, and Architecture at Classic Maya Courts and Households. In *Royal Courts of the Ancient Maya*, Vol. 1, edited by T. Inomata and S. D. Houston, pp. 84–129. Westview Press, Boulder, Colorado.

McCumber, J.
2011    *Time and Philosophy: A History of Continental Thought.* McGill-Queen's University Press, Montreal.

McGee, R. J.
1990    *Life, Ritual, and Religion among the Lacandon Maya.* Wadsworth, Belmont, California.

McGlade, J., and J. M. McGlade
1989    Modelling the Innovative Component of Social Change. In *What's New? A Closer Look at the Process of Innovation*, edited by S. E. v. d. Leeuw and R. Torrence, pp. 281–299. One World Archaeology 14. Unwin Hyman, London.

McGuire, R. H.
1983    Breaking Down Cultural Complexity: Inequality and Heterogeneity. *Advances in Archaeological Method and Theory* 6:91–142.

Medin, D. L., and B. H. Ross
1996    *Cognitive Psychology.* 2nd ed. Harcourt Brace, Orlando, Florida.

Mejía-Arauz, R., B. Rogoff, and R. Paradise
2005    Cultural Variation in Children's Observation during a Demonstration. *International Journal of Behavioral Development* 29(4):282–291.

Meskell, L. M.
2005    Objects in the Mirror Appear Closer Than They Are. In *Materiality*, edited by D. Miller, pp. 51–71. Duke University Press, Durham, North Carolina.

Milanović, B.
2005    *Worlds Apart: Measuring International and Global Inequality.* Princeton University Press, Princeton, New Jersey.

Miller, A. G.
1986    *Maya Rulers of Time.* University Museum, University of Pennsylvania, Philadelphia.

Miller, D.

1985        *Artefacts as Categories: A Study of Ceramic Variability in Central India*. Cambridge University Press, Cambridge.

1987        *Material Culture and Mass Consumption*. Blackwell, Oxford.

Miller, D., and C. Y. Tilley

1984        Ideology, Power and Prehistory: An Introduction. In *Ideology, Power, and Prehistory*, edited by D. Miller and C. Y. Tilley, pp. 1–16. Cambridge University Press, Cambridge.

Miller, H. M.-L.

2012        Types of Learning in Apprenticeship. In *Archaeology and Apprenticeship: Body Knowledge, Identity, and Communities of Practice*, edited by W. Wendrich, pp. 224–239. University of Arizona Press, Tucson.

Miller, M. E.

1986        *The Murals of Bonampak*. Princeton University Press, Princeton, New Jersey.

Miller, M. E., and S. D. Houston

1987        The Classic Maya Ballgame and Its Architectural Setting: A Study of Relations between Text and Image. *Res: Anthropology and Aesthetics* 14:46–66.

Miller, M. E., and S. Martin (editors)

2004        *Courtly Art of the Ancient Maya*. Thames & Hudson, New York.

Minsky, M. L.

1975        A Framework for Representing Knowledge. In *The Psychology of Computer Vision*, edited by P. H. Winston, pp. 211–277. McGraw-Hill, New York.

Misch, C. E.

2007        *Contemporary Implant Dentistry*. Mosby Elsevier, St. Louis, Missouri.

Mishra, P.

2014        Introduction *to The Time Regulation Institute*, edited by A. H. Tanpınar, pp. vii–xix. Translated by M. Freely and A. Dawe. Penguin Books, New York.

Mitchell, R. P.

1969        *The Society of the Muslim Brothers*. Middle Eastern Monographs 9. Oxford University Press, London.

Moholy-Nagy, H.

2003        *The Artifacts of Tikal: Utilitarian Artifacts and Unworked Material*. Tikal Report 27, Part B. University of Pennsylvania Museum of Archaeology and Anthropology, Philadelphia.

Monaghan, J. D.

1998        The Person, Destiny, and the Construction of Difference in Mesoamerica. *Res: Anthropology and Aesthetics* 33:137–146.

2000        Theology and History in the Study of Mesoamerican Religion. In *Ethnology*, Supplement 6 to the *Handbook of Middle American Indians*, edited by J. D. Monaghan, pp. 24–49. University of Texas Press, Austin.

Montgomery, J. E.

1995        Sculptors of the Realm: Classic Maya Artists' Signatures and Sculptural Style during the Reign of Piedras Negras Ruler 7, Department of Fine Arts, University of New Mexico, Albuquerque.

Morris, E. H., J. Charlot, and A. A. Morris
1931    *The Temple of the Warriors at Chichen Itzá, Yucatan.* Carnegie Publication 406. Carnegie Institution of Washington, Washington, D.C.

Morris, W. F., Jr.
1987a   *Living Maya.* Harry N. Abrams, New York.
1987b   *Symbolism of a Ceremonial Huipil of the Highland Tzotzil Maya Community of Magdalenas, Chiapas.* Notes of the New World Archaeological Foundation 4. Brigham Young University, Provo, Utah.

Morrison, D. E., K. Kumar, E. M. Rogers, and F. C. Fliegel
1976    Stratification and Risk-Taking: A Further Negative Replication of Cancian's Theory. *American Sociological Review* 41(5):912–919.

Munn, N. D.
1983    Gawan Kula: Spatiotemporal Control and the Symbolism of Influence. In *The Kula: New Perspectives on Massim Exchange,* edited by J. W. Leach and E. R. Leach, pp. 277–308. Cambridge University Press, Cambridge.
1986    *The Fame of Gawa: A Symbolic Study of Value Transformation in a Massim (Papua New Guinea) Society.* Cambridge University Press, Cambridge.
1990    Constructing Regional Worlds in Experience: Kula Exchange, Witchcraft and Gawan Local Events. *Man* 25(1):1–17.
1992    The Cultural Anthropology of Time: A Critical Essay. *Annual Review of Anthropology* 21:93–123.

Murata, K. J.
1940    Volcanic Ash as a Source of Silica for the Silification of Wood. *American Journal of Science* 238(8):586–596.

Muthukrishna, M., B. W. Shulman, V. Vasilescu, and J. Henrich
2013    Sociality Influences Cultural Complexity. *Proceedings of the Royal Society B: Biological Sciences* 281(1774):20132511.

Myers, N., R. A. Mittermeier, C. G. Mittermeier, G.A.B. da Fonseca, and J. Kent
2000    Biodiversity Hotspots for Conservation Priorities. *Nature* 403(6772):853–858.

Nabokov, V. V.
1992    *Pale Fire.* Everyman's Library 67. Alfred A. Knopf, New York.

Nash, J.
1967    The Logic of Behavior: Curing in a Maya Indian Town. *Human Organization* 26(3):132–140.

Nash, M.
1958    *Machine Age Maya: The Industrialization of a Guatemalan Community.* Memoir 87. American Anthropological Association, Menasha, Wisconsin.

Neisser, U.
1976    *Cognition and Reality: Principles and Implications of Cognitive Psychology.* W. H. Freeman, San Francisco, California.

Netting, R. M.
1982    Some Truths on Household Size and Wealth. *American Behavioral Scientist* 25(6):641–662.

Nickerson, D. W., and T. Rogers
2010    Do You Have a Voting Plan? Implementation Intentions, Voter Turnout, and Organic Plan Making. *Psychological Science* 21(2):194–199.

Nicklin, K.
1971    Stability and Innovation in Pottery Manufacture. *World Archaeology* 3(1):13–48.

Offit, T. A.
2008    *Conquistadores de la Calle: Child Street Labor in Guatemala City.* University of Texas Press, Austin.

Ortmann, C.
1996    Minnedienst—Gottesdienst—Herrendienst. Zur Typologie des Kreuzliedes bei Hartmann von Aue. In *Lied im deutschen Mittelalter: Überlieferung, Typen, Gebrauch,* edited by C. W. Edwards, E. Hellgardt, and N. H. Ott, pp. 81–99. De Gruyter, Tübingen, Germany.

Ortmann, C., and H. Ragotzky
1993    Das Kreuzlied. Minne und Kreuzfahrt. Albrecht von Johansdorf: "Guote liute, holt die gâbe." In *Gedichte und Interpretationen. Mittelalter,* edited by H. Tervooren, pp. 169–190. Reclams Universalbibliothek 8864. Reclam, Ditzingen, Germany.

Palka, J. W.
2002    Left/Right Symbolism and the Body in Ancient Maya Iconography and Culture. *Latin American Antiquity* 13(4):419–443.
2014    *Maya Pilgrimage to Ritual Landscape: Insights from Archaeology, History, and Ethnography.* University of New Mexico Press, Albuquerque.

Papadopoulos, J. K., and G. Urton
2012    Introduction: The Construction of Value in the Ancient World. In *The Construction of Value in the Ancient World,* edited by J. K. Papadopoulos and G. Urton, pp. 1–47. Cotsen Advanced Seminar Series 5. Cotsen Institute of Archaeology, University of California, Los Angeles.

Papousek, D. A.
1981    *The Peasant-Potters of Los Pueblos: Stimulus Situation and Adaptive Processes in the Mazahua Region in Central Mexico.* Studies of Developing Countries 27. Van Gorcum, Assen, The Netherlands.
1989    Technological Change as Social Rebellion. In *What's New? A Closer Look at the Process of Innovation,* edited by S. E. v. d. Leeuw and R. Torrence, pp. 140–166. One World Archaeology 14. Unwin Hyman, London.

Park, R. E.
1928    Human Migration and the Marginal Man. *American Journal of Sociology* 33(6):881–893.

Parmington, A.
2003    Classic Maya Status and the Subsidiary "Office" of Sajal: A Comparative Study of Status as Represented in Costume and Composition in the Iconography of Monuments. *Mexicon* 25(2):46–53.

Pauketat, T. R.

2001    Practice and History in Archaeology: An Emerging Paradigm. *Anthropological Theory* 1(1):73–98.

2007    *Chiefdoms and Other Archaeological Delusions*. University of Alabama Press, Tuscaloosa.

Pazos Garciandía, Á.

1995    El modelo del actor en Giddens: una exposición crítica. *Revista Española de Antropología Americana* 25:205–221.

Pendergast, D. M.

1970    Tumbaga Object from the Early Classic Period, Found at Altun Ha, British Honduras (Belize). *Science* 168(3927):116–118.

1979–1990    *Excavations at Altun Ha, Belize, 1964–1970*. Royal Ontario Museum, Toronto.

Percy, W.

1966    *The Last Gentleman*. Farrar, Straus, and Giroux, New York.

Pérez Martínez, V., F. García, F. Martínez Álvarez, and J. López y López

1996    *Diccionario del idioma Ch'orti,' Jocotán, Chiquimula*. Proyecto Lingüístico Francisco Marroquín, Antigua, Guatemala.

Pfaffenberger, B.

1992    Social Anthropology of Technology. *Annual Review of Anthropology* 21:491–516.

Piperno, D. R., E. Weiss, I. Holst, and D. Nadel

2004    Processing of Wild Cereal Grains in the Upper Palaeolithic Revealed by Starch Grain Analysis. *Nature* 430(7000):670–673.

Pohl, M. D., K. O. Pope, J. G. Jones, J. S. Jacob, D. R. Piperno, S. D. de France, D. L. Lentz, J. A. Gifford, M. E. Danforth, and J. K. Josserand

1996    Early Agriculture in the Maya Lowlands. *Latin American Antiquity* 7(4):355–372.

Pohl, M. E. D., K. O. Pope, and C. L. von Nagy

2002    Olmec Origins of Mesoamerican Writing. *Science* 298(5600):1984–1987.

Politis, G. G.

2007    *Nukak: Ethnoarcheology of an Amazonian People*. Translated by B. Alberti. Left Coast Press, Walnut Creek, California.

Popenoe, D. H.

1934    Some Excavations at Playa de los Muertos, Ulua River, Honduras. *Maya Research* 1(2):8–85.

Powell, A., S. Shennan, and M. G. Thomas

2009    Late Pleistocene Demography and the Appearance of Modern Human Behavior. *Science* 324(5932):1298–1301.

Prager, C. M.

2000a    Enanismo y gibosidad: las personas afectadas y sus identidad en la sociedad maya del tiempo prehispánico. In *La organización social entre los mayas prehispánicos, coloniales y modernos*, edited by V. Tiesler Blos, pp. 35–68. Memoria de la Tercera Mesa Redonda de Palenque. INAH, UADY, México, D.F.

2000b       Hofzwerge—Begleiter der Herrschenden und Boten der Unterwelt. In *Maya. Gottkönige im Regenwald*, edited by N. K. Grube, pp. 278–279. Könemann, Köln, Germany.

Prechtel, M., and R. S. Carlsen

1988       Weaving and Cosmos amongst the Tzutujil Maya of Guatemala. *Res: Anthropology and Aesthetics* 15:122–132.

Proskouriakoff, T. A.

1963       *An Album of Maya Architecture.* University of Oklahoma Press, Norman.

Putnam, R. D.

2000       *Bowling Alone. The Collapse and Revival of American Community.* Simon and Schuster, New York.

Quart, A.

2013       *Republic of Outsiders: The Power of Amateurs, Dreamers, and Rebels.* New Press, New York.

Rampal, A.

2003       The Meaning of Numbers: Understanding Street and Folk Mathematics. In *Reading beyond the Alphabet: Innovations in Lifelong Literacy*, edited by B. Kothari, P. G. Vijaya, S. Chand, and M. Norton, pp. 241–258. Sage, New Delhi.

Rands, R. L., and R. L. Bishop

1980       Resource Procurement Zones and Patterns of Ceramic Exchange in the Palenque Region, Mexico. In *Models and Methods in Regional Exchange*, edited by R. E. Fry, pp. 19–46. SAA Paper 1. Society for American Archaeology, Washington, D.C.

Rathje, W. L.

1971       Lowland Classic Maya Socio-Political Organization: Degree and Form through Time and Space. Unpublished Ph.D. dissertation, Department of Anthropology, Harvard University, Cambridge, Massachusetts.

Ratner, B. D.

2013       History of Biomaterials. In *Biomaterials Science: An Introduction to Materials in Medicine*, edited by B. D. Ratner, A. S. Hoffman, F. J. Schoen, and J. E. Lemons, pp. xli–liii. 3rd ed. Academic Press, Waltham, Massachusetts.

Redfield, R.

1955       *The Little Community: Viewpoints for the Study of a Human Whole.* University of Chicago Press, Chicago.

Redfield, R., and M. P. Redfield

1940       *Disease and Its Treatment in Dzitás, Yucatán.* Carnegie Institution of Washington Publication 523. Carnegie Institution of Washington, Washington, DC.

Redfield, R., and A. Villa Rojas

1934       *Chan Kom, a Maya Village.* Carnegie Institution of Washington Publication 448. Carnegie Institution of Washington, Washington, D.C.

Reents-Budet, D.

1998       Elite Maya Pottery and Artisans as Social Indicators. In *Craft and Social Identity*, edited by C. L. Costin and R. P. Wright, pp. 71–89. Archaeological Paper 8. American Anthropological Association, Washington D.C.

2006        The Social Context of Kakaw Drinking among the Ancient Maya. In *Choco-late in Mesoamerica: A Cultural History of Cacao*, edited by C. L. McNeil, pp. 202–223. University Press of Florida, Gainesville.

Reina, R. E.
1963        The Potter and the Farmer: The Fate of Two Innovators in a Maya Village. *Expedition* 5(4):18–30.

Reina, R. E., and R. M. Hill II
1978        *The Traditional Pottery of Guatemala*. University of Texas Press, Austin.

Renfrew, C.
2012        Systems of Value among Material Things: The Nexus of Fungibility and Mea-sure. In *The Construction of Value in the Ancient World*, edited by J. K. Pa-padopoulos and G. Urton, pp. 249–260. Cotsen Advanced Seminar Series 5. Cotsen Institute of Archaeology, University of California, Los Angeles.

Rheingold, H. L.
1982        Little Children's Participation in the Work of Adults, a Nascent Prosocial Be-havior. *Child Development* 53(1):114–125.

Rice, P. M.
1987        *Pottery Analysis: A Sourcebook*. University of Chicago Press, Chicago.
2004        *Maya Political Science: Time, Astronomy, and the Cosmos*. University of Texas Press, Austin.
2007        *Maya Calendar Origins: Monuments, Mythistory, and the Materialization of Time*. University of Texas Press, Austin.
2008        Time, Power, and the Maya. *Latin American Antiquity* 19(3):275–298.
2009        Late Classic Maya Pottery Production: Review and Synthesis. *Journal of Ar-chaeological Method and Theory* 16(2):117–156.

Ricœur, P.
1977        *The Rule of Metaphor: Multi-Disciplinary Studies of the Creation of Meaning in Language*. Translated by R. Czerny. University of Toronto Romance Series 37. University of Toronto Press, Toronto.

Riese, B.
1984        Hel Hieroglyphs. In *Phoneticism in Mayan Hieroglyphic Writing*, edited by J. S. Justeson and L. Campbell, pp. 263–286. Institute for Mesoamerican Studies Publication 9. State University of New York, Albany.

Ring, M. E.
1985        *Dentistry: An Illustrated History*. 2nd ed. Harry N. Abrams, New York.

Ringle, W. M., and E. W. Andrews V
1988        Formative Residences at Komchen, Yucatan, Mexico. In *Household and Com-munity in the Mesoamerican Past*, edited by R. R. Wilk and W. Ashmore, pp. 171–198. University of New Mexico Press, Albuquerque.

Riquelme, F., J. Alvarado-Ortega, M. Cuevas-García, J. L. Ruvalcaba-Sil, and C. Linares-López
2012        Calcareous Fossil Inclusions and Rock-Source of Maya Lime Plaster from the Temple of the Inscriptions, Palenque, Mexico. *Journal of Archaeological Sci-ence* 39(3):624–639.

Robb, J. E.
1998        The Archaeology of Symbols. *Annual Review of Current Anthropology* 27:329–346.
Robertson, J. S., D. A. Law, and R. A. Haertel
2010        *Colonial Ch'olti': The Seventeenth-Century Morán Manuscript.* University of Oklahoma Press, Norman.
Robertson, M. G.
1995        *Merle Greene Robertson's Rubbings of Maya Sculpture.* Pre-Columbian Art Research Institute, San Francisco, California.
Robertson, R. A.
1983        Functional Analysis and Social Process in Ceramics: The Pottery from Cerros, Belize. In *Civilization in the Ancient Americas: Essays in Honor of Gordon R. Willey,* edited by R. M. Leventhal and A. L. Kolata, pp. 105–142. University of New Mexico Press, Albuquerque.
Robicsek, F.
1975        *A Study in Maya Art and History: The Mat Symbol.* Museum of the American Indian, Heye Foundation, New York.
Robicsek, F., and D. M. Hales
1981        *The Maya Book of the Dead: The Ceramic Codex.* University of Oklahoma, Norman.
Robin, C.
2001        Peopling the Past: New Perspectives on the Ancient Maya. *Proceedings of the National Academy of Sciences of the United States of America* 98(1):18–21.
2002        Outside of Houses. The Practices of Everyday Life at Chan Nòohol, Belize. *Journal of Social Archaeology* 2(2):245–268.
2003        New Directions in Classic Maya Household Archaeology. *Journal of Archaeological Research* 11(4):307–355.
2006        Gender, Farming, and Long-Term Change: Maya Historical and Archaeological Perspectives. *Current Anthropology* 47(3):409–433.
2016        Neither Dopes nor Dupes: Maya Farmers and Ideology. *Ancient Mesoamerica* 27(1):221–230.
Robinson, W. S.
1951        A Method for Chronologically Ordering Archaeological Deposits. *American Antiquity* 16(4):293–301.
Robson, L. L.
1983        *A History of Tasmania.* Vol. I: *Van Diemen's Land from the Earliest Times to 1855.* Oxford University Press, Melbourne.
Rocha, O. d. l.
1985        The Reorganization of Arithmetic Practice in the Kitchen. *Anthropology & Education Quarterly* 16(3):193–198.
Rodas N., F., and O. Rodas Corzo
1938        *Simbolismos (maya quichés) de Guatemala.* Tipografía Nacional, Guatemala, C.A.
Rogers, E. M.
1995        *Diffusion of Innovations.* 4th ed. Free Press, New York.

Ross, N. O.

1994     Die Entwicklung der Blumenindustrie in Zinacantán. *Zeitschrift für Ethnologie* 119(1):59–73.

2004     *Culture and Cognition: Implications for Theory and Method*. Sage, Thousand Oaks, California.

Rowe, E. K.

2011     *Saint and Nation: Santiago, Teresa of Avila, and Plural Identities in Early Modern Spain*. Pennsylvania State University Press, University Park.

Roys, R. L.

1931     *The Ethnobotany of the Maya*. Middle American Research Series Publication 2. Tulane University, New Orleans, Louisiana.

1967     *The Book of Chilam Balam of Chumayel*. University of Oklahoma, Norman.

Rumelhart, D. E.

1980     Schemata: The Building Blocks of Cognition. In *Theoretical Issues in Reading Comprehension: Perspectives from Cognitive Psychology, Linguistics, Artificial Intelligence, and Education*, edited by R. J. Spiro, B. C. Bruce, and W. F. Brewer, pp. 33–58. Lawrence Erlbaum Associates, Hillsdale, New Jersey.

Ruz Lhuillier, A.

1952     Exploraciones en Palenque: 1951. *Anales del Instituto Nacional de Antropología e Historia* 5:47–66.

1959     *Palenque, Guía oficial*. INAH, México, D.F.

Sahlins, M. D.

1976     *Culture and Practical Reason*. University of Chicago Press, Chicago.

1999     Two or Three Things That I Know about Culture. *Journal of the Royal Anthropological Institute* 5(3):399–421.

Sanders, W. T. (editor)

1986–2000     *Excavaciones en el área urbana de Copán*. Instituto Hondureño de Antropología e Historia, Tegucigalpa, Honduras.

1989     Household, Lineage, and State at Eighth-Century Copan, Honduras. In *The House of the Bacabs, Copán, Honduras*, edited by D. L. Webster, pp. 89–105. Studies in Pre-Columbian Art & Archaeology 29. Dumbarton Oaks, Washington, D.C.

Sandstrom, A. R., and P. E. Sandstrom

1986     *Traditional Papermaking and Paper Cult Figures of Mexico*. University of Oklahoma Press, Norman.

Saramago, J.

1996     *The History of the Siege of Lisbon*. Translated by G. Pontiero. Harcourt Brace, Orlando, Florida.

Sassaman, K. E., and W. Rudolphi

2001     Communities of Practice in the Early Pottery Traditions of the American Southeast. *Journal of Anthropological Research* 57(4):407–425.

Saturno, W. A., K. A. Taube, and D. Stuart

2005     *The Murals of San Bartolo, El Petén, Guatemala*. Part 1: *The North Wall*. Ancient America 7. Center for Ancient American Studies, Barnardsville, North Carolina.

Saussure, F. d.

1966    *Course in General Linguistics.* Translated by W. Barkin. McGraw-Hill, New York.

Saxe, A. A.

1971    Social Dimensions of Mortuary Practices in a Mesolithic Population from Wadi Halfa, Sudan. *Memoirs of the Society for American Archaeology* 25:39–57.

Saxe, G. B.

1991    *Culture and Cognitive Development: Studies in Mathematical Understanding.* Lawrence Erlbaum Associates, Hillsdale, New Jersey.

Scarborough, V. L., and F. Valdez, Jr.

2009    An Alternative Order: The Dualistic Economies of the Ancient Maya. *Latin American Antiquity* 20(1):207–227.

Schachner, G.

2001    Ritual Control and Transformation in Middle-Range Societies: An Example from the American Southwest. *Journal of Anthropological Archaeology* 20(2):168–194.

Schele, L.

1991    An Epigraphic History of the Western Maya Region. In *Classic Maya Political History: Hieroglyphic and Archaeological Evidence*, edited by T. P. Culbert, pp. 72–87. University of Oklahoma Press, Norman.

1992    The Founders of Lineages at Copan and Other Maya Sites. *Ancient Mesoamerica* 3(1):135–144.

1993    *Creation and the Ritual of the Bakabs.* Texas Notes on Precolumbian Art, Writing, and Culture 57. Art Department, University of Texas, Austin.

Schele, L., and D. A. Freidel

1990    *A Forest of Kings: The Untold Story of the Ancient Maya.* William Morrow, New York.

Schele, L., and M. E. Miller

1986    *The Blood of Kings: Dynasty and Ritual in Maya Art.* George Braziller, New York.

Schellhas, P.

1897    *Die Göttergestalten der Mayahandschriften: Ein mythologisches Kulturbild aus dem alten Amerika.* Verlag von Richard Bertling, Dresden.

1904    *Die Göttergestalten der Mayahandschriften: Ein mythologisches Kulturbild aus dem alten Amerika.* 2nd rev. ed. Verlag von A. Asher, Berlin.

Schiffer, M. B.

2005    The Devil Is in the Details: The Cascade Model of Invention Processes. *American Antiquity* 70(3):485–502.

2011    *Studying Technological Change: A Behavioral Approach.* University of Utah Press, Salt Lake City.

Schmidt, P. R.

2006    *Historical Archaeology in Africa: Representation, Social Memory, and Oral Traditions.* AltaMira Press, Lanham, Maryland.

2010    The Play of Tropes in Archaeology. *Ethnoarchaeology* 2(2):131–152.

Scholes, F. V., and E. B. Adams
1938    *Don Diego Quijada, alcalde mayor de Yucatán, 1561–1565; documentos sacados de los archivos de España.* Biblioteca Histórica Mexicana de Obras Inéditas 14–15. Antigua Librería Robredo de J. Porrúa e Hijos, México, D.F.

Scholes, F. V., and E. B. Adams (editors)
1960    *Relación histórica-descriptiva de las provincias de la Verapaz y de la del Manché by Martín Alonso Tovilla and Relación que en el Consejo Real de las Indias hizo sobre la pacificación, y población de las provincias del Manché y Lacandón by Antonio de León Pinelo.* Editorial Universitaria, Guatemala City.

Schwarz, K. R.
2013    Architecture, Materialization and the Duality of Structure: A Maya Case Study of Structurally Shaped Innovation. *Cambridge Archaeological Journal* 23(2):307–332.

Scott, J. C.
1985    *Weapons of the Weak: Everyday Forms of Resistance.* Yale University Press, New Haven, Connecticut.
1990    *Domination and the Arts of Resistance: Hidden Transcripts.* Yale University Press, New Haven, Connecticut.

Scott, J. F.
2001    Dressed to Kill: Stone Regalia of the Mesoamerican Ballgame. In *The Sport of Life and Death: The Mesoamerican Ballgame,* edited by E. M. Whittington, pp. 50–63. Mint Museum of Art, Charlotte, North Carolina.

Scribner, S.
1984    Studying Working Intelligence. In *Everyday Cognition: Its Development in Social Context,* edited by B. Rogoff and J. Lave, pp. 9–40. Harvard University Press, Cambridge, Massachusetts.
1985    Knowledge at Work. *Anthropology & Education Quarterly* 16(3):199–206.

Seler, E.
1887    Namen der in der Dresdener Handschrift abgebildeten Maya-Götter. *Zeitschrift für Ethnologie* 19:224–231.

Sewell, W. H., Jr.
1992    A Theory of Structure: Duality, Agency, and Transformation. *American Journal of Sociology* 98(1):1–29.
1996    Historical Events as Transformations of Structures: Inventing Revolution at the Bastille. *Theory and Society* 25(6):841–881.
2005    *The Logics of History: Social Theory and Social Transformation.* University of Chicago Press, Chicago.

Shanks, M., and C. Y. Tilley
1987    *Re-constructing Archaeology: Theory and Practice.* Cambridge University Press, Cambridge.

Sharer, R. J.
1977    The Maya Collapse Revisited: Internal and External Perspectives. In *Social Process in Maya Prehistory: Essays in Honor of Sir J. Eric Thompson,* edited by N. Hammond, pp. 532–552. Academic Press, New York.
2006    *The Ancient Maya.* 6th ed. Stanford University Press, Stanford, California.

Sharer, R. J., and C. W. Golden
2004        Kingship and Polity: Conceptualizing the Maya Body Politic. In *Continuities and Changes in Maya Archaeology: Perspectives at the Millennium*, edited by C. W. Golden and G. Borgstede, pp. 23–50. Routledge, New York.

Sharp, L.
1952        Steel Axes for Stone-Age Australians. *Human Organization* 11(2):17–22.

Sharpe, A. E., and K. F. Emery
2015        Differential Animal Use within Three Late Classic Maya States: Implications for Politics and Trade. *Journal of Anthropological Archaeology* 40:280–301.

Shaw, R.
1992        Dreaming as Accomplishment: Power, the Individual and Temne Divination. In *Dreaming, Religion and Society in Africa*, edited by M. C. Jędrej and R. Shaw, pp. 36–54. Studies on Religion in Africa 7. E. J. Brill, Leiden, The Netherlands.

Shectman, J.
2003        *Groundbreaking Scientific Experiments, Inventions, and Discoveries of the Eighteenth Century*. Greenwood Press, Westport, Connecticut.

Sheehy, J. J.
1991        Structure and Change in a Late Classic Maya Domestic Group at Copan, Honduras. *Ancient Mesoamerica* 2(1):1–19.

Sheets, P.
2000        Provisioning the Ceren Household. The Vertical Economy, Village Economy, and Household Economy in the Southeastern Maya Periphery. *Ancient Mesoamerica* 11(2):217–230.

Sheets, P., C. Dixon, D. Lentz, R. Egan, A. Halmbacher, V. Slotten, R. Herrera, and C. Lamb
2015        The Sociopolitical Economy of an Ancient Maya Village: Cerén and Its Sacbe. *Latin American Antiquity* 26(3):341–361.

Shennan, S.
2011        Demography and Cultural Innovation: A Model and Its Implications for the Emergence of Modern Human Culture. *Cambridge Archaeological Journal* 11(1):5–16.

Shoaps, R.
2009        Moral Irony and Moral Personhood in Sakapultek Discourse and Culture. In *Stance: Sociolinguistic Perspectives*, edited by A. Jaffe, pp. 92–118. Oxford University Press, New York.

Silesius, A.
1675        *Cherubinischer Wandersmann oder Geist-Reiche Sinn- und Schluß-Reime zur Göttlichen beschaulitgkeit anleitende*. Schubarthus, Glatz, Poland.

Simondon, G.
1958        *Du mode d'existence des objets techniques*. Aubier-Montaigne, Paris.

Sirén, O.
1963        *The Chinese on the Art of Painting: Translations and Comments*. Schocken Paperbacks SB57. Schocken Books, New York.

Skeaping, J. R.
1953        *The Big Tree of Mexico*. Indiana University Press, Bloomington.

Smith, A.
1776        An Inquiry into the Nature and Causes of the Wealth of Nations. W. Strahan and
            T. Cadell, London.
Smith, A. L.
1932        Two Recent Ceramic Finds at Uaxactun. In Carnegie Publication 436, pp.
            1–25. Contributions to American Archaeology 5, No. 2. Carnegie Institution
            of Washington, Washington, D.C.
Smith, A. T.
2003        The Political Landscape: Constellations of Authority in Early Complex Polities.
            University of California Press, Berkeley.
Smith, M. E.
1987        Household Possession and Wealth in Agrarian States: Implications for Ar-
            chaeology. Journal of Anthropological Archaeology 6(4):297–335.
2009        V. Gordon Childe and the Urban Revolution: An Historical Perspective on a
            Revolution in Urban Studies. Town Planning Review 80(1):3–29.
Smith, M. E., T. Dennehy, A. Kamp-Whittaker, E. Colon, and R. Harkness
2014        Quantitative Measures of Wealth Inequality in Ancient Central Mexican
            Communities. Advances in Archaeological Practice 2(4):311–323.
Smith, P. E.
2005        Children and Ceramic Innovation: A Study in the Archaeology of Children.
            Archeological Papers of the American Anthropological Association 15:65–76.
Smith, R. E.
1955        Ceramic Sequence at Uaxactun, Guatemala. Middle American Research Insti-
            tute Publication 20. Tulane University, New Orleans. Louisiana.
Soleri, D., and D. A. Cleveland
1993        Hopi Crop Diversity and Change. Journal of Ethnobiology 13(2):203–231.
Sontag, S.
1977        On Photography. Farrar, Straus and Giroux, New York.
Spector, J. D.
1993        What This Awl Means: Feminist Archaeology at a Wahpeton Dakota Village.
            Minnesota Historical Society Press, St. Paul.
Sperber, D.
1975        Rethinking Symbolism. Translated by A. L. Morton. Cambridge University
            Press, Cambridge.
1996        Explaining Culture: A Naturalistic Approach. Blackwell, Oxford.
Spielmann, K. A.
1998        Ritual Craft Specialists in Middle Range Societies. In Craft and Social Identity,
            edited by C. L. Costin and R. P. Wright, pp. 153–159. Archeological Papers of
            the American Anthropological Association 8. American Anthropological As-
            sociation, Arlington, Virginia.
2002        Feasting, Craft Specialization, and the Ritual Mode of Production in Small-
            Scale Societies. American Anthropologist 104(1):195–207.
Šprajc, I., and A. Flores Esquivel
2010        El Zacatal Stela 1. Mexicon 32(1–2):1–5.

Stanton, T. W.

2004    Concepts of Determinism and Free Will in Archaeology. *Anales de Antropología* 38:29–83.

Stanton, T. W., M. K. Brown, and J. B. Pagliaro

2008    Garbage of the Gods? Squatters, Refuse Disposal, and Termination Rituals among the Ancient Maya. *Latin American Antiquity* 19(3):227–247.

Stone, A. J.

1989    Disconnection, Foreign Insignia, and Political Expansion: Teotihuacan and the Warrior Stelae at Piedras Negras. In *Mesoamerica after the Decline of Teotihuacan, A.D. 700–900*, edited by R. A. Diehl and J. C. Berlo, pp. 153–172. Dumbarton Oaks, Washington, D.C.

1995    *Images from the Underworld: Naj Tunich and the Tradition of Maya Cave Painting*. University of Texas Press, Austin.

Stone, A. J., and M. Zender

2011    *Reading Maya Art: A Hieroglyphic Guide to Ancient Maya Painting and Sculpture*. Thames & Hudson, New York.

Strathern, M.

1988    *The Gender of the Gift: Problems with Women and Problems with Society in Melanesia*. University of California Press, Berkeley.

1992    *After Nature: English Kinship in the Late Twentieth Century*. Cambridge University Press, Cambridge.

Strömsvik, G.

1952    *The Ball Courts at Copan, with Notes on Courts at La Unión, Quirigua, San Pedro Pinula, and Asunción Mita*. Carnegie Institution of Washington Publication 596. Carnegie Institution of Washington, Washington, D.C.

Stross, B.

1983    The Language of Zuyua. *American Ethnologist* 10(1):150–164.

1996    Mesoamerican Copal Resins. *U Mut Maya* 6:177–186.

1998    Seven Ingredients in Mesoamerican Ensoulment: Dedication and Termination in Tenejapa. In *The Sowing and the Dawning: Termination, Dedication, and Transformation in the Archaeological and Ethnographic Record of Mesoamerica*, edited by S. B. Mock, pp. 31–39. University of New Mexico Press, Albuquerque.

Stuart, D.

1984    Epigraphic Evidence of Political Organization in the Usumacinta Drainage. Unpublished manuscript. Mimeograph.

1987    *Ten Phonetic Syllables*. Research Reports on Ancient Maya Writing 14. Center for Maya Research, Washington, D.C.

1989    Hieroglyphs on Maya Vessels. In *The Maya Vase Book: A Corpus of Rollout Photographs of Maya Vases*, Vol. 1, edited by J. Kerr, pp. 149–160. Kerr Associates, New York.

1995    A Study of Maya Inscriptions. Unpublished Ph.D. dissertation, Department of Anthropology, Vanderbilt University, Nashville.

1996    Kings of Stone: A Consideration of Stelae in Ancient Maya Ritual and Representation. *Res: Anthropology and Aesthetics* 29–30:149–171.

1997     Kinship Terms in Maya Inscriptions. In *The Language of Maya Hieroglyphs*, edited by M. J. Macri and A. Ford, pp. 1–11. Pre-Columbian Art Research Institute, San Francisco, California.

1998     "The Fire Enters His House": Architecture and Ritual in Classic Maya Texts. In *Function and Meaning in Maya Architecture*, edited by S. D. Houston, pp. 373–425. Dumbarton Oaks, Washington, D.C.

2000     "The Arrival of Strangers": Teotihuacan and Tollan in Classic Maya History. In *Mesoamerica's Classic Heritage: From Teotihuacan to the Aztecs*, edited by D. Carrasco, L. Jones and S. Sessions, pp. 465–513. University of Colorado Press, Boulder.

2005     *The Inscriptions from Temple XIX at Palenque: A Commentary*. Pre-Columbian Art Research Institute, San Francisco, California.

2006     *The Palenque Mythology: Inscriptions and Interpretations of the Cross Group. Sourcebook for the 30th Maya Meetings*. University of Texas, Austin.

2012     The Name of Paper: The Mythology of Crowning and Royal Nomenclature on Palenque's Palace Tablet. In *Maya Archaeology 2*, edited by C. W. Golden, S. D. Houston, and J. Skidmore, pp. 116–141. Precolumbia Mesoweb Press, San Francisco, California.

Stuart, D., and S. D. Houston

1994     *Classic Maya Place-Names*. Studies in Pre-Columbian Art & Archaeology 33. Dumbarton Oaks, Washington, D.C.

Sugiyama, S., and L. López Luján

2007     Dedicatory Burial/Offering Complexes at the Moon Pyramid, Teotihuacan: A Preliminary Report of 1998–2004 Explorations. *Ancient Mesoamerica* 18(1):127–146.

Suhler, C. K., and D. A. Freidel

2003     The Tale End of Two Cities: Tikal, Yaxuna, and Abandonment Contexts in the Lowland Maya Archaeological Record. In *The Archaeology of Settlement Abandonment in Middle America*, edited by T. Inomata and R. W. Webb, pp. 135–147. University of Utah Press, Salt Lake City.

Suitably Dressed

2010     *The Economist* 397(8713):136.

Sullivan, J. J.

2014     "Please Don't Bury My Soul." Searching for Geeshie Wiley and Elvie Thomas, the Lost Geniuses of the Blues. *New York Times Magazine,* April 13, 2014:24–31, 38, 44–46, 49. New York.

Suskind, R.

2014     *Life, Animated: A Story of Sidekicks, Heroes, and Autism*. Kingswell, Glendale, California.

Tainter, J. A.

1978     Mortuary Practices and the Study of Prehistoric Social Systems. *Advances in Archaeological Method and Theory* 1:105–141.

Talese, G.

1966     Frank Sinatra Has a Cold. Electronic document, http://www.esquire.com/

news-politics/a638/frank-sinatra-has-a-cold-gay-talese/, accessed November 25, 2013.

Tambiah, S. J.
1985    *Culture, Thought, and Social Action: An Anthropological Perspective.* Harvard University Press, Cambridge, Massachusetts.

Tanpınar, A. H.
2014    *The Time Regulation Institute.* Translated by M. Freely and A. Dawe. Penguin Books, New York.

Taschek, J. T., and J. W. Ball
2003    Nohoch Ek Revisited: The Minor Center as Manor. *Latin American Antiquity* 14(4):371–388.

Taube, K. A.
1992    *The Major Gods of Ancient Yucatan.* Studies in Pre-Columbian Art & Archaeology 32. Dumbarton Oaks, Washington, D.C.
1998    The Jade Hearth: Centrality, Rulership, and the Classic Maya Temple. In *Function and Meaning in Classic Maya Architecture*, edited by S. D. Houston, pp. 427–478. Dumbarton Oaks, Washington, D.C.
2000    The Turquoise Hearth: Fire, Self-Sacrifice, and the Central Mexican Cult of War. In *Mesoamerica's Classic Heritage: From Teotihuacan to the Aztecs*, edited by D. Carrasco, L. Jones, and S. Sessions, pp. 269–340. University Press of Colorado, Boulder.

Taube, K. A., and M. Zender
2009    American Gladiators: Ritual Boxing in Ancient Mesoamerica. In *Blood and Beauty: Organized Violence in the Art and Archaeology of Mesoamerica and Central America*, edited by H. Orr and R. Koontz, pp. 161–220. Ideas, Debates, and Perspectives 4. Cotsen Institute of Archaeology Press, Los Angeles.

Taussig, M. T.
1993    *Mimesis and Alterity: A Particular History of the Senses.* Routledge, Chapman, and Hall, New York.

Tedlock, D.
1985    *Popol Vuh: The Mayan Book of the Dawn of Life.* Simon and Schuster, New York.

Tehrani, J. J., and M. Collard
2009    On the Relationship between Interindividual Cultural Transmission and Population-Level Cultural Diversity: A Case Study of Weaving in Iranian Tribal Populations. *Evolution and Human Behavior* 30(4):286–300.

Thaler, R. H., and C. R. Sunstein
2008    *Nudge: Improving Decisions about Health, Wealth, and Happiness.* Yale University Press, New Haven, Connecticut.

Thomas Aquinas
1964    *Summa theologiæ.* Blackfriars with Eyre & Spottiswoode, London.

Thompson, J. E. S.
1962    *A Catalog of Maya Hieroglyphs.* University of Oklahoma Press, Norman.

Thompson, R.
1969    Àbátàn: A Master Potter of the Ègbádò Yorùbá. In *Tradition and Creativity*

*in Tribal Art*, edited by D. P. Biebuyck, pp. 120–182. University of California Press, Berkeley.

Tiesler Blos, V.
1999 Rasgos bioculturales entre los antiguos mayas. Aspectos arqueológicos y sociales. Unpublished Ph.D. dissertation, Facultad de Filosofía y Letras, Universidad Nacional Autónoma de México, México, D.F.

Tiesler Blos, V., A. Cucina, T. K. Manahan, T. D. Price, T. Ardren, and J. H. Burton
2010 A Taphonomic Approach to Late Classic Maya Mortuary Practices at Xuenkal, Yucatán, Mexico. *Journal of Field Archaeology* 35(4):365–379.

Tilley, C. Y.
1999 *Metaphor and Material Culture*. Blackwell, Oxford.

Tokovinine, A.
2013 *Place and Identity in Classic Maya Narratives*. Studies in Pre-Columbian Art & Archaeology 37. Dumbarton Oaks, Washington, D.C.

Tonkinson, R.
2003 Ambrymese Dreams and the Mardu Dreaming. In *Dream Travelers: Sleep Experiences and Culture in the Western Pacific*, edited by R. I. Lohmann, pp. 87–105. Palgrave Macmillan, New York.

Torrence, R., and S. E. van der Leeuw
1989 Introduction: What's New about Innovation? In *What's New? A Closer Look at the Process of Innovation*, edited by S. E. van der Leeuw and R. Torrence, pp. 1–15. One World Archaeology 14. Unwin Hyman, London.

Tourtellot, G., III
1988 *Excavations at Seibal, Department of Petén, Guatemala: Peripheral Survey and Excavation. Settlement and Community Patterns*. Memoirs of the Peabody Museum of Archaeology and Ethnology 16. Harvard University, Cambridge, Massachusetts.

Tozzer, A. M. (editor)
1941 *Landa's Relación de las Cosas de Yucatan: A Translation*. Peabody Museum of American Archaeology and Ethnology, Cambridge, Massachusetts.

Treherne, P.
1995 The Warrior's Beauty: The Masculine Body and Self-Identity in Bronze Age Europe. *Journal of the European Association of Archaeologists* 3(1):105–144.

Tsukamoto, K., J. L. Camacho, L.E.C. Valenzuela, H. Kotegawa, and O. Q. Esparza Olguín
2015 Political Interactions among Social Actors: Spatial Organization at the Classic Maya Polity of El Palmar, Campeche, Mexico. *Latin American Antiquity* 26(2):200–220.

Turner, B. L., II
1990 Population Reconstruction of the Central Maya Lowlands: 1000 B.C. to A.D. 1500. In *Precolumbian Population History in the Maya Lowlands*, edited by T. P. Culbert and D. S. Rice, pp. 301–324. University of New Mexico Press, Albuquerque.

Turner, B. L., II, and J. A. Sabloff
2012 Classic Period Collapse of the Central Maya Lowlands: Insights about Human–Environment Relationships for Sustainability. *Proceedings of the National Academy of Sciences of the United States of America* 109(35): 13908–13914.

Turner, E. S., N. I. Turner, and R.E.W. Adams

1981        Volumetric Assessment, Rank Ordering, and Maya Civic Centers. In *Lowland Maya Settlement Patterns*, edited by W. Ashmore, pp. 71–88. University of New Mexico Press, Albuquerque.

Turner, T. S.

1991        "We Are Parrots," "Twins Are Birds": Play of Tropes as Operational Structures. In *Beyond Metaphor: The Theory of Tropes in Anthropology*, edited by J. W. Fernandez, pp. 121–158. Stanford University Press, Stanford, California.

1995        Social Body and Embodied Subject: Bodiliness, Subjectivity, and Sociality among the Kayapo. *Current Anthropology* 10(2):143–170.

Urban, G.

1996        *Metaphysical Community: The Interplay of the Senses and the Intellect*. University of Texas Press, Austin.

Urry, J.

1991        Time and Space in Giddens' Social Theory. In *Giddens' Theory of Structuration: A Critical Appreciation*, edited by C.G.A. Bryant and D. Jary, pp. 160–175. Routledge, London.

Vaesen, K., M. Collard, R. Cosgrove, and W. Roebroeks

2016        Population Size Does Not Explain Past Changes in Cultural Complexity. *Proceedings of the National Academy of Sciences of the United States of America* 113(16):E2241–E2247.

van der Leeuw, S. E., and R. Torrence (editors)

1989        *What's New? A Closer Look at the Process of Innovation*. Unwin Hyman, London.

Veblen, T.

2007        *The Theory of the Leisure Class*. Oxford University Press, Oxford.

Velásquez García, E.

2006        The Maya Flood Myth and the Decapitation of the Cosmic Caiman. *PARI Journal* 7(1):1–10.

Viel, R. H.

1983        Evolución de la cerámica en Copán, resultados preliminares. In *Introducción a la arqueología e historia de Copán, Honduras*, Vol. 1, edited by C. F. Baudez, pp. 471–549. Proyecto Arqueológico Copán; Secretaría del Estado en el Despacho de Cultura y Turismo, Tegucigalpa, Honduras.

1999        The Pectorals of Altar Q and Structure 11: An Interpretation of the Political Organization at Copán, Honduras. *Latin American Antiquity* 10(4):377–399.

Villalobos, J. P.

2013        *Quesadillas: A Novel*. Farrar, Straus and Giroux, New York.

Vogt, E. Z.

1969        *Zinacantán: A Maya Community in the Highlands of Chiapas*. Harvard University Press, Cambridge, Massachusetts.

1976        *Tortillas for the Gods: A Symbolic Analysis of Zinacanteco Rituals*. Harvard University Press, Cambridge, Massachusetts.

Vygotsky, L. S.
1962        *Thought and Language*. Translated by H. Eugenia and G. Vakar. MIT Press, Cambridge, Massachusetts.

Wagner, E.
2000        An Alternative View on the Meaning and Function of Structure 10L-22a, Copán, Honduras. In *The Sacred and the Profane: Architecture and Identity in the Maya Lowlands*, edited by P. R. Colas, K. Delvendahl, M. Kuhnert, and A. Schubart, pp. 25–49. Acta Mesoamericana 10. Verlag Anton Saurwein, Markt Schwaben, Germany.

2006        White Earth Bundles: The Symbolic Sealing and Burial of Buildings among the Ancient Maya. In *Jaws of the Underworld: Life, Death, and Rebirth among the Ancient Maya*, edited by P. R. Colas, G. Le Fort and B. L. Persson, pp. 55–69. Acta Mesoamericana 16. Verlag Anton Saurwein, Markt Schwaben, Germany.

Wagner, R.
1977        Analogic Kinship: A Daribi Example. *American Ethnologist* 4(4):623–642.

Walker, D. S.
1998        Smashed Pots and Shattered Dreams: The Material Evidence for an Early Classic Maya Site Termination at Cerros, Belize. In *The Sowing and the Dawning: Termination, Dedication, and Transformation in the Archaeological and Ethnographic Record of Mesoamerica*, edited by S. B. Mock, pp. 81–99. University of New Mexico Press, Albuquerque.

Walker, W. H., and L. J. Lucero
2000        The Depositional History of Ritual and Power. In *Agency in Archaeology*, edited by M.-A. Dobres and J. E. Robb, pp. 130–147. Routledge, London.

Walker, W. H., and M. B. Schiffer
2006        The Materiality of Social Power: The Artifact-Acquisition Perspective. *Journal of Archaeological Method and Theory* 13(2):67–88.

Warren, K. B.
1978        *The Symbolism of Subordination: Indian Identity in a Guatemalan Town*. University of Texas Press, Austin.

1995        Each Mind Is a World: Dilemmas of Feeling and Intention in a Kaqchikel Maya Community. In *Other Intentions: Cultural Contexts and the Attribution of Inner States*, edited by L. Rosen, pp. 47–67. School of American Research Press, Santa Fe, New Mexico.

Washburn, D. K.
1983        Toward a Theory of Structural Style in Art. In *Structure and Cognition in Art*, edited by D. K. Washburn, pp. 1–7. Cambridge University Press, Cambridge.

1999        Perceptual Anthropology: The Cultural Salience of Symmetry. *American Anthropologist* 101(3):547–562.

Watanabe, J. M.
2000        Maya Anthropologists in the Highlands of Guatemala since the 1960s. In *Ethnology*, Supplement 6 to the *Handbook of Middle American Indians*, edited by J. D. Monaghan, pp. 224–247. University of Texas Press, Austin.

Wauchope, R.

1938      *Modern Maya Houses: A Study of Their Archaeological Significance*. Carnegie Institution Publication 502. Carnegie Institution, Washington, D.C.

1948      *Excavations at Zacualpa, Guatemala*. MARI Publication 14. Middle American Research Institute, Tulane University, New Orleans, Louisiana.

Weber, M.

1991      *From Max Weber: Essays in Sociology*. Translated by H. H. Gerth and C. W. Mills. Routledge, London.

Webster, D. L. (editor)

1989a      *The House of the Bacabs, Copan, Honduras*. Studies in Pre-Columbian Art & Archaeology 29. Dumbarton Oaks, Washington, D.C.

1989b      The House of the Bacabs: Its Social Context. In *The House of the Bacabs, Copan, Honduras*, edited by D. L. Webster, pp. 5–40. Studies in Pre-Columbian Art & Archaeology 29. Dumbarton Oaks, Washington, D.C.

1992      Maya Elites: The Perspective from Copan. In *Mesoamerican Elites: An Archaeological Assessment*, edited by D. Z. Chase and A. F. Chase, pp. 135–156. University of Oklahoma Press, Norman.

2000      The Not So Peaceful Civilization: A Review of Maya War. *Journal of World Prehistory* 14(1):65–119.

2002      *The Fall of the Ancient Maya: Solving the Mystery of the Maya Collapse*. Thames & Hudson, London. Webster, D. L., B. W. Fash, R. J. Widmer, and S. Zeleznik

1998      The Skyband Group: Investigation of a Classic Maya Elite Residential Complex at Copán, Honduras. *Journal of Field Archaeology* 25(3):319–343.

Webster, D. L., W. L. Fash, and E. M. Abrams

1986      Excavaciones en el conjunto 9N-8: patio A (Operación VIII). In *Excavaciones en el área urbana de Copán*, Vol. 1, edited by W. T. Sanders, pp. 155–317. Instituto Hondureño de Antropología e Historia, Tegucigalpa, Honduras.

Webster, D. L., and A. Freter

1990      Settlement History and the Classic Collapse at Copan: A Redefined Chronological Perspective. *Latin American Antiquity* 1(1):65–85.

Webster, D. L., A. Freter, and N. Gonlin

1999      *Copan: The Rise and Fall of a Classic Maya Kingdom*. Harcourt College, Fort Worth, Texas.

Weiner, J. F.

1988      *The Heart of the Pearl Shell: The Mythological Dimension of Foi Sociality*. University of California Press, Berkeley.

Weishampel, D. B., P. Dodson, and H. Osmólska (editors)

2004      *The Dinosauria*. 2nd ed. University of California Press, Berkeley.

Wendrich, W.

2012      Archaeology and Apprenticeship: Body Knowledge, Identity, and Communities of Practice. In *Archaeology and Apprenticeship: Body Knowledge, Identity, and Communities of Practice*, edited by W. Wendrich, pp. 1–19. University of Arizona Press, Tucson.

Wentzlaff-Eggebert, F.-W.

1960        *Kreuzzugsdichtung des Mittelalters; Studien zu ihrer geschichtlichen und dich-
terischen Wirklichkeit.* De Gruyter, Berlin.

White, L. A.

1943        Energy and the Evolution of Culture. *American Anthropologist* 45(3):335–356.

Whiting, A. F.

1939        *Ethnobotany of the Hopi.* Museum of Northern Arizona Bulletin 15. Northern
Arizona Society of Science and Art, Flagstaff.

Whittaker, A., and V. Warkentin

1965        *Chol Texts on the Supernatural.* Summer Institute of Linguistics Publications
in Linguistics and Related Fields 13. Summer Institute of Linguistics of the
University of Oklahoma, Norman.

Widmer, R. J.

2009        Elite Household Multicrafting Specialization at 9N8, Patio H, Copan. *Archeological Papers of the American Anthropological Association* 19(1):174–204.

Wiessner, P.

2002        Vines of Complexity: Egalitarian Structures and the Institutionalization of
Inequality among the Enga. *Current Anthropology* 43(2):233–269.

Wilk, R. R.

1983        Little House in the Jungle: The Causes of Variation in House Size among Modern Maya. *Journal of Anthropological Archaeology* 2(2):99–116.

1991        *Household Ecology: Economic Change and Domestic Life among the Kekchi
Maya in Belize.* University of Arizona Press, Tucson.

Wilk, R. R., and W. L. Rathje

1982        Household Archaeology. *American Behavioral Scientist* 25(6):617–639.

Willey, G. R.

1972        *The Artifacts of Altar de Sacrificios.* Papers of the Peabody Museum of Archaeology and Ethnology 64, No. 1. Harvard University, Cambridge, Massachusetts.

Willey, G. R., T. P. Culbert, and R.E.W. Adams

1967        Maya Lowland Ceramics: A Report from the 1965 Guatemala City Conference. *American Antiquity* 32(3):289–315.

Willey, G. R., and R. M. Leventhal

1979        Prehistoric Settlement at Copán. In *Maya Archaeology and Ethnohistory*, edited by N. Hammond, pp. 75–102. University of Texas Press, Austin.

Willey, G. R., R. M. Leventhal, A. A. Demarest, and W. L. Fash

1994        *Ceramics and Artifacts from Excavations in the Copan Residential Zone.* Papers
of the Peabody Museum of Archaeology and Ethnology 80. Harvard University, Cambridge, Massachusetts.

Willey, G. R., and D. B. Shimkin

1973        The Maya Collapse: A Summary View. In *The Classic Maya Collapse*, edited
by T. P. Culbert, pp. 457–502. University of New Mexico Press, Albuquerque.

Willis, P.

1977        *Learning to Labour: How Working Class Kids Get Working Class Jobs.* Saxon
House, Farnborough, UK.

Wilson, B. R.

1970        *Rationality*. Blackwell, Oxford.

Wilson, W. J.

1999        *The Bridge over the Racial Divide: Rising Inequality and Coalition Politics*. Aaron Wildavsky Forum for Public Policy 2. University of California Press, Berkeley.

Winner, L.

1986        *The Whale and the Reactor: A Search for Limits in an Age of High Technology*. University of Chicago Press, Chicago.

Wisdom, C.

1950        *Materials on the Chorti Language*. Microfilm Collection of Manuscripts on Middle American Cultural Anthropology 28. University of Chicago, Chicago.

Wittgenstein, L.

1980        *Remarks on the Philosophy of Psychology*, 2 vols. Translated by G.E.M. Anscombe. University of Chicago Press, Chicago.

2001        *Philosophical Investigations: The German Text, with a Revised English Translation*. 3rd ed. Translated by G.E.M. Anscombe. Blackwell, Malden, Massachusetts.

Woolley, A. W., C. F. Chabris, A. Pentland, N. Hashmi, and T. W. Malone

2010        Evidence for a Collective Intelligence Factor in the Performance of Human Groups. *Science* 330(6004):686–688.

Wright, D. R., R. E. Terry, and M. Eberl

2009        Soil Properties and Stable Carbon Isotope Analysis of Landscape Features in the Petexbatún Region of Guatemala. *Geoarchaeology: An International Journal* 24(4):466–491.

Wu, X., C. Zhang, P. Goldberg, D. Cohen, Y. Pan, T. Arpin, and O. Bar-Yosef

2012        Early Pottery at 20,000 Years Ago in Xianrendong Cave, China. *Science* 336(6089):1696–1700.

Yaeger, J.

2000        The Social Construction of Communities in the Classic Maya Countryside: Strategies of Affiliation in Western Belize. In *The Archaeology of Communities: A New World Perspective*, edited by M. A. Canuto and J. Yaeger, pp. 123–142. Routledge, London.

2003        Internal Complexity, Household Strategies of Affiliation, and the Changing Organization of Small Communities in the Upper Belize River Valley. In *Perspectives on Ancient Maya Rural Complexity*, edited by G. Iannone and S. V. Connell, pp. 42–58. Cotsen Institute of Archaeology, University of California, Los Angeles.

Yaeger, J., and M. A. Canuto

2000        Introducing an Archaeology of Communities. In *The Archaeology of Communities: A New World Perspective*, edited by M. A. Canuto and J. Yaeger, pp. 1–15. Routledge, London.

Yaeger, J., and C. Robin

2004        Heterogeneous Hinterlands: The Social and Political Organization of Commoner Settlements near Xunantunich, Belize. In *Ancient Maya Commoners*, edited by J. C. Lohse and F. Valdez, Jr., pp. 147–173. University of Texas Press, Austin.

Yoffee, N.
2005        *The Myth of the Archaic State*. Cambridge University Press, New York.

Yuedi, L.
2011        Calligraphic Expression and Contemporary Chinese Art: Xu Bing's Pioneer Experiment. In *Subversive Strategies in Contemporary Chinese Art*, edited by M. B. Wiseman and L. Yuedi, pp. 87–108. Philosophy of History and Culture 31. Brill, Leiden, The Netherlands.

Zaro, G., and J. C. Lohse
2005        Agricultural Rhythms and Rituals: Ancient Maya Solar Observation in Hinterland Blue Creek, Northwestern Belize. *Latin American Antiquity* 16(1):81–98.

Zender, M.
2004        A Study of Classic Maya Priesthood. Unpublished Ph.D. dissertation, Department of Anthropology, University of Calgary, Alberta.

# Index

Royal headbands, 58, 58*f*, 76, 141, 155
Royal symbols: ballgames as, 155–56; head-
    bands as, 58, 76, 141, 155; mats as, 148–49,
    156; nonroyals and, 155–56, 159–160; power
    and, 159; scepters as, 151–52, 154–56
Rules: of knowledge, 97; language and, 36–37,
    195; nature of, 14; schemas and, 53–54;
    social, 28, 35; social interactions and,
    92; structures and, 7–9, 14, 107, 138, 179;
    sumptuary, 165
Rumelhart, D. E., 12

Saak Chin, 114
Sacred ideals, 114
*Sajals* (governors), 77
San Bartolo murals, 1–2, 2*f*, 4, 208
Santiago, Diego de, 100
Santiago Matamoros, 59
Saussure, F., 36, 62, 104, 201, 205
Scepters, 151, 152*f*, 153, 153*t*, 154–55, 155*f*, 190
Schemas, 14; classification in, 13–14, 55–56;
    conditions in, 13; context and, 102; creation
    myths and, 51–52; defining, 12; framing
    in, 13–15; nature of, 14–15; organization of,
    197; as real world exemplars, 53–54; shared
    values in, 53; symbolic generalizations in,
    52–53; technology and, 54; worldviews
    and, 53
Schooling, 96
Scribes (*Aj tz'iib*): hieroglyphic writing and,
    18; in Itzamnaaj's court, 33, 66–67, 67*f*, 117;
    priests ("daykeepers") as, 24; status and, 18;
    as superhuman, 166
Selection, 34
Self-body, 40, 44–45
Self-sacrifice, 57
Sewell, W. H., Jr., 15, 101–2, 108, 169
Shared values, 53
Sharp, L., 10
Sihyaj Chan K'awiil, 58
Silesius, 38–39
Similarity: opposition and, 35; relationships
    of, 33–34; selection and, 34; substitution
    and, 34
Similarity disorders, 34
Simondon, G., 9
Situated learning, 72–73, 75, 90, 96–97, 100,
    123

Skull masks, 199–200
Social agency: as ability, 11; creativity and, 32;
    structure and, 16; technology and, 10
Social change: agency and, 16, 32, 101; new
    norms for, 33; public discourse and, 31
Social control, 142
Social diversification, 88–89, 98–99
Social groups: individuals in, 72; norms of,
    71–72; organization of, 65–66
Social inequality, 83–89
Social interactions: authority ranking, 92–93;
    commitment and, 169, 171; communal
    sharing, 92–93; culture-specific, 197;
    equality matching, 92–93; formalized, 42;
    innovation and, 90–91; market pricing, 92,
    95; situated learning and, 90; transforma-
    tion of personal beliefs and, 65
Social knowing: cultural context of, 41–43;
    embodied experiences and, 43; empathic,
    41, 44; opacity in, 42–43
Social learning: autonomous, 196; in-
    complete copying in, 194–96. *See also*
    Learning
Social mobility, 78, 88–89
Social opacity, 42–43
Social roles, 73
Social structures: consumption and, 162;
    cultural capital and, 167, 169; individual
    choice and, 140; innovation and, 138–39;
    pottery design and, 179
Social systems: changes in, 8; human
    behavior and, 35; individuals in, 15–16;
    reproduction of, 7–8, 17; resources in, 14;
    rules in, 14; structure of, 101
Society: dissonance and, 6; habit-based
    models of, 111, 203; individuals in, 7; inno-
    vation and, 6–7, 98; learning in, 96; social
    inequality in, 83; social learning and, 98;
    structure-based models of, 201; structures
    in, 7–8, 107; technology and, 9–10, 17
South Plaza (Dos Ceibas), 81*f*, 86, 89, 91–93
Space-time, 194, 204*f*, 205–6
Spanish: conquest of, 14, 24; on Maya cal-
    endars, 206; prohibition of native rituals
    by, 51; on ritual drinking, 68; scurvy and,
    100–101
Speech: context and, 35–36; defining, 34;
    figures of, 33–35; language-games in, 36;

Markus Eberl, associate professor of anthropology at Vanderbilt University, is the author of *Community and Difference: Change in Late Classic Maya Villages of the Petexbatun Region* and *Muerte, entierro y ascención: Ritos funerarios entre los antiguos mayas.*

*Approaches to Monumental Landscapes of the Ancient Maya*, edited by Brett A. Houk, Barbara Arroyo, and Terry G. Powis (2020)

*The Real Business of Ancient Maya Economies: From Farmers' Fields to Rulers' Realms*, edited by Marilyn A. Masson, David A. Freidel, and Arthur A. Demarest (2020)

*Maya Kingship: Rupture and Transformation from Classic to Postclassic Times*, edited by Tsubasa Okoshi, Arlen F. Chase, Philippe Nondédéo, and M. Charlotte Arnauld (2021)

*Lacandón Maya in the Twenty-First Century: Indigenous Knowledge and Conservation in Mexico's Tropical Rainforest*, by James D. Nations (2023)

*The Materialization of Time in the Ancient Maya World: Mythic History and Ritual Order*, edited by David A. Freidel, Arlen F. Chase, Anne S. Dowd, and Jerry Murdock (2024)

*El Perú-Waka': New Archaeological Perspectives on the Kingdom of the Centipede*, edited by Keith Eppich, Damien B. Marken, and David Freidel (2024))

www.ingramcontent.com/pod-product-compliance
Lightning Source LLC
Chambersburg PA
CBHW020829270326
41928CB00006B/467